POWER AND STATUS

POWER AND STATUS
Officeholding in Colonial America

Edited by Bruce C. Daniels

Essays by

Grace L. Chickering   Richard Alan Ryerson
Bruce C. Daniels   Ronald K. Snell
A. Roger Ekirch   Alan Tully
Jessica Kross   Lorena S. Walsh
Thomas L. Purvis   Richard Waterhouse
Thomas Wendel

Wesleyan University Press   Middletown, Connecticut

Distributed by Harper & Row Publisher, Keystone
Industrial Park, Scranton, Pennsylvania 18512.

LIBRARY OF CONGRESS CATALOGING IN PUBLICATION DATA
Main entry under title:
Power and status.
    Includes bibliographies and index.
    1. United States—Politics and government—Colonial
period, ca. 1600–1775—Addresses, essays, lectures.
2. Politicians—United States—History—18th century—
Addresses, essays, lectures.   3. Elite (Social sciences)
—United States—History—18th century—Addresses,
essays, lectures.   I. Daniels, Bruce Colin.
JK54.P68   1986   973.2   84-21023
ISBN 0-8195-5118-X (alk. paper)

Manufactured in the United States of America
First edition

With love to my three daughters
Elizabeth, Abigail, Nora

Contents

At the Pinnacle of Elective Success: The Speaker of the
House in Colonial America

INTERCOLONIAL LEADERSHIP

"Patronage Most Ardently Sought": The New York Council, 1665–1775

A Beleaguered Elite: The New Jersey Council, 1702–1776

Founders of an Oligarchy: The Virginia Council,
1692–1722

Figures and Tables

At the Pinnacle of Elective Service: The Speaker of the House in Colonial America

"Patronage Most Ardently Sought": The New York Council, 1665–1775

A Beleaguered Elite: The New Jersey Council, 1702–1776

Acknowledgments

In almost all cases, a large number of people lend their time and expertise to an academic book. For a book that has many authors, the number is probably larger than usual. Over two dozen scholars and friends have generously assisted in the development of this book from conception to publication. It gives me great pleasure to thank them on behalf of myself and my coauthors. The following people read one or more essays and made suggestions for improvement: Alfred A. Aya, Jr., Lois Carr, David Chestnut, Paul Clemens, Stanley Engerman, Douglas Greenberg, P. M. G. Harris, John Hemphill, Edward Hundert, Herbert Alan Johnson, David Kaplan, Milton M. Klein, Leonard Krueger, Jack Marietta, Whitman Ridgway, Carol Shammas, Jean Ruth Suderland, and James Taylor.

I wish also to thank three historians who read the entire manuscript and offered advice on its organization as well as on individual essays: Robert Dinkin of Fresno State University, Jack P. Greene of Johns Hopkins University, and Harry S. Stout of the University of Connecticut. Jeannette Hopkins, director of Wesleyan University Press, supported this project from its inception, and with characteristic intelligence and frankness suggested ways in which the manuscript could be improved. María Élida Bottino, production editor at the press, tolerated my many phone calls and letters without once losing her good humor and eased a complicated book through the various prepublication stages. The University of Winnipeg Research and Travel Committee was, as usual, generous in its support, supplying funds for typing and an index. President Robin Farquhar, Vice-President A. Ross McCormack, Dean of Arts and Sciences Michael McIntyre, and history department chairmen Walter Stein and Herbert J. Mays have each in different ways contributed to a climate at the University of Winnipeg that makes research and publication easier: for this, I am grateful. Kate MacFarlane and Janice Stasiewski typed the manuscript with skill and speed, and always insisted on paying for their portions of the pizzas we shared.

The members of my family also deserve recognition: they have contributed little to the book but much to its editor. My mother, Willa Daniels; my brother, Roger Daniels; and my sister and brother-in-law, Lea and Daniel Riccio, are decent, loyal people. I confess unabashedly that I love them. My three daughters, Elizabeth, Abigail, and Nora, are more valuable and contribute more to the world than anything I have ever published or ever will. They will enjoy *Power and Status* far less than my more successful bedtime stories, "Bow Woof," "Frannie and Freddie Frog," and "Eddie Eagle." Despite its unworthiness, I dedicate this book to them.

Bruce C. Daniels

POWER AND STATUS

BRUCE C. DANIELS

Introduction

LEADERSHIP IS BY definition elitist. Leaders may form an elite only temporarily, they may be recruited from a wide spectrum, and they may share their power with many; but to be a leader is to be separated by some marks of distinction from "the rest" of society. Theoretically the distinctive attributes of leaders need not be economic success, social status, or political or personal ability; merely occupying a position of power could be the only distinctive attribute a leader enjoyed, and once removed from that position a leader would be just like everyone else. Except for a few societies that have chosen their leaders by random lot, however, this is not the case; leaders are usually distinguished by either high social status arising from birth or work, economic advantages above the average, exceptional ability, or exceptional character. Because of these factors, everyone does not have equal access to positions of power.

It should come as no surprise, therefore, that historians of early America have found that, despite a wide voting franchise, officeholding in the colonies was dominated by the upper elements of society and a few men occupied many offices for substantial periods. Voters elect whom they perceive will do the best job, and a person who appears successful in private life would naturally be considered a more likely candidate to be successful in public life than one who was not. Voters also usually maintain people in office whom they perceive are performing well, so it is reasonable to expect that some people will stay in office for long periods. Of course, voters sometimes elect people who reflect their own personal attributes, and it is not unknown for an electorate composed of lower-class people to elect to office one of their number with great ability or character but little social status or economic advantage. Usually, however, the choice of the working classes is some figure from a social and economic class higher than theirs who is sympathetic to their needs. Nor is it unknown for an electorate to consider frequent reelection to office a dangerous phenomenon and to systematically turn incumbents out of office. Yet we know from a wide variety of sources that colonial voters did not usually choose their leaders from the bottom of society and did not automatically refuse to reelect them; the prevalent values of the early modern Western world inculcated respect and deference for the "better sort" of society. And, despite the present pejorative connotations of the words "discriminate" and "elite", few people today would argue against the concept of a discriminating electorate voting for elite officeholders if the people understood the proper meaning of these words. Thomas Jefferson, regarded by most as an apostle of democracy, had no problem accepting that leaders should come from the better sort; but he defined the "better sort" as a natural aristocracy distinguished by ability, character, experience, and training, not an artificial aristocracy distinguished by birth and wealth.

The natural aristocracy, of course, cannot easily be separated from the artificial aristocracy; the superior connections and economic advantages of the artificial aristocracy, as well as its differing socialization process, give its children more of an opportunity to develop into natural aristocrats than other children have. Hence, in any society with social and economic distinctions we should normally expect these distinctions to be reflected in the officeholding patterns characteristic of that society. Thus it would be utterly improbable not to find some degree of artificial elitism in an examination of colonial officeholding. And, without a shadow of a doubt, social and economic distinctions were translated into political distinctions, and an elite did rule colonial America. But to say this is not to add much to our knowledge. A variety of much more specific questions must be asked of the officeholding structure before we can gain an understanding of the world of power and status in the colonies. We need to know how relatively closed or open the colonial elite was, what occupations were most likely to provide a springboard to political office, how much of the elite was native to the colonies and how much was native to England or elsewhere, how the elite was recruited and trained, where leaders tended to live. In answering these and the many other questions that a study of elites involves, we must bear in mind that colonial America was not a static society, but one undergoing considerable change in response to demographic, economic, and political stimuli. And we must also remember that the colonial world was far from being homogeneous—each colony had a unique social structure and unique constitutional arrangements deriving from differing political origins and settlement patterns. Moreover, as does any complex society with several layers of institutions, the colonies had a hierarchy of elites. Thus there is no reason to think that a common experience characterized all of the colonies or all of the eighteenth century or all of the levels of leadership. The job of describing and analyzing the attributes of men of power and status in colonial America will be complex and time-consuming and will require the energies of dozens of scholars trained in numerous methodologies. Already in the last decade a significant start has been made, but I think most historians will agree that only the surface has been scratched.

It is to scratch a little deeper into the power structures of colonial America that the eleven original essays presented in this volume have been compiled. They range from an examination of a county elite in Massachusetts to a prosopographical study of the New York council to an analysis of the membership of the South Carolina assembly. The methodologies employed vary greatly as do the questions asked, but most of the essays are largely quantitative in approach and employ the innovative techniques of recent social history. All of the authors have written extensively on their subjects, and I think it would be accurate to say that the total research involved in the eleven essays would be beyond the capacities of most individuals in a lifetime. This is not to say that these essays are in any way a full treatment of the subject. They constitute the most comprehensive treatment yet achieved, but they do not begin to exhaust the subject. Yet I believe that every succeeding serious analysis of officeholding in the colonies and elsewhere will find them invaluable for points of reference and comparison.

Usually, collections of essays that span the colonial spectrum are arranged in geographical order or categories in order to dramatize differences among the three major mainland regions. Regional comparisons are salutary to any study of colonial American society—indeed, in the present one they are crucial—but the essays in this collection have been grouped by levels of leadership, in order to highlight the fact that one can divide colonial society by horizontal lines demarcating planes of activity and influence as readily as one can divide it by geography. Within each region—New England, the Middle Colonies, or the South—at least three strata of leadership can be identified: local, colony-wide, and intercolonial. While these strata were discrete, each affected the others in basic and profound ways, and the lines between them were often blurred, because some men functioned in two, or even all three, of the strata.

Three essays are on local leadership: Ronald K. Snell examines the major county officeholders in Hampshire County, Massachusetts, and their relations with the colonial government above them and the town government below them; Bruce C. Daniels's essay identifies patterns of officeholding among selectmen in thirty Connecticut towns; Lorena S. Walsh analyzes local power structures in late seventeenth- and early eighteenth-century Maryland. Five essays are on colony-wide leadership: Alan Tully and Richard Ryerson both assess the role of the Quaker Party in providing leadership to the Pennsylvania assembly, Tully from a primarily qualitative perspective and Ryerson from a quantitative one; A. Roger Ekirch's and Richard Waterhouse's essays provide profiles of the members of the assemblies in North and South Carolina; Thomas Wendel collects and analyzes data on the 275 Speakers in the assemblies of the thirteen colonies. And, finally, three essays are on intercolonial leadership: Jessica Kross, Thomas L. Purvis, and Grace L. Chickering examine the memberships of the New York, New Jersey, and Virginia governors' councils.

Identifying members of the assemblies as a colony-wide elite and members of the governors' councils as an intercolonial elite creates categories too rigidly defined to correspond perfectly with reality. An assembly often dealt with issues beyond its colony's borders, and sometimes assembly members were well known and influential outside of their colony; conversely, the council often dealt with internal affairs, and a few councillors were not known beyond their own colony. Nevertheless, colonists thought and modern historians agree that the council constituted a higher level of elitism than the assembly; and the council was much more likely than the assembly to be directly involved in relations with other colonies or with officials in England.

Surveying the conclusions of the eleven essays, one is struck by the diversity of the colonial elite. The two case studies of local leadership—Snell's on Hampshire County, Massachusetts, and Walsh's on Charles County, Maryland—both stress the uniqueness of their subjects. Hampshire County, isolated from the crosscurrents of eastern Massachusetts, developed an elite much smaller, more interrelated, and more successful in quelling opposition than any of the county elites along the seacoast. The average member of the Hampshire County elite may not have been as prominent as most members of eastern-county elites, but a smaller leadership pool in the west resulted in less competition and diminished access to the ruling circles. Paradoxically, in one sense—wealth and social status—Hampshire County possessed a lesser elite than counties in the east; but in another sense—power and access—Hampshire County displayed a greater degree of elitism. Walsh's analysis of Charles County and its neighboring counties shows how varying local economic and religious circumstances resulted in differing patterns of leadership. Calvert and Prince George counties had better soils and hence greater prosperity than Charles County. This produced more men of substantial fortunes in Calvert and Prince George counties who were much more influential in colony-wide matters than the leaders of Charles. In all of Maryland, the elite grew progressively more exclusive and powerful in the late seventeenth and early eighteenth centuries, but in Charles County the stages of development lagged twenty or thirty years behind those of Calvert and Prince George. In another neighboring county, St. Mary's, elite development was retarded more than in Charles, because most of the wealthy planters who had the social and economic attributes essential for leadership were Catholics and hence barred from office.

Daniels's essay on Connecticut selectmen, which compares office-holding in thirty towns, deals explicitly with the diversity of local leadership patterns. As other historians have shown, some of this variety derives from identifiable social and economic variables. Daniels argues, however, that these standard variables do not explain most of the diversity. Frequently, towns of similar age, economic function, size and location had dramatically different patterns of officeholding derived from idiosyncrasies that became hardened into local custom. Two or three forceful leaders, a quarrel between neighborhoods, the absence or presence of group migration, all might alter election patterns in the first decade of a town's history and lead to patterns that persisted long after the original reasons ceased to exist. Daniels also shows that each type of locally elected office had distinctive patterns of recruitment. In nearly all towns, treasurers and clerks had long tenures in office; once elected, a treasurer or clerk who did his job well was often reelected every year for the rest of his life. The officeholding patterns of deputies to the general assembly were less oligarchical than those of treasurers and clerks but more so than those of selectmen. The election patterns of deputies also correlated more significantly with economic and social variables than selectmen's patterns did, and hence were more predictable and less erratic. All of this diversity—created by local circumstances, the nature of the office, and the type of town—means that any analysis that tried to fashion a uniform picture of local officeholding in Connecticut without paying full attention to these details would be doomed to failure.

The variety of patterns in local officeholding paralleled a variety of institutions. Local government was diverse, ranging from the town meeting in New England to the parishes and county courts in the south. At the colony level more institutional similarity was evident: each colony had an assembly, elected by the freemen, that provided a forum for debate and action on matters of concern to the entire colony. Some institutional differences among the assemblies did exist. The qualifications of the electorate, frequency of elections, size of membership, internal proceedings, and relationships with the governor and council varied from colony to colony, but these differences were substantially less than those that characterized local constitutional arrangements. The growth of the assembly as a parliamentary body representing similar forces and aspirations in all of the colonies has been the central factor in most explanations of colonial politics.

The essays in this collection that analyze colony-wide leadership, however, find each assembly unique. The Quaker Party in Pennsylvania controlled elections to the assembly and influenced its procedures to a remarkable degree. Although pressure groups or partisan factions existed in other colonies, most notably New York and Rhode Island, none of them could begin to approach the power of the Quaker Party to define the colony-wide elite. Similarly, orthodox Puritans may have closed ranks on a few issues in the Connecticut and Massachusetts assemblies, but they never formed a cohesive group that could control those assemblies' actions and personnel.

Profiles of the members of Virginia's, North Carolina's and South Carolina's assemblies suggest little similarity between neighbors. The colony-wide elite in North Carolina was less wealthy, less educated, less bound by ties of kinship, and less native to the colony than its counterparts in other colonies. It was an emergent elite that did not take on the attributes of the gentry or become very exclusive during the colonial period. Members of South Carolina's assembly had many of the classic characteristics of an entrenched elite: wealth, kinship ties to each other, and a reluctance to admit outsiders. In these attributes, South Carolina's colony-wide elite resembled Virginia's. In other ways, however, the two differed. Most leaders in the South Carolina assembly were merchants or lawyers, in Virginia most were planters. Members resident in Charlestown dominated the South Carolina assembly; Virginia had no urban entrepot to exercise similar power.

Thomas Wendel's study of the 275 Speakers of the assemblies finds that, although certain common patterns obtained throughout the colonies, substantial variations in the types of Speakers elected occurred among the three major regions. Speakers in New England were almost always native to their colony, but in the Middle and Southern colonies only one-fourth and one-third, respectively, were natives. New England Speakers usually had some college education, most of those in other colonies did not. Not surprisingly, the religion of the Speakers reflected the differing religious orientations of the three main regions.

Within regions variations in the attributes of Speakers were also evident. In New England—probably the most homogeneous region in terms of social structure—Connecticut and Rhode Island, the two corporate colonies, elected Speakers with much less prior experience and less wealth than the two royal colonies, Massachusetts and New Hampshire. Speakers in Rhode Island, however, tended to be from the urban centers of Newport and Providence, Connecticut drawing many more of its legislative leaders from rural areas. Rhode Island differed sharply from the rest of New England in the religious affiliation of its Speakers.

As in the case of the assemblies, the governors' councils had similar constitutional roles in all of the mainland colonies. Advisors to the governor, they functioned both as the upper house of a bicameral legislative system and as the highest court in each colony. Members of the council were, in royal colonies, appointed by the Board of Trade and, in the corporate colonies, elected. They were part of an intercolonial elite in the sense that they usually had important connections outside of their own colony and were invariably drawn into the vortex of imperial politics. Despite the structural similarities of the various councils, the nature of their memberships varied greatly, receiving its form from the specific social, economic, and historical circumstances that characterized each colony. New Jersey's council, for example, was far more of an artificial elite grafted on the colony's political system by outside forces than either the New York or Virginia councils were. Prior to 1740 most New Jersey councillors appointed had been born outside of New Jersey and many were connected by kinship ties to the great families of New York and Pennsylvania. By contrast, as early as 1700 most members appointed to the Virginia council had been born in Virginia and were deeply rooted in the Tidewater social structure. The development, in late seventeenth-century Virginia, of an indigenous gentry that could supply leaders of high social status meant that the council no longer needed to recruit members from outside the colony. New York also developed a native intercolonial elite at the beginning of the eighteenth century, one that was much less closed than the Virginia one, reflecting the heterogeneous political and social milieu of New York. Other differences existed among the three councils whose memberships are analyzed in this collection. For instance, New Jersey councillors were substantially less wealthy than those of New York and Virginia, and, although merchants dominated New York's council, planters dominated Virginia's, and lawyers dominated New Jersey's.

Despite the diversity of the colonial elite and the fact that the eleven essays leave large gaps in our knowledge, some reasonably firm officeholding patterns do emerge. It is clear that the elite of early America in all regions and at all levels was an English elite. New York was the only colony with a substantial number of non-English in its elite, and even there the English constituted a majority of the council members and were increasing in proportion throughout the eighteenth century. In ethnically heterogeneous New Jersey, the council was not heterogeneous but was overwhelmingly English in origin. It is also clear, however, that the colonial elite, although English in origin, did not contain many placemen. Every colony wished its leaders to be selected by colonists, and allowed only a very few to be placed in high position by English power and connections. Whether or not leaders were native to the colony in which they served varied from colony to colony and from region to region. Most of New England's leaders were indigenous New Englanders, but less than half of the leaders in other regions were native to their particular colony. Within regions, patterns of nativity also varied. Sixty-one percent of South Carolina's assembly were from families that had been in South Carolina before 1700, while 73 percent of the leaders of North Carolina's assembly were not born in North Carolina. Overall, the nativity of the leaders, not surprisingly, followed immigration patterns: New England, with the lowest rate of immigration in the eighteenth century, had the highest percentage of leaders born in the region; the Middle Colonies, with the highest rate of immigration, had the lowest percentage of leaders born in the region; and the South fell between these two regions in terms of both immigration and non-native leaders. In all regions, however, the percentage of leaders not native to the colony declined over the course of the eighteenth century.

Although some essays do not provide data on the occupations of leaders, all those that do suggest that merchants, lawyers, and large landholders were most likely to achieve positions of power. For the colonies as a whole, merchants were by far most numerous in positions of leadership, but a career in law may have been the best springboard to power and status. Lawyers were considerably fewer in number than merchants, but a proportionately much larger percentage of them achieved high office. Even among the Quaker Party in the Pennsylvania assembly, which had a traditional suspicion of formal legal training, lawyers were extremely influential, and everywhere in the colonies they were becoming more influential as the eighteenth century progressed. Finally, large landholding was most likely to lead to political success in the South, but it also gave a person credentials to seek office in the Middle Colonies and New England. Only occasionally did physicians, prosperous artisans, or placemen penetrate into the preserve of merchants, lawyers, and large planters. All of the essays that examine occupations, however, are studies of colony-wide or intercolonial elites; at the town, parish, or county levels, prosperous farmers and moderate planters were undoubtedly represented in large numbers.

Most members of the colony-wide and intercolonial elites had previously served in lesser offices. In New England, deputies to the assemblies had almost invariably held town office; the vast majority of the Speakers of the assemblies had served in lesser offices outside the assembly; and most leaders in the South had been vestrymen or justices of the peace. In Virginia, members of the council frequently held other offices at the same time. Two exceptions to this practice of leaders serving a political apprenticeship are worth noting: high-ranking Maryland local officers in the seventeenth century and New Jersey council members prior to 1750 usually did not have officeholding experience previous to their service. In both cases these exceptional patterns were products of the founding experience and did not persist throughout the colonial period. Important leaders in the colonies usually were tested in some lesser capacity before being entrusted with major responsibilities. This finding should do much to dispel the notion that office in colonial America was a privilege foreordained by birth.

Having said the above, it is necessary to emphasize that family connections and proper social status were important criteria in leadership selection. The various contributors to this volume employ differing methodologies to study family connections, but with only two exceptions all emphasize the importance of kinship networks among the elite. The most striking exception, North Carolina, had the newest and most fluid elite; for example, only 17.8 percent of North Carolina's assembly leaders had the same surname as another assembly leader compared to 53.4 percent of Virginians. In the other exception, Maryland, high mortality rates precluded family dynasties: when mortality rates began to decline to normal levels, kin connections became much more important. In Connecticut, family connections were important at the local level but less so than at the colony level. Of the forty-three councillors examined in Virginia, twelve of them succeeded their fathers on the council. In Hampshire County, Massachusetts, six families held two-thirds of the county's major offices at midcentury. Most of the kinship networks were formed within the confines of one colony, the major exception being New Jersey's conciliar elite. Befitting a small colony located between the influential colonies of New York and Pennsylvania, many of New Jersey's council members in the first half of the

eighteenth century were part of the elite of her two more powerful
neighbors. This changed over the course of the eighteenth century,
and increasingly New Jersey's elite came to be a native elite rather than
an intercolony one.

As family connections helped a man achieve power and status, so
also did urban residence. We know from previously published work
that New England drew a disproportionate number of its major leaders
from its main urban centers. Despite an urban population in the colonies that comprised less than 10 percent of the population, 46 percent
of the Speakers of the assemblies were urban residents. In New York
and Pennsylvania, New York City and Philadelphia both produced
many more colony leaders than their respective populations warranted.
Thirty-six percent of New Jersey's councillors lived in the urban centers
of Perth Amboy and Burlington. Maryland, Virginia, and North Carolina, on the other hand, had almost no urban centers to furnish leaders. As noted earlier, one southern urban center did exercise a strong
influence on positions of power; Charlestown dominated the elite of
South Carolina, and many outlying parishes were represented by men
resident there.

From all of the above, we can form a picture of a typical member of
the colonial elite. He would be of English descent but native to his
colony; a merchant, large landholder, or lawyer; connected to a prominent and wealthy family. He would have proven himself in lesser
offices to be a man of ability and would be likely to live in an urban
center. As several of the essays show, he would not likely be a university
graduate, but, if he were, his access to the elite would have been made
easier. If he lived in New England, he would probably be a Congre-
gationalist; if in the South, an Anglican; and if in Pennsylvania, a
Quaker. Although a majority of leaders in New York and New Jersey
were Anglicans, being a member of a dissenting church was a lesser
handicap for entry to the elite in these two colonies than it was elsewhere.

Having developed this group portrait, it is appropriate to enter two
disclaimers. First, important differences existed among and within different colonies; the elite of no two colonies were identical, and within
colonies differing levels of government, regions, and types of settlements had differing patterns of officeholding. The heterogeneous nature of the colonial social structure created heterogeneous patterns of
elite formation. Second, despite the presence of an identifiable elite in
every colony, several of the essays show that a high degree of upward
mobility into the elite was possible. Perhaps this was most true for
small colonies such as North Carolina and Connecticut, but, even in
the powerful New York council, leadership was achieved not ascribed.

To return to Jefferson's distinction between types of aristocracy, each of the elites had many artificial qualities, but they combined them with many natural ones.

The ratio between artificial qualities and natural qualities increased over the course of the colonial portion of the eighteenth century. Maryland, for example, having had one of the most fluid power structures in the seventeenth century, underwent a dramatic metamorphosis between 1690 and 1720, emerging as part of the tidewater aristocracy so familiar to the folk image of the South. In all of the colonies, elites became more Americanized, but, as they matured, turnover rates among elected officials declined, so that fewer men served and those that did served longer terms; kinship networks became more entangled and important among the elite; and officeholders became progressively wealthier relative to the rest of the population. In other words, the lines separating the elite from the rest of the population hardened and entry into leadership ranks became more restricted. In many ways this is not surprising, inasmuch as a certain amount of flux within the social structure was a necessary consequence of the settlement process in each colony. As each colony's society matured, a leavening occurred within it: the further a colony was from its frontier period, the more rigid were its social and economic class lines, and the more directly were social and economic distinctions translated into political distinctions. Elites take time to form, but by mid-eighteenth century, the fluidity associated with nascent societies had subsided, and an increasingly entrenched group of officeholders dominated positions of power and status.

The agenda for expanding our knowledge of early American elites contains three essential items. First, the present essays are but signposts between large gaps, and much similar work needs to be done on all of the colonies. Second, historians of the Revolution and early national period have lagged behind colonial historians in analyzing leadership. We know much about the fifty most important Revolutionary and early national leaders, but we know little about officeholding patterns after the colonial period. Investigations of the Revolutionary and early national elites are not only valuable for their own sake; they will in turn enhance our understanding of the colonial period. And, finally, colonial historians should become imaginative and daring enough to compare patterns of leadership in the colonies to patterns in other societies. Not until we fill in more of the details and place them in comparative historical context, will we be entitled to feel secure in our knowledge of colonial American elites. This volume of essays is offered as a step in that direction.

LOCAL
LEADERSHIP

RONALD K. SNELL

"Ambitious of Honor and Places":
The Magistracy of Hampshire County,
Massachusetts, 1692–1760

EIGHTEENTH-CENTURY Hampshire County in Massachusetts witnessed the development of a political and social elite group which in its
coherence and compactness provides a useful model for assessing the
nature of elites elsewhere in colonial New England. The Hampshire
elite centered on the county judiciary, whose importance in colonial
Massachusetts has attracted a number of recent scholars.[1] The focus of
this paper is county officeholding as one expression of the unitary authority of a small group of county families. It seeks answers to the questions of the extent of their authority within Hampshire; the degree to
which they composed an identifiable political and social elite beyond
their simply sharing the authority of county government; the degree to
which the elite was other than the sum of town elites; and the way such
an elite might come into being and maintain itself.[2]

County government in eighteenth-century Massachusetts provided
a potential for elite-group control which had not existed under the
seventeenth-century charter. The charter of 1691 caused the replacement of once-elective offices with a form closer to that of England,
according to which the governor and his council appointed justices to
control the county. Justices of the peace individually exercised statu-
tory criminal and civil jurisdiction. Together the justices composed the
court of general sessions, which exercised more extensive criminal, administrative, and regulatory authority than an individual justice. Its ju-

17

risdiction included the hearing of appeals from individual justices'
decisions; extensive control over criminal and antisocial behavior; the
regulation of such enterprises as taverns, mills, and fisheries; and the
construction of highways and bridges. The court had the authority to
supervise the work of town officials as well, a power that was little used
in practice. Some of the justices held the distinction of being appointed "of the quorum" which entitled them to somewhat greater
powers than other justices had; a justice of the quorum had to be
present for a court of sessions to convene. A greater distinction was
appointment as one of the four justices of the court of common pleas,
who shared the civil jurisdiction of the county. The greatest place in
county government was that of judge of probate, one such sitting in a
county at a time. County government was rounded out with a sheriff,
who was primarily an administrative officer of the courts, and a clerk-
ship for each court. In Hampshire it was customary for one man to
hold both clerkships and as well to be elected by the county freemen to
the two minor positions at their disposal, those of treasurer and of
registrar of deeds. [3]

The principal rewards of county office were power and status. Although justices received a nominal salary and some fees, these taken
all together seem to have been slight, at least in Hampshire. Only the
justices of common pleas, the sheriff, and the judge of probate were
likely to receive enough pay to make the office worth holding for its
income. For all the justices, however, there were important nonmone-
tary rewards. Justices were relatively few and held great power over
their neighbors. Office meant a connection with the royal government, the title of "esquire," precedence in local assemblies, and the
regular opportunity to associate with other men of high status. Such
rewards were of consequence in a status-hungry society with few hon-
ors or titles. [4]

Throughout the century, observers of the colonial scene agreed on
the enviable status of a justice's appointment. In 1774 John Adams
remarked that "the Office of a Justice of the Peace, is a great Acquisition . . . enough to purchase and corrupt allmost any Man." [5] Earlier
Dr. William Douglass had noted that the appointment of justices was a
tool for governors to use in extending their political influence: "We are
all ambitious of honor and places." [6] And in 1709 Cotton Mather analyzed the subject thoroughly: "The Influence which Preferments and
Commissions have upon little Men, is inexpressible. It must needs be
a Mortal Sin, to Disoblige a Governour, that has Inabled a Man to
Command a *Whole Country Town* and to strut among his Neighbours
with the Illustrious Titles of, *Our Major,* and *the Captain,* or *His*

Worship. Such magnificent Grandeurs, make many to Stagger Egregiously!"[7]

Although Mather notes that status flowed as readily from a military title as from a civil, he, like the others quoted, slights the power that these appointments also conveyed. Held together, they meant substantial power as well as status. In Hampshire, therefore, it is notable that military and civil status tended to be associated with each other and with service in the general governing authority that rested with a few men. The examination of appointive and elective office in Hampshire shows the extent to which a county political elite existed.

Military office was of particular importance in Hampshire because of the county's situation and history. Colonial Hampshire made up the western third of Massachusetts, with the oldest and principal settlements lying in the Connecticut River Valley. King Philip's War in 1675 and 1676 brought the devastation of the valley; because of subsequent wars some of the towns abandoned in 1676 were not resettled until the 1720s. In subsequent wars Hampshire was invaded from Canada along the convenient Connecticut River route, and the county consequently remained something of a garrison into the 1740s. Even in the 1750s rumors of invasion caused the abandonment of some outposts. Hampshire was not expected to provide its defense unaided, but its distance from the other settled areas of the colony increased its exposure (the area east of the Connecticut Valley was settled only in the 1730s and 1740s). Other than towns on the Maine coast, no long-settled area of Massachusetts was as risky a spot as Hampshire during an Indian war. Thus a responsible and able local military command was a necessity, and civil and military command were the two faces of the coin of authority, with a clarity sharper than in the other, less endangered, older settlements of the colony.[8]

Hampshiremen held roughly comparable ranks in their county's civil and military structures. In the 1690s, as in earlier decades, John Pynchon of Springfield presided in the three county courts and commanded the county regiment. His rank of colonel and his role as presiding justice passed to Samuel Partridge when Pynchon died in 1703. The same positions went to John Stoddard as Partridge retired from office in the 1730s and to Israel Williams upon Stoddard's death in 1749. Lesser military rank corresponded to lesser civil rank; justices of the peace tended to be captains and lieutenants, with a sprinkling of majors, mostly in wartime. With allowance made for the practical difficulties of matching rank in one hierarchy with that in the other, civil and military authority in Hampshire marched along together.[9]

The same officeholders dominated the county's representation in the colonial legislature, the general court (see tables 1 and 2). The few Hampshiremen who became members of the Governor's Council, or upper house, were the leaders previously named: Pynchon, Partridge, Stoddard, and Williams. Other county officeholders had to be content with the House of Representatives where they held an increasing proportion of the seats for which their residences made them eligible. The proportion of representatives who were county officials when they were elected grew from 17 percent in the years before 1726 to 33 percent between 1726 and 1760. Such men's share of all the terms served grew from 29 percent to 47 percent, indicating Hampshire's increasing dependence on their leadership. The proportion of terms served by men who would at some time in their lives be county officials was considerably larger: 51 percent in the earlier period and 68 percent in the later.

The county's political elite was characterized by family ties among its members as well as by multiple officeholding. Men who were close relatives of other representatives dominated the town's representation through the period. (For this paper, "close relatives" designates the relationship of father and son, brothers, brothers-in-law, or uncle and nephew.) Further exploration of the importance of these family ties comes below; at present it is also important to note that a majority of the men appointed to county office received their first appointments before they were elected to the house. The governors' choice of appointees at least at first appointment was thus a recognition of something other than services performed in the legistlature. Some Hampshiremen belonged to a group in which authority was seen properly to rest, a view shared by the county's voters and by those who controlled appointments to county office and the militia. The members of this group were largely from the older Hampshire towns, were usually county officials and representatives, and were drawn from a few families.[10]

Hampshire representatives demonstrated their ties to each other through their voting record in the House of Representatives. They formed a permanent bloc in support of the governors' position on issues from the beginning of roll-call votes through those of the 1750s, voting together 88 percent of the time. Differences between the majority and dissenters within the delegation paralleled differences in residence and family connections. Although some dissenters were county officials, they were without exception representatives of towns—Brimfield, Enfield, and Suffield—that were not dominated by the extensive family connections from which most county officials came, and, individually, they were unrelated to those families. Such divisions appeared in all three of the roll-call votes in which more than one Hamp-

TABLE 1

Hampshire representation in the General Court

	Founding to 1726			1726–1760		
	% of total terms (N = 155)	% of men (N = 70)	Average number of terms	% of total terms (N = 234)	% of men (N = 87)	Average number of terms
County officials at time of service	29	17	3.8	47	33	3.8
County officials at time of service or later	61	28	4.7	68	36	5.2
County officials at time of service or later, or close relatives of other legislators	72	0	4.0	74	45	4.4
All others	28	60	1.0	26	55	1.3

NOTE: Terms and men are counted for all towns with resident county officials in the period. The county officials included are justices of the peace, justices of common pleas, probate judges, clerks, and sheriffs.

TABLE 2

County officials' service in the House of Representatives prior to appointment,
1696–1760

	Years of service in House						
	0	1	2	3	4	5	6–9
Percentage of county officials (N = 54)	52%	11%	15%	4%	7%	—	11%

NOTE: This tabulation includes appointments to judicial and sheriff's positions. It excludes officers appointed in 1692, because of their long previous records in office, and it excludes appointments to clerkships, because of the extreme youth at which men became clerks.

shire delegate differed with the majority of the county's representatives. Two of these, in 1740 and 1741, concerned the land bank, most Hampshire delegates agreeing with Governor Belcher in opposing it. The third occurred in 1754 on the question of increasing Governor Shirley's salary, which most Hampshire delegates favored. A similar division along residential and family lines characterized each instance in which there was only one dissenter.[11]

Robert Zemsky has recently suggested that the Hampshire County bloc voting was the expression of rural conservatism, an ideological

TABLE 3
Hampshire towns represented in the General Court,
1726–1760

Towns (with date of incorporation)	Number of resident county officials	Terms represented	Percentage served by officials and close relatives
Springfield (1636)	8	34	74
Northampton (1654)	9	34	88
Hadley (1661)	3	34	65
Westfield (1669)[a]	6	34	68
Hatfield (1670)	4	30	90
Suffield (1675)[a,b]	4	22	36
Enfield (1683)[a,b]	2	22	9
Deerfield (1684)	6	23	96
Northfield (1713)[a]	1	1	—
Sunderland (1718)[a]	1	7	—
Brimfield (1722)[a]	1	12	29
Sheffield (1733)	4	12	50
Somers (1734)[b]	—	—	—
Stockbridge (1739)	1	4	100
Blandford (1741)	—	—	—
Pelham (1743)	—	—	—
Palmer (1752)	—	—	—
Grenville (1754)	—	—	—

[a] Towns in which fewer than one-half the county officials were closely related to the six principal Hampshire families.
[b] Part of Connecticut after 1749.

position, but there is a well-documented alternative explanation: such voting was Hampshire's responsibility in a longstanding and honorably maintained bargain in which Hampshire delegates' support for governors was repaid with local control of patronage offices. Hampshire control of Hampshire office was of old origin; in 1691 Governor William Phips was being respectful of tradition when he appointed justices whom Colonel John Pynchon nominated for the county. Governor Jonathan Belcher's arrangement with John Stoddard was quite explicit, Belcher writing typically, "If you can propose any thing for your reasonable Advantage, You'll find me ready to serve you, and God Sparing your Life and Health, I desire you would not fail to be here with all your Friends on the Election Day" (in reference to the representatives' election of the councillors). On another occasion Belcher assured Stoddard, "The Officers of your County are settled as you have desired." Belcher's successor William Shirley similarly reached agreement with Stoddard: "I will take care of your own Interest." After Stoddard's death in 1748, his successor as master of patronage in Hampshire, Israel Williams, also had a comfortable relationship with

Shirley and Francis Bernard, despite difficulties with the intervening governor, Thomas Pownall.[12]

The coincidence of the military and civil hierarchies in Hampshire, the county officials' domination of the delegations to the House, and the patronage arrangements between Hampshire leaders and colonial governors indicate the existence of an enterprising and authoritative county elite. A further manifestation of the elite's authority and prestige was its individual members' role in the government of their towns. County officials inevitably were important local figures. A great number of them served as moderators of their town meetings, as lifetime clerks or treasurers of their towns, and as committeemen who decided such sensitive issues as the division of common lands or the seating arrangements in the meetinghouse, the latter requiring the wisdom to assign every family in the parish according to its social rank.

Such responsibilities did not necessarily extend to a town's requiring justices or other county officials to participate in the routine administration of affairs that fell upon town selectmen.[13] The smaller and newer towns that had a single justice of the peace were likely to impose a heavy burden of officeholding upon him, but older towns were more likely to spread the burden of town office. In some towns county officials were the most frequently elected selectmen, but more often they fell within the group of from fifteen to twenty men who in each town made up the top 25 percent of selectmen in terms of number of years in office. At Springfield, Pynchon family members' service as selectmen ranged from none at all to three years, an extreme example of escaping the job, though Pynchons who were not county officials spent long years in town offices. There were other comparable examples. They are of interest not only because of the generally unitary nature of authority that has been shown to exist in Hampshire, but also because county officials, who were invariably from the more prominent town families and thus were offered town office at early ages, had more opportunity than other men for long runs of service.[14]

Unpopularity may have kept some of the selectmen from long terms in town office, but it was probably not an important consideration. The Springfield men elected for six, three, and no terms were among the town's most frequently elected representatives. The Westfield man who served only one term as selectman had nine in the general court between 1713 and 1735, and was frequently called upon for committee service. The weight of other responsibilities could be a consideration in freeing county officials from town office; for example, Samuel Partridge rarely was reelected as Hatfield selectman after he became major of the regiment and probate court judge in 1703, though he had previously been a selectman twelve years in a row.[15]

TABLE 4

Service as selectmen of county officials and others, 1701–1750

Town	Average number of terms, all selectmen	Average number of terms of 25% serving most often	Range of number of terms, top 25%	Number of terms for each county official
Deerfield	3.9	9.6	5–16	2, 2, 8, 11, 11
Hadley	3.6	8.3	6–14	0, 1, 7, 12
Hatfield	5.2	12.5	7–20	3, 10, 11, 15, 16
Northampton	4.4	11.1	6–18	0, 6, 10, 17, 18
Springfield	4.1	11.0	5–20	0, 2, 3, 3, 6
Westfield	3.8	8.8	5–17	1, 8, 9, 14, 17

SOURCE: Town records listed in note 13.
  NOTE: This tabulation includes all terms a justice, clerk, or sheriff served within the period before and after appointment to office. It excludes men who died before 1710 and those born after 1720, to allow reasonable opportunity for election to office. The towns included are those that had at least four officials falling within those limits.

The variation in county officials' service to their towns indicates that they were freer than other men to refuse office, though the refusal perhaps need not be explicit. Town records do not indicate such refusals. Instead, in a society that recognized high status with officeholding, the voters' failure to choose some county officials for town office indicated respect for the higher status and responsibilities appointive office carried. County officials who were willing to accept town office could receive long terms if they chose; others continued to win election as representatives when they apparently chose to avoid local responsibilities. Appointive office carried enough status to distinguish its occupants from other members of town elites and to give them the privilege of refusing office.

The most distinguishing characteristic of the Hampshire elite was not the varieties of office its members held, but the extent to which the political elite of the county was coextensive with six interrelated Hampshire families. By midcentury, the men of these families held two-thirds of the county offices and a comparable proportion of Hampshire's general court seats. County government was dominated by the pursuit of family interest; leaders saw the furtherance of their relatives' status and power as a means of augmenting their own. The conversion of the county magistracy into a family magistracy began late, but proceeded rapidly. Only eight of the twenty-three men named as justices from 1692 through 1730 were closely related (in the sense defined earlier) to previously appointed justices. But from 1731 through 1760 the proportion doubled to twenty-three out of thirty-three (from 35 percent to 70 percent). Nearly three-quarters of the county officials of the latter period were closely related to the Dwights, Partridges, Porters, Pynchons, Stoddards, or Williamses. After 1740 men with those family names held all of the more prestigious or profitable county offices—those of justice of the quorum, common pleas justice, judge of probate, sheriff, and clerk. Their county status extended to military office—they supplied most of the captains, colonels, and majors—and to the general court, where Hampshiremen who became leaders in the house, or councillors, bore those family names. The late seventeenth- and early eighteenth-century circumstances of these six families show how a county elite came into being.[16]

They rose to prominence in Hampshire at different times and in different ways. The oldest county family was the Pynchons, whose first American representative led the settlement of the northern Connecticut Valley in the 1630s. John Pynchon dominated western Massachusetts through the second half of the seventeenth century and provided a substantial landed fortune to cushion his descendants in the eighteenth century. Because his only son to survive youth spent most of his life in Boston, the family suffered something of a diminution of its authority in the county after John Pynchon's death in 1703. Later generations provided numerous officeholders for Springfield and several justices of the peace, and the family remained the most notable in the southern part of the county.[17] Competition for status came from the later settlements further north along the Connecticut River.

The competitors appeared in Hatfield, Hadley, and Northampton in the late seventeenth century. The prominent family heads there at the turn of the century were Samuel Partridge of Hatfield, Samuel Porter of Hadley, Joseph Hawley of Northampton, and the Dwight brothers, Henry and Nathaniel, from Hatfield and Northampton. The first three were second-generation Hampshiremen; the Dwights arrived from Dedham in the 1690s. Samuel Partridge's father had built a substantial estate in land and through trade, which Samuel had to share with only one sister and which he increased with land speculation, trade, and the provisioning of troops.[18] Hawley, another trader and landowner, was the third-generation heir of what was by Hampshire standards a mercantile fortune.[19] Porter's fortunes similarly rested on a solid paternal foundation. Although he had numerous brothers with whom to share his inheritance, he seems to have gained control of his brothers' and his mother's shares and went on to amass a fortune comparable to those of Boston merchants of his time.[20] The Dwight brothers came to Hampshire to manage land their family owned in frontier towns and quickly married into the families of their important neighbors. Henry married Samuel Partridge's daughter Mehitable, and Nathaniel chose Joseph Hawley's sister Lydia. These ties secured a social position while the Dwights enriched themselves by land speculation, financed through trade, moneylending, and their occupation as surveyors.[21] With the exception of Joseph Hawley, whose career was hampered by his mental illness, these men and the Pynchons took the military and civil leadership of Hampshire in the early decades of the eighteenth century.

Their ability to prosper in the difficult decades after King Philip's War distinguished these leaders from their former equals. The 1690s brought wartime destruction to Hampshire, in addition to the high taxes and general economic difficulties the entire colony suffered. Hampshire met still further economic troubles. By the 1690s, due to plant disease, wheat, which had formerly been the county's major export and the source of its agricultural prosperity, could no longer be grown profitably. The wheat blight and the declining fertility of the Connecticut Valley soils encouraged a shift to livestock production. Cattle and packed meat would become its major eighteenth-century export. This business involved a larger investment of capital than grain production had, so served to shift control to a few wealthy men, such as Samuel Partridge and Samuel Porter. Their ability to prosper in changed circumstances indicated an eye for the main chance that served them politically as well as economically.[22]

Two other families, the Stoddards and the Williamses, complete the array of Hampshire's eighteenth-century gentry. These were originally ministerial families. Their Hampshire progenitors were the clergymen Solomon Stoddard of Northampton, John Williams of Deerfield, and John's cousin William Williams of Hatfield. They were similarly, though unequally, prominent figures in their time, alike in being prolific fathers and in amassing substantial estates.

Stoddard would have been the most prominent of them even without his well-known theological innovations. He was from a prominent Boston family that was connected with such families as the Belchers and was an ambitious and imperious man. He ruled his church firmly and attempted to extend his control to the other county churches through the Hampshire Association, which he envisioned as something of a presbytery.[23] John Stoddard's later control of the county was a secularized version of his father's ambition. The Williamses were also men of ability and tenacity. Though they lacked Stoddard's elevated family connections, once in Hampshire they made up for it. John Williams married Stoddard's stepdaughter, Eunice Warham Mather, the descendant of two noted clerical families. William Williams found his first wife among the Cottons, another old and prominent ministerial family. Such marriages united them to the galaxy of venerated fathers of New England, already in their time a matter for pride.[24]

Besides creditable ancestry and good local connections, the three clergymen provided their children with affluence in youth. Each of the Williamses put four sons through Harvard; Stoddard had only two to see through college. Presumably the Williamses provided their daughters with the dowries their status required; those Stoddard gave for his six daughters each amounted to the value of a substantial house. Such circumstances gave these three men's children marital prospects that extended far beyond their native towns. None of John Williams's seven children married within Deerfield. Only one of William Williams's seven married children chose someone from Hatfield—one daughter married a son of Samuel Partridge. Similarly, the only one of Stoddard's nine to marry within Northampton chose the most eligible man in town, Joseph Hawley.[25]

The other children, like their contemporaries among the Dwights, Partridges, Porters, and Pynchons, married across Hampshire among the families named, into other landed or clerical families in the county, or into similar Connecticut families. The children of John and William Williams married Partridges, Stoddards, Porters, Pynchons, and Dwights, and an occasional Ashley from Westfield. One of Samuel Partridge's sons married the sister of his pastor, William Williams; others married other Williamses and Dwights. Three of Samuel Porter's children married Williamses, and a thicket of connections united the Dwight and Pynchon families. Even marriages outside Hampshire could further complicate the relationships among these families, as when John Stoddard and his nephew Israel Williams married sisters from the Chester family of Connecticut. Succeeding generations duplicated and reduplicated the resulting tangle of connections, especially as the Williamses, who favored close family ties, developed the practice of marrying first cousins. In 1699 Solomon Stoddard's daughter Christian became William Williams's second wife; around 1712 Christian's sister Hannah married William's son. This sort of thing was unusual, but suggests the intensity of the family ties that turned the six major Hampshire families into one cousinry, extending through the older county towns.[26]

This array of connections encompassed the clergymen of the older and more prosperous Hampshire towns. Strong-minded ministers like Solomon Stoddard were quite capable of imposing their choice of successor upon a church, as Stoddard did at Northampton with Jonathan

Edwards. Important families elsewhere had college-educated sons, sons-in-law, and nephews to place in parishes. The lifelong tenure clergymen enjoyed by custom did not provide easy access to convenient parishes, but by 1740 six of the ten Hampshire churches that had been founded before 1700 had ministers who were closely related to the county's six important families. Numerous ties of marriage existed among the clergymen themselves, suggesting the beginnings of a parallel to the family control of the Hampshire magistracy. At Springfield, Robert Breck's marriage to his predecessor's daughter linked him to other clerical families as well as to the Pynchons. Ebenezer Devotion of Suffield married a daughter of Edward Taylor, the poet-pastor of Westfield, and thus gained brothers-in-law among two families productive of county officers, the Pynchons and the Taylors. Other ministers of 1740 with magisterial family ties were Jonathan Ashley of Deerfield, Chester Williams of Hadley, Samuel Hopkins of the west parish at Springfield, and Jonathan Edwards.[27]

This close alliance of ministers and magistrates did not reach to the newer Hampshire churches. In 1740 none of the churches organized since 1700 had clergymen who were related to the six leading county families. This remained true in 1760. Except for Northampton, the churches that in 1740 had had ministers closely related to the leading families still had one, and only one of the newer churches had gained one. The exception was Sunderland, which by 1760 was far from being a frontier town.[28]

The ministerial-magisterial connection did not ensure theological harmony within either group or between them, but, in towns where it was pronounced, the relationship lent stability to the churches. Springfield and Northampton provide examples. The oldest congregations in each town endured bitter internal disputes in the 1730s and 1740s. That at Springfield led to the Pynchons' attempt to use the court of general sessions to dismiss a clergyman and to the General Court's interference. The dispute at Northampton was the famous controversy which led to Jonathan Edwards's dismissal in 1749. Neither of these dramatic quarrels produced a congregational schism, however. Though other Hampshire churches underwent secessions in the period, they were in towns that lacked the important county families. Where the family magistracy was present in force—in Hadley, Hatfield, Deerfield, Westfield, Northampton, and Springfield—quarrelsomeness stopped short of physical division.[29]

Those circumstances bespeak a social authority used in the interests of social unity. The clearest expression of that authority was the Hampshire elite's control of officeholding, most marked after 1730.

Jonathan Belcher's appointment as governor in that year followed by a few months John Stoddard's rise to the top civil and military posts in Hampshire after Samuel Partridge's retirement. Belcher carried patronage politics to new heights in the colony. Stoddard's alliance with him gave Stoddard the power to recognize the status of his cousins among the Williamses and Dwights and the related families.[30]

Although previous Hampshire leaders had practiced nepotism, they had not done so with Stoddard's thoroughness. In John Pynchon's time, all of his available relatives had held county posts, but there had not then been enough Pynchons to dominate the government. Pynchon's lack of an heir of the age and inclination to assume his offices had made room for men from other families to rise; Samuel Partridge was one of those.[31] Partridge had dominated Hampshire for nearly thirty years, from 1703 to 1729. His position as royal councillor, in addition to his county offices, put him in a strong position to control appointments, but he had used his power to disperse appointments widely. One-third of the twelve justices appointed in his time were closely related to previous appointments, but none of them were Partridges, and the twelve all bore different family names. Though there were a Stoddard, a Pynchon, a Porter, and a Dwight among the appointments of Partridge's time, it was only after 1730 that the newer county families commanded county office almost as a matter of right.[32]

Under Stoddard and his like-minded successor, his nephew Israel Williams, county officeholding became a family matter: the proportion of county offices the six related families held rose to two-thirds of the total from 1730 through 1760. By 1740 all of the more important or profitable places in government had fallen into the hands of Dwights, Partridges, Pynchons, Stoddards, and Williamses, where they rested into the revolutionary period. Stoddard's consciousness of family and his patronage arrangements with the governors made the county magistracy into a family magistracy. Israel Williams preserved it as such after Stoddard's death in 1748.[33]

The growth of the county's population and of the number of towns brought little strain to the magisterial elite. It admitted some talented outsiders and gave office only to the more competent family members from within the elite. The ruling clique extended its influence in the county by presiding over the settlement of new towns. Aside from questions of personal rivalry, there were no issues to divide the elite for long: members' economic interests were alike bound in land speculation and trade, and the unity of their political views was demonstrated in their votes in the house of representatives. Rivalries themselves were few, if bitter. As Perry Miller pointed out, personal and family feuding appears to have been at the root of Jonathan Edwards's difficulties at Northampton, where John Stoddard defended Edwards until Stoddard's death in 1748, and where Israel Williams then intervened to engineer Edwards's removal. Some degree of bad feeling continued between Williams and Edwards's adherents, Timothy Dwight and his sons, though it did not hinder the Dwights' regular promotion in the county hierarchy. Another family quarrel, that between Joseph Hawley III and Israel Williams in the 1750s, assumed importance only because of the direction that colonial and imperial politics took in the 1760s. The traditional variety of authority Israel Williams and his predecessors had in Hampshire took on the appearance of authoritarianism in the light of colonial resistance to British policy. But before Revolutionary ideology entered local politics in Massachusetts, such authority as Williams's and Stoddard's had too solid a base in tradition, social expectations, and family connections to be legitimately challenged.[34]

The magistracy also, as noted above, remained somewhat available to outsiders qualified by status and ability, warding off a possible source of discontent. In the 1750s and 1760s, it was in the process of absorbing two new families, the Ashleys and the Woodbridges, who had earlier provided an occasional justice of the peace, a number of county clergymen, and some in-laws for the six principal families. This example and others demonstrate that with a sufficient show of ability and willingness to serve in office, the handicap of not being related to the county's principal families could be overcome. It also appears that without ability and willingness to accept office, even the best family connections would not bring a man's appointment to office.

The demonstration of ability that most facilitated appointment as a county official was a college education. Graduates, whether or not they were closely related to the leading families, became justices at a much earlier age than other men. The median age for college graduates appointed between 1730 and 1760 was thirty; that for other men was forty-seven. Of the seven men who became justices in that period without a close relationship to a leading family, four were college graduates. Even more indicative of the value of a degree is that there appears to have been only one man from a Hampshire family who retuned to the county after graduation who failed to become either a minister or a county official by the time he was forty.[35]

Good family connections led graduates and even college students into careers of public service at early ages. John Pynchon III's grandfather took him from college to become clerk of courts when he was eighteen. Israel Williams (Harvard, 1729) later got the job when he

TABLE 5
Age of county officials at appointment, 1730–1760

	College Graduates (N = 12)	Others (N = 15)
Range of ages	25–36ᵃ	31–55ᵇ
Mean	31.2	47.4
Medians:		
All officials	29.5	47.0
Those from, or closely related to, six important families	29.5 (N = 8)	47.0 (N = 12)
Those not so related	30.5 (N = 4)	52.0 (N = 3)

NOTE: This tabulation includes all justices, clerks, and sheriffs appointed in the period for whom ages are known: twenty-seven of the thirty-five appointments of the period. Before 1730, only two college graduates entered the magistracy, one at twenty-nine and the other at an unknown age.
ᵃExcludes one man aged 50 at appointment; he is included in calculations of mean and median.
ᵇExcludes one man aged 70 at appointment; he is included in calculations of mean and median.

was twenty-two, and Timothy Dwight II (Yale, 1744) became clerk of probate at the same age. Williams subsequently became a justice of the peace when he was twenty-four, and Dwight when he was twenty-seven. Joseph Hawley III, Israel Williams's and John Stoddard's nephew, became a justice of the peace three years after graduating from Yale, when he was only twenty-five.[36]

It followed that without such family connections a graduate's appointment as a justice would come somewhat later in life. Seth Field of Northfield graduated from Yale in 1729 and returned to his native town where he married the minister's daughter and became a local potentate—principal landowner, schoolmaster, town clerk for life, most frequently reelected selectman, and captain in the militia. He did not become a justice of the peace until he was thirty-six despite all that, for lack of family connections. Joseph Lord of Sunderland did better. A Harvard graduate in the class of 1726, he came to Hampshire where he had no previous family ties when Sunderland invited him to settle as its physician. He became a justice of the peace when he was about thirty, perhaps helped by his distinguished ancestry in Plymouth Colony.[37]

In the absence of family connections and of a college education, some unusual show of distinction was necessary for men to receive a county office. Richard Crouch of Hadley did so on the basis of being a physician and a man of wealth from England; John Sherman of Brimfield was a physician and a schoolmaster. Samuel and John Kent of Suffield, and Thomas and David Ingersole of Westfield, came from families long established in those towns, were men of considerable property, and had long records in local office. Both families were remotely related to families of greater county note and lived in towns where at the time of their appointments there were no justices from the six greater families of Hampshire. The Ashleys and Woodbridges, mentioned earlier as coming to prominence in the county in the 1750s and 1760s, rose on the basis of college educations and numerous connections with the ministers and magistrates of the county.[38]

Among the leading families themselves, some show of distinctiveness was also necessary for a man to win a magisterial appointment. Within the six elite families, the number of men who lived in obscurity was greater than the number who became clergymen or who attained county offices. The Williams family was exceptional in that all of the twelve sons of John, William, and William's brother Ephraim were clergymen, county officials, or soldiers with at least the rank of captain by the age of thirty. This was an unmatched record. Samuel Partridge's two sons who survived their twenties rarely held office even in their towns. A number of Pynchons held very few town offices, and no county office. Seth Dwight and Elisha Hawley, brothers of justices of the peace, made good soldiers but never became county officials. The historian of the Porter family at Hadley has noted that Porters either were conspicuous for their public careers, or barely in evidence even on the town level.[39] There seems to have been a winnowing of the magisterial families to keep the less able and the uninterested out of office. County office in practice was no sinecure; officials generally were diligent and responsible, and men who were not thought to be so were unlikely to join them in office.[40]

Acquiring or having wealth was not in itself the show of ability that could lead to county office. Wealth augmented the qualifications described so far, but could not substitute for them. It was part of the foundation of the status of the leading county families; Samuel Porter's and John Stoddard's estates, both over £10,000, were probably the largest in Hampshire before midcentury. Henry Dwight, two justices from the Pynchon family, and Thomas Ingersole of Westfield all were among the wealthiest men in the county. Samuel Partridge's will indicates that he ranked with them. But the status that led to office required more than wealth. Such county officials were only a part of a larger group of well-to-do landowners, merchants, and speculators, most of whom failed to have noteworthy careers in office. Of the thirty-five men whose estates were worth over £1,500 from 1729 through 1751 (taking inflation into account), only six were county officials. Four of the others were clergymen. Of the remaining twenty-five, only six ever won elec-

TABLE 6
Distribution of wealth of Hampshire estates, 1729–1751

Amount (1730 pounds)	Distribution (N = 303)	Number of county officials' estates
1–199	22.4%	—
200–499	33.0	—
500–999	21.8	1
1,000–1,999	14.8	1
2,000 and over	7.9 (N = 24)	6

NOTE: This table is based upon the analysis of 303 entries for completely inventoried estates in Hampshire Probate Records, IV through VII. The inflation of the Massachusetts currency in which the estates were valued made it necessary to adjust them to one level; I chose 1730 and used the scale in Bureau of the Census, *Historical Statistics of the United States: Colonial Times to 1970* (Washington, D.C., 1975), II, 1199, series Z, 586. The inventoried price of silver demonstrates that Hampshire inventories were valued in currently depreciated Massachusetts pounds. Because my purpose was principally to identify propertied men who had the opportunity through length of life to serve in office, I have not taken the biases of probated inventories further into account. Other than the county officials and the clergymen, these men have been traced through the records of the towns where they resided at the date of their death. In most cases the presence in their towns of others of the same family name indicates they were likely to be of that town throughout their lives; records of lawsuits in the Hampshire County Court Records also indicated that they tended to be life-long residents of one town. For those about whom I was uncertain, I examined recorded of other towns.

TABLE 7
Careers of wealthy men not clergy or county officials

	Number of terms						
	0	1	2	3	4	5–10	over 10
Service in the House of Representatives	19	5	—	—	—	1	—
Service as Selectman, Town Clerk, or Town Treasurer[a]	13	4	—	1	2	2	2

NOTE: This tabulation is based on the careers of thirty-five men whose estates exceeded £1,500. Six of them were county officials, and four were clergymen. The public careers of the other twenty-five are recorded in the table above. See note 41.

[a] Unknown for one individual.

tion to the House of Representatives, and only one of them for more than one term. Thirteen were never chosen as town selectmen, and only seven of the twenty-five had more than one term as a selectman. While county officials sometimes evaded town office because of their other duties, the poor showing of these twenty-five men indicates that they lacked the confidence of their townspeople. Wealth itself did not carry the kind of status that produced office.[41]

Though the elite families of Hampshire were originally based in a few towns, they extended their control of the county through direction of, and participation in, the settling of new towns. From the mid-1670s until the 1730s, the General Court gave committees of county leaders oversight of the new towns opened to settlement in the region. John Pynchon, Samuel Partridge, and John Stoddard chaired many such committees, and the membership generally was drawn from the county justices.[42] These committees were not proprietors in the later manner of individuals who bought a township to parcel out for resale; they were instead supposed to supervise settlement and be personally disinterested. They platted towns, admitted inhabitants, granted land, apportioned the costs of settlement among the grantees, issued ordinances, planned roads, and in general governed the settlement as its town meeting later would do. Supervisory committees played a far from perfunctory role in many late seventeenth-century and early eighteenth-century settlements. The committeemen's involvement brought them rewards in land in the new town, opportunity for investment in mills, and the chance to lend the settlers money for developing the place. During and after their service, committee members were the obvious choice as agents to represent the new town's interests in the county courts or the General Court; their role helps explain why new towns rarely elected formal representatives.[43]

The major county families also invested heavily in the private proprietorships that became the chief form of settling new towns in the 1730s and after. Such ventures have often been characterized as nothing more than speculation in land; at minimum they were nothing more than the purchase and subdivision of a township for resale. In Hampshire the county magistracy as a rule did more than the minimum. Partly this was an expression of financial self-interest, because an early influx of financially able settlers meant quick returns, and partly the magistrate's activity in their new towns reflected their concern to maintain and expand their role as county leaders. Some members of magisterial families led substantial numbers of men from their original towns to new settlements, as David Ingersole and the Ashleys led Westfield men to found Sheffield and Great Barrington. John Stoddard fostered his investment at Pittsfield by encouraging Colonel William Williams to settle there, in the hope that the presence of a gentleman would invite other settlers of rank. Other Williamses moved to what became Williamstown and Stockbridge; they encouraged the settlement of their enemy Jonathan Edwards at Stockbridge because they expected his presence to raise land values. Place names such as Hawley, Partridgefield, and Worthington reflect the similar ventures of other magisterial families in the expansion of Hampshire west to the Berkshire Hills. The personal participation of the magistracy made this expansion far from the coldly capitalistic enterprise it is sometimes described as having been.[44]

The Hampshire magistracy's extension of its authority to the frontier was a striking success. When the western towns of Hampshire were formed into the new county of Berkshire in 1761, four of the five of the new county's justices were representatives of the Hampshire magisterial families. Ashleys, Dwights, Stoddards, and Williamses took the place in Berkshire their relatives had had for years in Hampshire, and the county remained their preserve into the revolutionary era. The Hampshire elite in effect watched its colony gain independence.[45]

The success of the leading Hampshire families in transferring their authority to the frontier and in supervising the establishment of a new county can be taken as the final indication that they were an elite by the customary measures of class, status, and power.[46] While they did not monopolize wealth in the county, they tended to be among the wealthiest members of their society. Their status was unassailable, short of a revolution. Their concern with family, with marriage among their peers, and with their social role as decision makers were indicators of their sense of their status. Their power and, more importantly, the way they gained power mark them as an elite; family and status conveyed the social power that originally led men to office. Their intricate family ties along with the independence of their authority from town officeholding mark them as more than a coalition of local leaders: they were a county-wide family magistracy.

As such, the Hampshire magistracy may well have been unique in eighteenth-century Massachusetts. The importance of family connections to political and social careers was certainly not limited to Hampshire County; the Hutchinson-Oliver connection alone would make that point. But there does not seem to have been another group precisely like the Hampshire magistracy in its geographic extent, its organization in the House of Representatives, its control of local patronage, its ecclesiastical influence, and its ability to replicate itself in another county. Isolation, military need, the resources to dominate expansion, and of course the Stoddard-Belcher tie help account for this remarkable efflorescence of a gentry. By 1760 the county had become a measure of the extent to which a traditionally elitist society could evolve within the republican traditions of colonial Massachusetts.

BRUCE C. DANIELS

Diversity and Democracy:
Officeholding Patterns among Selectmen
in Eighteenth-Century Connecticut

TWO CONFLICTING IMAGES of colonial New England towns have enjoyed a high visibility in the American past and persist in the present.
The first image is that of nearly autonomous little city-states holding
open town meetings to shape policy and to elect leaders according to
natural ability. This is the vision of the fabled democratic town, and it
is central to the American folk culture. The second image is that of the
repressive Puritan community dominated by a clique of ministers and
magistrates who suppressed all dissent. This is the vision of the auto-
cratic Puritan village and, while one would not say this vision was
fabled, it certainly has been central to the iconoclastic tradition of the
twentieth century. One cannot assign the first image to the general
public and the second one to professional historians. Despite the patriotic fervor mention of the colonial New England town can inspire,
much of the general public's reaction has been conditioned by books
such as Nathaniel Hawthorne's *The Scarlet Letter* and Anya Seton's
The Winthrop Woman or by plays such as Arthur Miller's *The Cru-
cible*, all of which stress the authoritarian nature of the Puritan village.
Similarly, despite a proclivity for debunking myths, much of the historical profession does pay homage to the democratic town meeting.

Most obviously, the truth of the matter lies somewhere between
these two extremes. Almost every historian would acknowledge this,
and yet, most tend to place themselves closer to one extreme than to
the other. Nearly as obviously, the question of definition is crucial to

where one places oneself on the continuum between democracy and autocracy. Since the publication in 1955 of Robert Brown's book on colonial and Revolutionary politics in Massachusetts,[1] much of the research on this subject has been quantitative; but precisely the same data can lead historians with differing criteria for what constitutes democracy or autocracy to opposite choices of terminology. All too frequently, the criteria are determined by personal predilection. In the era of the cold war of the 1950s and the reform movements of the 1960s and 1970s, the choice of adjectives used by colonial historians to describe the New England town has been a handy index to their present ideological commitments. The result has become a tiresome and utterly inconclusive debate.

Besides the language problem, that is, how does one label the data after they are collected, there has also been a problem with the data themselves. Most of them have been collected for community studies, and thus the data base for much of the argumentation has been unacceptably small. Moreover, most of the data collected are for short periods and do not comment meaningfully on change—after all, New England was over one hundred fifty years old by the end of the colonial period. Also, no New England colony was homogeneous, each contained towns of various ages, locations, economic functions, and populations. Why should we logically expect that such a variegated social and economic structure would necessarily produce similar political structures? Each type of town might be placed on different parts of the continuum; and these placements might change over time.[2]

The present study of officeholding patterns among selectmen in Connecticut's towns does not solve all of these problems, but it does address them all, with the hope that this will move us nearer to a sophisticated appraisal of colonial politics. Officeholding patterns are not the only way to measure the degree of democracy in society but they are one of the best ways. Whom a society elects to office and how long they continue to serve tells us much about that society. Probably no one could develop a definition of democracy or autocracy that could satisfy everyone and this essay will not try to; instead, the essay will compare selectmen's officeholding patterns in eighteenth-century Connecticut with data in other eras and societies to arrive at a relative appreciation of how Connecticut towns compared to other political systems. The data base for this study consists of records of selectmen's elections in thirty Connecticut towns from 1701 through 1780. The thirty towns comprised over half of the number of towns in the colony in 1701 and over one-third of them in 1780, and the time span is sufficiently long to examine changes over time and to establish existing trends. Finally, the sample of thirty towns is heterogeneous enough to permit an analysis of how the important variables that distinguished towns from each other affected the officeholding pattern among the selectmen.

Selectmen varied in number from three in some towns to seven in others. Like all town-meeting officers, they were elected annually. In the first generation after the settlement of the colony, when towns elected only a small number of officers, and the Puritan impulse was strong, the selectmen had the powers of the magistracy and functioned as village elders; they not only administered almost all of the affairs of local government, but also heard petty criminal and civil legal cases and watched over the moral lives of their fellow townsmen. In the last quarter of the seventeenth century, as the Puritan ethos weakened, the towns became more populous and heterogeneous, and the nucleated village gave way to the farmstead, the selectmen began to function much more as local political leaders and much less as moral guardians. One should not overstate this change; throughout the colonial period it was difficult to separate political and moral functions, and selectmen would not look the other way from unacceptable social behavior. But, increasingly after the late seventeenth century, selectmen were more concerned with poor relief, local finances, and supervising lesser officers than with questioning children on the street about their catechism or inquiring about young men's tavern haunting. As a symbol of this transition, the powers of the local magistracy were transferred from the selectmen to colony-appointed justices of the peace in 1698. This decline in moral authority was more than compensated for by an increase in political power, as eighteenth-century towns, grown more socially and economically complex, needed a secular government of increasing complexity. By the outbreak of the Revolution, most town meetings elected a large variety of officers, usually more than seventy-five and occasionally as high as two hundred. It was the selectmen who oversaw and unified this burgeoning bureaucracy. Without any doubt, they were the most important officers elected by the town meeting; their position represented the pinnacle of community political leadership. One had to move from town to county or colony politics and serve as a justice of the peace or deputy to the General Assembly to gain more influence or prestige.[3]

Three statistics can tell us much about the pattern of officeholding among selectmen: average number of terms served per selectman, turnover rate in the annual elections, and the percentage of the total terms served by the five most politically powerful families in each town.

The method of computing average terms needs some explanation: selectmen who appeared in the records in the first ten years of the period 1701–1780 or who appeared for the first time in the last ten years have not been included in the calculations, since some of them could quite possibly have served terms before or after the period under study and including them would have slightly understated the overall average. For example, since only the records for 1701–1780 were consulted, a man might first appear in my data sheets in 1703 but in reality might have been elected a selectman in 1698. Similarly, a man first elected in 1778 may have been reelected several times after 1780, but since the records after 1780 were not consulted, these latter terms would not show up in the data. (Probably a few men included in the data analysis served terms before 1700 and after 1780, but their number could only be very small, and the omission of a term or two would not significantly affect the calculations.)

Turnover rates were calculated by examining the percentage of men not reelected from one year to the next; a turnover rate of 100 percent would mean that no selectmen were reelected, and a rate of 0 percent would mean that all of them were reelected. If, as occasionally happened, a man was elected but chose not to serve, he was treated in the data as if he were not reelected.

The family dominance factor is determined by dividing the number of terms served by members of the five leading families into the total number of terms; the higher the percentage, the more dominant these five families were.

After assessment of such data for all thirty towns from 1701 to 1780, the period was subdivided into four equal intervals (1701–1720, 1721–1740, 1741–1760, and 1761–1780) for the purpose of analyzing changes over time.[4] These periods are somewhat artificial, designed primarily for convenience of analysis, yet they are not without some relationship to Connecticut's development: the first two periods embrace the maturing years of colonial society, the third corresponds to the Great Awakening struggles and their aftermath, and the fourth encompasses the pre-Revolutionary debates and early Revolutionary years.

The sample of thirty towns, besides being large enough to give weight to the results, permits us to isolate certain variables and measure how they affected local officeholding. The crucial attributes that distinguished towns from each other were population, age, and location. On the eve of the Revolution, Connecticut towns ranged from urban centers to isolated rural villages, with populations of 1,000 to 7,000; founding dates from the 1630s to the 1750s, and locations from the borders of Rhode Island to the borders of New York. It is worth investigating if these factors affected power relationships manifested in the officeholding patterns of selectmen.

The overall data from 1701 to 1780 yield few dramatic conclusions. For all thirty towns, the selectmen averaged 4.7 terms per man. Although one town ranged as high as 9.4 and another as low as 2.3, twenty of the towns were clustered between 3.7 and 5.7. The 4.7 average is neither high enough to suggest that a few men monopolized the offices nor low enough to suggest that the towns tried to spread the offices around to most responsible men. Approximately 25 percent of the selectmen served single terms, but the thirty longest-serving selectmen—one from each town—averaged 18.4 terms, and one man served 32 terms. The moderate average number of terms served thus included many men serving once and several men serving a large number of terms. Each selectmen's board could usually be depended upon to have a combination of experienced and inexperienced men. Few large aggregates of comparable data exist, but those that do suggest that Connecticut's selectmen had a less oligarchical officeholding pattern than was commonly found in other systems and with other officers. Rhode Island's town-councilmen, also elected annually, averaged nearly six terms per man in the eighteenth century, a significant increase. Data on officeholding for selectmen in Massachusetts, the colony most similar to Connecticut in social structure and governing arrangements, has been collected by Edward Cook, Jr., for 36 towns. Cook found that the average selectman in eighteenth-century Massachusetts served 4.4 terms, but this figure should be adjusted upward because Cook did not figure into his calculations the certainty that some selectmen in the period sampled would have held office before or after the period ended.[5] If this adjustment were made, Massachusetts selectmen would have averaged at least five terms per man, a slight but significant increase over Connecticut's average.

Other important officers elected in Connecticut also averaged longer tenures in office. Deputies to the General Assembly averaged approximately nine terms in office. Of course, the significance of this long tenure is lessened by the fact that deputies' terms were for six months, or half as long as selectmen's terms; nevertheless, despite facing election twice as often, deputies served as many years in office as selectmen, testimony to a more stable officeholding pattern among deputies than among selectmen. Town clerks, officeholders who had very different responsibilities than selectmen but were elected by the same body, the town meeting, averaged 21.4 terms per man. One might expect, given the fact that there was only one clerk per town and that clerks were not in policy-making positions, that they would have longer tenures in office than selectmen; but the difference between the selectman's average term and the clerk's is extreme.[6]

When we turn from average terms served to the turnover rate, our picture sharpens. From 1701 to 1780, Connecticut's selectmen experienced a turnover rate of 51.3 percent; slightly over one half of the incumbent selectmen were not reelected. This measurement varied greatly among the towns: only thirteen of the thirty towns clustered between 40 percent and 60 percent, and the towns ranged from Saybrook's high of 93 percent to Fairfield's low of 26 percent. What the turnover rate does tell us clearly, when analyzed along with the average number of terms served, is that men frequently served for a term, did not serve for an ensuing period, and then were again elected. With a 93 percent turnover rate, Saybrook's selectmen averaged 2.4 terms per man. Norwalk, with a turnover rate of 75 percent, averaged 4.7 terms per selectman. Thus, a rotation of sorts was widely practiced by the towns, although the 51.3 percent turnover rate viewed in isolation would disguise the fact that usually a majority of the men on each selectmen's board had served previously in the office. The turnover rate does tell us that many, probably most, of the men who served multiple terms as selectmen did not serve them consecutively.

A comparative view helps us to see how high the turnover rate was for Connecticut's selectmen. The colony's deputies had a turnover rate of 44 percent. Rhode Island's town councilmen had a dramatically lower turnover rate of 27.3 percent. A sample of fifteen Massachusetts towns had a turnover rate of 46.2 percent among selectmen. Unlike the case of average terms per officeholder, modern data do exist for turnover rates among city councillors, and a large sample in the 1970s reveals a turnover rate of 44 percent among officeholders who were almost always serving terms of either two or four years as compared to the one-year terms of Connecticut's selectmen.[7] In comparison to the other New England colonies and to modern American local governments, the officeholding patterns of Connecticut's selectmen were relatively democratic.

The dominance of elite families on selectmen's boards is more difficult to measure comparatively because almost no similar data exist. The five leading families in each town served an average of 46 percent of all the terms in the thirty towns; this ranged from a high of 71 percent in Canaan to a low of 24 percent in Hartford. Twenty of the towns ranged between 36 and 56 percent. These high figures seem at first to argue against a democratic model of officeholding—and indeed they certainly do qualify the above findings of average numbers of terms served and turnover rates—but we must be careful not to place too heavy a burden of interpretation upon the absolute quality of these data. Obviously family names and connections were important assets to have for aspiring selectmen, making access to office much easier for some than for others; but we do not know what percentage of each town's population these five families constituted. It is fairly certain that five families did not constitute 46 percent of each town's population, but, with the reluctance of young men to leave their hometowns before the 1760s and with high fertility rates, the proportion of a town's population furnished by the five leading families may have been surprisingly high by today's standards. Politically powerful families did not dominate the office of selectman as much as they did that of deputy to the General Assembly, where the five leading families in the same time period served 66 percent of the terms.[8]

When turnover rates and average numbers of terms served are compiled for four twenty-year periods, they yield a rather clear conclusion: officeholding patterns of selectmen grew progressively more oligarchic and less democratic over the course of the colonial portion of the eighteenth century. Turnover rates declined from a high of 68 percent in 1701–20 to a low of 41 percent in 1761–80, and average numbers of terms served for these twenty-year blocks increased from 2.7 to 3.5. The trend was clear, constant, and rather dramatic. Nor was it a result of any drastic drop in a few individual towns, producing statistical anomalies that disguise reality. Of the eighteen towns for which data are available for the entire period, sixteen of them experienced a decline in turnover rates, one experienced an increase, and one stayed the same. More men were being reelected at the end of the eighteenth century than at the beginning, and they were serving more terms. A smaller percentage of men therefore could hope to be selectmen in 1780 than in 1701.

This change in the officeholding pattern indicating a lessened accessibility to high local office must be evaluated in light of the sizable growth occurring in each town's population in this period. Not only were fewer men serving in office from 1761 to 1780 than from 1701 to 1720, but there were many more potential officeholders in each town. In other words, the chances for an adult white male to serve as a selectman in 1780 were even more reduced from 1701 than the changes in the data on officeholding reveal. Connecticut's population grew from approximately 38,000 inhabitants in 1710, the midpoint of the first twenty-year period, to 181,000 inhabitants in 1770, the midpoint

TABLE 1

Overall data for selectmen by town, 1701–1780

Town	Average number of terms served per officeholder	Percentage not reelected (turnover rate)	Percentage of total terms served by five leading families	Most terms served by any individual
Branford	5.0	39	41	15
Canaan	5.9	44	71	24
Derby	4.5	49	43	17
Durham	6.9	32	66	24
Fairfield	6.1	26	48	29
Farmington	3.6	62	40	18
Goshen	5.2	46	48	14
Groton	4.8	44	46	22
Hartford	2.3	78	24	9
Hebron	9.4	34	59	23
Killingworth	4.2	78	48	17
Lebanon	5.6	50	55	21
Mansfield	5.1	30	62	20
Middletown	4.2	53	25	28
Milford	3.0	39	36	14
Newtown	4.0	72	37	12
New Hartford	3.7	38	53	9
New Haven	3.6	41	30	15
New London	4.6	37	38	19
Norwalk	4.7	75	38	20
Norwich	2.5	91	46	13
Ridgefield	3.4	82	59	10
Salisbury	4.3	42	48	14
Saybrook	2.4	93	32	11
Sharon	4.6	41	48	14
Simsbury	4.9	50	64	23
Stonington	6.1	37	47	32
Stratford	5.0	40	40	20
Waterbury	4.9	51	44	18
Windham	5.3	45	40	26
Average per town	4.7	52	46	18

of the last twenty-year period.[9] In Hartford, for example, during the period from 1701 to 1720, 66 men became selectmen out of an adult white male population of approximately 310, whereas from 1761 to 1780, 41 men did so out of approximately 1184 adult white men. An eligible man's chances of being elected to the top local office in early eighteenth-century Hartford was thus 1 out of 4.7, a figure that could easily be seen as remarkably democratic. His grandson's chances to serve in the same office were reduced to 1 out of 28.9, a figure that might look democratic by today's standards but must certainly have represented diminished aspirations in eighteenth-century Connecticut.

TABLE 2

Changes in patterns of officeholding among selectmen, 1701–1780

	1701–20	1721–40	1741–60	1761–80
Turnover rates (Percentage not reelected)	68	63	50	41
Average number of terms served	2.7	2.9	3.3	3.5

Perhaps to counteract the lessened opportunity for major office, and almost surely to meet the expanding governmental needs of their growing populations, most Connecticut towns between 1701 and 1780 increased the number of selectmen elected annually. The eighteen towns whose records are complete usually elected three or five selectmen annually in the 1701–1720 period, five or seven in the 1761–1780 period. The increase in the number of selectmen elected annually did not keep pace with the growing population, however, and when this growth is coupled with the increased propensity to reelect incumbents, a man's chances of being elected a selectman in these eighteen towns decreased from one out of 4.1 in the earlier period to one out of 20.8 in the latter. Of course, by itself this does not mean that Connecticut's local politics were growing less democratic; one would hardly say that because the United States has tripled in population in the twentieth century, but still only elects one president, it is less democratic in 1980 than it was in 1900. But these data do mean that it was much more of a real possibility for a given individual to be elected a selectman at the beginning of the eighteenth century than it was at the end.

The effects of the population growth on the possibilities of serving as selectmen are important but hardly surprising. It does seem surprising that after 1740 the officeholding patterns themselves were more oligarchic and less democratic. The forty-year period from 1741 to 1780 embraced the eras of the Great Awakening and the American Revolution, two phenomena which are generally regarded as having advanced the ideology of both social and political democracy. Why then would a people becoming more assertive against an established church and a mother country tend to defer more to local leaders? There are three plausible explanations none of which are mutually exclusive and all three of which probably worked together to produce this result.

First, the towns grew tremendously in social and economic complexity in the eighteenth century, and many more distinctions of status and wealth could be made at midcentury than could be earlier. Connecticut was never a homogeneous society of equals who all made their living farming, but it was much more homogeneous in 1701 than it was in 1741 or 1780. The eighteenth century witnessed a transition from a basically internal economy to an external one: trade grew in volume, merchants and artisans in number; large estates were amassed, distinctions made within towns between early and late arrivals; and in general the social structure became much more variegated and heterogeneous.[10] It is logical to expect that a more egalitarian social structure in the early eighteenth century would produce a more egalitarian officeholding pattern and a less egalitarian social structure late in the century, a less egalitarian one. As it became increasingly possible to make social and economic distinctions, it would be surprising if it did not become increasingly likely that political distinctions would be made.

Second, as the towns grew in size and complexity, the job of the selectmen grew more complex, required more ability and more time, and benefited more from having an experienced man serve in it. An intelligent and pious farmer, familiar with the town's history and people, might well feel qualified to deal with the problems arising in a small agricultural village of the early eighteenth century. He might increasingly feel out of his depth as the town became populated to the extent that he did not know a substantial percentage of its inhabitants and as transportation systems became well developed, external and internal commerce placed new demands on local government, taxing policy and problems grew more contentious, and relations with the colonial government became more formal and less personal. Moreover, the political problems caused by the Awakening and the Revolution were frequently colony-wide, requiring more sophistication to handle than the more local problems he would have been called upon to solve earlier in the century. Even more likely, this same farmer would not have the time to devote to all of these new duties, and, as the Puritan sense of corporate responsibility waned, to be replaced by a headier individualism, he might not have the inclination to sacrifice his own time for the benefit of the community. The demands of the selectman's job were increasingly likely to require the free time, as well as the social confidence, of a member of the privileged class. And, if many of the problems towns faced were increasingly unfamiliar to many people, it became imperative to retain in office a larger number of men who had gained some expertise in dealing with these problems.

Finally, the tumultuous quality of the Great Awakening and the American Revolution may have caused the towns to reelect more men and create more of a local elite.[11] In circumstances that cause great contention and threaten the social fabric, as both the Awakening and Revolution did, one can postulate two extreme possible effects on leadership: voters can arise in anger, effect an electoral revolution, and elect almost all new leaders or fearing for their security, they can elect respected and proven leaders who can be trusted to guide them through the crisis. The latter seems to have been the case in Connecticut's towns. Connecticut men had two primary focuses of loyalty beyond their local community, colony, family, and personal friends: the Congregational Church and England. When the integrity of both of these bonds was threatened, it was not surprising that they may have felt bewildered, in need of the reassurance that the stability of an elite could provide. Moreover, we should not overstate the change in officeholding patterns that did take plce. The freemen still could and did turn selectmen out of office and still had a chance to bring them to an annual accounting on election day. Nor should we assume that a more elite pattern of officeholding was inconsistent with a rising curve of democratic political and social ideology: the always delicate relationship between voter and officeholder may have changed, and the personal merit of good leaders may have become more highly prized by the freemen. What we can assume is that democratic ideological thrusts and social upheaval did not manifest themselves in the election of larger numbers of men to the position of selectmen.

Connecticut's towns were not only growing internally more heterogeneous in the eighteenth century but were also growing more heterogeneous in relation to each other. The Connecticut River had always been (and still is today) seen as a cultural, as well as a physical, dividing line, and it became much more so at midcentury, as eastern Connecticut became identified with the New Lights in the Great Awakening and Revolutionary eras and western Connecticut became identified with the Old Lights.[12] Towns on and off navigable water also developed differing economic functions which became more pronounced as trade expanded at midcentury. Aggregate population and population density are other ways that Connecticut's towns increasingly became distinguished from each other. Towns ranged from the thirteen with populations of over 4,000 in the census of 1774 to the more numerous middle-sized ones of between 2,500 and 4,000 to still more numerous ones of less than 2,500. Within the large towns a distinction can be made between the five that had very densely populated centers and well-developed business districts, and hence were real urban centers, and the other large towns, which were populous but, lacking the same concentration of people and business in one compact area, were not urban to the same degree. Finally, Connecticut's towns were not all founded at the same time. Many dated their settlement to the 1630s, Connecticut's founding decade, but others were being founded continually, if irregularly, until the settlement of Litchfield County from the 1730s to 1750s. Towns at mid-eighteenth century thus ranged from frontier[13] towns to communities in their fourth generation of settlement.

Surprisingly, given the ideological positions usually associated with the east and the west in Connecticut, geography had no apparent effect on the officeholding pattern of selectmen. Eastern towns may have been more radical religiously in the Great Awakening, and more radical politically in the Revolution, than the western towns, but this radicalism was not reflected in more democratic officeholding patterns among selectmen. Turnover rates, average numbers of terms served, and family dominance rates were nearly identical in the two sections. Similarly, a town's location on or off navigable water had no measurable effect on the election of selectmen; when inland towns and coastal towns of similar populations were compared, the differences were too slight to be significant.

Population size and the presence of a high degree of urbanization, however, did, at first analysis, appear to have a clear effect on the distribution of selectmen's offices. The five urban centers of Connecticut— Hartford, Middletown, New Haven, New London, and Norwich— when grouped together had a significantly less oligarchic pattern than the rest of the towns in the colony: their turnover rate of 60 percent, average number of terms served of 3.4, and family dominance factor of 32 percent, contrast sharply with the 49 percent turnover rate, 5.1 average terms served, and 47 percent family dominance factor of all the rest. Small towns had a higher turnover rate, lower average number of terms served, and higher family dominance factor than either the large nonurban or medium-sized towns, both of which were nearly identical in all their measurements. These latter distinctions were not, however, as great as those between the urban towns and the rest.

There is a problem with drawing hard conclusions about the local politics of towns of various sizes. Grouping towns together by size disguises the extraordinarily full range of experiences that took place within the same category. The clearly more democratic pattern of the turnover rates in the five urban towns, for example, is a sum of Norwich's and Hartford's rates of 91 percent and 78 percent respectively, much higher than the average for all towns; Middletown's rate of 53 percent, which is marginally higher than the average for all towns; and New Haven's and New London's rates of 41 percent and 37 percent, which are markedly lower than the average for all towns. Thus, to say that the urban towns have a substantially higher turnover rate than the average is accurate for them *as a group* but is accurate for only two of the five within the group, and hence the overall statement disguises the individual experiences of the five which were extremely varied. On the other hand, the statements that selectmen in the five urban towns served fewer terms and that the family dominance rate was lower in these towns is true for four of the towns, and the fifth had the same measurements as the average of all of the towns: none of them was higher than the mean. Similarly, although the small towns do as a group differ slightly from the large and medium-sized towns, the most oligarchic of any town, Hebron, and the least oligarchic, Saybrook, were both small in population. Obviously, the generalizations made about the effects of population size and density upon selectmen's officeholding patterns are at best very tenuous guides for predicting political behavior.

It is impossible to say with absolute certainty what factors worked to produce differences in these patterns, but the division between the urban towns and the rest in average number of terms served and in family dominance, the only striking contrast in the measurements, is a division that Edward Cook, Jr., in his studies of officeholding in general, found characterized all of New England.[14] Cook's explanation of this phenomenon is applicable to Connecticut: the urban towns attracted men of talent, wealth, and good family connections from the surrounding countryside and thus had a substantially larger pool of potential officeholders with superior ability and economic and social connections than other towns. Thus, while the number of men serving, the length of time they served, and the number of families they represented may appear more democratic in the urban towns than in the rest, the actual men serving in the selectmen's offices in the urban towns could easily be more wealthy and socially prominent—and indeed probably were—than the men in the other towns of the colony. There were just many more such men in the five urban towns because they were centers of social and economic power and opportunity. The differences between the small towns, on the one hand, and the medium and large ones, on the other, were too slight to be more than suggestive. The biggest difference, that of the higher rate of family dominance in the small towns, is explicable in terms of demography, so does not indicate the unusual influence of a few elite families. Since there were fewer people in the small towns, five large families would constitute a much larger percentage of the population; naturally these families also constituted a larger percentage of the selectmen. The

TABLE 3
Officeholding among selectmen by town population and population density

Type of town	Turnover rate (percentage not reelected)	Average number of terms served	Percentage of terms served by five families
Urban (N = 5)	60	3.4	33
Large (N = 5)	48	5.1	43
Medium (N = 5)	48	5.4	45
Small (N = 15)	51	4.8	50

other measurement that distinguished small from medium and large towns, the lower average number of terms served in the former, undoubtedly relates to two factors: first, the small towns were the least commercially developed of all the towns in the colony and had the most egalitarian social and economic structures, so selectmen's jobs were less complicated and could be handled by a larger percentage of men. Second, the small towns of the late eighteenth century had similar social, economic, and political structures to most of the towns of the early eighteenth century, the changes that took place in Connecticut's economy over the course of the eighteenth century affected these towns much less than the others. Their selectmen's officeholding patterns, therefore, remained closer to the democratic patterns of the early eighteenth century.

Surprisingly, the date of settlement did not affect the pattern of selectmen's officeholding. If one compared all the towns settled in the seventeenth century with those settled in the eighteenth century, differences would emerge; but this is because the five urban towns all fall in the first group, skewing the measurements. When towns of similar populations were compared, settlement dates had no measurable effect on the election of selectmen. Saybrook and Milford, for example, two small towns settled at nearly the same time, had turnover rates of 93 percent and 39 percent, respectively. Norwalk and Fairfield, two large towns with similar locations and social structures, were both settled in the early years of the colony but had contrasting turnover rates of 75 percent and 26 percent. Similarly, Mansfield and Ridgefield, small farming towns with little commercial development, were founded within three years of each other but had turnover rates of 82 and 30 percent respectively.

These great variations occurring among towns of similar circumstances lead us to one of the most important conclusions the data suggest: local circumstances—the interaction of unique individuals,

histories, and traditions—affected the officeholding patterns of selectmen more than did identifiable variables applicable to most towns.
Even when the behavior of the five urban towns is taken into account,
the officeholding patterns of selectmen in the various towns was highly
idiosyncratic. For example, Norwich and New London, two of the
urban towns, were adjacent to each other; were both founded in the
first wave of settlement; were similar in population size, density, and
composition and in economic function; and yet had turnover rates of
91 percent for the former and 37 percent for the latter and average
numbers of terms served of 2.5 and 4.6, respectively. New Haven and
Hartford, the two co-capitals, contrast nearly as much in these two
measurements. The presence or absence of a few prestigious men, a
tradition started in the first decade of a town's history, continuing problems of where to locate a meetinghouse, and all the other possible
phenomena that we can imagine occurring in the towns, affected the
pattern of choosing selectmen more than whether or not the towns were
New Light or Old Light, new towns or old towns, and urban entrepots or
isolated farming villages. We should not completely discount the possibility of classifying a town's political behavior by social and economic
variables, but we should be aware that these variables were not the
dominant force affecting the officeholding patterns of selectmen.

This emphasis on the unique local circumstances affecting the
choice of selectmen contrasts to my earlier study of the officeholding
patterns of deputies elected by Connecticut towns to the General
Assembly; clearer and less ambiguous correlations could be obtained
between the variables of geography and population and the election
patterns of deputies to the assembly. These contrasting patterns of electoral behavior are not necessarily inconsistent. The position of deputy
to the General Assembly and the position of selectman placed different
demands upon an officeholder. Being a deputy to the assembly en-
tailed much more contact on a wider scale with issues and men from
other towns than being a selectman did; despite the growth in complexity of the selectman's job, it was essentially local in scope. Deputies had to leave their hometowns to travel to the capital for several
sessions a year, but selectmen were seldom required to travel outside
their town on political business. Furthermore, there were only two
deputies to the General Assembly, but there were usually five or seven
selectmen. Probably for all of these reasons and perhaps for others, the
political behavior of Connecticut towns in electing deputies to the
General Assembly lends itself much more readily to classification by
town types than does the political behavior of these same towns when
electing selectmen.

To return to the question raised in the introductory pages of this essay, which of the two visions of the New England town, the democratic open model or the elite closed model, does the foregoing analysis seem to suggest? Despite the inherent danger of moving from a description and analysis of data to a value-laden term, one is tempted to say that by most definitions there was much that was democratic about the officeholding patterns of selectmen. Turnover rates that exceed 50 percent, average numbers of terms served that are less than other neighboring colonies and lower than today's towns, and a one out of five chance for inhabitants of becoming a selectman, suggest that, although they may fall short of textbook definitions of democracy, Connecticut's towns maintained a comparatively open and democratic system.

To this limited endorsement of the democratic image of Connecticut's towns, four important qualifications must be added. First, although many men moved freely in and out of the selectman's office, family prestige and connections did account for a high percentage of each town's selectmen. Until the family networks of towns' populations are more carefully studied, we will not know how significant this family influence was, but certainly the right family name increased one's chances of being elected, as the wrong family name decreased one's chances. Second, during the eighteenth century, a change in the pattern of the election of selectmen and the rapid growth of population severely reduced a man's chances of becoming a selectman and so participating directly in decision making at the highest level in his hometown. Both political and demographic changes made the selectmen's boards of 1780 more elite than those of 1701. Third, the fact that the towns had relatively democratic patterns of elections to the selectmen's boards does not mean that their politics were consistently democratic. In their elections of town clerks, deputies to the General Assembly, and moderators of town meetings, towns appear to have been much more elitist and restrictive than in their election of selectmen: different offices elicited differing election patterns. Fourth, none of the data in this essay speak to the social and economic characteristics of the men who were elected—they speak only to the pattern of election. From every analysis we have of colonial New England officeholding, we know that major officeholders were usually from the upper half of the economic class structure. Of course, to retreat to a comparative position, data for officeholding today suggest the same phenomenon, and it would be surprising to discover any communities that elected as many poor and middle-income men to major office as prosperous ones. Economic well-being not only breeds confidence and prestige, but also serves to many people as a sign of success and ability. Fifth and finally, if we placed Connecticut's towns on an ideal scale ranging from very oligarchic to very democratic, some properly would be placed near one end and some near the other. The political behavior of these towns in electing selectmen was highly idiosyncratic. Although the overall figures justify the label of "comparatively democratic," these aggregate totals disguise the behavior of towns that deviated substantially from the mean.

Perhaps this idiosyncratic pattern is characteristic of local politics in eighteenth-century Connecticut. Although their data cluster around a mean, Connecticut's towns felt free to shape their own policies when they elected their major local executives. Eclectic patterns of office-holding reflect eclectic patterns of thought, indicating that the most important dynamic behind the forces operating in each town's choice of selectmen was local circumstance and tradition. In the final analysis, each Connecticut town was as democratic as it chose to be.

LORENA S. WALSH

The Development of
Local Power Structures: Maryland's Lower
Western Shore in the Early
Colonial Period

———————•◉•————————

MOST STUDENTS OF colonial Chesapeake politics agree that political stability and social order emerged but slowly in the region. Through most of the seventeenth century, even on the provincial level, both Maryland and Virginia lacked a knowledgeable, sustained political leadership enjoying widespread public acceptance and capable of governing without provoking intrigue, disruption, and periodic rebellion. Not until the turn of the century did an educated, affluent, and well-connected native-born gentry class secure political dominance.[1] These conclusions are drawn largely from studies of provincial leaders. Especially in many of the earlier works, similar and parallel changes are assumed to have been happening in lesser administrative units as well. However, the few county-level studies now available suggest that some local units may have achieved a degree of stability and responsibility not yet found at the provincial level, while others lagged markedly behind in recruiting local leaders who could bolster their political positions with the weight of immense social authority.[2]

If Maryland's founders had had their way, they would have re-created in the colony the kinds of social relationships and governmental institutions that structured and ordered life in the Old World. Immigrating gentlemen were expected to take their place at the top of a rigidly stratified hierarchic society, controlling land and trade and governing localities through a succession of manorial, borough, and county courts. Broad political authority vested in local rulers was to be reinforced by broader social authority drawn from established wealth, high birth, and educational accomplishments. This planned social arrangement quickly disintegrated during the difficult years of early settlement. Financial disappointment, political squabbles, and early death soon dispersed the colony's intended rulers, and, given the new settlement's halting economic beginning and peculiar religious orientation, few other English gentlemen could be enticed to replace those who died or left.[3] The transfer of governmental institutions was also incomplete, as the county court alone emerged as an effective agency of local government, absorbing the duties of other English lower jurisdictions.[4]

This paper will discuss the development of local power structures twenty-odd years after Maryland's founding, when settlement had spread about forty-five miles, as the crow flies, up the Potomac and Patuxent rivers from the original seat near the base of the lower western shore. Immigrants both bound and free were pouring into a now rapidly growing region and had begun to carve isolated farmsteads out of the wilderness. From the outset tobacco dominated the economy of the colony, and relatively high profits obtained from growing the weed, even on a small scale, permitted rapid expansion of small, independent, landowning planters. By the late 1650s yeoman farmers predominated in Maryland—numerically, economically, and politically.[5]

It was under these conditions that the early ruling class of Charles County emerged, and it is primarily on its members that I will concentrate.

When the county was established in 1658, it was bounded on the east by the Wicomico and on the south and west by the Potomac, "up as high as any Plantation is now seated."[6] Charles was a frontier county, its jurisdiction expanding as the line of settlement moved up the Potomac and its tributaries. Near the end of the century, a new county was erected out of the northwesternmost settlements, and thereafter Charles consisted of a five hundred-square-mile expanse along the mid-Potomac.

The county is reasonably representative of tobacco-growing areas settled around the middle of the seventeenth century and has one of the fullest sets of surviving colonial records for any Maryland jurisdiction.[7] In 1658 it was home to about 300 settlers. Population grew rapidly into the late 1670s, reaching about 1,250 in 1675; thereafter growth was slower.[8] By 1704 residents numbered nearly 3,000 and by

1720, about 5,000.[9] Until the 1690s most adult residents were immigrants, and not until the turn of the century did a native-born majority emerge among adults. This was due to the peculiar demographic structure of early Maryland. First, exceedingly high mortality decimated the population. Immigrant men who survived their initial seasoning could not expect to live beyond age forty-three, and 70 percent would die before age fifty. The native-born did only a little better. Second, perhaps 85 percent of the immigrants arrived as indentured servants and consequently married late. Family groups were never predominant in the immigration to Maryland and were a significant part for only a brief time at midcentury. Finally, many more men than women immigrated throughout the period, and the resulting sexual imbalance meant that many men would never marry at all. Consequently, for a long time immigrants failed to reproduce themselves and population growth was possible only through continued influxes of new settlers.[10]

Among colonial leaders—those men who held positions of major local or provincial power—were justices of the peace, sheriffs, burgesses, and members of the colony's council.[11] The justices of the peace were the effective rulers of the county. As administrators they regulated local economic activity, determined what public services would be provided, and apportioned the costs of these services, both in time and taxes, among county residents. The justices were also the main conservators of order in the community. In addition to jointly trying all cases brought before the county court, individual justices had a number of powers designed to keep the peace. Each had the power to demand a peace bond or recognizance from anyone who broke or threatened to break the peace, and the power to require bond for good behavior. In the absence of any police force, it was the justice who interrogated those accused of offenses by their neighbors and either bound the accused to appear in court for trial or ordered him to prison. From the 1690s the single justice heard and determined small civil cases, and two justices together performed functions ancillary to litigation in the higher courts. The extensive judicial and administrative powers of these men, especially when acting together as a court, were augmented by seventeenth century Maryland's highly decentralized governmental authority. For many Charles County planters the local rulers were the only rulers. The county court's power could theoretically be checked by the higher courts, by the governor and council, and by the assembly, but these appellate remedies were slow, time-consuming, and often too expensive for smaller planters. For many there was probably no effective appeal from the decisions of the local court.[12]

The sheriff was, equally with the justices, a county ruler. He was both the servant of the justices and an independent power, commissioned by, and representing, the central government. As the one major local office of power which also supplied a considerable income, the shrievalty was a position to be sought after. While the net profit accruing to the office was not enormous—about £100 per year at the turn of the century—this was sufficient inducement to prompt already substantial men to seek the post.[13]

Both the justices and sheriffs were chosen by the colony's governor after consultation with his councillors, and they in turn perhaps seeking advice from leading county residents. The burgesses were the only elected local officers. We know almost nothing about nomination and election procedures in this period.[14] However, the men selected to represent the county were by and large the men who already ruled it. Of the forty-four Charles County delegates elected before 1721, thirty-three (75 percent) had previously held appointive offices, and seven of the remaining eleven became justices or sheriffs after their election to the assembly.

Provincial councillors stood at the apex of power and authority in the colony. Intimate advisers to the governor, they also constituted the upper house of the legislature and sat on the provincial court until 1695. In their own counties they had some of the powers of a single justice, could sit as quorum magistrates, and had considerable say over the appointment of commissioned county officers. Few men from Charles were named to this prestigious position, and only three served for any length of time before 1689. On the whole, Charles County leaders (except as delegates to the assembly) were purely local rulers.[15]

What populace were these men to govern? Charles County's early settlers came largely from middle- or lower-class English backgrounds. At least a quarter, and probably just over one-third, of the adult male residents in 1660 had arrived in the colony as servants. Even among those who had paid their own passage, most brought only modest capital with them, and few could claim the lowest honorific title of "mister."[16] Subsequently, some men of more substantial backgrounds—primarily representatives of English mercantile families and established landowners from Virginia and Barbados—contributed an element of gentility which had previously been missing. By the 1680s white immigration had declined, and population increase slowed. While a few well-capitalized merchants continued to arrive, a growing proportion of later settlers were former servants who stayed on after serving their time in the county. In 1690 just over half of the county's free adult male population was foreign-born, and of these more than half are known to have been servants. Since the records are incomplete, the true proportion of ex-servants may have been even higher. In an area where land was cheap and plentiful, access to labor made the difference between relative prosperity or rude sufficiency. Until the mid-1670s the bound-labor force was composed almost entirely of white indentured servants, fairly broadly distributed among most established planters. Beginning in the late 1670s, slave labor became more important, and by the 1690s the transformation to a slave-labor system was nearly complete. This change greatly widened the gap between the county's large and small planters, as at first only the wealthy could afford the high initial cost of slave labor. In addition, beginning in the 1680s, a thirty-year-long depression in tobacco prices brought hard times to the county. Lesser planters, now effectively cut out of the labor market, found only slight opportunity for advancement through small-scale production of the weed. Meanwhile, large planters, less drastically affected by adversity, solidified their economic and social dominance.[17]

In the county's early years, there were few settlers of great wealth, gentle origins, or formal education available to assume customary leadership roles (see table 1). Consequently, the county's first rulers were a most untraditional lot. The men initially appointed to the county bench were, with one exception, immigrants whose origins were very similar to those of most of the settlers they were to govern. Six of the twelve justices appointed by 1660 had arrived as indentured servants, and four of the remaining six had immigrated with little capital. Probably only one merchant was called "Mister" upon arrival. Neither were the justices exceptionally wealthy. Excluding one unusual settler who had already accumulated 2,500 acres, the mean landholding of all justices at appointment was only 464 acres. At least one-quarter of the justices were illiterate, and even those who were literate probably had little formal education.[18]

Some of these first appointees had perhaps demonstrated some abilities and qualities of leadership which had come to the ears of the governor. Others were perhaps simply the most prosperous settlers living in a particular area of the county.[19] The authority with which these men governed did not depend on deference automatically accorded to rank, but arose instead from respect for native ability and judgment earned over a period of time in daily intercourse with men who were their equals—or at least near-equals. To ensure the effective rule of a frontier community, it was critical that rulers brought to their offices the added weight of community respect. Officers who were openly

TABLE 1

Characteristics of major officeholders in Charles County, Maryland, 1658–1720

Period of first service[a]	N	Social and economic background at immigration or majority				Landholding		Personal estate at death (Mean £)[f]	% literate
		Immigrant[b] (%)	Ex-servant (%)	Son of former officer[c] (%)	Possessing capital at age or arrival[d] (%)	Mean acres at appointment	Mean acres at death or maximum held[e]		
1658–59	12	100	50	0	17	1458	1706	227	92
1660–69	21	100	24	5	24	923	1987	352	76
1670–79	14	86	7	29	64	777	2067	342	86
1680–88	13	92	21	0	29	2076	2798	643	69
1689–95	13	77	8	25	31	1006	2086	694	89
1696–1700	9	54	11	44	67	732	1727	748	100
1701–09	12	42	8	33	58	2356	3467	788	100
1710–20	13	31	8	69	85	1019	2094	706	100

SOURCE: See notes 11 and 29.

[a] Table 1 begins in 1658 when Charles County was erected. Subsequent divisions are by decade with the exception of the years 1680–1700. Here the periods are divided between 1688 and 1689 to highlight changes associated with the Revolution of 1689, and between 1695 and 1696 to facilitate comparison with other counties in tables 2 and 3. Tabulations for Calvert County (established 1654, but most known appointments date from 1655) and for St. Mary's County (established 1637) begin in 1655 to include a representative group of contemporary officeholders. Dates of initial service were not bunched in 1658–1659 in these counties as was the case in newly organized Charles County. Tabulations for Prince George's County (established 1695) begin in 1696 when the county court was first organized.

[b] Includes all men who were not born in Maryland.

[c] Includes children who immigrated with their parents.

[d] Economic status at arrival for immigrants, at majority for native-born.

[e] Category includes land held at death or maximum amount held earlier in career, if greater than holdings at death.

[f] Since there was little inflation in Maryland before 1720, inventories prior to that year were not deflated. The table includes inventories of officeholders who died through 1735. Those for 1721–1735 were adjusted according to a deflator developed by the St. Mary's City Commission.

held in contempt by their neighbors could do little to uphold the authority of the government. A few such men served for a time, but were replaced as soon as appointees of better character could be found.[20]

Most of the men Governor Charles Calvert named justices or sheriffs, after his arrival in Maryland in 1661, had immigrated with more economic resources than the earlier appointees. They included the son of a former governor, a merchant with connections in England, a well-educated attorney, and two substantial landowners, who probably came from respectable English families.[21] The real and personal wealth amassed by officers newly appointed during the 1660s and 1670s edged upward; there was not yet, however, an unbridgeable gulf between the wealth of most of these gentlemen justices and other leaders—including sheriffs and burgesses—and that of many middling planters in the county. Also, while by the 1670s more of the leaders could sign their names, as yet it is likely that few had had much formal education.

By the mid-1680s the distance between many of the county rulers and the families they ruled increased. Some ex-servants and ordinary free immigrants were still selected, but many of the new appointees were of extraordinary backgrounds. A former West Indian planter, an extremely successful creole planter-merchant, and a prominent English immigrant who entered office in the mid-1680s all became councillors, and a well-schooled lawyer quickly rose to the posts of justice, burgess, and attorney general of the colony.[22] Such men, being among the wealthiest and best educated in Maryland, brought added social and economic authority to their offices, making it more difficult for ordinary settlers to question their actions. The Lord Proprietary undoubtedly felt such qualities essential in a period when his subjects were growing increasingly restive and dissatisfied with the policies of the central government.[23] Only a few years before, some citizens had openly complained, "what pittiful Justices . . . they [have] picked up for us."[24] No one could characterize the owners of dozens of slaves and thousands of acres as pitiful.[25] After the Revolution of 1689 the characteristics of newly appointed justices were much more diverse. With the exclusion of Catholics from office, more positions became available to qualified Protestants. In addition, the deaths of a number of men who had served ten to fifteen years in office created an unusual number of new openings. Although some of the officers chosen during the 1690s were men of background and fortune, others were modest planters who gained appointment from their support of the revolution or who were selected simply because there were no men with greater qualifications available.[26]

The beginning of the eighteenth century marked a return to more consistent appointment or election of the wealthy and better educated. Every leader chosen after 1695 was literate. For the first time, native-born residents held a majority of local positions of power. This change reflected shifts in the make-up of the county's free adult population; by 1705 half of the free adult males were native-born, and by 1720, nearly two-thirds. As heirs to established estates, with blood ties to many county residents, these leaders brought a new element of family stability and social authority to their positions. The creole was surer of his status, having inherited rather than acquired it, and perhaps more comfortable in the colonial environment, the only one he had ever known. He almost invariably stayed in the locality in which he had been born and in the community to which he was tied by expectations of future inheritance and kin relationships in a way few immigrants ever were.[27]

Changes in the status of leaders is most apparent among burgesses. Prior to the late 1680s the men elected were on the average no more or less wealthy or educated than other local officers. One result of Maryland's revolution in government and subsequent period of royal rule was a growth in power and procedural sophistication in the lower house of the assembly. Thereafter, the men who represented the county in the legislature were among the richest and best-educated county residents. Mean real and personal estates of delegates rose to three times the mean estates of the more important local officers who did not serve in the assembly. The cream of the elite was coming to seek—and to be elected to—an office of growing influence and prestige.[28]

While the preceding discussion has emphasized differences across time in the background and wealth of Charles County's rulers at the time of their first selection, it is equally important to note that differences in wealth diminished as the leaders' careers progressed. By the time of their death or departure from the county, most of the political rulers were also among the county's leading land and labor owners.

Established wealth—or the potential for acquiring a fortune—seems then to have been the primary quality that governors and their advisors looked for when they chose local rulers, and that voters considered when electing representatives. The governors' increasing tendencies from the mid-1680s to select men who had already made their fortunes suggests that they thought of local offices of power as an obligation or honor which fortune and status conferred. There is evidence that this was in fact the case, for in Charles County three-quarters or more of the richest men dying after 1680 were officers, as were two-fifths to two-thirds of decedents well off enough to own a slave.[29] Certainly naming the already wealthy simplified the selection process, once there was a large enough pool of men of fortune to fill most of the openings. Before this occurred, a keen insight into men's abilities and potentials was required in order to determine who among a group of relatively poor, newly established planters would become the county's major wealth-holders. Perhaps it was considered fairer, as well, to assign weighty and time-consuming duties to such men as could most easily afford to put aside private pursuits.

In this newly settled area, economic success was the one sure attribute that carried social authority. Title undoubtedly commanded some respect, but since there were never enough settlers who could claim gentle or near-gentle status, acquired, rather than inherited, position remained a sufficient qualification. Although literacy was an advantage, learning, of itself, usually carried little social weight unless it could be readily turned to economic advancement.[30] Age and experience, too, may have counted for something, but were not primary considerations. For one thing there were few patriarchs around. In a society where most men died young, leaders began serving early, and many died before they reached fifty. The tendency for governors to drop from commissions older men whose economic careers had failed to advance, in favor of younger, wealthier appointees further suggests that even when older men were available, age and experience carried less weight than economic resources. Simple longevity gave most men an advantage, however, in that wealth usually did continue to increase with age.

Kin connections, especially in the early years, were of little importance. Not many immigrants to the lower western shore had blood relatives in Maryland, and given that many early settlers failed to generate progeny, there were few established families for newcomers to marry into. The more usual connection achieved was through marriage to the widow of a former officeholder. Some men acquired ties to a widow's powerful relations by this means, but more often they simply gained control of the valuable economic assets of her former husband. Of the forty-eight county-level officers serving before 1681, only eight may have owed their appointment to powerful relatives in the colonies. The one connection necessary to retain office was continued support of the proprietary government. More than a few local leaders found their careers abruptly terminated as a result of their injudicious support of the county's perennial revolutionary, Josias Fendall.

In contrast with many New England towns where future rulers often proved themselves through service in minor local office, there was very little working up through the ranks, especially in the early years.[31] Only five of fifty-three Charles County leaders chosen before 1681 served in any local conscriptive office other than that of juryman before becoming county rulers, and just two others first held minor offices of profit. Of the fifty-four men entering office between 1681 and 1720, about half had seen minor service (e.g., as undersheriff or county clerk), but only a quarter first performed unsalaried duties. A belief that men should serve only in offices appropriate to their status may have contributed. Local magistrates decided who should carry out the sometimes burdensome duties of constable, overseer of the highways, or pressmaster, and they usually selected neither substantial immigrants nor sons of current or former leaders for such posts. Instead, these duties were reserved for more ordinary residents.[32]

Leaders were recruited from a variety of occupations, although planters and planter-merchants predominated. Planter-merchants were always an important element among local leaders, and overrepresented in proportion to their numbers in the population. Some were selected for their English ties, others simply because their fortunes had been suitably augmented through mercantile pursuits. In a society where geographic mobility was usually quite limited, however, all merchants had much wider communication networks than most other residents. Traders maintained contacts in many parts of one and sometimes in two or three counties, and were thus more widely known than men who had less reason to travel far from their own plantations.[33] Other leaders combined planting with additional pursuits, including those of attorney, physician, clerk, surveyor, cooper, carpenter, tanner, and innkeeper. During the period studied, none of these subsidiary occupations provided regular avenues to either economic or social status.[34] However, such activities did tend to bring their practitioners into contact with customers living in several parts of the county, and thus, when combined with landed wealth, contributed to a county-wide reputation.

Finally, residence was always a criterion for selection of justices. If order was to be effectively maintained, all residents had to have relatively convenient access to a magistrate. As a consequence, county commissions usually included a representative from each district. It might happen that some otherwise qualified men were passed over because their locality was already well represented on the bench, men of more marginal status being named to provide necessary services to unrepresented portions of the county.[35]

Justices remained in power so long as the governor continued to include them in the county commissions. Tenure was long in the sense that three-quarters of the rulers continued in office until they retired, died, or left the area. However, because of high mortality, virtual "life-long" tenure amounted to an average of only nine years in office.[36] As a consequence, the number of experienced leaders at any given time remained small, and the burden of maintaining some continuity fell on a very few shoulders. From the 1670s until the turn of the century, mean years of cumulative experience among magistrates ranged from six up to ten years, reaching a high of fourteen in only one year before 1721. The contrast with some New England boards of selectmen is stark. Mean years of experience ranging from twenty to fifty could not be achieved in the Chesapeake environment.[37]

Because of early death, the county's rulers were unable to hold power for long. And, because most died so young, few were able to successfully bequeath positions of power to their heirs. Nearly half (twenty-four) of the leaders serving before 1681 in fact left no male heirs at all. Fifteen others did have sons who reached majority, but either the fathers had not accumulated sufficient fortunes to sustain the position of the family into the next generation, or their heirs were barred from office after 1689 on account of their religion. Only one-quarter (fourteen of the fifty-three early rulers) left heirs who later held offices of power.[38]

Men who became leaders during the 1680s and 1690s did better. Most left male heirs, and about half of these sons eventually assumed an economic and political position equivalent to that of their fathers. Such inheritance was far from automatic, however, because many of the fathers died while their sons were still young minors.[39] Even when there was continuity among officeholding families, effective power relationships could seldom be maintained during the minority of the founder's heir. Before 1700 most sons of officeholders did not begin to serve until a full eighteen to thirty-two years after their fathers had died. Even after that date only a handful of adult sons were ready to take office when their fathers retired or died. In fact, it was not until the 1760s that a majority of lower western shore decedents lived to see at least one child reach majority.[40] In the early eighteenth century, instrumental relationships tended to be intragenerational rather than intergenerational. In general, the crucial connections were between brothers, brothers-in-law, and cousins, rather than between fathers or uncles and sons or nephews.

If local power remained dispersed among a number of families—with very few lines able to maintain a continuous hold on offices—it was concentrated, nonetheless, in a few hands at any one time. About half of the local leaders taking office before 1720 held more than one office of power during their careers, no trend toward greater concentration or diffusion being evident over time. Appointment to the bench was generally the initial step in an officeholder's career; sheriffs were usually chosen from among the justices, and the county's voters almost invariably reaffirmed the leadership of the appointed officers by electing them to the assembly. This situation seems more to reflect the usually small number of county residents possessing requisite status and resources than partiality on the part of governors, or tight control of positions by those already occupying office. Maryland justices never gained control of the shrievalty as magistrates did in Virginia.[41] Conceivably they did control elevation to the assembly through self-nomination and *viva-voce* voting—here the historical record is silent. Magistrates might have maintained power through profits gained from their office, but there is little evidence to support this supposition, at least in the case of Maryland. Officers other than sheriffs were expected to serve without fees or salary, and there were few opportunities for magistrates to increase their fortunes in the course of carrying out their official duties.[42] Neither was county office likely to lead to lucrative provincial positions of profit. During the proprietary period such posts were reserved largely for relatives and friends of the Calverts (very few of whom lived in Charles County), and under royal rule, wealthier, better-connected men from other counties had the advantage.[43] Apparently some combination of a sense of obligation to serve the community and of the honor conferred by important local office, coupled with a desire to wield power over the locality and its residents, was enough to induce most appointees to take on the responsibilities of office.

Whatever their motivations, Charles County's leaders had little leisure to bask in the prestige of their positions. Forces for disorder were many, and were not limited to the period of early settlement. Shortly after the county was established, the handful of men who were supposed to rule—most of them with little experience in leadership and precious little economic or social authority—were faced with keeping order within an unsettled, widely dispersed group of settlers of diverse economic, social, and religious backgrounds.[44] Once immigration slowed and white society had a chance to coalesce, county leaders had to cope with an economic depression that widened the gap between rich and poor, and with the stresses associated with the introduction of a racially alien, unfree labor force. The central government was periodically disrupted by a series of attempted coups, efforts with which many county residents sympathized and which a number actively supported. Such disruptions at the colony level periodically left open to question the authority by which local rulers might act. High mortality continually robbed the county of its few experienced leaders, and cut short the lives of ordinary settlers at mid-career, interrupting the orderly accumulation and transference of wealth, and disrupting and stunting family life. Religious differences were another source of instability, for despite the official policy of religious toleration, deep-seated antagonisms and prejudices among both Protestants and Catholics periodically threatened the peace.[45]

Yet county leaders did succeed, even to the extent of keeping local government functioning smoothly when the central government fell. Almost certainly this could have been achieved only with the active support of ordinary residents. We have become accustomed to attributing a yearning for good order and stability to the settlers of New England. Historians of the Chesapeake have generally failed to explore the consensual dimension of a society in which most leaders were appointed rather than elected, or have emphasized instead the exploitation of the powerless by the powerful, or the inability of those at the bottom of a firmly established hierarchy to do anything but acquiesce in the rule of their betters.[46] Certainly these elements were present. But the county's government functioned as much from the bottom up as from the top down. Government began in the household, and a belief in the centrality of good family government to good religious and civil government was as much a part of the cultural baggage of Chesapeake settlers as of those who migrated elsewhere. No man was considered fit to lead others who could not maintain order in his family, and the very act of setting up a household made a man an undisputed member of the polity, with recognized rights and obligations to the wider community.[47] Beyond the family, rural neighborhoods exerted strong controls on individual behavior. It was at this level that proper conduct was defined, admonition informally offered to those who transgressed the social code, violations of the law detected and reported, and many disputes settled by private mediation. Neighborly pressures were sufficient to regulate the behavior of the great majority who were unwilling to risk continued behavior "tending much to the breach of . . . comfortable living amongst [their] neighbors."[48] Of course few neighborhood leaders ever achieved the economic status that would create a county-wide reputation and bring possible appointment to an office of authority. Instead they contributed to community order in the less elevated capacities of juror, constable, and highway overseer. While such men had little formal say in who their rulers would be, I suspect they had much greater influence over these decisions than they are generally given credit for. Local reputation prompted the selection of many leaders in the first place, and the central government was never secure enough to risk continued support of men who fell into disrepute with their neighbors.

In order to place this study in a broader perspective, I have compared the leaders of early Charles County with those of the three other contiguous counties (the older St. Mary's, contemporaneous Calvert, and later-established Prince George's) that make up a subregion within Maryland—its boundaries the Chesapeake Bay on the east and the Potomac on the west—known as the lower western shore (see tables 2 and 3).[49] Within this geographic unit, soils were similar (although the quality varied); residents uniformly pursued plantation agriculture based on tobacco, corn, and livestock; settlers were drawn from the same migration stream (but with variation in the proportions of various religious groups between counties), and the labor forces were similar (initially, indentured servants, followed by a switch to predominantly slave labor). If common patterns can be found in the development of local colonial power structures, these should be most in evidence within a subregion.[50]

Indeed, leaders in all four counties had many common characteristics. In the formative years, each county was ruled primarily or exclusively by immigrants. In the three counties settled by the 1650s, early leaders were drawn from diverse economic, social, educational, and religious backgrounds, and, though they were wealthier than the majority of local residents, they were not extravagantly rich. Subsequently, the pool of men with larger estates and some education increased in each county, and leaders came usually to be selected from a group more distinctly set apart from ordinary settlers. A good proportion of the early leaders failed to produce heirs, those who did often dying too soon to leave their heirs either a secure status or estate, much less assured access to political office. Finally, in all the counties, once a native-born adult majority began to emerge, power was shared between a few wealthy newcomers, many of them merchants, and a growing number of native-born sons, including many second-generation officeholders.

This comparison also establishes the fact that special local conditions could redirect the general pattern. Two differences are worthy of note here. Calvert and Prince George's counties had soils more uniformly suited to high-quality tobacco production than did either Charles or St. Mary's. Mean and median wealth were higher in these better-endowed counties, and in Calvert, the older of the two, there emerged such a large pool of relatively wealthy residents that governors had the luxury of choice among a number of qualified candidates.

TABLE 2

Characteristics of major officeholders in St. Mary's County, Maryland, 1655–1720

Period of first service	N	Status at immigration or majority				Landholding		Personal estate at death (Mean £)	% literate
		Immigrant (%)	Ex-servant (%)	Son of former officer (%)	Possessing capital at age or arrival (%)	Mean acres at appointment	Mean acres at death or maximum held		
1655–59	28	100	25	0	32	2271	3071	154	86
1660–69	19	100	11	11	59	2081	2992	673	89
1670–79	22	82	9	27	57	1487	2343	500	95
1680–88	9	78	22	44	56	2264	3406	612	100
1689–95	24	88	21	8	33	709	1021	765	92
1696–1700	10	70	10	20	20	552	993	222	100
1701–09	10	50	10	30	30	1184	1898	1189	100
1710–20	11	27	9	36	36	662	723	303	100

SOURCES AND NOTES: See table 1, p. 58.

TABLE 3

Characteristics of major officeholders in Calvert and Prince George's counties, Maryland, 1665–1720

Period of first service	N	Status at immigration or majority				Landholding			% literate
		Immigrant (%)	Ex-servant (%)	Son of former officer (%)	Possessing capital at age or arrival (%)	Mean acres at appointment	Mean acres at death or maximum held	Personal estate at death (Mean £)	
CALVERT COUNTY									
1655–59	23	100	0	9	13	731	1726	379	78
1660–69	20	100	0	10	45	2727	2933	458	95
1670–79	29	86	17	21	28	1238	2895	578	97
1680–88	5	40	20	60	20	2233	3825	775	100
1689–95	14	64	14	38	57	1553	1788	1292	100
1696–1700	10	30	0	20	40	627+	1020+	1060	100
1701–20	15	37	0	40	40	632+	1931+	668+	100
PRINCE GEORGE'S COUNTY									
1696–1700	18	67	6	33	61	1884	2678	953	100
1701–09	16	31	0	31	50	1387	3009	1379	100
1710–20	9	67	0	22	78	655	1794	1557	100

SOURCES AND NOTES: See table 1. Information on Calvert County officers after 1700 is incomplete. The county's records have been destroyed, and it is difficult to reconstruct individual careers. For officers serving from 1696 on, figures for landholding include all holdings for which records have survived. The plus signs indicate that some officers are known to have held additional land for which the acreage cannot be determined. Similarly, probate records could not be located for all the men serving after 1700, and some of the available inventories were incomplete.

Newer Prince George's County also fostered men of great fortune, but population there was yet so small that almost all wealthy residents were recruited for office. The greater resources of the Calvert and Prince George's leaders afforded them an increasing colony-wide influence seldom matched by the less wealthy rulers of Charles and St. Mary's.[51]

St. Mary's presents one of the most interesting departures from the general pattern. At the turn of the century nearly half of the white inhabitants and probably a disproportionate number of wealthy county residents were Catholics, all of whom were barred from holding office.[52] Legal constraints thus caused the economic and political elite of the county to diverge. After 1689 less than half of the county's political leaders were members of the economic elite. Very marginal slaveowners became rulers, and in St. Mary's after 1700 it was still possible for the posts once occupied by a titled lord of a manor to be subsequently filled by his former indentured servant.[53]

The first twenty years of the eighteenth century marked the beginnings of gentry dominance on the lower western shore, yet sixty or more years after initial settlement, the process was far from complete. Especially in St. Mary's and Charles counties, the number of positions to be filled continued to exceed the supply of very rich, politically eligible men. Consequently, it was often necessary to dip much lower into the wealth structure, selecting some men of quite ordinary means to fill the remaining slots. In St. Mary's a close relationship between political and economic power was not possible. Great disparities in wealth, variations in education and style of life,[54] and, probably, marked differences in social influence persisted among the cadre of leaders in both counties. These circumstances, coupled with continued high mortality, impeded the development of a strong sense of group unity among leaders.

In better-endowed Calvert and Prince George's counties, conditions were more favorable to the emergence of gentry rule. Continued economic growth produced a large body of substantial wealthholders, almost all of them Protestants,[55] who controlled offices of power and who were well placed to form alliances and begin developing a style of life appropriate to their elevated position in society.[56]

Scholars of the Chesapeake are not in full agreement as to exactly when the creole gentry assumed control of the region; however, a range of dates between 1690 and 1720 encompasses most estimates. To quote from two representative accounts: (1) "by the end of the century . . . there was an acceptance of the fact that [in Virginia] certain families were distinguished from others in riches, in dignity, and in access to political authority,"[57] or (2) "In the fifteen years after 1700 a con-

TABLE 4

Relationship between personal wealth and officeholding among inventoried decedents by county, 1658–1720

		Counties							
	Total estate value in # Maryland currency (£)	Charles		St. Mary's		Calvert[a]		Prince George's[b]	
Years		N	Officer (%)	N	Officer (%)	N	Officer (%)	N	Officer (%)
1665–1679	0–50	76	4	139	1	95	0	—	
	51–225	47	19	84	20	51	23	—	
	226–490	7	57	19	47	4	50	—	
	491+	2	50	12	50	2	50	—	
1680–1691	0–50	50	0	97	2	63	0	—	
	51–225	37	19	44	5	40	0	—	
	226–490	6	67	7	0	10	30	—	
	491+	3	100	9	67	7	29	—	
1692–1705	0–50	118	0	145	1	107	1	51	0
	51–225	48	15	76	12	76	1	38	3
	226–490	10	40	15	33	31	16	7	14
	491+	9	78	15	64	17	47	5	60
1706–1720	0–50	179	2	218	1	—		124	0
	51–225	122	6	130	4	—		78	1
	226–490	23	4	35	20	—		19	11
	491+	10	70	15	40	—		21	83

SOURCES: See note 29.

NOTES: Cut-off points for wealth were selected as follows: at £50 because this was close to the median through the 1720s; at £225 because investment patterns changed at this point across the whole colonial period; at £490 because inventories worth more represent the top wealth group in divisions based on 9 groups of approximately equal size. Ns are inventoried decedents in each county.

[a] Inventories for Calvert County were analyzed only through 1705.

[b] Prince George's County was established in 1696.

stellation of new families would assume their places [in Maryland] in a rapidly emerging oligarchy."[58] On the other hand, the contrast between these descriptions and some eyewitness accounts generated between 1694 and 1709 is marked. The governors, Nicholson and Seymour, who served the King in Maryland between those years found the character and competency of many Maryland justices scandalous and felt it necessary to institute a variety of reforms, ranging from dictating how many hours justices must sit to actively discouraging nonquorum magistrates, considered totally unqualified to try any case, from attending sessions of the court at all.[59] In 1708 Ebenezer Cook, who was well acquainted with the whole of the lower western shore, painted a vivid picture of local leaders—crude, unlettered, inept, and frequently intoxicated.[60] Even if we grant that these latter commentaries were colored with a cosmopolitan Englishman's contempt for things colonial, and in Cook's case, with poetic license, it is still difficult to reconcile the contemporary accounts with those of the historians. Local studies such as this one can help to bridge the gap. In Maryland and Virginia, the men who sat in the council and assembly were by the turn of the century or shortly after something of a provincial elite. However, on Maryland's lower western shore at least, in the early eighteenth century men fitting this description were spread thinly indeed. The gentlemen who would "dominate provincial affairs in the eighteenth century's golden age of deferential politics"[61] shared power in their home counties with leaders still close enough to the "planting rabble" as to be virtually indistinguishable to the unpracticed observer.

COLONY-WIDE LEADERSHIP

ALAN TULLY

Quaker Party and Proprietary Policies: The Dynamics of Politics in Pre-Revolutionary Pennsylvania, 1730–1775

———————•◉•———————

OVER THE PAST thirty years numerous monographs have been published on pre-Revolutionary Pennsylvania politics. From them we have learned a good deal about the institutional development of colonial government, the diverse political aims of Pennsylvania's Quakers, the course of proprietary affairs, the organization of political parties, the politicization and mobilization of the electorate, and the characteristics of those who wielded political power.[1] As varied as discussions of these and related themes have been, there is one thread that runs through them all—the interplay between Quaker Party and proprietary policies.[2] Clearly this relationship constitutes the principal dynamic of pre-Revolutionary provincial politics as the Quaker Party coalesced, consolidated power, and attempted to maintain its presence in electoral politics, and as the proprietors formulated policies, pressed for their implementation, and tried to recruit support in Pennsylvania. Because of the fundamental importance of this relationship for our understanding of Pennsylvania politics, it deserves the kind of systematic historical treatment it has not hitherto been accorded.

The most important political organization in pre-Revolutionary Pennsylvania politics was the Quaker Party. For approximately four-and-a-half decades prior to Independence, almost all those who gained election to provincial office were sponsored by this informal county-based organization. In the case of the four old counties of Bucks, Chester, Philadelphia and Lancaster, it mattered little how well a man's family connections, wealth, education, occupation, style of life, prior political experience, religious affiliation, or capacities appeared to fit him for high political office. Without the endorsement of a significant proportion of his county's party organizers, the aspiring politician would remain that—aspiring. In the newer, underrepresented western and northern counties of York, Cumberland, Berks, and Northampton successful independent candidacy was possible and, at times, an asset. Even those who were independents, however, postponed until they were seated in the assembly what successful opposition candidates in the old counties had already begun—the process of directly confronting and coming to terms with Quaker Party men and policies.

The Quaker Party was one of the very few colonial political organizations that, from a modern perspective, deserves the term "party" rather than the epithet "faction." The party had a continuing informal membership of "weighty" men who broadly agreed on political policies—policies that were whiggish and antiproprietary in nature. While the most visible party members were those who were elected to the Pennsylvania assembly, others filled lesser county offices or simply participated in party affairs as supporters and promoters. Among all party adherents, loyalty was held in high regard. Although important political differences occurred among Quakers (most notably in 1756, when a small number of conscientious Quakers withdrew—some temporarily, some permanently—from political affairs, and in 1764, when some Quakers chose to support, others to oppose, the campaign to replace proprietary with royal government in Pennsylvania), at no time between the 1730s and the Revolution did the Quaker Party split into opposing factions.

Paradoxically, one important source of the party's strength was its decentralization. Much has been made of the supposed supervisory role of the Philadelphia Yearly Meeting in drawing up slates of candidates for the annual October 1 election.[3] Yet it is clear that this superintendency, on the few occasions when it occurred, never went beyond Philadelphia County. Only in one situation did a *provincial* body impose what was in effect a party decision on the whole organization; that was in the choice of a new Speaker of the assembly who, through his office, became the acknowledged party leader. Beyond this, party affairs in the outlying counties were left to the appropriate county politicians. The weighty men of Bucks, Chester, Lancaster, and Philadelphia recruited new men to ensure continuity and generational succession; they congregated yearly in homes and taverns to put together slates of candidates for provincial and county offices, ranging from assemblyman and sheriff down to county commissioner, assessor, and coroner;[4] they mobilized voters throughout the towns and countryside to support the men of their choice. In so doing, the Quaker politicians controlled popular government in eastern Pennsylvania.

The term "Quaker Party" gained currency between 1739 and 1742 and continued to be used through 1776.[5] It orginated in 1739 with the voluntary retirement from the assembly and from pre-election negotiations over candidates in Philadelphia County, of Andrew Hamilton and a sprinkling of his non-Quaker supporters. Into the vacuum crowded Philadelphia Quakers who, according to William Allen, "were for choosing none but people of that persuasion."[6] Hence the name.

In fact, the groundwork for the Quaker Party had already been well laid in the 1730s. It was during these years that a strong county-based Quaker interest really emerged. In Lancaster County, a small handful of Friends led the defense of Pennsylvanians' property rights in the border war with Maryland. In Chester and Bucks, pro-proprietary Quakers who had opposed Governor William Keith's city-based faction in the 1720s gradually began to reflect an antiproprietary bias. In addition, the Quakers began adjusting to their growing minority position in Pennsylvania society. No longer could they afford to split into opposing political factions if they were to remain the preponderant force in Pennsylvania politics.

It is strange that these political adjustments took place under the leadership of a non-Quaker, but Andrew Hamilton was unique. Of Scottish descent and an avowed freethinker, Hamilton was Speaker of the assembly from 1729 to 1739. In that role, he ardently defended the Pennsylvania Charter of Privileges; assembly rights, as they had developed under that constitution; the Pennsylvania heritage of religious liberty; and freedom of the press. Yet there was another side to Hamilton: his whiggish respect for property and his gratitude for the proprietary favors he had won led him to insist that the Penns be treated equitably on their quitrent and property sales income. Thus, Hamilton was a proprietary man, as well as popular spokesman—a feat no other leading Pennsylvania politician was ever able to accomplish.[7]

When Hamilton and his cronies withdrew from the assembly in 1739, there began fifteen years of unqualified Quaker Party dominance. Between 1740 and 1756, the Pennsylvania assembly was overwhelmingly Quaker in its religious composition.[8] In no county was any person who ran against the Quaker slate of candidates elected. During the first ten years of this period, John Kinsey, the Speaker of the assembly, personified the Quaker Party.[9] As Speaker of the assembly and clerk of the Philadelphia Yearly Meeting, Kinsey bridged the gap between Statehouse and meeting house, keeping a rein on those who would channel their religious commitment into extreme and prolonged political contention with the colony's chief executive.[10] A lawyer by profession, Kinsey was able to keep lines of communication open with the executive and proprietary while serving as a proprietary placeman, first as attorney general, then as chief justice of the Pennsylvania Supreme Court. Yet Kinsey's underlying political sentiments were never really in doubt. He used both posts more often to thwart the proprietary will than to advance the interests of the Penn family. Kinsey also used his power as Acting Trustee of the Loan Office (the most powerful patronage position in Pennsylvania, one conferred on him with the blessings of Andrew Hamilton and William Allen) in a blatantly political fashion.[11] By favoring as many as possible with the mortgages that Pennsylvanians needed to buy their freeholds and by granting unending extensions to delinquent mortgagors, Kinsey markedly strengthened the foundations of Quaker Party political support.[12]

When Kinsey died in 1750, his successor as party leader was Isaac Norris, Jr.[13] Like Kinsey, Norris was a moderate politician. He pushed for a firm defense of existing assembly practices and for an extension of legislative powers, should circumstances allow it. Despite the threat of war and the growing restiveness of a small but influential set of conscientious Quakers who were growing more critical of many Friends' worldliness, the first five years of Norris's party leadership saw a continuation of Quaker dominance both in and out of the assembly. With the French and Indian War, came change.

Seventeen fifty-six has often been described as a crucial year in the history of the Quaker Party. Reacting to pressure from England and dictates of conscience, the self-styled "sober sort" of Friends withdrew from the Pennsylvania assembly rather than be a party to military appropriations and militia laws.[14] As a result of this, and because of the recent creation of four new counties that were either on the fringes of or beyond the old Quaker political network, Quakers suddenly became a minority in the thirty-six-seat legislature.[15]

The eight remaining years (1756–1764) of Isaac Norris' speakership were unlike his first six. Formerly the spokesman for a nominally pacifist assembly, Norris became the leader of a legislature committed to fighting a war; accustomed to working out compromises with legislative dissidents who were Quakers, once past 1756, Norris had to deal with outsiders representing the west (although not necessarily western-

TABLE 1
Quakers in the assembly, 1756–1775

Year	Number of Quakers	Number of Assembly seats	Year	Number of Quakers	Number of Assembly seats
1756	11	36	1766	18	36
1757	12	36	1767	17	36
1758	14	36	1768	17	36
1759	13	36	1769	15	36
1760	14	36	1770	18	36
1761	18	36	1771	17	38
1762	18	36	1772	18	39
1763	16	36	1773	17	40
1764	15	36	1774	15	40
1765	17	36	1775	13	41

ers) and a hotheaded element of non-Quakers—most of whom were churchmen—from Philadelphia City and County. Yet the Quaker Party had by no means disappeared. The Quaker organization in the four old counties continued to function in the election of assembly-men much as it had in the past. With the exception of defense, it stood for the same policies it had in preceding years—continued resistance to proprietary-executive claims and augmentation of assembly powers. Historians differ in their assessments of how much Benjamin Franklin, Joseph Galloway, and their small contingent of Philadelphia church-men usurped Norris's role as the major party leader. Certainly the ill-thought-out campaign for royal government of 1764–1765 took place at their behest, though it was an old Quaker Party idea. But Norris was never openly challenged for party leadership until then, and the Franklin-Galloway interest continually had to court the old county-based Quaker contingent from the mid-fifties through early sixties.[16]

The true strength and resilience of the Quaker Party in the late 1750s and early 1760s cannot be measured simply by the number of Quakers who sat in the legislature. Provincial Secretary Richard Peters made an apt point after the 1756 election when he pointed out that the resignation of conscientious Quakers made little difference when they were replaced by "Quakerized Churchmen" and "Quakerized Pres-byterian[s]."[17] In addition to these hybrids, there were the relatively large number of assemblymen who attended Friends' meetings but did not belong to the Society or who, after having been raised as Quakers, frequented no religious society. James Pemberton attested to this sev-eral times. In 1756 he stated there were "12 [Assemblymen] under our [the Quakers'] care" but "our adversaries reckon them 16"; in 1762 "a large majority of [Assemblymen did] not qualify by the oath"; in 1764 there were "14 Quakers . . . but others [were] said to be so."[18]

In recruiting for provincial office, the Quaker Party simply broadened its scope. In the 1730s to 1750s, there had always been some Anglicans, Presbyterians, Mennonites, Lutherans, and German and Dutch Reformed who had periodically cooperated with Quaker leaders in organizing slates of candidates for county and provincial office. The promotion of men of differing religions to a share of provincial office after 1756 was a logical and necessary step, given the withdrawl of the "sober sort" of Friends.[19] Clearly this strategy strengthened the Quaker Party in the short run, enabling it to survive a war and retain its broad popular base.

Despite Norris's successful leadership of the party in difficult times, 1764 did bring change and defeat. After persuading the assembly over Norris's protests and eventual resignation (in the spring of that year), that Benjamin Franklin should go to England to petition for royal government, Franklin, Galloway, and their Philadelphia County Quaker Party supporters were ousted from the assembly by the proprietary supporters in the annual October election. This was the only sizable Quaker Party electoral defeat in the four old counties during the forty-five years prior to the Revolution. It did not last long. The following year the Quakers regained their political dominance and defended it successfully for ten years against both proprietary men and a newly emerging but still tiny opposition group in Philadelphia County referred to by contemporaries as the "Presbyterian Party." After witnessing the Quaker Party victory in 1766, Governor John Penn described the party as a "Macedonian phalanx," unbreakable and carrying all before it.[20] Throughout the late sixties and early seventies, under the leadership of Joseph Fox and Joseph Galloway, the party was not quite that, but it clearly remained the most successful and coherent political organization in Pennsylvania politics.[21]

Given the central role of the Quaker Party in pre-Revolutionary Pennsylvania politics, it is important to have some sense of why it was so successful and so long-lived. Why was it able to retain its cohesiveness, its vitality, and its appeal?

Historians have paid a great deal of attention to the tensions and divisions among Pennsylvania's Quakers. The best known of these was the withdrawal of the "sober sort" from political affairs in 1756. Large as this episode looms in historiography and as important as it was for the long-range development of the Society of Friends, it is important to remember that the vast majority of Quakers always supported the Quaker Party. Although the Quaker reformers included such well-known men as the three Pembertons, Anthony Benezet, John Woolman, and Isaac Zane, they were a small minority. For all their prominence and influence, they could never dissuade many politically active Friends from voting their traditional support for Quaker Party candidates.[22] Only a year after the withdrawal of these Quakers, Friends having again turned out at the October election to support Friends, Israel Pemberton lamented that "the number of Assemblymen bearing our name [were] . . . increased and those appointed to levy, assess and collect the tax in the three old counties [were] generally such."[23] Five years later, brother James confirmed their failure: "There are now, as last year, very near an equal number of our society [and non-Quakers in the Assembly] . . . and a large majority of such [i.e., the Assemblymen] who do not qualify by the oath."[24]

There were always political differences among Quakers, not just in the mid- to late 1750s: witness the disagreements among Bucks and Philadelphia County Friends over the desirability of war preparations between 1740 and 1743; witness the divisions among Quakers over the advisability of petitioning the Crown for royal government in 1764 and 1765; simply witness the erratic, noisy gambolings of Israel Pemberton, Jr., who attempted to set up an independent partial slate of Quaker candidates for Philadelphia County in 1744, and who supported what concerned Friends called the Presbyterian Party in 1766. And there was always the sprinkling of Friends who, time after time, supported the proprietors and governors in their differences with the assembly.[25] Knowledge of these divisions, however, should not obscure the fact that the Quaker Party continually held the political confidence of the bulk of the Quaker community.

Just as in religious affairs, political unity among Friends rested to a large degree on their concern for consensus. It was one thing for Quakers to disagree among themselves quietly and in the proper forums; it was quite another for them to have "a public declaration of differing sentiments." That was to be avoided, not at all costs, but if at all possible.[26]

What gave this concern for consensus additional weight in political affairs was the Quakers' fierce possessiveness about Pennsylvania. Pennsylvania was *the* Quaker province. It was William Penn's land, with the fine constitution and libertarian heritage he had conferred on them in trust. With the defection of the Penn children from the Quaker fold, the guardians of his land felt themselves to be the true Quakers—the sons of those who had walked with Penn and shared his dreams in their new land. In the minds of most Quakers, their identity depended on continued political control of Pennsylvania.[27] The alter-

native version of an inward-looking Quaker society offered by the sober
sort in 1755–1756 did not appeal beyond a limited circle. Even some
of those initially persuaded that the Society's interests lay outside politics returned to the old course in the mid-sixties and early seventies.[28]
It took the Revolution to convince large numbers that the political
route was no longer possible.

By the beginning of the second quarter of the eighteenth century,
Friends began to realize that they would face growing difficulty in re-
taining their self-appointed role as political guardians of the "Holy Experiment." The continued immigration of Scotch-Irish, Germans,
and others made it clear that Quaker political power could be continued only if Quakers were politically cohesive and if they followed an
inclusive policy towards the newcomers. As non-Quakers interspersed
themselves among pockets of old settlers and took up whole townships
in frontier areas, Quaker politicians reached out to influential individuals, incorporating them within the political process. The Quaker
meeting house and township had always been centers for political
activities from the earliest days. By the 1730s and 1740s notices of
Friends' political organization meetings were going out to the meeting
houses and township gathering points of other religious groups. This
organizational incorporation of outsiders into the Quaker Party was
one of the first and most important steps in the generation of Quaker
Party supporters among non-Quakers, and, ultimately, of "Quakerized" politicians.[29]

A second step was convincing those of other persuasions, particularly those of non-English stock, that the Quakers had a special role to
play in Pennsylvania government. That proved relatively easy. The
Germans and Scotch-Irish had come to Pennsylvania because of the
religious liberties, civil freedoms, political rights, and economic opportunity that the Quaker province offered. It was a Quaker, William
Penn, who had conceived of this society, and it was Quakers who had
protected that vision. Surely with such a record they should continue
to govern. When Quakers claimed they had the right as well as the
capacity and experience to continue to have a strong voice in the governing of Pennsylvania, there were many who were quick to assent.[30]
And they were not just the few German sectarians often cited as
Quaker allies. Quaker Party support cut across all religious denominations and ethnic groups—Anglican, Presbyterian, Lutheran, Reformed, Moravian, and Mennonite; English, Scotch-Irish, German,
and Dutch.[31] Of course it was easy for outsiders to accord the Quaker
Party the special role it played. Not only was the proprietary no longer
Quaker after the 1720s—and thus a Quaker assembly could claim to

be the sole guardian of William Penn's trust—but also the Quaker Party stood for popular principles. As the voice of the assembly, the Quaker Party defended Pennsylvanians' property rights. One example of this was their concern for freeholders' titles during the boundary dispute with Maryland; another was their support of masters whose servants were enlisted for wartime service against Spain in 1740.[32] At the same time, assemblymen were not quite so concerned about proprietary property rights. They continually refused legislation requiring that all quitrents be paid according to the current sterling rate; and in trying to establish assembly control over the proprietors' land office, they attempted to vest property rights in warrants for survey rather than only in fully-paid-for patented lands.[33]

Beyond the question of property rights, and with the exception of one or two cases of individual rights, assembly policies were whiggish. The Quaker Party passionately defended the assembly's power of sole appropriation of the provincial revenues, its right to control its own adjournments, its policy of promoting voluntary militias with elected officers, its conviction that judges should be appointed for "good behaviour" and not "at pleasure" and its claim that equitable taxation involved the taxing of all lands (including the proprietors') by elected assessors. The extension and defense of assembly powers and the curtailment of proprietary-executive ones were the Quaker Party's basic policies. And in large measure the party was successful. If the gains the assembly made during the fifties and sixties (such as control over the Indian trade, the right to tax proprietary land, the laying of provincial taxes by elected assessors, and provision for increasing the degree of popular government in Philadelphia City) seem minor, that is in large measure because the assembly had already successfully claimed far-reaching powers by 1730.[34]

With policies such as these, the Quaker Party had little difficulty in commanding substantial electoral support. They had, as Richard Peters pointed out, "the ears of the people."[35] And, because Quaker Party representatives were listened to, they could and did spread rumors that strengthened their position even more: The governor, if he gained appointive power over a regular militia, would force conscientious objectors to drill, march, and fight. A militia would be used to collect delinquent quitrents. Increased proprietary power would lead to the conscription of labor to work the Penn manors. Germans and Scotch-Irish not long removed from the shadows of harsh European landlords were influenced by such charges. Quakers who went "often into the country and [knew] men better than [the proprietor's] Friends" exploited those fears in deliberate fashion.[36]

So deeply were the Quakers trusted, and so fully did they control the information networks outside of Philadelphia, that they could do a complete somersault on a policy question and still be elected. In 1764, the country Quakers in the assembly agreed with their Philadelphia counterparts that they should petition the King for a change to royal government. On returning to the counties, Quaker Party representatives soon realized that their constituents were adamantly opposed. Very quickly the assemblymen then changed positions; they argued that *they* were the defenders of proprietary government and their proprietary opponents the proponents of change. Incredible as it sounds, they were believed. Once safely back in the assembly, the country Quakers began to soft-pedal the change of government idea and gradually the issue faded away.[37]

Any political party, if it is to remain a strong force in public affairs, must have patronage to dispense. By colonial standards, the Quaker Party had more than its share. The most important figure in dispensing political patronage was the party leader, the Speaker of the Assembly. Within the legislature he chose the committee members for both standing and ad hoc committees. Such appointments conferred no monetary benefit, but they did confer power both within the legislature and in assembly relationships with constituents, office holders, chief executive, and proprietor.

When Andrew Hamilton resigned from the assembly in 1739, he remarked that one of the most important privileges Pennsylvanians enjoyed under its unique constitution was the legislative appointment of many provincial officers.[38] The most important such office was one that Hamilton knew well, for it was one that he had held, one that John Kinsey held after him and that Isaac Norris's brother Charles occupied during Norris's speakership.[39] That position was Acting Trustee of the Loan Office. Beginning in 1723, the Pennsylvania assembly had provided for the printing of paper currency, which was to be loaned out in amounts up to £100. This was normally done through 5 percent mortgages, with payment of interest and repayment of principal to be spread over a specified number of years. The individual in charge of these operations was known as the Acting Trustee of the Loan Office.

The personal advantages to such an office are obvious. An Acting Trustee received a high salary per annum;[40] more importantly, he had a fund of ready cash at his disposal. The fact that *all* of the long-standing Acting Trustees—William Fishbourne (in the 1720s), Andrew Hamilton, John Kinsey, and Charles Norris—died owing substantial sums to the Loan Office, demonstrates that they used the income as a fund of convenience.

More importantly for the purposes of the Quaker Party, however,

were the larger patronage possibilities that all Acting Trustees exploited. Those who borrowed money in order to finance initial land
purchases from the proprietor—and loans of this category constituted
about half the Loan Office business in 1755[41]—were reminded that it
was an assembly agency, not the proprietary, that allowed them to become freeholders. When the demand for loans outstripped the existing
money supply, or when the mortgage schedule became so contracted
that potential borrowers could no longer afford the payments, it was
the assembly that pushed for more money or a new Re-Emitting Act to
extend the term of mortgages. The proprietor, on the other hand, with
his determination to prevent inflation (to protect the sterling value of
his quitrents and property purchase income), his concern not to offend
British politicians who periodically frowned on such issuances, and his
desire to curb assembly powers, very often resisted this popular course.

The Acting Trustee also had the power to play favorites. For instance, he could advance one person over another on the mortgage
waiting list, or he could raise enough questions about the legitimacy of a
particular title to disqualify, or at least slow down, a potential mort-
gagor's application.[42] Generally, the Acting Trustees did not worry about
delinquent mortgagors. By midcentury numerous borrowers had not
made a payment in ten years. Some contemporary observers estimated
that if foreclosure proceedings were begun against all delinquent debtors,
economic hardship would be widespread. Although the Loan Office's
policy was generally that of leniency, the Acting Trustee had the discretionary power of deciding against whom to initiate proceedings.[43]

Along with the Acting Trustee, the assembly appointed four additional trustees (usually one each from the three old counties and one
from the southwestern back country) to evaluate lands that were offered as security for loans. Again, the trustees were paid a substantial
annual salary and given a great deal of discretionary power. There was
no appeal from their recommendations and valuations. An anonymous petitioner to the assembly put the case succinctly: "The important station of a Trustee of the General Loan Office is attended with
such influence and power upon the persons and estates of the inhabitants of this Province and upon the votes in elections, that it is highly
unreasonable they should sit or act as Representatives in the General
Assembly."[44] Only in Philadelphia County in the 1750s was there any
indication that the Quaker Party heeded this cry.[45] There, on one occasion, two trustees disqualified themselves from elective office. More
characteristic were the periodic disagreements (usually every four years)
over who among assemblymen or staunch party supporters should get
the posts.[46]

In addition to these key positions, the assembly controlled many others. Each county had a collector of the excise appointed by the assembly (before 1756, for the duration of each Excise Act, after that date, annually) whose duty was to collect the excise on wines and spirits. Collectors received up to 10 percent of what they collected and, like the Acting Trustee, had the use of any collected funds until their accounts were settled.[47] The assembly also appointed signers of all the paper currency emitted; a provincial treasurer, inspectors of flour, staves, and lumber; collectors of tonnage duties and of duties on convicted criminals, servants, and slaves imported into Pennsylvania; a provincial health officer and others.[48] During war years, provincial commissionerships for Indian affairs and for appropriating military funds were additional lucrative posts. With the money the assembly raised from its loan office and excise taxes, it bought further good offices. Contracts for the construction of the Statehouse, for the supplying of Indian-trade goods, for the outfitting of British or militia troops and for the building of British troop barracks were awarded with an eye to the political advantage they might bring. In these matters there was far more self-interest than Quaker Party leaders would have cared to admit.[49]

Of all the prerequisites for Quaker Party success, the most important was the existence of a strong minority of Quakers in the basic provincial electoral units—that is, in the different counties and in Philadelphia City. In the three old counties of Chester, Bucks, and Philadelphia, each with its eight assembly seats, and in Philadelphia City with its two, Quaker residents were plentiful. In Lancaster, York, Berks, and Northampton, however, Quakers were never more than a handful. That made the west the Achilles heel of the Quaker Party.

In the first stages of westward expansion that was not so apparent. During the 1720s and 1730s, as farmers began to occupy the Lancaster plain in southeastern Pennsylvania, a small but very influential pocket of Quakers established itself on the banks of the Susquehanna River, close to the present-day towns of Columbia and Wrightsborough, in what was to become Lancaster and York counties. The leading Quakers among this group—Samuel Blunston, John Wright, and the latter's two sons, John and James—are most aptly described as tough-minded Quakers. John Wright, Sr., and Samuel Blunston were alleged to have been involved in violent altercations between Pennsylvanians and Marylanders during the days of the Pennsylvania-Maryland boundary dispute. Whether or not such charges were true, these Quakers certainly took a leading role in organizing Pennsylvanians in defense of their property claims and acted as mediators between the proprietary and local settlers. In doing so, they worked closely with the Scotch-Irish and Germans who mostly peopled the area. They were dependent on these groups for election to county and provincial office at the same time as they shared these offices with the Scotch-Irish and a small sprinkling of Germans. Through the 1730s, 1740s, and early 1750s, the Quaker Party network in Lancaster County held strong, even though it was composed mainly of non-Quakers.[50]

With the French and Indian War changes occurred. Out in the west, in Lancaster, York, Berks, Cumberland, and Northampton, friends, neighbors, and kinfolk were left homeless, injured, or killed while a Quaker assembly and a governor argued over the terms of wartime appropriations. Certainly anti-Quaker sentiment began to accumulate, but it did not immediately burn through the west. Under Isaac Norris, and with Benjamin Franklin's collusion, the Quaker Party did become a defense party, and assembly members who supported the old party traveled through the back country from 1755 to the end of the decade, inspecting forts and organizing militia, settling accounts, distributing arms and letting contracts. At the Susquehanna, the Quaker Wright brothers James and John, Jr., were involved in distributing military supplies. Thomas Minshall supported defensive measures, and the Warrington Monthly Meeting rebuked John Pope and John Blackburn for their aggressive response to Indian attacks. The actions of Pope and Blackburn lent credibility to the Quaker Party as an able defender of Pennsylvania society. These men were heirs to Blunston and Wright, carrying out the tough Quaker tradition born of the frontier.[51]

Where there was a handful of Quakers, accompanied by men who had worked closely with the Quaker Party over the years, the party kept its credibility in the early stages of the war. Back-country folk listened to those whom they had trusted in the past maintaining that proprietary duplicity in land purchases had caused the war. Insofar as the assembly was implicated, the complaint was that they had not provided enough money for defense, nor sufficient relief once war had broken out. As Conrad Weiser stated, when he informed his neighbors that no scalp bounty and no regular pay for provincial rangers was immediately forthcoming in the fall of 1755, "they began, some to curse the Governor, some the Assembly."[52] These were cries against the government, not against the Quakers.

That was not to last. As the war went on, as the Indian attacks continued during 1757 and 1758, and as governmental squabbling failed to abate, Quakers began to attract more and more of the back-country hostility. The lightning rod in this situation was the Friendly Association, a Quaker philanthropic association founded in 1756 to promote peace between Pennsylvanians and Indians. The association was the idea of that small Philadelphia-centered group of sober Friends who had cooperated with like-minded "public Friends" (i.e., Quaker ministers) in organizing the Quaker withdrawal from provincial politics in 1756. The self-appointed conscience of the Society of Friends, this minority saw the Friendly Association as a means of demonstrating that they, not the Quaker assemblymen, were the true heirs of William Penn—the promoters of peaceful relationships in Indian affairs. Having temporarily abandoned politics, they were anxiously searching for new public expressions of a renewed Quakerism. Vocal, intolerant, and judgmental, the Friendly Association Quakers embarked on their private diplomatic crusade: plying the Delaware Indians with gifts, seeking praise for Quaker land policies of the past, and stirring up anger at recent proprietary diplomacy. At the Easton Indian Conferences of 1757 and 1758, for example, the Friendly Association Quakers appeared in force; propped up a drunken Delaware chief, Teedyuscung; and prompted him to denigrate the current proprietors and extol the days of William Penn.[53]

Given the common interest of the Friendly Association and the Quaker Party in blaming the proprietors for the Indian war against Pennsylvania, Quaker politicians openly cooperated with the association. This collusion reached its high point in 1759 when, under the new bill to regulate the Indian trade passed by the assembly, most of the commissioners appointed to oversee the provincial trading stores at Fort Pitt and elsewhere were Quakers who had subscribed to the Friendly Association.[54] Increasingly, Quakerism came to be associated in back-country minds with extravagant charity to the Indians, the building-up of Indian strength through trade, and support of Indian positions against those of white settlers, as opposed to the rigorous defense of western lives and property that they desired.[55]

With the outbreak of Pontiac's Rebellion in 1763, and a new bloodying of the Pennsylvania frontier, anger at the Quakers reached a new pitch. When back-country residents of Paxton and Hanover townships in Lancaster saw that a Quaker Assembly was prepared to protect the Christian Conestoga Indians—whom the frontiersmen believed to be spies and whom they had tried to kill—they massacred those who were still within reach and marched on Philadelphia. The so-called Paxton Rebellion arrayed a Quakerized assembly, backed by a wasp's nest of weighty nonpolitical Quakers, against non-Quaker frontiersmen.[56] The former called for the latter to be arrested and tried; the latter castigated the former for its insensitivity to the lives of western Pennsylvanians. After the assembly had promised to entertain their grievances, the frontiersmen departed for home. Immediately thereafter, a vitriolic pamphlet war broke out. Unlike the case in the 1750s, the westerners' hostility was not directed towards governor and assembly. In the eyes of the Paxton Boys' supporters, it was the Quakers alone who had betrayed their interests, showing more concern for Indian well-being than for the lives and estates of white Pennsylvanians. Out in Lancaster County, Susanna Wright fearfully reported that her brother James's efforts to protect the Conestoga Indians had endangered his life, despite his well-deserved reputation as a hard and practical frontier Quaker whose roots went back to the old Blunston-Wright days of the thirties.[57]

The Paxton affair was not the only event to dramatize the conflict between western settler and Quaker easterner. In early 1765 a group of charcoal-blackened men from Cumberland County, allegedly encouraged and abetted by some of the magistrates of that county, intercepted a wagon train containing £20,000 of trade goods. These goods, including barrels of scalping knives, were destined for trade with western Indians who had yet to conclude peace with the colonists. The goods were owned by the Baynton, Wharton, and Morgan firm of Philadelphia, whose chief partners were connected with the Quaker Party. Again in the case of "the Black Boys," as this escapade became known, a howl went up from the west against the Philadelphia Quakers and their merchant friends.[58]

As the differences between Quakers and frontiersmen grew in intensity, the systematic underrepresentation of the western counties that had begun in 1729 and continued to the Revolution became an increasingly important means by which the Quaker Party retained its political power.[59] Yet, to emphasize this theme of western disenfranchisement and alienation too insistently would be as misleading as to omit it. Despite the periodic outburst of western complaint against Quaker domination, the outlying counties continued to elect assemblymen who could and did work with the majority group in the assembly. Habit and deference prompted this; so too did the continued good reputation of local Quakers in Lancaster, York, Berks, and Northampton. Moreover, the association of Quakerism with whiggism remained intact, as the Quaker Party had continued to protect popular government and the Pennsylvania constitution throughout the fifties and sixties. In 1767, for example, against the objections of Governor John Penn and his council, the Quaker Party, led by Joseph Galloway, pushed through an act requiring the Supreme Court to ride circuit through the back countries. In that one piece of legislation that brought appellate courts to the county seats rather than forcing back-country people to travel all the way to Philadelphia for access to the Supreme Court, the Quaker Party helped and favorably influenced many westerners.[60] Friends' actions in office continually reinforced a perception that Quakers were special and therefore had a justified claim to running the province. Such psychological positioning of Quakers as the rightful leaders of society provided Friends with a significant advantage when wavering voters made their final choices.

What we find on the level of provincial politics, then, was the continued existence of Quaker Party influence throughout the fifties and sixties in the back-country area. For example, in Lancaster County, at least two Quakers or Quakerized men were returned to the assembly in each session until the Revolution. In York, one of the two representatives was almost always a Quaker. Berks and Northampton voting was only slightly less regular. The western independents formed no coherent groups, no caucus of any force or strength. Critical of the Quaker Party at one moment, they participated on committees with powerful party men in the next.

Assembly politics do not tell the whole story. When we look closely at county politics in Lancaster, the most Quakerized of the western counties, for example, we can see important changes taking place. From the 1730s to 1750s, the important political conflicts took place *within* the organizational framework of the Quaker Party. There were two notable exceptions: in 1741, when a slate of prodefense candidates challenged the incumbent, and in 1756, when Edward Shippen, Jr., and Alexander Stedman ran as proprietary supporters. But neither of these was more than a momentary aberration. The real change came about in 1764. In that year the so-called Proprietary Party tried to organize opposing tickets in all of Pennsylvania's counties. While in the three old counties the contest was described as one between Quaker Party and Proprietary Party, in Lancaster it was referred to as a battle between Old Side and New Side. The names are important because they describe accurately what had happened—a new, outside coalition of weighty men had challenged the old dominant group of power brokers. And unlike the situation in the three eastern counties, the electoral contests did not end with the 1765 or 1766 election.

Until the Revolution, Old Side fought New Side in every election. Significantly, they usually only disagreed on one or two of four assemblymen. The real disputes occurred over county commissioners, assessors, and sheriffs, the major prize being control of the board of county commissioners and the local patronage that board could dispense. At the heart of each coalition was a small group of German managers—the Old Side more closely attuned to the Mennonite Germans and the small Quaker coterie that remained a real presence in Lancaster politics, the New Side clearly oriented more towards the German Church people. Both vied for support of the Presbyterians and

TABLE 2

Quaker assembly representation in Lancaster, York, and Berks counties, 1755–1775

	Lancaster	York	Berks
1755–56	Q, Q, Q, Q	Q, NQ	Q
1755–56[a]	Q, Q, Q, NQ	Q, NQ	Q
1756–57	NQ, Q, Q, NQ	NQ, Q	NQ[b]
1757–58	Q, Q, NQ, NQ	Q, NQ	NQ[b]
1758–59	NQ, NQ, Q, Q	Q, NQ	Q
1759–60	Q, NQ, NQ, Q	Q, NQ	Q
1760–61	NQ, NQ, Q, Q	NQ, Q	Q
1761–62	NQ, Q, Q, NQ	Q, NQ	Q
1762–63	NQ, Q, NQ, Q	NQ, Q	NQ[c]
1763–64	NQ, Q, NQ, NQ	NQ, Q	NQ[c]
1764–65	NQ, Q, NQ, Q	NQ, Q	NQ[c]
1765–66	NQ, Q, Q, NQ	Q, NQ	NQ
1766–67	NQ, Q, Q, NQ	Q, NQ	NQ
1767–68	NQ, Q, NQ, Q	NQ, NQ	NQ[d]
1768–69	NQ, Q, NQ, NQ[e]	Q, NQ	NQ[d]
1769–70	NQ, Q, NQ, NQ[e]	NQ, Q	NQ[d]
1770–71	NQ, NQ[e], Q, NQ	NQ, Q	NQ[d]
1771–72	NQ, NQ[e], NQ, Q	NQ, NQ	NQ[d], NQ[f]
1772–73	NQ, NQ, Q, Q	NQ, Q	NQ[d], NQ[f]
1773–74	NQ, Q, NQ[e], NQ	NQ, Q	NQ[d], NQ[f]
1774–75	Q, NQ, NQ, NQ[e]	NQ, NQ	NQ[d], NQ[f]
1775–76	NQ, NQ, NQ[e], Q	NQ, NQ	NQ[d], NQ[f]

NOTES: Q = Quaker, NQ = non-Quaker. Representatives are listed in the order in which they appear in the records. In 1771 Berks County representation was increased by one member.

[a] After the Quaker withdrawal and by-elections of 1756.

[b] Thomas Yorke was a member of the Church of England with strong Quaker Party ties.

[c] John Ross was another Church of England member known to have close connections with the Quaker Party.

[d] Although Edward Biddle was a member of the Church of England, he was from a Quaker family, with close Quaker political connections.

[e] George Ross, John Ross's brother, was also a member of the Church of England whose Quaker Party affiliations were well known.

[f] Henry Chreist was a German Lutheran whose family had been Quakers.

churchmen; both were in some measure successful. What determined their respective successes was how they spread their candidates among religious, ethnic, and geographical groups. The formation of each ticket became a juggling match among local interests.[61]

The importance of this change in the organization of Lancaster County politics is obvious. This was the western county with the strongest Quaker party ties, yet notwithstanding continued Quaker representation in the assembly and continued cooperation of most Lancaster provincial representatives with the Quaker Party, that party had lost control of local politics. And because the Quaker presence had been so strong, Lancaster was the last western county in which this occurred. Gradually, beginning in the 1750s (and in Cumberland's case, because there were no visible Quakers or Quakerized politicians there, beginning with its creation in 1752), the western counties began to float on their own peculiar bases of factionalized local politics. Each county had its own configuration, its own balancing of interests, its own particular foci of conflict and conciliation. Ultimately, the reaches of the Quaker party were determined by residency patterns.

Try as one might, it is impossible to understand the success of the Quaker Party simply by looking at it in isolation. Provincial politics in Pennsylvania at all times included, and many times centered on, the relationship between Quaker Party supporters and a handful of proprietary spokesmen. The proprietary family, with its vast holdings of land, its control over the executive part of government, and its political support among some Pennsylvanians, was the counterpoint to the Quaker Party. Or, perhaps more correctly, Thomas Penn was the counterpoint to the Quaker Party.

Born in 1702, the second son of William and Hannah Callowhill Penn, Thomas was the main proprietary voice in Pennsylvania affairs from 1732 through 1775.[62] Not surprisingly, there was a striking parallelism between the career of Thomas Penn and the trials of the Quaker Party. While the Quaker Party was forming in the 1730s, Thomas Penn was serving his nine-year apprenticeship in Pennsylvania—reorganizing proprietary affairs and forming his own opinions on how the colony should be run. As the Quaker Party matured in the 1740s and early '50s, so did Thomas Penn, taking sole control of the colony in 1746, with the death of his elder brother John, and charting proprietary policy for the next three decades. Like the Quaker Party, Penn had to deal with war and adjust to it; he had to confront the varied problems that westward expansion brought; and continuously he had to face the prospect of diminished political control over his increasingly far-flung province.

When Thomas Penn had arrived in Pennsylvania in 1732, his priorities were clear. The proprietary of Pennsylvania was deeply in debt; Penn's primary order of business was to reduce the burden. The means of doing so and of supporting the proprietary family lay before him. Hundreds of settlers who had bought land from his father William, before William's death in 1718, owed back quitrents of one or two shillings per hundred acres. Hundreds more settlers had poured into the colony during the succeeding fourteen years and, because the succession of the Penn property was not clear, had neither paid for land nor begun payment of their rents. Thomas Penn's self-appointed job was to make them pay.

One of the major problems Penn faced was the lack of rent rolls for the colony—a detail that William Penn had overlooked! There was no indisputable record of who among owners of patented land had kept their quitrent payments up to date. For all those others who occupied warranted or surveyed but patented land, and for those who held only "improvement" (i.e., squatters) rights to land, important questions had to be resolved. What price would be paid? What should the quitrent rate be? What interest rate should be paid on the purchase price and back quitrents, and from what date should it be paid? Further compounding the problem were the Pennsylvania-Maryland boundary dispute and the issuing of Pennsylvania paper money in the 1720s. In the case of the boundary dispute, Lord Baltimore claimed much of the rich farmland of southwestern Pennsylvania, thus Penn could not in good faith give patents or collect back quitrents in this area. Nor would settlers volunteer payment when Penn's ownership was in doubt. The case of the Pennsylvania currency was somewhat more complicated. Prior to 1732, patentees were required to pay one or two shillings per hundred. Through the early 1720s it was self-evident what that meant— one or two shillings sterling. With the printing of paper money that was no longer the case. Pennsylvania currency was declared legal tender, yet it depreciated compared to sterling and fluctuated in value. Although the 1729 assembly had openly declared that all quitrents should be in sterling valuation, most Pennsylvanians argued that the proprietors should accept Pennsylvania currency at par or at least discounted only 33½ percent, the rate at which British law had pegged colonial currency.[63]

By 1739 both of these difficulties had apparently disappeared. Lord Baltimore and the Penns had agreed on a temporary boundary line, and the line had been surveyed almost to the limits of western settlement. On the question of the pre-1732 quitrent arrears, the Pennsylvania assembly had reached a settlement with Penn. Afraid that if Pennsylvania currency could not pass at a rate close to par with sterling, it would depreciate even more and willing to acknowledge that Penn's claim was a legitimate property right, Andrew Hamilton pushed through the assembly a quitrent arrears settlement: those who owed pre-1732 quitrents could discharge them and the interest accrued thereon in Pennsylvania currency at the rate of Proclamation Money, i.e., 16 pence on the shilling. In compensation, the assembly paid Penn a lump sum of £1,200 and promised £130 per annum to run for the length of the new currency emission (eventually to 1756).[64] With the prospect of these settlements in sight, Penn wrote (as gleefully as he ever wrote), "I shall lose no time to seize on the tenants and use all methods the laws allow to make a speedy collection of the whole."[65]

And he did just that. Receiver General James Steel had never been as busy as he was in late 1739.

Penn's dealings with the Land Office in the 1730s demonstrate how his greatest successes were also his greatest failures. Many of those old settlers who had bought land prior to 1732 had paid only a part of the purchase price and no quitrents for years. The truth was that most landholders in the three old counties had enjoyed a free ride at the Penns' expense for some years. Rather than grateful, they were now resentful. Every shilling Penn collected in those back rents cost him good will among the elder settlers in the east. Penn's statement that the people could owe him no ill will because "justice" was on his side meant little to thrifty Quaker farmers when justice was at their expense.[66]

Had the old quitrent arrears question been the only land-related source of friction between proprietor and people, Penn might have received more of the respect and support to which he felt entitled. It was not, however. As soon as Penn arrived in his colony, he raised the price of land by 50 percent, to £15 10s. per hundred acres, and doubled quitrents by raising them to one halfpenny per acre. The new terms produced what any price rise does—grumbles and complaints. These were kept alive and increased in frequency by the stipulation in new patents that all quitrents should be paid at the sterling exchange. John Penn expressed the proprietary position succinctly: the quitrents were "so plainly expressed to be according to the exchange that . . . there will be no occasion to make any allowance on them."[67] Pennsylvanians resisted this measure tenaciously, refusing to see Pennsylvania currency discounted so low. And in 1739 they found additional grounds for their case. If the pre-1732 quitrents could be paid at the rate of Proclamation Money, why should not all others? And the 1739 Currency Act was ambiguous; it seemed to sanction payment of quitrents "according to the tenor of the grant" with "regard being had to the rates of exchange between Philadelphia and London," commanding debtors to pay their arrears "in bills of credit of this province" (suggesting the bills were good at face value) before moving on to state that Pennsylvania currency was legal tender "at the Rates ascertained in the said Act of Parliament" (the Proclamation Money Act). Here were enough ambiguities to make reluctant quitrent debtors intransigent.[68]

Finally, Thomas Penn found that he had to come to terms with a great number of settlers who prior to 1732 had settled land without purchasing it. As a rule, he let those who had warranted the land prior to 1732 purchase it under the old price and terms. But those many who had not even bothered to take this first step towards patenting were to pay the new high rates. Penn held to some version of this policy even in cases in which settlers maintained that special terms had been granted to them. Such was the case of the Donnegalians, a group of Scotch-Irish who had settled in what were to become Donnegal, Paxton, and Hanover townships in Lancaster County at the invitation of James Logan in 1719. In 1733 Penn tendered them the first of a series of offers incorporating higher purchase prices, quitrents, or both than the old rate to which they felt they were entitled. The dispute continued throughout Thomas Penn's residency in Pennsylvania and as late as 1743 there was still disagreement over the terms of settlement both in this area and immediately across the Susquehanna River in what was to become York County.[69]

Thus Pennsylvanians were first introduced to Thomas Penn through his land policies. Accustomed to the less than vigorous collection methods of William Penn and the long interlude of freedom from proprietary exactions after William's death, many resented his son's attempts at renewed control. Thomas collected rents as his father had not, set stiff purchase terms beyond that of any neighboring colony, and demanded the letter of the law wherever he could. The alienation of Pennsylvanians from the proprietary is best demonstrated by the comment of Presbyterian minister Samuel Thomson of Pennsborough who, when brought before the Donnegal Presbytery for writing "some things which were very offensive" to the proprietors, pointed out that they were not his ideas but the "thoughts of the people."[70]

The ground swell of antiproprietary feeling soon made itself felt in political affairs. When, in 1740, Governor George Thomas broke with the Pennsylvania assembly over what he construed as the unwillingness of a Quaker legislature to provide for colonial defense, popular opinion provided a very different explanation. During the dispute, which lasted through 1742, Governor Thomas apparently disregarded the property rights of masters in individual servants when he defended the Crown's rights to enlist such servants; he tried to destroy the whole concept of a Quaker colony when he pleaded to the Crown that Quakers should be disqualified from government; and he attacked the Pennsylvania constitution outright by arguing that he needed a militia with his appointed officers in command, a chancery court to offset the bias of common law courts, power to prorogue and dissolve the assembly, and joint control with the assembly over all appropriations.[71]

Throughout this dispute, Thomas Penn at no point dissociated himself from the words and actions of his deputy governor. Not only was Penn in agreement with Thomas's general sentiments (with the exception of the disqualifying of Quakers from public office) but he also seemed to agree with Thomas on tactics. At one point, Governor

Thomas started a rumor that he had a legal opinion sanctioning his right to prorogue and dissolve the Pennsylvania assembly, despite the Pennsylvania Charter of Privileges, which vested that power in the assembly.[72] Some time earlier when the issue of the chancery court—to be made up of provincial councillors, beholden to Penn—had first been posed, Penn remarked to his brother that "some people whisper that we intend to make use of that Court to recover our arrears and if they conceive it likely, they may think it much more proper to comply."[73]

The problem with a policy of intimidation is that out of the fear it generates defiance can come as easily as submission. And that is precisely what happened in Pennsylvania. Threatened Quakers led the political fight against Thomas Penn and his governor while the German and Scotch-Irish immigrants, with their abiding hatred of landlords, supported the Quakers fully. Those who stood by the proprietary as "Governor's men" or "Friends of the Proprietary" destroyed whatever hopes they had for elected political office. Although still able to attract a respectable number of votes in the 1740 provincial election, the Proprietary Party completely discredited itself by its election tactics and its continued espousal of unpopular policies in 1741 and 1742. One of the greatest strengths of the Quaker Party from this moment on, then, was the widespread dislike of proprietary policies and distrust of proprietary policies and their spokesmen.[74]

When Thomas Penn returned to England in 1741, his ideas on Pennsylvania government were well formulated. He believed that the executive share of government had been sadly reduced by an aggressive assembly and that somehow the balance had to be righted.[75] With the death of his brother John in 1746, Thomas became Pennsylvania's chief proprietor, with the full opportunity to pursue what course he would. That course was to be clearly marked by a series of confrontations between the governor, acting under Penn's instructions, and the assembly.

"The first cause of all" for Penn was some measure of executive control over appropriations.[76] This power had been given up in the 1720s to the assembly, and Penn hoped to regain it. From the late forties through the sixties Pennsylvania's governors were bound by proprietary instructions requiring that all taxation bills should provide for joint appropriation by executive and legislature. This issue came to the fore again and again in the late 1750s and early '60s because wartime expenses required taxation and appropriation of money for military defense. Ultimately Penn won his point through sheer tenacity, only to abandon it as political circumstances changes in the late 1760s.[77]

In addition to joint appropriation, Penn never gave up hope of seeing a regular militia organized under the direction of the governor. A point of contention in the late forties and early to mid-fifties, it gradually became less so in the late fifties and early sixties. By that time, the governor did issue commissions to provincial officers, but in practice he did so only very carefully, to those who could command support in their own community, men who would otherwise have been chosen officers by their own recruits.[78]

Finally, Penn's chancery court schemes were always in the back of his mind. The fact that magistrates, sheriffs, and juries shared the prejudices of their communities put too much popular influence into the common law courts. A chancery court would right the balance. So too would a greater executive voice in appointments to offices created by act of the legislature. In too many instances the popularly elected body used its appointments to influence important public offices. At one point, Penn even toyed with the idea of submitting the Charter of Privileges to Parliament for amendments that would formally establish what he viewed as his prerogatives.[79]

Penn's policies, conceived in the thirties and early forties and promulgated during the fifties and sixties, generated deep rancor in public affairs. And, as if Penn's demands were not provocative enough, a sprinkling of his supporters in Pennsylvania resurrected Governor Thomas's line from the early forties—that the Quakers should be disqualified from office. Again, as earlier, this suggestion led to the branding of Penn and his executive-proprietary men as potential tyrants. Pennsylvania's existing constitution was the best colonial constitution in existence. It afforded rights enjoyed by no other colony. Pennsylvania's remarkable prosperity, its religious and political liberties all stemmed from that constitution. To allow any diminution of assembly powers was to sanction the degeneration of that constitution. And the connection between the Quakers and the Charter of Privileges was organic—to attack Quakerism was to attack assembly rights, the constitution, and the whole Pennsylvania tradition of new-world freedom.[80]

This was the popular view of the confrontation between assembly and proprietor. And on the strength of it the Quaker Party answered proprietary policies with renewed attention to power, seeking to deny the validity of proprietary instructions, pressing to take over the administration of the Land Office, reaching for control of the Indian trade, and conspiring to set up a new civil appellate court staffed by assembly appointees.[81] Rather than strengthen Penn's political position in Pennsylvania, his policies worked to the advantage of the Quaker Party, consolidating and broadening its basis of popular support. As Governor

James Hamilton saw it, the assembly was "backed and applauded by the whole province."[82]

Proprietary goals in the 1740–1760 period were not limited to governmental affairs. As Thomas Penn indicated during his residency in Pennsylvania, he was determined to protect proprietary property rights and to generate more income from them. Consequently, his instructions to his governors included requests that all paper-money bills stipulate that quitrents should be paid at the rate of exchange and in sterling, not at face value. This would clear up the ambiguity in the 1739 act and, Penn hoped, force reluctant landholders to pay quitrents at the sterling exchange rate rather than at the Proclamation Money rate. In practice, the proprietors admitted that working with a floating exchange rate was an administrative nightmare.[83] Neither receiver general nor tenant knew what amount of Pennsylvania currency would have to be tendered to discharge the yearly debts until payment was due. But Penn was determined to have the last farthing.

With Thomas Penn's departure from Pennsylvania in 1741 and Receiver General James Steel's death in the same year, collections of quitrents and purchase money on land sales declined.[84] During the next ten years the receiver general's office was reorganized under Lynford Lardner, with new deputies appointed for the various counties, and, once Penn became chief proprietor in 1746, Land Office activity accelerated. Proprietary Secretary Richard Peters organized the burning out of frontiersmen who had settled on unpurchased Indian land;[85] ejectments were brought against those who squatted on proprietary manors but resisted entering into leaseholds;[86] and commands were issued to Land Office officials to distrain for rents and sue for trespass in order to recover quitrents and outstanding debts for land purchase.[87]

Penn's agents in the colony pointed out the hostility and intransigence that they found.[88] Richard Hockley, for example, reported that settlers continued to refuse to pay off their quitrents at anything more than the 33½ percent Proclamation Money rate and clearly could argue that they were allowed to do so, for "the law was very lame."[89] Others refused to comply at all until they were hauled into court.[90] Yet financially the new toughness paid off.[91] On April 2, 1757, Edward Physick reported to Penn that his agents were "taking in more" than at any time since Penn had established residence.[92]

Although Penn's policies were productive monetarily, they certainly brought the proprietary no new popularity.[93] On the one hand, the proprietor kept currency scarce by forbidding the issuance of new paper currency save on grounds the assembly would not accept, while, on the other, Penn demanded payment of debts. And at the same time his agents were pressing people to pay—even under the war-time conditions of the fifties—Penn was fighting against taxation of his own land. Beginning in 1756, when the assembly first formed a bill taxing proprietary property along with that of other individuals, Penn used his position as proprietor to fight against such exactions. First, he argued that his lands should be exempt; then, that only his rents and quitrents (not his land) ought to be taxed; and, finally, that his land should be taxed below the level of others. Only in 1764 did he accept parity in taxation rates.[94]

While Penn was trying to avoid taxation in the fifties and early sixties, the colonists were paying unprecedented taxes to support the war effort. And, despite voicing sympathy for their continued difficulties, Penn insisted on suing for proprietary debts. Even his apparent acts of generosity proved hollow. A supposedly free gift of £5,000 in 1756 to support the war effort was, in fact, ordered to be paid out of quitrents collected during the war years.[95]

Such policies brought the proprietary nothing but scorn and hatred. Compared to Penn the assembly-run Loan Office, with its record of overlooking late payments and failing to foreclose, looked like an angel of mercy. Assemblymen were not slow to exploit this difference between assembly and proprietary policy. They felt that Penn was using the governorship as a private interest to protect his proprietary claims. Thus the executive had forfeited its right to speak for the people; it was the legislative assembly, Pennsylvanians believed, not the legislature and executive together, that represented the "whole body of the People."[96]

It is often assumed that, despite Penn's land policies, the French and Indian war brought new political support for the proprietary in the western counties. The evidence offered for this is usually Chief Justice William Allen's election as a representative for Cumberland County, along with the assumption that other western representatives were of similar political leanings. The assembly records between 1755 and 1763, however, indicate no such phenomena. Although outside the network of the Quaker Party, most western representatives were pro-defense politicians, not proprietary, and they cooperated with eastern assemblymen in their antiproprietary stance. Western representatives shared committee appointments on bills which encroached on proprietary prerogatives or were highly critical of the proprietary record.[97] According to William Allen, who stood alone on a number of instances during these years, "many of my . . . old friends [in the assembly] . . . [had been] cowed."[98] There was no proproprietary rump or cabal because there was so little in the way of popular support for the proprietary.[99]

Nor did the Paxton Rebellion bring about any proprietary-western alliance. True enough, Governor John Penn forbore public condemnation of the rioters, and, more important, he did not acquiesce to assembly demands that the rioters be apprehended and interrogated by the courts.[100] But that was a long way from the open championing of their actions that would have been required to build political bridges. The chasm between proprietary and people was too wide to be affected by any backhanded recognition of the frontiersmen's cause.

The chief reason why this gulf remained so great was the hatred that proprietary land policy continued to inspire. The great bulk of warranted and unpaid-for land was located in the frontier counties of Cumberland, Lancaster, and York. Much of this land could only be patented at the new quitrent level of one penny per acre that Penn had instituted in 1762.[101] Consequently, this was the area that bore the brunt of proprietary exactions, though it was precisely the area in which money was the most scarce.[102] It was the frontier settlers, too, who saw at first hand the favoritism of the Land Office—the reserving of prime land for eastern proprietary favorites, for proprietary reserve lands, and for large group purchases.[103]

The Scotch-Irish, often cited as being friends to the proprietary, demonstrated again and again their abiding hostility to the Penn claims and exactions. In the 1730s and '40s they fought for their homes in Paxton, Derry, and Donnegal against the land purchase terms Penn demanded.[104] In the 1750s it was the Scotch-Irish assessors of Cumberland County who stung the proprietors by overassessing their land, thinking, as William Smith reported to Thomas Penn, that it was "justice to do him injustice."[105] And then in the 1760s and early 1770s these same Scotch-Irish left upper Lancaster and Cumberland counties to support Connecticut's claims to the Wyoming Valley and joined with Virginians in Redstone Valley on the Monongahela and at Fort Pitt to resist the hated Penn terms for land.[106] Just as the west floated free of the Quaker Party, so did it stay free of proprietary loyalties. The allegiances that underlay administrative ties with the proprietary government were not strong.[107]

In the east, the proprietary fared only marginally better. The year 1764 did bring a temporary change in the distribution of political power. Franklin and Galloway's wild scheme of petitioning the Crown to take over the Pennsylvania government ran into such resistance that the proprietary supporters and placemen challenged the Quaker Party with opposing slates of candidates in the election of that year. For the first time in memory, the proprietary supporters had a truly popular issue, and they were not about to waste the opportunity. Yet their victory was momentary. Stung by the electoral defeat of Franklin, Galloway, and four of their supporters in Philadelphia County and City, and forced to repudiate its petition for royal government in other counties, the Quaker Party closed ranks, agreed to soften its demand for a change of government, and subsequently carried the 1765 election. The proprietary success of the previous year had been based on one issue—the deep-seated wish of most Pennsylvanians to keep their Charter of Privileges inviolate. It certainly signified no great surge of proprietary feeling.[108]

The notion of a proprietary party, however, was exceedingly important for the dynamics of Pennsylvania politics throughout the second and third quarters of the eighteenth century. Quite simply, it provided a political straw man for the popular Quaker Party. Proprietary supporters suggested by their presence and political activities the dangerous marriage of private interest to executive power. The very name "Proprietary Party" or "Governor's Party" denoted that. Yet as Isaac Norris pointed out, "it [was] indeed absurd to call the opposition a party; a few men only compose[d] it."[109] Only in five years 1740, 1742, 1756, 1764, and 1765 did the proprietary men mount anything like a major attempt to provide alternate assembly candidates for three or four counties. And these efforts occurred only when they felt they had a popular cause—the issue of military defense, or political protection of the Charter of Privileges. These moments when they did find an appealing issue were never enough, however, to dispel the overwhelming distrust Pennsylvanians felt for proprietary and executive power.

The failure of the Proprietary Party as a political party went beyond its lack of popularity and electoral weakness. It was basically a loose aggregation of proprietary placemen—provincial councillors, Supreme Court judges, members of the Philadelphia Corporation and such public officials as the attorney general, the provincial secretary, and the prothonotaries and clerks of the county courts—with no cohesion and little in the way of consistent leadership. Men such as William Allen, Richard Peters, and Benjamin Chew were important as proprietary advisors at different times and in different capacities, but no individual ever provided the moderate leadership that Andrew Hamilton had done in the 1730s. The correspondence of Thomas Penn with his governors and close advisors, whether in the 1740s, 1750s, or 1760s, reveals a constantly weak provincial council, plagued with interminable backbiting, antipathy, disorganization, jealousy, double-dealing, and pique among proprietary supporters. The election tactics they followed were often ill advised, ranging from ineffective cooperation[110] to outright advocacy of the use of force.[111] And despite the various tensions within the Quaker Party over the years, proprietary men could never more than briefly exploit those differences for their own political advantage.

The absence of leadership in proprietary ranks can in large part be traced to Thomas Penn—not just in reference to his unpopular policies but to his conception of the proprietor as correctly standing above local politics rather than becoming directly involved in them. In the 1730s, Penn cut himself off from close association with local political allies, and that was the stand he continued to take through the 1760s. He maintained that the proprietary should deal with all groups equally and, in so doing, try to generate independent recognition of proprietary justice. Partisanship should be avoided.[112] When Thomas Penn's nephew John Penn took over the governorship in 1763, he realized with some shock that his uncle had indeed tried to implement such a policy. Patronage, John charged, had not been effectively used to build up a political party of consequence. There was some truth to his observations; most deputy surveyors were Quakers whose associations were with the Quaker Party;[113] magistrates' commissions were most commonly issued on a nonpartisan basis;[114] and the patronage possibilities in the granting of tavern licenses had never been exploited.

Although John argued that his uncle Thomas should abandon his nonpartisan policy in making appointments,[115] and although, as governor, John made some small headway in this regard,[116] the complexion of proprietary appointments changed very little. The chief surveyor, John Lukens, "as thorough pac'd a Quaker as any in the County," remained in his office;[117] Quaker Party members were still solicited for magistrates;[118] Quakers still headed the commissions of the peace even in some of the frontier counties;[119] and in Chester County the well known "hot" Quaker Henry Hale Graham was appointed to the important office of clerk of courts and prothonotary.[120]

The truth was that in making such appointments as magistrate, or even in granting commissions to militia officers, the proprietary had to pay due regard to eminence within local communities. Only if they had respect could magistrates command respect; only under popular officers would militia men enlist and march.[121] Perhaps the point can best be made by reference to John Armstrong, Scotch-Irishman, resident of Cumberland County, and favorite proprietary contact in that area. A local hero of the French and Indian War and a justice of the peace, Armstrong blamed the assembly for the failure to provide adequate defense for the west.[122] According to Richard Peters, it was this anger that prompted Armstrong to use his interest to secure the election of William Allen to the assembly as a Cumberland County representative during the late fifties and early sixties.[123] But, in 1765, when Chief Justice Allen issued a writ to remove one Frederick Stump (a man guilty of murdering a number of Indians) from Cumberland for questioning in Philadelphia, Armstrong challenged Allen.[124] Allen's writ seemed to prepare the way for changing trial locations from west to east, a contravention of basic constitutional rights, and the frontiersman would have none of it: Armstrong was his own man. Local officials, whether in Cumberland or Chester County owed their first allegiance to the community in which they lived.[125] In such a society, and given the unpopularity of the proprietary, it is not at all clear that more concerted attempts to secure partisan appointments would have borne fruit. Certainly John Penn had little enough success with his modest efforts in the mid-1760s.

Until 1766, the profile of Pennsylvania politics remained much as it had been since 1740. During that quarter century, the lines of division among politicians were relatively clear. The relationship between the Quaker and Proprietary parties, however heated or placid, had always been a symbiotic one. The former fed on the threat of the latter, the latter serving as a catchall for those who resisted the process of Quakerization. In the late sixties and early seventies, however, the distinct lines between Quaker party friends and proprietary men began to blur in a way that was reminiscent of the 1730s. The policy of the proprietors, their governors, and what might best be referred to (although with some inaccuracy) as the Church of England branch of the Proprietary Party sought to come to terms with the Quaker Party. Governor and assembly compromised their differences over such issues as joint appropriation of revenue and the taxation of proprietary lands and became increasingly unsympathetic to the western problems of Indian relations and proprietary land policy.[126] In the old Quaker areas in Philadelphia, Chester, and Bucks quitrent arrears had largely been paid, and farmers objected but little to the annual one or two shillings per hundred acres that Penn's receiver general, James Tilghman, argued were not even worth the trouble of collection.[127] Given this closing of ranks and the abating of antiproprietary feeling, the proprietary men simply gave up the organization of elections and tickets in the three old counties to the Quaker Party.[128]

But this turn did not bring unanimity. In Philadelphia County, beginning in 1764 with the Paxton disturbance and reinforced in 1765 with the Stamp Act crisis, in 1768 with conflict between Church of England men and Presbyterians in the College of Philadelphia over the prospect of an American bishopric, and in 1769–1770 with the nonimportation issue, the spectre of a Presbyterian, or Whig, party began to appear. This new political entity was only cohesive enough to contest one or two seats in Philadelphia in 1766 and again in 1770.[129] It hardly seemed to threaten the Quaker Party-proprietary détente or

Quaker Party control in the old counties. As long as the back country continued to be underrepresented, and as long as western politicians accepted their traditional relationship to the Quaker Party, no effective political alliance between a nucleus of whiggish Philadelphia Presbyterians and some of their back-country coreligionists could emerge. Such an alliance, however, was not as far in the future as Quaker Party men hoped.

Close examination of the relationship between the Quaker Party and the proprietary spokesmen during the four-and-a-half decades before the Revolution clearly reveals that, in electoral politics, Pennsylvania was totally dominated by one party. The Quaker Party stood for popular issues, was accorded special status as the custodian of the Friends' "Holy Experiment," and, through a network of meeting houses, could control information and turn out the vote. Organized as it was and wielding power as it did through continuous control of the most powerful assembly among the thirteen colonies, the party defied traditional labels. It was too long-lived, too well-organized, and too consistent in policy to be dismissed as a "faction."[130] Superficially, with its rural roots, its legislative base, and its rhetorical defense of mixed government, the Quaker Party seems to have been very much a "country" party. Yet its "court" characterisics were legion: its highly organized political machine, its use of patronage, its monopoly of legislative power, its acceptance of credit financing through the Pennsylvania land bank, and its Philadelphia members' involvement in business and commerce.[131] Clearly the Quaker Party was *sui generis*.

The party did not, of course, draw the allegiance of all of the politically active populace. Some gravitated towards the proprietor in order to defend either, in most instances both, proprietary or executive powers, or to press for a more vigorous defense policy than the Quaker Party legislators were willing to pursue. Proprietary support foundered on proprietary policies. Thomas Penn's tough land policies and his efforts to strengthen the executive sharply alienated many Pennsylvanians, as the visible marriage of private interest to executive power in the proprietor raised fearsome specters of tyranny in their minds. Unpopular, numerically weak, rife with dissent, disorganized and suffering from want of leadership, the Proprietary Party was never a successful political party: electorally the party had destroyed itself for fifteen years through its election tactics in 1742; party members failed to gain legislative power in the defense crisis of the mid-1750s; their one electoral victory in Philadelphia County in 1764 was fleeting because the Party's unpopularity ran so deep; and in the west there was always at least as much antipathy to proprietary men as there was to their Quaker opponents. In truth, the Proprietary Party was so weak electorally and so completely dependent on proprietary and executive power for its continued existence as to make a mockery of the "court" party terminology occasionally accorded it.

Given the unpopular character of the proprietary men, all that the Quaker Party had to do to maintain its legislative power was to evoke its own traditions, in contrast to proprietary policies, and to adjust to new political developments. Quaker Party spokesmen were very successful in remaining visibly faithful to their popular heritage. They so pre-empted the politically popular ground that there was little left for other groups to cultivate. Outsiders either accepted exclusion from assembly power, as most proprietary supporters continuously did, or allowed themselves to be coopted by the Quaker Party, the fate of some non-Quaker western representatives in the 1750s and early 1760s and of some eastern-based proprietary men in the late sixties and early seventies.

To adjust to new political developments was a far greater challenge for the Quaker Party, a challenge that it was ultimately unable to meet. In the 1730s and 1740s the party was an open, representative organization observing the niceties of the deferential politics while being firmly grounded in local communities. In the old counties of Bucks, Chester, and Philadelphia that did not immediately change. At times, the leadership ossified; certainly there were moments when too much was assumed by the Philadelphia contingent. But, overall, the Party reflected rather than frustrated local opinion—until the late 1760s and early 1770s. Only then did imperial issues, which cut across existing party lines at the same time as they began to destroy the all-important intraparty consensus, seriously undercut the Quaker Party's political effectiveness.

In the western areas of Pennsylvania the adjustment was even less successful. Because Quakers did not move in any strength into the newly settled areas of the colony, the Quaker Party was denied the organizational base that made it so durable in the east. Slowly, during the 1750s and 1760s, the ability of the party to reach out into the back-country areas and reflect opinion over a wide range of issues disappeared. The power brokers of the east never completely lost touch with the west—there were far too many sources of Quaker Party information and far too many genuine reasons why back-country settlers could identify with the party for that. But, by the early 1770s, the west was without any deep Quaker Party allegiances. Bereft of grassroot support and unwilling to give expression to incipient Revolutionary feeling, the Quaker Party had become too narrow in its base and in its interests to survive as a popular political party.

RICHARD ALAN RYERSON

Portrait of a Colonial Oligarchy:
The Quaker Elite in the Pennsylvania
Assembly, 1729–1776

———————•◉•———————

"OUR HONORABLE HOUSE made a scurvy appearance. . . . it was enough to make one sweat to see a parcel of countrymen sitting with their hats on, in great coarse cloth coats, leather breeches, and woolen stockings in the month of July. . . . there was not a speech made the whole time, whether their silence proceeded from their modesty or from their inability to speak I know not."[1] This vivid description of Pennsylvania's assemblymen, stolid members of the Society of Friends who made no concessions either to the refined manners of their bareheaded worldly colleagues or to the heat of a Philadelphia summer, richly confirms the familiar view of eighteenth-century Quaker political culture. The dominance of men from the meeting house in both the counting and the state house, from the colony's founding until the sudden withdrawal of Quakers from politics in 1756, is one of our clearest images of colonial Pennsylvania.[2] Our anonymous observer, however, was not speaking of the 1730s or the 1750s, but of July 21, 1774, eighteen years after Quakers had supposedly abandoned public office rather than prosecute an imperial war, and less than seven weeks before the gathering of the First Continental Congress. Did Pennsylvania's Quaker oligarchy in fact survive, as a *Quaker* oligarchy, down to the American Revolution? If it did survive, how did it do so, and what can its survival tell us about eighteenth-century American politics?

The existence of a native American oligarchy on the eve of the Revolution is no occasion for surprise; detailed studies of Massachusetts,

Virginia, and the Carolinas, and surveys of all of the colonies have firmly established the widespread growth of American oligarchies in the eighteenth century.[3] A fresh look at the Pennsylvania assembly, however, suggests that for at least one province the argument for a growing demobilization of American politics has not been made strongly enough. Pennsylvania's Quaker Party was no ordinary colonial elite; its primary power base—English and Welsh Quakers—was a shrinking religious minority living in an increasingly pluralistic society. Moreover, while this durable party frequently sought British support in its protracted struggle with Pennsylvania's proprietors, it never became so dependent upon the British establishment as Thomas Hutchinson's "court" in Massachusetts, or so imitative of the British gentry as the "country" legislative oligarchy in Virginia. Finally, unlike the pro-imperial cliques in the Wentworths' New Hampshire and in Massachusetts, Pennsylvania's pro-imperial legislative oligarchy did not lose electoral support after the Stamp Act crisis.[4] So striking a political phenomenon deserves an attempt to explain its particular character and its singular durability. This essay will examine the Quaker oligarchy within the Quaker, or Assembly, Party, that alliance of Quaker and "Quakerized" non-Quaker legislators who bonded together to control Pennsylvania's political life for over half a century.

The key to the Quaker Party's domination of Pennsylvania politics, particularly after 1756, the year in which many historians have seen an irreversible decline in Quaker power, lies in the manner in which it controlled the assembly. This powerful legislature early became the focus of political activity in the province, the center of an elaborate political structure that extended from local Quaker meetings and county courthouses to the governor's chair. To understand the Quaker Party's domination of this body, one must examine the assembly's structure and assess the legislative behavior of its members. To what degree did the size of the House, the geographical distribution of its seats, and the extent of its powers favor a legislative obligarchy; and how strong a foundation did local Quaker meetings and county governments provide for that oligarchy? To what extent did the legislators become a clique of veterans of many years' service? What role did geographic distribution, seniority, and religious identification play in shaping the membership of the assembly's standing and ad hoc committees, those small bodies which powerfully shaped the behavior of the whole chamber? Finally, how did each of these factors change over time, particularly after 1756, and can these developments help to explain the nature of the Quaker party's continued domination of Pennsylvania's pluralistic society?

A view of the assembly from outside the chamber suggests its suitability as the home of a political oligarchy. Pennsylvania had an exceptionally small legislature for so large a land area and population. With thirty members between 1729 and 1749, thirty-six between 1752 and 1771, and only forty by 1775, the House had the highest ratio of constituents to representatives of any Anglo-American colony.[5] These few lawmakers were slow to extend representation to Pennsylvania's recently settled but rapidly developing interior regions. In the 1760s, Bucks County, on the Delaware River, enjoyed four times the legislative voice accorded to the newer Lancaster County, on the basis of their taxable populations. As late as 1770, the older eastern, heavily Quaker counties elected twenty-four lawmakers, while the equally populous western, non-Quaker counties chose only ten.[6] Yet this small chamber possessed extraordinarily large powers, even by the standards of British North America's aggressive assemblies. Pennsylvania's legislature, unicameral after 1701, had become one of the most powerful in America by the mid-1720s; it increased those powers still further over the next half century.[7]

Quaker legislators could not easily have dominated this assembly into the 1770s if Pennsylvanians had formed a highly mobilized citizenry. Quakers diminished from perhaps one-third of the colony's population in the 1720s to only one-eighth in the 1770s; even combined with their Anglican allies they had lost their numerical dominance of Pennsylvania's voters by 1750, a full generation before their party lost control of the province. But as the best study of the Quaker oligarchy before the Seven Years' War convincingly argues, Pennsylvanians were not highly mobilized citizens; they were instead among the most passive and deferential constituents in British North America. To a remarkable degree, they remained so until 1774.[8]

Pennsylvanians had not always been so docile. The colony's first generation, although heavily Quaker, was most contentious. Wealthy urban Friends often allied with the founding proprietor, William Penn, in a struggle against their less affluent country brethren—who adopted a more whiggish, antiproprietary stand—for control of the assembly. But in the mid-1720s this Quaker strife ended. A secure, now largely antiproprietary Quaker elite emerged to take command of the whole Quaker electorate, which was itself rapidly becoming a political elite within Pennsylvania's ever more pluralistic society.[9] For the next fifty years, Friends occupied a special position in the province. Wealthier than their immigrant neighbors, enjoying the prestige of native, and then of second- and even third-generation American birth, and steadily diminishing in relation to the larger community, they lost remarkably little political power.

The transition from founding majority to minority elite did not prove difficult. Quakers established Pennsylvania's county governments, and to supplement the narrowly circumscribed role which late seventeenth-century whiggish dissenters expected government to play, they provided many desired social services through their own religious meetings. As several of these functions passed to the civil government in the eighteenth century, Friends often continued, as public officeholders, to perform them. In the three eastern counties the whole ladder of public service from township constable to county sheriff, and ultimately to assemblyman, remained thoroughly under Quaker control.[10] In Berks, Lancaster, and York counties to the west, where Friends were few, Anglican, German, and even Presbyterian voters, impressed with the Quakers' determined opposition to war, high taxes, and the sometimes heavy hand of British authority and proprietary greed, voted accordingly, and swelled the ranks of Quaker legislators still further.[11]

Between 1726 and 1755, in nearly every part of Pennsylvania, and for twenty years thereafter in Chester, Bucks, and Philadelphia counties, local leaders from established political families continued to nominate unopposed lists of assembly candidates, most of whom were Friends. To give the voters a choice, they presented just a few more names than the number of seats to be filled.[12] Contested elections and years of significant turnover were rare in the House between 1726 and 1756, and after the massive but quite temporary Quaker withdrawal in 1756 and 1757, they remained rare until the Revolution.[13] In the 1760s, as in the 1740s, Pennsylvania's Quaker legislators were riding a strong and steady wave of deference, whiggish sentiments, and their own faithful performance of their duties at low cost to the voters, who in turn enjoyed personal freedom, economic prosperity, and enduring peace.

It was a political formula that guaranteed success. And it remained, to a degree that historians of colonial Pennsylvania have seldom appreciated, a Quaker formula, whose effectiveness was limited to the boundaries of the Quakers' local meetings and governments.[14] The manner in which Friends built upon local foundations to dominate the assembly, and the nature of that domination's limits, become clear when one opens the doors of the legislative chamber, doors that Quaker legislators traditionally kept closed to their constituents.[15]

A visitor entering the eighteenth-century Pennsylvania assembly would first be struck by the simple, almost rustic dress of several of the members, by their broad-brimmed hats planted firmly upon their heads, and above all by their long silences, those inner dialogues that were central to the Quaker decision-making process.[16] In its formal organization, the Pennsylvania House resembled many another colonial American legislature; in its members' personal style, it was unique.[17] But what of the assembly's substance: how did this legislature really work, who controlled it, and how did they effect that control? To answer these questions, one must determine how often House seats changed occupants, and perhaps more important, how often men who were new to the chamber took up seats. One must also calculate the members' cumulative seniority over time. Most important, one must study the composition of the legislature's standing and ad hoc committees. The electoral district, seniority, and religious identification of committee members help to make clear what kind of legislator possessed the greatest power in the House, and thereby suggest the contours of Pennsylvania's oligarchy.[18]

Oligarchies base a large measure of their power upon the stability of their membership, and the Pennsylvania House was no exception. The basic index of *carry-over*, the proportion of seats in any session held by members who had sat in the previous session, points to an impressive stability in the chamber's membership over five decades. In only six of the first twenty annual sessions of the assembly under the Constitution of 1701 with extant membership lists (1704–1723) did the carry-over exceed 50 percent, but in the next fifty-two sessions (1724–1775) it never fell below 56 percent. In the period 1746–1775, the Pennsylvania House had the highest legislative carry-over rate in British North America.[19] A more compelling challenge to the traditional argument that the Quaker Party changed fundamentally after 1755 lies in the timing of the two periods of greatest stability. The first is exactly where historians have led one to expect it, at the height of the almost purely Quaker oligarchy in the speakership of John Kinsey; in the years 1740–1748, carry-over ranged between 80 and 100 percent. But the second peak occurred after the great Quaker withdrawal of 1756. Following the return of several veteran Quaker lawmakers to public life and the recruitment of several other Friends, the years 1758–1771 had a carry-over that ranged from 72 to 94 percent. Alan Tully, the leading historian of the assembly in the years 1729–1755, finds an average carry-over, in those years, of 77 percent; but the average carry-over for 1756–1775, which includes the Quaker withdrawal of 1756, is 79 percent. Finally, the average carry-over for the eleven years of John Kinsey's speakership (1739–1749) is 83 percent and for the eight years of Joseph Galloway's speakership (1766–1773) is 82 percent. The Quaker oligarchy may have changed dramatically after 1755, but the assembly's membership remained stable until Independence.[20]

TABLE 1

Three indices of stability in the Pennsylvania assembly, 1729–1775

	Carry-over	Veterancy	Seniority		Carry-over	Veterancy	Seniority
1729	57%	70%	4.7 yrs.	1753	83	89	5.3 yrs.
1730	63	77	4.2	1754	94	94	6.2
1731	67	83	4.5	1755	83	87	5.9
1732	70	87	5.3	1756	58	67	5.4
1733	73	87	5.0	1757	78	86	5.1
1734	70	83	5.8	1758	81	86	5.8
1735	73	87	6.2	1759	89	97	6.6
1736	87	97	7.2	1760	75	81	6.9
1737	77	93	7.6	1761	75	81	6.9
1738	67	90	6.9	1762	81	83	6.6
1739	63	80	6.3	1763	83	86	6.9
1740	87	90	5.7	1764	72	81	6.1
1741	87	90	4.7	1765	75	86	6.4
1742	100	100	5.7	1766	86	92	6.3
1743	87	90	6.4	1767	75	83	5.6
1744	93	97	7.2	1768	86	89	6.0
1745	83	83	7.5	1769	94	97	6.6
1746	80	83	6.6	1770	78	89	6.8
1747	87	90	7.3	1771	87	87	6.6
1748	87	90	7.7	1772	69	74	6.0
1749	56	72	6.6	1773	83	88	6.2
1750	75	78	6.0	1774	80	85	6.1
1751	74	85	5.9	1775	76	83	6.1
1752	71	74	5.3				

A better test of long-term legislative stability is *veterancy*, the proportion of seats in any session held by members who had sat in any previous session. The assembly's veterancy rate, too, was consistently high; veteran lawmakers held more than 80 percent of the chamber's seats in every session after 1730 except five: 1749, 1750, 1752, 1756, and 1772. Periods of high veterancy occurred both before the Quaker withdrawal of 1756, in the second speakership of Andrew Hamilton (1734–1738: 90 percent) and in the tenure of John Kinsey (1739–1749: 88 percent); and after that event, in the second half of Isaac Norris Jr.'s speakership (1757–1764: 85 percent) and in the speakership of Joseph Galloway (1766–1773: 87 percent). Tully found an average veterancy of 86 percent for the years 1726–1755; for the years 1756–1775, again including the Quaker withdrawal of 1756, veterancy drops only to 85 percent.[21] Stability of this order seems remarkable in an oligarchy whose character is thought to have changed fundamentally near the midpoint of its domination.

The *seniority* of Pennsylvania's assemblymen, expressed in their

TABLE 2

Quakers in the Pennsylvania assembly, 1729–1775

	Number	%		Number	Number below one-half of all assemblymen	%
1729	19	63	1756	11	−7	31
1730	19	63	1757	12	−6	33
1731	19	63	1758	14	−4	39
1732	21	70	1759	13	−5	36
1733	23	77	1760	14[b]	−4	39
1734	20	67	1761	18[b]	even	50
1735	17	57	1762	16[b]	even	50
1736	16	53	1763	15[b]	−2	44
1737	18	60	1764	17[b]	−3	42
1738	22	73	1765	18	−1	47
1739	24	80	1766	17	even	50
1740	27	90	1767	17[b]	−1	47
1741	27	90	1768	15	−1	47
1742	27	90	1769	18[b]	−3	42
1743	26	87	1770	17[b]	even	50
1744	25	83	1771	18	−2	45[a]
1745	26	87	1772	17	−2	46[a]
1746	25	83	1773	15	−3	43[a]
1747	25	83	1774	13	−5	38
1748	25	83	1775		−8	32[a]
1749	24	75[a]				
1750	25	74[a]				
1751	24	71				
1752	26	72[a]				
1753	27	75				
1754	27	75				
1755	27	75				

[a] The assembly increased in size in these years, thus altering the percentages.
[b] In each of these years the assembly had one member who is here counted as a Quaker, but who may not have been.

average number of years served at the opening of each annual session, closely parallels the legislature's other indices of stability. As carry-over and veterancy increased in the first three decades of the eighteenth century, seniority steadily mounted; after 1731 mean seniority fell below five years only once. There were four peak periods of seniority, 1736–1738, 1744–1749, 1759–1763, and 1769–1771, one each in the speakerships of Hamilton, Kinsey, Norris, and Galloway. Comparatively, Hamilton's later years (1734–1738) had the highest mean veterancy and seniority, although the lowest carry-over; Kinsey's term (1739–1749), the high point of Quaker power in the assembly, had the second highest veterancy and seniority and the highest carry-over, with Norris's early years, through 1757, the low point of veterancy and seniority. Norris's later years (1758–1764) saw a dramatic recovery in veterancy and seniority but a low carry-over, because several long-term veterans returned after the withdrawal of 1756. Galloway's years (1766–1773) recovered nearly to Kinsey's levels on all indices—within one percentage point on carry-over and veterancy, and three months on seniority.[22]

Yet another measure of stability in the Pennsylvania assembly is the high frequency of familial interrelationships among its members. One hundred of the 265 legislators who served between 1729 and 1776 (38 percent) shared their surnames with one or more other members. There were ten groups of three sharing surnames, four groups of four, and one of five. The vast majority of these men were in fact related to one another. Total familial relatedness, of course, ran much higher. Thomas Purvis, in his study of New Jersey's colonial assembly, found that nearly 43 percent of the members serving between 1722 and 1776 shared surnames, but that total familial relatedness, by blood or marriage, calculated for each session, ranged from 65 to 96 percent. The Pennsylvania assembly's somewhat lower frequency of shared surnames suggests interrelationship levels of 55 to 85 percent.[23]

These measures of stability suggest that the Pennsylvania assembly passes the first test of an oligarchy: it was a small body of men who wielded political power over long, generally unbroken terms of years and whose membership changed both slowly and fairly evenly, except during the mid-1750s. Neither carry-over nor veterancy nor seniority, however, demonstrate that the assembly formed an oligarchy in the second, more popular sense of that term: a body of men set apart in some key respect—wealth, membership in a prominent old family, education, ethnic background, or religious identification—from most members of the society they govern. More specifically, these indices do not show that the legislature was a Quaker oligarchy, or that if it was Quaker in one period, it remained so in another. To settle this question, one must first determine how many Quakers sat in the House in any given year.

Although historians have studied the Quakers' role in early Pennsylvania politics for two centuries, no systematic attempt to count Quaker assemblymen appeared in print before 1971, but in the following decade several scholars working independently identified nearly every Quaker legislator who served between 1729 and Independence.[24] This research suggests a quite different view of the Quaker role in late colonial politics from that which prevailed until very recently. Between 1729 and 1755, Quaker assemblymen always held a majority of the assembly's seats; after 1755, as historians have always argued, they

never held a majority. If one looks at this pattern in some detail, however, a more complex picture emerges. Between 1729 and 1740,
Quaker assemblymen increased from 63 to 90 percent of the House;
they then held steady at 83 to 90 percent until 1748, and sank slightly
to a 71 to 75 percent range through 1755. In 1756, Quaker membership dropped from 75 percent to 31 percent, and it remained under 40
percent until 1761. But in the 1760s several Friends entered the
House, and between October 1761 and September 1774, they held between 42 percent and 50 percent of the chamber's seats. Only in October 1774 did Quaker assemblymen again decline to well under 40
percent of the legislature. Pennsylvania's Quakers, then, easily dominated their assembly between 1729 and 1755, were in a poor position
to do so between 1756 and 1760, and were numerically able to do so,
under favorable circumstances and astute leadership, from 1761 to
1774.[25] To determine whether circumstances favored them, whether
they received the leadership that they needed, and whether they manifested the will to dominate their polity, one must carefully analyze the
internal leadership structure of the House.

From its earliest years under the Constitution of 1701, Pennsylvania's assembly performed many of its duties through the use of committees, and by the 1740s the Speaker routinely divided up nearly all
House business among four standing and several ad hoc committees.
The most important standing committee, appointed regularly beginning in 1716, audited the assembly's accounts. Ad hoc committees appointed to revise the minutes of the House for publication led to a
second standing body in 1735. A committee appointed to correspond
with the legislature's agent in London became permanent by 1739 and
included the Speaker himself. Finally, in 1740 Speaker John Kinsey
appointed a grievances committee to read all petitions to the House
and make recommendations to the full chamber on an appropriate response to each. This body occasionally acted as a committee on elections as well. From 1740 to Independence, the audit, correspondence,
minutes, and grievances committees remained the legislature's only
standing bodies.[26]

As the Pennsylvania assembly became a more active legislative body,
its leaders assigned a greater share of its work to ad hoc committees,
groups of between two and over a dozen men whose work on a specific
problem might last a few days or extend over several months. Most of
these bodies drew up reports on pressing issues or bills for immediate
consideration by the House. Others drafted answers to governors' mes-
sages, welcoming addresses to visiting proprietors, and, on one occa-

sion, congratulations to a victorious British general; they investigated the merits of petitions from individuals involving bankruptcy, imprisonment for debt, or insanity; they formed delegations to confer with the governor and his council on matters of defense, or to negotiate treaties with Indian tribes; they examined new inventions and supervised construction projects; and they tallied up the chamber's incidental expenses at the close of each session.[27]

As Pennsylvania grew in population, increasing legislative activity demanded more and larger committees, and both the standing grievances committee and the number of ad hoc committee seats expanded dramatically. In the 1730s, Andrew Hamilton named an average of only thirteen committees each year, with just over four members per committee, for a total of fewer than two seats per member. In the 1740s, John Kinsey only slightly expanded the number of committees per year (13.5), the members per committee (5), and the total seats per member (2.3). In Isaac Norris's fifteen years (1750–1764) of imperial war and conflict with the proprietors, however, committees multiplied to over twenty-nine per session with over six seats on each; they provided more than five seats per legislator. Joseph Galloway's eight years (1766–1773) saw less conflict with the proprietor, and, in the legislature, fewer imperial problems, but rapid population expansion and vigorous economic development stimulated even greater assembly activity. Galloway named an average of thirty-three committees per year, again with over six members on each, thereby creating nearly six seats for every member of the House.

The Speakers of the Pennsylvania assembly distributed seats on both standing and ad hoc committees quite unevenly. In 1746, a quiet year, Speaker John Kinsey filled 18 standing seats with 12 men and 38 ad hoc seats with 18 men; 10 legislators, exactly one-third of the House, received no seats. In 1756, one of the legislature's most active years, Speaker Isaac Norris filled 22 standing and 328 ad hoc committee places. Seventeen legislators, just under one-half of the chamber, shared the standing committee posts, but 5 legislators each held over 20 ad hoc seats, 7 others received between 10 and 20, and 3 men received no seats at all. In any series of annual sessions, the assembly's leaders and back-benchers can be readily identified. In 11 years (1739–1749), Kinsey awarded Thomas Leech, Isaac Norris Jr., and Israel Pemberton, Sr., 88 standing and 208 ad hoc places; in the same period Thomas Chandler, Owen Evans, and Joseph Trotter received only 2 standing and 43 ad hoc seats. A generation later, Speaker Joseph Galloway assigned Joseph Fox, Michael Hillegas, and Isaac Pearson 45 standing and 232 ad hoc committee seats in eight years (1766–1773),

TABLE 3
Ad hoc committee assignments, 1729–1774

Year	Number of committees (Total seats)	Seats per committee/ per member	Year	Number of committees (Total seats)	Seats per committee/ per member
1729	16 (51)	3.2/1.8	1752	10 (85)	8.5/2.4
1730	16 (63)	3.9/2.1	1753	20 (145)	7.3/4.1
1731	12 (44)	3.7/1.5	1754	40 (287)	7.2/8.1
1732	4 (16)	4.0/0.6	1755	42 (280)	6.7/7.9
1733	12 (41)	3.4/1.4	1756	51 (328)	6.4/9.3
1734	22 (94)	4.3/3.2	1757	36 (231)	6.4/6.5
1735	19 (92)	4.8/3.2	1758	29 (185)	6.4/5.3
1736	4 (18)	4.5/0.6	1759	21 (116)	5.5/3.3
1737	8 (36)	4.5/1.2	1760	30 (198)	6.6/5.6
1738	13 (66)	5.1/2.3	1761	31 (163)	5.3/4.6
1739	18 (92)	5.1/3.2	1762	30 (177)	5.9/5.1
1740	8 (34)	4.2/1.1	1763	37 (254)	6.9/7.3
1741	16 (88)	5.5/3.0	1764	28 (130)	4.6/3.7
1742	16 (73)	4.6/2.5	1765	25 (139)	5.6/4.0
1743	12 (60)	5.0/2.1	1766	35 (195)	5.6/5.6
1744	10 (49)	4.9/1.7	1767	25 (160)	6.4/4.6
1745	24 (109)	4.5/3.7	1768	34 (175)	5.1/5.0
1746	7 (38)	5.4/1.3	1769	28 (178)	6.4/5.1
1747	12 (59)	4.9/2.0	1770	31 (197)	6.4/5.6
1748	11 (53)	4.8/1.8	1771	50 (343)	6.9/9.3
1749	14 (79)	5.6/2.5	1772	34 (201)	5.9/5.3
1750	17 (121)	7.1/3.7	1773	26 (213)	8.2/5.4
1751	17 (112)	6.6/3.2	1774	39 (271)	6.9/6.9

while giving Benjamin Chapman, John Minshall, and Henry Pawling only 9 standing and 48 ad hoc seats.[28]

The traditional portrait of Pennsylvania's legislators suggests that representing the City or County of Philadelphia, belonging to the Society of Friends, and serving for several years would increase a member's likelihood of obtaining a committee seat, but a close look at the delegates' committee activity shows that the matter was not so simple.[29] Of the legislators named above, assembly leaders Leech and Hillegas were not Quakers, and Fox had been disowned by Friends in 1756, while the backbenchers Chandler, Evans, Trotter, and Minshall were Friends. Among these twelve lawmakers, those who sat for the City and County of Philadelphia were more active than their country colleagues, but leader Pearson represented Chester County, while Evans, Pawling, and Trotter were Philadelphia County backbenchers. Seniority also played a role, but Norris, Hillegas, and Pearson were quite new to the House when they became leaders, and Chandler was an eleven-year back-bencher when Kinsey became speaker. Only a comprehensive survey of every legislator's committee service can begin to explain why the assembly distributed its leadership positions to certain men rather than to others.

The first factor determining the number of committee posts that a member held was the district that he represented. This was particularly true of standing committee seats because the audit and minutes commitees had to perform regular service between sittings of the legislature, and the correspondence committee was most effective when it could meet with the Speaker on short notice at any time during the year. For this and probably other reasons, the City of Philadelphia's two burgesses and the Philadelphia County delegation nearly always received a greatly disproportionate share of both standing and ad hoc seats. These ten delegates held a majority of standing committee places every year from 1732 to 1769, except for 1735 and 1765, and received one-third or more of the ad hoc seats from 1729 to 1772, although after 1749 they were less than one-third of the House. In contrast, from 1730 to 1773 the eight-man Bucks and Chester delegations never held the number of either standing or ad hoc seats to which their numbers would have entitled them. The four-man Lancaster County delegation did better, usually receiving roughly its fair share of committee seats. The one- and two-man delegations from the newer western and northern counties fared better still in securing ad hoc seats from the time of their formation, and after 1756 they received several seats on the standing grievances committee as well.

Viewed over time, the pattern of geographic distribution is one of considerable stability, with one important exception. The Philadelphia County delegation began losing strength on both standing and ad hoc committees gradually after 1760 and more precipitously after 1770. The activity of the City burgesses varied greatly but also declined on ad hoc committees in the 1770s. The Bucks and Chester delegations gained the places that their Philadelphia colleagues had lost. The assembly distributed its leadership positions more broadly and evenly in the 1760s and early 1770s than it had before the Quaker withdrawal of 1756; nevertheless, until Independence, members from the City and County of Philadelphia, along with a few from Chester and, to a lesser extent, Bucks County, secured most leadership positions in the chamber.

Seniority played a strikingly different role in the distribution of committee posts. An increasing use of seniority to determine the distribution of power in lawmaking bodies often accompanies increasing carry-over and veterancy in their membership. Several scholars have associated these developments with the professionalization of legis-

TABLE 4
Standing committee assignments, by district, 1729–1774

Year	Phila.	Bucks	Chester	Lancs.	West	Year	Phila.	Bucks	Chester	Lancs.	West
1729	3	1	1	—	—	1752	6	1	2	2	—
1730	4	2	2	1	—	1753	13	1	2	1	—
1731	3	1	1	4	—	1754	13	1	2	1	—
1732	3	1	1	4	—	1755	15	1	2	1	—
1733	3	1	1	—	—	1756	14	2	2	1	3
1734	6	2	1	—	—	1757	16	3	2	1	4
1735	4	2	2	1	—	1758	16	3	2	1	1
1736	8	1	1	—	—	1759	15	3	2	1	4
1737	8	1	1	—	—	1760	16	3	2	1	4
1738	6	1	1	1	—	1761	15	2	3	1	4
1739	12	1	1	—	—	1762	12	2	3	1	6
1740	13	3	3	2	—	1763	17	2	5	1	5
1741	12	2	2	2	—	1764	15	2	4	1	7
1742	12	2	2	2	—	1765	12	3	5	1	5
1743	13	3	2	—	—	1766	14	1	4	1	5
1744	13	2	2	2	—	1767	15	3	3	1	5
1745	12	2	2	2	—	1768	16	3	3	1	5
1746	12	2	2	2	—	1769	15	3	3	1	5
1747	10	2	2	2	—	1770	11	4	3	1	4
1748	11	2	2	2	—	1771	13	5	3	2	6
1749	12	2	2	1	1	1772	11	5	4	2	4
1750	12	2	2	2	—	1773	11	5	6	2	3
1751	12	2	2	2	—	1774	11	4	6	1	10

latures, not only in the present century, where the practice has reached its apotheosis in the United States Congress, but in colonial America as well.[30] Not all colonial legislatures were being professionalized in this way, however; Robert Zemsky found that seniority played little role in the mid-eighteenth-century Massachusetts assembly.[31]

In the Pennsylvania assembly, with one important exception, seniority was not a factor determining the assignment of ad hoc committee seats. Between 1729 and 1740, the correlation of seniority with committee activity exceeded .200 only twice, and only in 1729 (.378) does it appear to have been statistically significant. Between 1750 and 1774, as well, this correlation exceeded .200 just twice; the correlation was negative in twelve of these twenty-five years, and in 1750 it plummeted to −.256, a marginally significant negative relationship between these two factors. The highest of these correlations (.378) explains no more than 14 percent of the observed variance in committee assignments.

Again, however, as in such legislative features as carry-over, veterancy, and the proportion of Quakers in the chamber, the Kinsey

TABLE 5
Ad hoc committee assignments, by district, 1729–1774

Year	Phila.	Bucks	Chester	Lancs.	West	Year	Phila.	Bucks	Chester	Lancs.	West
1729	17	11	17	6	—	1752	32	9	8	7	29
1730	31	9	15	8	—	1753	59	17	17	16	36
1731	21	9	9	5	—	1754	105	33	31	34	84
1732	9	3	2	2	—	1755	101	35	34	34	76
1733	26	9	5	1	—	1756	170	26	32	22	78
1734	45	21	19	9	—	1757	109	25	29	21	47
1735	44	14	23	11	—	1758	71	22	25	22	45
1736	6	4	4	4	—	1759	55	12	12	13	24
1737	19	5	6	6	—	1760	82	21	25	18	52
1738	37	11	9	9	—	1761	85	12	17	14	35
1739	56	12	14	10	—	1762	92	17	21	14	33
1740	18	6	6	4	—	1763	108	25	31	23	67
1741	50	14	12	12	—	1764	65	11	17	12	25
1742	38	12	12	11	—	1765	77	11	21	10	20
1743	25	12	11	12	—	1766	94	29	29	16	27
1744	28	7	7	7	—	1767	61	24	28	11	36
1745	51	27	17	14	—	1768	94	24	27	14	16
1746	15	7	9	7	—	1769	61	26	37	16	38
1747	30	9	11	9	—	1770	76	31	36	18	36
1748	25	9	10	9	—	1771	131	52	49	29	82
1749	43	9	9	10	8	1772	70	28	33	20	50
1750	49	16	16	16	24	1773	56	37	35	21	64
1751	49	15	15	13	20	1774	86	36	57	20	72

years stand in sharp contrast to those around them. From 1741 to 1749, the correlation between the legislators' seniority and the number of their ad hoc committee assignments ranged from .363 to .598. Eight of these nine sessions produced correlations with a statistical significance of 95+ percent, two reached 99 percent, and 1749 exceeded 99.9 percent; the observed variance in committee assignments explained by seniority ranges from 13 to 36 percent. Speaker John Kinsey must have taken seniority into account when assigning committee seats. Like other quantitative measures of the character of the House, the high correlation between seniority and committee activity fell sharply in the 1750s; unlike each of those former measures, this correlation never returned to its earlier level. For most of the colonial era, Pennsylvania's Speakers ignored seniority when awarding ad hoc committee seats.[32]

The picture of the Pennsylvania assembly taking shape under our analysis of its readily quantifiable features is clear in its general outlines: the high levels of carry-over, veterancy, and seniority, and the

TABLE 6

Correlations between seniority and ad hoc committee assignments, 1729–1774

Year	Pearson's r (correlation)	Pearson's r^2 (variance explained)	Year	Pearson's r (correlation)	Pearson's r^2 (variance explained)
1729	.378	.143	1752	−.122	−.015
1730	.037	.001	1753	−.057	−.003
1731	.081	.007	1754	−.031	−.001
1732	.148	.022	1755	−.118	−.014
1733	.292	.085	1756	.069	.005
1734	.035	.001	1757	.013	.0002
1735	.092	.008	1758	.055	.003
1736	.020	.0004	1759	.123	.015
1737	−.061	−.004	1760	.247	.061
1738	.168	.028	1761	.031	.001
1739	.144	.021	1762	.022	.0005
1740	.141	.020	1763	−.126	−.016
1741	.466	.217	1764	−.216	−.047
1742	.456	.208	1765	−.204	−.042
1743	.488	.238	1766	.093	.009
1744	.450	.202	1767	.099	.010
1745	.465	.216	1768	−.024	−.001
1746	.526	.276	1769	.210	.044
1747	.411	.169	1770	−.056	−.003
1748	.363	.132	1771	.070	.005
1749	.598	.358	1772	−.077	−.006
1750	−.256	−.066	1773	.089	.008
1751	−.186	−.034	1774	.140	.020

continued prominence of certain religious and ethnic minorities—particularly Quakers, but also Anglicans; the English and the Welsh—delineate a legislature that was highly oligarchical from the 1730s to Independence. What is not yet clear is the configuration of social and cultural factors that shaped the leadership of this oligarchy. From the perspective of the members' legislative committee activity, the districts they represented, and the number of terms they served, one sees two simple behavioral patterns. First, the assembly's Speakers concentrated legislative power in the delegations representing the City and County of Philadelphia until the 1760s, and then began to apportion it more evenly throughout the chamber until Independence. Second, with the exception of the 1740s, seniority appears to have played no significant role in the distribution of legislative power. To gain a deeper understanding of the leadership of the Pennsylvania assembly, one must know something about the leaders as individuals.

Two factors that might be expected to play a major role in the selection of assembly leaders—differences in wealth and in ethnic background—probably did not. Nearly all assemblymen were drawn from the highest economic levels of Pennsylvania society: from the 1730s to the 1770s it was the most prosperous farmers, millers, and iron founders of the countryside; Philadelphia's major merchants; and a few prominent lawyers from across the colony who held nearly all assembly seats. This was as true for the newer western as for the older eastern counties.[33] Nor do leaders' ethnic backgrounds reveal much about their selection, because most assemblymen were of English or Welsh stock. Yet ethnicity probably was a factor in determining leadership; among the handful of Scotsmen and Germans in the House, only two were prominent leaders—Andrew Hamilton in the 1730s and Michael Hillegas in the 1770s—and no delegate of Scotch-Irish or Dutch background ever became an assembly leader.

Occupation was of greater importance. The few lawyers in the House were nearly always influential, despite the Quaker bias against attorneys. Indeed, the most powerful of all assemblymen were Quaker lawyers: David Lloyd in the generation before 1730; John Kinsey in the 1740s; and Joseph Galloway, who was born a Quaker and maintained close ties with the Society of Friends, in the 1760s and 1770s.[34] Merchants and other urban delegates who were widely read in law, history, and political science, or were otherwise "men of parts," also enjoyed great advantages. Isaac Norris Jr. and Benjamin Franklin come readily to mind. The occupational basis of legislative leadership, however, is not sufficient to explain the larger pattern. Several leaders of the assembly were not urban, and several were not lawyers; while a few lawyers and several urban delegates were not leaders. Although a broad, sometimes self-acquired, education seems to have been an important factor in determining leadership, it is difficult to distinguish from other factors that cannot be measured precisely—intelligence, general ability, and ambition. Despite being the most difficult to measure, these last ingredients of political leadership were certainly the most important of all. Before commenting upon the role of individual personality in the activities of the House, however, one must return to a factor earlier discussed—religious identification—to determine whether it also played a role in the selection of the assembly's leaders.

Quaker members, we have shown, numerically dominated the legislature until 1756, and were a large minority from 1761 to 1773. One may consider their corresponding representation on assembly committees from two perspectives. In counting the number of committee seats held by Quaker and non-Quaker members, one sees that in the years in which Quakers held a majority in the House (1729–1755), they dominated standing committees in every year except 1738, and ad hoc

TABLE 7
Assignment of committee seats to Quakers and non-Quakers, 1729–1774

	Standing		Ad Hoc			Standing		Ad Hoc	
Year	Q	NQ	Q	NQ	Year	Q	NQ	Q	NQ
1729	4	1	47	4	1752	15	6	48	37
1730	6	3	43	20	1753	13	5	103	42
1731	5	4	27	17	1754	13	4	177	110
1732	4	1	9	7	1755	13	6	140	140
1733	4	1	26	15	1756	5	17	50	278
1734	6	3	70	24	1757	5	21	52	179
1735	6	3	57	35	1758	6	17	44	141
1736	7	3	11	7	1759	4	21	16	100
1737	6	4	23	13	1760	4	22	48	150
1738	4	5	42	24	1761	6	19	65	98
1739	9	5	72	20	1762	7	17	58	119
1740	16	5	31	3	1763	11	19	69	185
1741	15	3	74	14	1764	10	19	30	100
1742	15	3	60	13	1765	10	16	64	75
1743	16	3	48	12	1766	10	15	105	90
1744	16	3	40	9	1767	12	15	71	89
1745	15	3	83	26	1768	13	15	85	90
1746	15	3	31	7	1769	12	15	78	100
1747	12	4	48	11	1770	11	12	102	.95
1748	12	5	41	12	1771	15	14	163	180
1749	13	5	55	24	1772	15	11	105	96
1750	16	2	92	29	1773	12	15	82	131
1751	12	5	74	38	1774	12	20	82	189

committees in every year except 1755. Between 1756 and 1765, when they were at first a small and then a steadily growing minority, they never dominated committee posts. Between 1766 and 1773, when they averaged just under half of the legislature, Quaker members held over half of the standing seats in 1771 and 1772. They also filled over half of the ad hoc seats in 1766, 1770, and 1772. After October 1774, they were heavily outnumbered on both standing and ad hoc committees.

The pattern of Quaker committee activity, it is clear, loosely corresponds with the Friends' strength in the whole House, but does not fit that pattern exactly. If one considers the average number of standing and ad hoc seats awarded per Quaker and non-Quaker member, a more complex picture emerges. Under Speaker Andrew Hamilton, Quaker and non-Quaker legislators filled seats with roughly equal regularity. Between 1729 and 1738, Quakers held more standing seats per member in six years, but filled either the same number, or fewer, in four. Quakers dominated ad hoc seats by the same margin, although in

TABLE 8

Committee assignments, per member, 1729–1774

Year	Standing Q	Standing NQ	Ad Hoc Q	Ad Hoc NQ	Year	Standing Q	Standing NQ	Ad Hoc Q	Ad Hoc NQ
1729	.21	.09	2.5	.4	1752	.58	.60	1.9	3.7
1730	.32	.27	2.3	1.9	1753	.48	.56	4.0	4.7
1731	.26	.36	1.4	1.6	1754	.48	.44	6.6	12.2
1732	.19	.11	.4	.9	1755	.48	.66	5.6	12.2
1733	.17	.14	1.2	2.1	1756	.45	.68	4.7	11.1
1734	.30	.30	3.5	2.7	1757	.42	.88	4.3	7.7
1735	.35	.23	3.4	2.9	1758	.43	.77	3.4	6.4
1736	.43	.21	.7	.5	1759	.31	.91	1.3	4.5
1737	.33	.33	1.3	1.2	1760	.29	1.00	3.5	6.8
1738	.18	.62	1.9	3.4	1761	.33	1.06	3.6	5.4
1739	.37	.83	3.1	3.3	1762	.39	.94	3.4	6.6
1740	.62	1.25	1.2	1.0	1763	.69	.95	4.6	9.3
1741	.58	.75	2.8	4.7	1764	.67	.90	2.1	4.9
1742	.58	.75	2.3	4.3	1765	.59	.84	3.8	4.2
1743	.62	.75	1.9	3.0	1766	.56	.83	5.8	5.3
1744	.64	.60	1.6	1.8	1767	.71	.79	4.2	4.9
1745	.58	.75	3.3	6.5	1768	.76	.79	5.0	5.0
1746	.60	.60	1.3	1.4	1769	.80	.71	5.2	5.0
1747	.48	.80	2.0	2.2	1770	.61	.67	5.7	5.5
1748	.48	1.00	1.7	2.4	1771	.88	.70	9.6	9.0
1749	.54	.62	2.4	3.0	1772	.83	.55	5.8	4.8
1750	.64	.22	3.8	3.2	1773	.71	.68	4.8	5.9
1751	.50	.45	3.1	3.8	1774	.80	.80	5.5	7.9

a different set of years. Under John Kinsey (1739–1749), although Quakers enjoyed a heavy majority in the House, non-Quakers garnered more standing seats per member in every year but two, and more ad hoc seats in every year except one. In the early Norris years (1750–1755), the activity of Quakers and non-Quakers was more even: Quakers held the edge on the standing committees in three of the six sessions. Non-Quakers continued to dominate ad hoc committees in five of the six sessions, however, and in the decade following the Quaker withdrawal of 1756, non-Quakers always held more seats per member on both standing and ad hoc committees.

Under Speaker Joseph Galloway (1766–1773), Quakers again became prominent members of the legislature. In 1766, and again in 1770, they filled just half of the seats in the assembly; in other years they were in a slight minority. Yet they received more standing committee posts per member than non-Quakers in four of those eight years: 1769, and 1771–1773. They filled more ad hoc seats in five years—1766, and 1769–1772—and received an even share of seats in 1768.

At no time under Galloway did Quaker members take a back seat in the assembly, but their domination from 1768 to 1773 is particularly striking.

Taken together with what is known about the assembly and its activities from other sources, these patterns of legislative activity have the power to illuminate the inner workings of the chamber's leadership. Before attempting this synthesis, however, one must probe a little deeper into the role of religion in the life of the assembly. The central question is this: what does it mean to say that the Pennsylvania assembly was firmly under the control of a Quaker oligarchy between 1729 and 1774? The answers to three questions may bring the character of Quaker dominance into sharper focus.

First, what was the character of the relationship between Quaker assemblymen and their non-Quaker colleagues? The evidence on this question is rather slight, but what is known does afford a further perspective on the political and social attitudes of Pennsylvania's Quaker lawmakers. Anglican legislators were always acceptable leaders to their Quaker colleagues, whether Quakers were in the majority or the minority. These Anglicans included Andrew Hamilton (1727–1738), John Kearsley (1722–1740), Thomas Leech (1730–1761), John Hughes (1755–1764), and Michael Hillegas (1765–1775). Presbyterian aspirants to leadership were another matter. In the 1730s, when there were few Presbyterian legislators, only one member of that denomination, William Allen (1730–1738; 1756–1775), achieved even moderate power in the House. But most Presbyterian lawmakers sat between 1750 and 1775, in a period when Quaker-Presbyterian relations were becoming increasingly strained, and most sat for the newer, increasingly underrepresented western counties. A few of these delegates, such as John Montgomery (1763–1775), accumulated considerable seniority, regularly sat on the standing grievances committee, and filled many ad hoc posts, yet they were never major leaders of the House. The only Presbyterian member ever to attempt to dominate the House was the aforementioned William Allen, who, after a brief retirement in 1739, sought to reenter the assembly, now in opposition to the Quaker lawmakers with whom he had earlier cooperated. He was defeated in 1740 and again in the riotous election of 1742, after which he was shut out of the house for fourteen years. Upon his return in 1756, he became an active but not especially powerful lawmaker.[35] The only legislator to gain great power in the assembly who was neither a Quaker nor an Anglican was Benjamin Franklin (1750–1763, 1773, 1775), whose religious identification defies precise location.

Second, did the relationship of Quaker legislators to the Society of

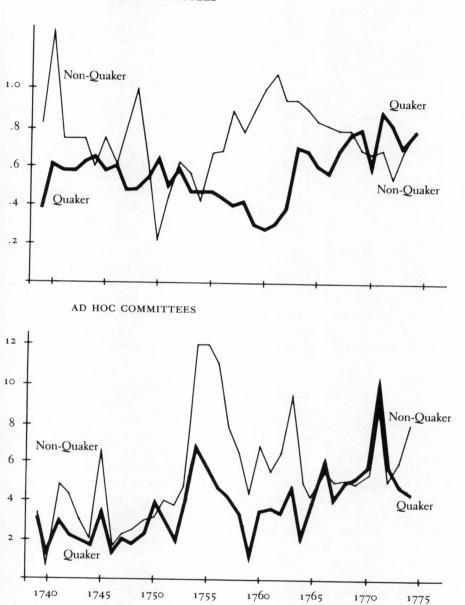

STANDING COMMITTEES

AD HOC COMMITTEES

FIG. 1 Standing and ad hoc committee assignments per member, by religious affiliation, 1739–1774

Friends change between the 1730s and the 1770s? Within the Society, as within the assembly, there were active, weighty members—delegates to Friends' quarterly and yearly meetings—and religious backbenchers. Recent scholarship has demonstrated that in Pennsylvania the Society's backbenchers included not only the lowly and obscure but, especially after 1756, Friends of high social standing who were now too worldly to lead their rapidly reforming sect.[36] A summary view of the religious careers of Quaker assemblymen strongly confirms this picture. In our three speakership periods between 1729 and 1756, between 25 and 35 percent of all Quaker lawmakers were frequently named delegates to the Philadelphia Yearly Meeting (of which Speaker John Kinsey was for twenty years the clerk), and between 66 and 74 percent were at least occasionally chosen to attend yearly or quarterly meetings by their monthly meeting. After the Quaker withdrawal of 1756, however, most Quaker legislators were viewed by their coreligionists as too worldly for religious duties. In each of our two last periods (1756–1765, and 1766–1773) only between 12 and 14 percent of Quaker assemblymen were frequently selected as delegates to the yearly meeting, and well under half of all Quaker legislators were ever sent to yearly or quarterly meetings.[37] Before 1756, disowned or lapsed Quaker lawmakers were almost unknown; by the 1760s there were at least four such legislators, including the perennial leaders Joseph Fox (1750–1771; disowned in 1756), and Joseph Galloway (1756–1763, 1765–1774).

Finally, did Quaker assemblymen act in concert in legislative business? No matter how many Friends sat in the House or on its various committees, they could not control the chamber unless they allied with one another against all potential or real non-Quaker opposition. The only testimony that speaks to this issue are a few widely scattered sets of roll-call votes.[38] To test Quaker voting power, four questions have been put to this evidence: (1) What proportion of voting members were Quakers? (2) How often did the majority of Quaker members side with the majority of the whole House? (3) How often did the Quaker members cohere more strongly than the non-Quaker members? (4) How often did the majority of Quaker legislators oppose the majority of non-Quaker members?

The results of these tests suggest that after the Quaker withdrawal of 1756, the remaining Friends did become a coherent block in the assembly. In the 1738 and 1753 sessions, when they were in a comfortable majority, Quakers neither voted in a higher proportion than their strength in the House nor cohered as strongly as non-Quaker members, despite the fact that on most of the war-financing votes of the

TABLE 9

The religious status of Quakers in the Pennsylvania assembly, 1729–1773

| Period | Most active[a] | Current Quakers | | Total | Disowned | Lapsed |
		Active[b] (Percentages)	Inactive[c]			
1729–38	18 (35)	16 (31)	17 (33)	51	0	0
1739–49	14 (25)	27 (49)	14 (25)	55	1[d]	0
1750–55	13 (31)	17 (40)	12 (29)	42	0	0
1756–65	5 (12)	11 (27)	25 (61)	41	2[e]	2[f]
1766–73	5 (14)	12 (32)	20 (54)	37	2	2

[a]Represented a quarterly meeting in five or more Philadelphia Yearly Meetings.
[b]Represented a monthly meeting in one or more quarterly meetings; or a quarterly meeting in between one and four yearly meetings.
[c]No record of attending a quarterly or yearly meeting.
[d]Oswald Peele.
[e]Joseph Fox (disowned 1756) and Charles Humphries (disowned 1751).
[f]John Dickinson (1762–1764, 1770, 1774–1775) and Joseph Galloway (1756–1763, 1765–1774).

1753 session the non-Quaker members sharply opposed them. In the 1760 and 1764 sessions, in a minority but with the Quaker Party still strong, Quakers abstained or were absent as much as their non-Quaker colleagues. Their coherence, however, was now consistently higher than that of non-Quakers, and they always voted with the majority, even though they were often opposed by most non-Quaker legislators. In the 1772 and 1773 sessions, when the Quaker Party had become weaker but enjoyed the energetic leadership of Joseph Galloway, Friends voted more frequently than non-Friends, their coherence remained high, and they continued to vote with the majority, whether they concurred with, or opposed, the majority of non-Friends. The 1774 session shows starkly the decline of Quaker power during the Revolutionary crisis: although Quaker lawmakers continued to vote as often as non-Quakers and sharply opposed them, their high coherence no longer exceeded that of their opponents. As a result, on most roll calls they failed to vote with the majority—for the first time in the history of the Pennsylvania assembly.

The behavioral patterns which demonstrate the interplay of the Pennsylvania lawmakers' religious identification and political activities all argue that a powerful Quaker oligarchy dominated the assembly between 1729 and 1755 *and* between 1766 and 1773. Four of these patterns also point to a radical transformation in the nature of that oligarchy, beginning in 1756 and fully realized a decade later. First, the Quaker lawmaker played a diminished leadership role within his own sect; while still a leader in the assembly he became, probably involuntarily, a backbencher—or a nonattender—at Friends' major business meetings. Second, perhaps as early as 1740, Quaker legislators appear to have developed a resistance to any leadership role in the assembly for Presbyterians. Third, most Quaker members usually opposed most non-Quakers on roll call votes after 1753, cohered more strongly than non-Quakers after 1760, voted more regularly than their opponents after 1765, and voted steadily with the majority until early 1775. Finally, in the late 1760s the Quaker legislators' chief spokesman, the lapsed Quaker Joseph Galloway, began awarding more committee posts to Quakers than to non-Quakers. This trend is so striking, coming after a quarter-century in which non-Quakers regularly received more than their share of committee posts, that one suspects the emergence of a deliberate new policy. To explain the significance of this development, and of several others that accompanied it, we will return to 1729 and proceed to examine the role of each quantitative feature of the assembly's behavior in the larger history of that body.

The narrative analysis that follows is not a history of the Pennsylvania assembly between 1729 and Independence,[39] but an interpretation of several behavioral characteristics of the assembly, organized around one central hypothesis: that committee activity and the structure of leadership in Pennsylvania's legislature were determined by Speakers who were chosen for their impressive leadership capacity, forceful personality, and ability to translate the will of the whole chamber into directed, and normally unanimous, action. This hypothesis assumes that patterns in the selection of assemblymen for committee posts were rarely accidental, but rather an expression—whether conscious or not—of the Speaker's, and his colleagues', convictions about the proper weight to give each member's district, seniority, and religion in considering him for a particular committee seat. While these questions were being addressed, openly or tacitly, the selections presumably also proceeded upon the basis of the energy and ability of forward members who sought office and of the Speaker's desire to involve more backward members in the full legislative process.

Andrew Hamilton (Speaker, 1729–1738), David Lloyd's protégé, was a remarkably successful politician by any standard. A free-thinking Anglican immigrant, he presided over a legislature that was increasingly native born, and two-thirds Quaker. A defender of assembly

TABLE 10
Roll calls and Quaker coherence in the Pennsylvania assembly, 1738–1774

Session	Roll calls	Quakers voting (%)	Roll calls with higher Quaker coherence (%)	Quakers voting with majority (%)	Quakers and non-Quakers polarized (%)
1738/39	1	21 (81)	0 (0)	1 (100)	0 (0)
1753/54	12	24–26 (75–76)	0 (0)	10 (83)	10 (83)
1760/61	1	8 (30)	1 (100)	1 (100)	1 (100)
1764/65	7	11–13 (36–42)	7 (100)	7 (100)	6 (86)
1765/66	2	15–16 (50–53)	2 (100)	2 (100)	0 (0)
1772/73	9	16–18 (55–61)	8 (89)	8 (89)	2 (22)
1773/74	5	15–16 (45–59)	4 (80)	5 (100)	3 (60)
1774/75	5	12–15 (39–41)	2 (40)	2 (40)	4 (80)

rights, he got on well with both the Penns and their governors; during his speakership, legislative-executive relations were unusually harmonious. At the same time, the Quaker oligarchy that would soon struggle with proprietor Thomas Penn for dominance in Pennsylvania was steadily building power. The carry-over, veterancy, and seniority of the legislators all rose dramatically. The proportion that was Quaker rose and fell, but by Hamilton's last year in office was 73 percent, and growing. In his first years as Speaker, Hamilton, a Bucks County delegate with strong Bucks County alliances, awarded more committee seats to Bucks and Chester delegates than had his predecessors, but he soon returned to the older pattern of favoring Philadelphia members. Perhaps because seniority was initially low, he paid little attention to it in awarding committee seats; perhaps because he was an Anglican in a Quaker world, he awarded Quakers just over their share of committee seats.[40]

If Hamilton moved easily to the New World, geographically and politically, his designated political heir, John Kinsey (1739–1749), a native New Jersey Quaker, based his position on an astonishing number of powerful local and provincial offices. He was clerk of the Philadelphia Yearly Meeting (1730–1750), attorney general of the province (1738–1741), acting trustee of the Pennsylvania Loan Office (1739–

TABLE 11

Assembly characteristics, 1729–1773

			Speakerships			
	Hamilton (1729–1738)	Kinsey (1739–1749)	1st Norris (1750–1755)	2nd Norris (1756–1760)	3rd Norris (1761–1765)	Galloway (1766–1773)
Carry-over (%)	57–87	56–100	72–94	58–89	72–83	69–94
Veterancy (%)	70–97	72–100	74–94	67–97	81–86	74–97
Seniority (years)	4.2–7.4	5.1–7.8	5.1–6.6	4.7–7.0	5.9–7.5	5.7–7.6
Quaker members (%)	53–77	75–90	71–75	31–39	42–50	42–50
Seniority/committee membership correlation	.02–.38	.14–.60	−.26––.03	.01–.25	−.22–.03	−.07–.21
Q/NQ committee activity by session[a]						
Standing:	6/4	1/10	3/3	0/5	0/5	4/4
Ad hoc:	6/4	1/10	1/5	0/5	0/5	5/3
Quaker assemblymen active in religious meetings (%)	66	74	71	39		46

[a] The figures under this heading show the number of annual sessions in each speakership in which members of each of the tw[o] major religious affiliations were more frequently appointed to the chamber's committees than those of the other religious affilia tion. Thus the figure of "6/4," appearing for both the standing and ad hoc committees under Andrew Hamilton, means that i[n] six of the ten years, Quakers received more committee assignments *per member* than did non-Quakers.

1750), and chief justice of the Supreme Court of Pennsylvania (1743– 1750). Kinsey developed the Quaker oligarchy to the peak of its power. His speakership saw the highest carry-over of Pennsylvania legislators in the eighteenth century and the highest proportion of Quakers in the assembly. As Speaker, he departed from several policies of his mentor, Andrew Hamilton. Under his leadership, the legislature immediately became embroiled with Governor George Thomas—and then with the Penns—over vital issues of war and finance, a struggle from which both he and the Quaker party emerged triumphant in 1743. There- after, Pennsylvania politics was quiet; John Kinsey and his assembly reigned unchallenged. Kinsey also exercised his authority within the House in different ways than Hamilton had. Alone among mid- eighteenth-century speakers, he consistently rewarded seniority with committee seats, a policy that fit his stable chamber well. He also fa- vored Philadelphia delegates, assigning his non-Quaker colleague Thomas Leech (1730–1761) an unusually large share of commit- tee seats.[41]

Kinsey's protégé, Isaac Norris Jr., a native Pennsylvania Quaker of high social standing, was even better placed for assembly leadership, although he never matched Kinsey's array of powerful offices. Nor, during his long tenure as Speaker (1750–1764), did circumstances permit him to maintain so purely Quaker an oligarchy. In the first period of his speakership (1750–1755), the Quaker party continued to enjoy a high continuity of carry-over and veterancy, and a heavy Quaker majority in the House; but, as the legislature entered disputes with Governor James Hamilton, son of Andrew, and with the proprietor, Thomas Penn, and as the great war with France loomed on the horizon, the volume of vital and often divisive legislative business rose sharply. Perhaps this growing contention, the retirement of several veteran legislators, and Norris's personal isolation from proprietary leaders with whom Kinsey had been on close terms made the new Speaker less secure than his predecessor. For whatever reason, Norris abandoned two of Kinsey's appointment policies: he quite ignored—or even slighted—seniority in awarding ad hoc committee seats, and he began favoring Quakers for standing committee posts.[42]

The resignation of six Quakers from the House in April 1756, and the refusal of several others elected the following October to serve, sharply altered Norris's political world. Quaker membership in the chamber fell from 75 percent to 31 percent in that year, and the remaining Friends enjoyed less influence within the Society than had their predecessors. Yet Norris survived the withdrawal, to remain Speaker of a heavily non-Quaker chamber for nearly a decade of intense legislative activity that centered upon imperial war and a struggle for power with proprietor Thomas Penn. With the carry-over, veterancy, and seniority of both Quaker and non-Quaker members fluctuating sharply, and with Quakers usually well below a majority, Norris worked closely with new, non-Quaker members, including several lawmakers from the recently created western counties, and continued to ignore seniority, as did his ally, Joseph Fox, who completed a term as Speaker for the ailing Norris and served another (1765) in his own right.

When Joseph Galloway (1766–1773) became Speaker, Quakers had not enjoyed a majority in the House for ten years, had not been strongly favored on standing committees for sixteen years, and had not been favored on ad hoc committees for two consecutive years since 1737. By 1766, however, several patterns of the old oligarchical dominance had reappeared in the House. Legislative carry-over, veterancy, and seniority reached levels not seen since the 1740s. From 1766 to 1773, Quakers averaged 46 percent of the chamber's membership; having gained just half of the seats in the assembly in 1766, they would fall no lower than three votes short of control until the convening of the First Continental Congress eight years later. Joseph Galloway soon moved Quakers into a commanding position in the chamber, awarding them more than their share of standing committee posts in four of his eight sessions (1769, 1771–1773), and of ad hoc committee seats in 1766 and from 1769 to 1772. He also awarded more standing committee posts to Chester County lawmakers and more ad hoc seats to Bucks County men than had Norris. When he moved his own electoral seat to Bucks in 1770, that county's delegation gained standing committee posts as well. Seniority, however, was no more important to Galloway than it had been to Hamilton or Norris.

Viewed quantitatively, Joseph Galloway's favoring of Quaker legislators and, to a lesser extent, his favoring Bucks and Chester assemblymen were the most radical departures from Pennsylvania's traditions of legislative leadership in the fifty years before the Revolution. Two recent studies of Pennsylvania politics, Alan Tully's analysis of the 1730s and 1740s, and James Hutson's reading of the 1750s and 1760s, afford a key to understanding this new policy.[43] Galloway was perhaps more conservative—and certainly more rigid, contentious, and personally disagreeable—than his predecessors Kinsey and Norris. He was also the first important Speaker in several decades who was not a protégé of his predecessor in the chair—Isaac Norris in fact quite disliked him. Yet Galloway fully shared Norris's primary political goals: the protection of Pennsylvania's Quakers, and of the province's Quakerized polity and society, from outside interference and burdensome exactions. Kinsey had been able to fend off the Penns with one hand in the 1740s. Norris needed both hands to keep Thomas Penn and the Crown within tolerable limits in the 1750s, and was finally worn down trying to restrain the pugnacious Benjamin Franklin and his young protégé, Joseph Galloway, in the early 1760s. Yet neither Kinsey nor Norris suffered any lack of popular support among Quakers, Anglicans, and many other Pennsylvanians for their assembly policies.

The Quaker Party's control first weakened under the political pressures generated by Franklin's rash plan to end Thomas Penn's power by royalizing the province, and by the frontier's explosive reaction to the assembly's perceived neglect of their defense against Indian raids that culminated in the angry march of the Paxton Boys in 1764. While the party quickly recovered from these shocks, and had by 1766 gained back every assembly seat lost in 1764 and 1765, Galloway found himself, upon assuming the Speaker's chair, in a radically different situation from that of his predecessors. Pennsylvania's popular rejection of the proposal to royalize the colony and its angry reaction to the Stamp Act the following year evidently taught Galloway a powerful lesson. In 1766, unlike the case in 1756, only Quaker legislators and Quaker voters could be trusted to defend the province against its real enemies: the proprietors, Presbyterian politicians, Scotch-Irish frontier bullies, and military enthusiasts of all descriptions. Galloway's distribution of committee seats to Bucks and Chester Quakers, particularly after 1768, suggests that he was thinking along these lines. It also reveals the oligarchy's precarious position in the late 1760s. Before 1764, the Quaker Party was without fear, confident of popular support for its positions in nearly every part of the province. By 1768, the year in which Philadelphians began agitating for the Townshend Act boycott, the party leadership was on the defensive, awarding committee seats to safe men and relying heavily upon its control of its two safe districts, Bucks and Chester counties.

By 1770 the oligarchy's position, still impregnable within the House, had unraveled a little more outside its doors. Galloway had long sat for Philadelphia County, which included hundreds of city voters who were becoming more alienated from his pro-British policies with each passing year of rising imperial tensions. In 1770 his constituents rejected him at the polls, forcing him to join his party's Bucks County ticket at the last minute to ensure that he could continue to lead his colleagues in the House. Ironically, his last four sessions as Speaker, running from October 1770 to September 1774, saw the most widely dispersed and even-handed distribution of committee seats among the assembly's county delegations in the colonial era. Galloway, no longer able to trust new Philadelphia delegates, quickly became dependent upon the support of Bucks, Chester, and even Lancaster legislators, mostly Quakers, to maintain control of the Assembly.

This strategy, however, had a built-in limitation. As Alan Tully has noted, only counties that had Quaker meetings and well-entrenched Quaker populations returned Quaker legislators.[44] Bucks, Chester, and Philadelphia counties were covered with meetings, and Berks, Lancaster, and York had a few. But Cumberland and Northampton counties, lacking Quaker populations, had fallen under the control of the proprietary Allen family and other anti–Quaker Party Presbyterian leaders in the late 1750s. Immediately after moving his seat to Bucks County, Galloway faced the necessity of creating new counties that would be even farther north or west of the Quaker Party's power base, and even more hostile to its antifrontier, anti-Presbyterian biases. To ignore these rapidly developing regions would entail the risk of losing them to Connecticut's Wyoming colony and to Virginia's designs on the Monongahela and upper Ohio valleys.[45] The assembly created three new counties in the north and west between 1771 and 1773, giving each a single assemblyman, and granted Berks County a second representative. Galloway set these four new delegates to work on several ad hoc committees but kept them out of standing committee posts and other positions of great influence. Thus the oligarchy held on to its power until that summer of 1774 when our amazed visitor to the assembly observed its members' country, Quaker ways.

Had the Quaker oligarchy been able to freeze demographic developments in Pennsylvania, and political developments in Massachusetts and London, as they were in 1770, it would have continued to enjoy an adequate power base from which to dominate the province. But, as Quaker lawmakers responded to political necessity by creating new counties and admitting new, non-Quaker members, they unavoidably began losing their grip on the House. The frontier of Quaker meetings had been reached, and crossed.[46] In October 1770 the House resolved, for the first time, that it would admit voters from time to time, upon a motion and vote, to witness debates.[47] Beginning in January 1773, the assembly's minutes recorded the first roll-call votes since 1765, and the first in the history of the House in which the lawmakers were nearly evenly divided on a range of domestic issues of the sort that Kinsey and Norris had always been able to resolve without a recorded division.[48] In October 1773, Friends fell to 43 percent of the chamber, and, even with Galloway still at the helm, they lost control of both standing and ad hoc committees. Had events in Boston Harbor and in Westminster not intervened between December 1773 and May 1774, the Quaker Party would perhaps have had another five to ten years of life. The Revolution merely brought on the oligarchy's final hours more swiftly.[49]

The Quaker oligarchy had a profound impact upon Pennsylvania in every decade of its existence; it was the essential ingredient in the colony's distinctive political life. The deep and abiding stability of the legislature both arose from, and in turn protected and reinforced, a stable, orderly local political world. The durable oligarchy produced by that world made the Pennsylvania assembly perhaps the most powerful of all colonial legislatures. Quaker leaders, in so ably protecting both their coreligionists and the society that they had created, insulated Pennsylvania from the factional squabbles and imperial interventions suffered by other colonies. They also insulated Pennsylvania from most political developments occurring outside its borders. The oligarchy had some success in defending its colony from the imperial exactions of the Seven Years' War; it was far more successful, for nearly a decade, in shutting out the Revolutionary turmoil that was deeply agitating several other colonies and nearly tearing apart the political fabric of Massachusetts. In the last analysis, the Quaker oligarchy ensured that when the Revolutionary crisis finally did break upon Pennsylvania's legislature, that body would be unready to face the task that lay before it. The oligarchy made Pennsylvania the most tranquil of all polities in British North America between 1766 and 1773; the Quaker Party's rapid demise after that year left the new state the most troubled of all American polities for over a decade after Independence.[50]

The power and durability of the Quaker oligarchy, with its rich, often paradoxical political and social legacy, should suggest to historians the need for looking at Pennsylvania in a new way. It will no longer do to repeat the familiar tales about a peaceful, quasi-democratic Quaker domination that ended voluntarily in 1756, to be followed by a more secular political alliance that presided over a more worldly, contentious two decades until the Revolution. The character of the assembly simply does not support this myth. Pennsylvania was neither a "Holy Experiment" nor a Quaker province after 1756 in the same way that it had been before that year. Politically, however, it was still Quaker in a profound sense, and it would remain so during the following two decades until, in the 1770s, two historical processes over which it had no control, one at home and one abroad, terminated Pennsylvania's Quaker century.

A. ROGER EKIRCH

"Hungry as Hawks": The Social Bases of Political Leadership in Colonial North Carolina, 1729–1776

A CENTRAL DEVELOPMENT in the public life of eighteenth-century America was the emergence of fully articulated political elites. Previously distinct interest groups, such as merchants and planters, Anglicans and Dissenters, and rival cliques of land speculators, became increasingly interlocked by midcentury. Nearly every colony produced a governing elite, distinguished not only by its cohesion and shared interests but by its wealth, education, ancestry, and native origins. The authority of political leaders was consequently well established and widely acknowledged. Further, these elites, unlike prior generations of political leaders, did not have to view politics in essentially opportunistic terms. No longer members of competing factions struggling to establish themselves at the center of provincial life, they brought a new sense of responsibility to their official duties, assuring a greater degree of stability in public affairs than in earlier decades.[1]

This paper seeks to study the political elite of colonial North Carolina. My focus is on the leaders of the lower house of assembly who served while North Carolina was a Crown province. From 1729 to 1776 approximately 550 men sat in the lower house, of that number only 73 members occupying major positions of responsibility. Beyond the post of Speaker, legislative power was usually wielded by a select few who chaired, or sat on, a handful of key committees. Other assemblymen, of course, received committee posts, but these routine assignments were neither as numerous nor as powerful as those held by the seventy-three key figures. Among the most important committees were such standing bodies as Public Accounts, Privileges and Elections, and Propositions and Grievances. After the Speaker appointed these and other committees at the beginning of each new session, they conducted most of the business of the lower house.[2]

Few leaders exercised authority for extended periods. The typical individual served a total of only seven years in the assembly, fewer than four of those years spent in a position of leadership. Fourteen men remained leaders for more than five years, only six for more than ten. Still, collectively, these men dominated the lower house. As Jack P. Greene has described in the case of Virginia's assembly leaders,[3] they formulated legislation, drafted petitions and addresses, and helped to adjudicate differences of opinion within the house. Consequently, they were among the most powerful men in the colony, for the lower house during this period was quickly expanding its influence in the political arena. An analysis of the seventy-three and their principal characteristics should illuminate not only the social bases of power but also the very character of politics in eighteenth-century North Carolina.[4]

Working the land was by far the most common occupation among leaders in this still very rural colony. Exact figures are difficult to obtain, but perhaps as many as two-thirds depended directly on agriculture and forest-related industries for their livelihood. Tobacco cultivation was especially common among representatives from the northeast, while in the Cape Fear region to the south several individuals grew either rice or indigo. In fact, three of the colony's seven principal indigo producers as of 1749—Maurice Moore, John Swann, and John Ashe—were one-time leaders.[5] Many leaders also produced naval stores and lumber products. Otherwise, a disproportionately large number were lawyers, no doubt because their skills were highly valued in such committee matters as drafting bills and preparing formal addresses. As late as the mid-1760s, there were only about forty-five lawyers in the entire colony,[6] yet as many as thirteen leaders during the mid-eighteenth century considered law their primary profession. Then, too, attorneys like Blake Baker, Alexander Elmsley, and William Hooper were joined by others, such as John Hodgson and William Downing, who supplemented their planting interests with a legal practice. Due to such a preponderance of attorneys, it seems likely that legal expertise, as much as any other single factor, insured a leadership role. Lower-house leadership also included one doctor—

Patrick Maule—and approximately ten merchants. Probably the most successful trader was Thomas McKnight, an overseas merchant who by the eve of the Revolution amassed commercial holdings worth roughly £11,000 sterling. One man, Francis Corbin, was a professional land agent for Earl Granville's proprietary district in the northern half of the province; a second, Richard Caswell, served in a lesser capacity, as a proprietary surveyor.

As planters, most of the seventy-three possessed ample tracts of land, especially since land was still reasonably plentiful in North Carolina. With rapid population growth, conditions did not remain what they were when Governor George Burrington wrote in 1733, "Land is not wanting for men . . . but men for land," yet even by the 1780s, about 70 percent of all adult white males still possessed land, with about 5 percent having over one thousand acres.[7] Based on quitrent lists, land grants, wills, and tax lists, rough estimates are possible for the landholdings of forty-nine leaders. Of these, thirty-three, or 67.4 percent, possessed over one thousand acres, with as many as eleven, or 22.5 percent, owning in excess of three thousand. Few men, on the other hand, had truly imposing holdings; only six, or 12.3 percent, owned over ten thousand acres, Robert Jones, Jr., Edward Moseley, and Thomas Pollock being the leading owners. Moreover, the value of all these estates, however large, should not be exaggerated. Not only was land generally plentiful in North Carolina, and its value correspondingly low, but the colony's lack of good harbor facilities lessened the worth of large holdings. The high costs associated with overland transportation and hazardous shipping channels significantly undermined the value of Carolina property. Further, much of these larger tracts probably consisted of waste land or wilderness acreage, unworked because of a shortage of labor. Unlike other Southern colonies, North Carolina had a relatively small number of slaves. As late as the 1760s, Blacks only constituted around 26 percent of the colony's total population. In most of the coastal plain counties, where the economy was more developed than in other regions, over 60 percent of all households were without taxable slaves (slaves twelve years and older), and less than 1 percent of all households had more than twenty.[8]

Like many Carolinians, leaders may have owned ample amounts of land, but very few possessed large numbers of slaves. With the aid of tax lists, wills, inventories, and headrights, individual holdings can be determined for fifty-one men. Of these, eleven, or over one-fifth, owned ten or fewer slaves; less than half, only twenty-four, had over twenty slaves; while probably only three leaders—Maurice Moore, Abner Nash, and Francis Corbin—owned over one hundred. Both in

TABLE 1
Land ownership among assembly leaders 1729–1776
(N = 49)

Acres	Assembly leaders (% in parentheses)	Acres	Assembly leaders (% in parentheses)
0–500	8 (16.3)	3,001–4,000	1 (2.0)
501–1,000	8 (16.3)	4,001–5,000	1 (2.0)
1,001–2,000	16 (32.7)	5,001–10,000	3 (6.1)
2,001–3,000	6 (12.3)	10,000+	6 (12.3)

land and slaves, North Carolina's leadership was a pale replica of neighboring Virginia's. Nearly three-fourths of Virginia assembly leaders in the mid-1770s owned over ten thousand acres, and well over a third possessed more than fifty slaves.[9]

Nearly every member of the seventy-three had some practical preparation for his stint as leader. Most had previously held positions in local government—as justices of the peace, sheriffs, building commissioners, and court clerks. At least fifteen men had also served on the provincial level, in such capacities as general court justice, attorney general, councillor, vice-admiralty judge, and surveyor-general. An exceptional case was Joseph Anderson of Chowan County. By the time he became a leader in 1743, Anderson had served as provincial secretary, vice-admiralty judge, and attorney general. Prior experience in the assembly itself was more restricted among leaders. Only thirty-nine, slightly more than half, had spent an apprenticeship period of at least one year before ascending to leadership status.

Far less impressive than their practical experience was the meager level of education attained by most leaders. Very few (only six) had ever attended a university. One possible reason is that there were none in the province until after the Revolution, but it's more probable that most leaders did not have parents who could afford formal instruction for their children. Of the exceptions, John Ashe and William Hooper had both attended Harvard, though Ashe left after his first year; Edmund Fanning was a graduate of Yale; and Princeton had two alumni among the seventy-three, Alexander Martin and Joseph Hewes. Despite its proximity, not a single leader had attended William and Mary. Some men did receive educational instruction through studying law with local attorneys. Samuel Johnston, Jr., for example, studied for several years at the side of the Edenton attorney, Thomas Barker, himself an assembly leader. Interestingly, only one individual, Richard Everard, Jr., had attended the Inns of Court, normally a popular place

TABLE 2
Slave ownership among assembly leaders 1729–1776
(N = 51)

Slaves	Assembly leaders (% in parentheses)	Slaves	Assembly leaders (% in parentheses)
0–10	11 (21.6)	41–50	5 (9.8)
11–20	16 (31.4)	51–75	3 (5.9)
21–30	5 (9.8)	76–100	1 (2.0)
31–40	7 (13.7)	100+	3 (5.9)

of study for young southern gentlemen. Furthermore, though Edward Moseley had supposedly been "bred in Christ's Hospital,"[10] no leaders had ever attended Oxford or Cambridge.

In contrast to political elites of other colonies, North Carolina's assembly leaders were predominantly newcomers to their province. A decided minority—notably members of the Swann, Harvey, and Pollock families—could root their ancestral trees in seventeenth-century Carolina. Others, like John Ashe, Blake Baker, Cornelius Harnett, and Robert Howe, were second-generation settlers whose parents had immigrated between 1710 and 1730. Most leaders, however, were themselves newcomers, without a longstanding record of family precedence; this was true of perhaps as many as thirty-seven, or 72.6 percent, of the fifty-one leaders whose native origins can be determined with any accuracy. The men who occupied the highest assembly posts constituted an extraordinarily youthful elite, drawn from all parts of the Atlantic world. The greatest number, around ten, came from England, although as many as eight were from neighboring Virginia. Others immigrated from South Carolina, Rhode Island, New Jersey, Massachusetts, Maryland, Pennsylvania, Ireland, Scotland, and the West Indies.

This preponderance of first-generation leaders resulted partly from the colony's rapid growth in population and settled territory during the mid-eighteenth century.[11] With the extension of assembly representation to newly settled localities, the number of aspiring newcomers rose in the political arena. In the rapidly growing Cape Fear region, leaders like John Starkey, Hugh Waddell, Lewis DeRossett, William Faris, and William Hooper were all first-generation immigrants, as was nearly every leader from the backcountry once it became populated in the 1750s and 1760s.

But political fluidity was not simply the product of expanding settlement patterns, for a majority of leaders from older regions were also newcomers. Immigrants to the Pamlico Sound area who ultimately penetrated the assembly's inner circle included Richard Caswell, Jr., from Maryland and Alexander Elmsley from England. Albemarle leaders in the northeast were no more exceptional in this regard. In fact, as late as the 1760s and 1770s, most individuals from the old Albemarle counties were still newcomers, including Thomas Barker, John Campbell, Francis Corbin, Joseph Hewes, Robert Jones, Jr., Thomas McKnight, and Joseph Montfort.

Several circumstances contributed to such quickly achieved prominence. Together with the heady share of ambition that probably propelled most of these men to North Carolina in the first place, some leaders initially benefited from practical advantages which could be parlayed into political power. Formal education or legal training doubtless helped some to cut an imposing figure, in addition to providing the knowledge and expertise that would later prove useful in assembly proceedings. Of the six leaders with a university education, five were first-generation immigrants who had attended school before settling in North Carolina. At least a few individuals came from families of some wealth and distinction. Robert Jones, Jr., and Abner Nash, for instance, were both sons of Virginia assemblymen. Still other leaders had arrived as merchants who, besides whatever wealth they may have possessed, had access to credit and capital through preexisting commercial contracts. Upon immigrating to North Carolina in 1742, John Campbell of Ireland, a self-made man, could count on trading ties to his brother, a Liverpool merchant. William Faris and Joseph Hewes were both merchants on arrival, their commercial connections and skills helping to assure them future success. Some men also benefited from political acquaintances, either in North Carolina or in Britain. Hugh Waddell's Irish father left him propertyless but did provide him with a good contact in Governor Arthur Dobbs. At the same time, Francis Corbin and Richard Caswell, Jr., probably profited from the proprietary positions they held under Earl Granville.

The ascendancy of first-generation immigrants into the upper echelons of the assembly was also abetted by the truncated structure of provincial society. No indigenous elite of sufficient strength to block the entrance of newcomers existed, so the pathways to political preferment were extraordinarily open. Had native members of North Carolina's upper class been sufficiently distinguished by their wealth and education, standards of admission would have been considerably more difficult.

Though not natives of North Carolina, a large majority, perhaps two-thirds, of the seventy-three were nevertheless of English descent. Most others were from families that had originated elsewhere in the British Isles. At least eight leaders were of Irish descent, four of Scottish, and one—Abner Nash—of Welsh. The only known representative from continental Europe was Lewis DeRossett, the son of a French Huguenot. More difficult to determine, given the colony's religious diversity, was the religious orientation of most leaders. In addition to its weak Anglican establishment, North Carolina contained a wide range of sects and denominations. Both the absence of church records and the not uncommon presence of dissenters on ostensibly Anglican vestries seriously complicate attempts to identify religious affiliation. Probably most leaders were nominal Anglicans, though the lack of concrete evidence may reflect the general weakness of religious activity in the colony.

If these men are typical, North Carolina's political leaders were less bound by elaborate kinship ties than most colonial elites. Only small clusters of family clans existed, notably in the Cape Fear area, where leaders like Samuel and John Swann, Robert Howe, and John Ashe were all linked by their common ties to the Moore family. With the near constant influx of new men and the colony's comparatively laggard development, the complex web of interrelated families so common to other upper classes did not have the chance to develop. Of Virginia's eighty-eight assembly leaders from 1729 to 1776, as many as ninety-eight, or 53.3 percent, had the same surname as at least one other leader.[12] In contrast, only thirteen, or 17.8 percent, of leaders in North Carolina shared the same surname with another leader.

Previous studies of colonial North Carolina have stressed the importance of sectional animosities during the eighteenth century, yet regionalism was only partly reflected in leadership patterns. In the 1730s a majority of leaders naturally came from the Albemarle counties in the northeast, where most settlers still resided. The so-called Great Schism, of course, radically redressed this imbalance, as Albemarle representatives unanimously refused to attend Assembly sessions from 1746 to 1754. In later years, up to and through the period of the Regulator disturbances, all regions were adequately represented. Not only did the Pamlico Sound, Cape Fear, and Albemarle regions have at least several leaders apiece in the assembly, but so too did the rapidly growing Piedmont, with representatives like William Eaton and Robert Harris of Granville County and John Frohock of nearby Rowan. Significantly, only one of the eleven leaders who represented Piedmont counties—Joel Lane, from Wake—came from an eastern family; the rest were newcomers to North Carolina. In contrast to Virginia's experience, western leadership did not represent an extension of tidewater authority but the inability of any one section in the province to monopolize political power.

In personal conduct and style of life, these men hardly possessed meek temperaments. According to assembly journals and scattered court records, they preferred force at times to ordinary legal processes. Maurice Moore, who in 1764 broke the arm of a British naval officer, was only one of several leaders capable of violent behavior. John Campbell's hot temper earned him the nickname, the "Bear," while James Castellaw once was described as "commonly Mad or Drunk." [13] On another occasion, Castellaw assaulted the colony's receiver general, William Little. Edward Moseley struck Chief Justice William Smith in 1735, after Smith had accused Moseley of corrupt land dealings. Speaker John Hodgson, several years later, allegedly attacked John Montgomery, the attorney general and himself a onetime leader. Another fracas between two assembly heavyweights occurred when Samuel Benton stabbed Thomas Person with a bayonet, because of a legal dispute and Person's refusal to leave Benton's chambers. Still other leaders who at one time or another displayed few inhibitions about resorting to violence included Edmond Porter, who attacked both Councillor John Lovick and Sir Richard Everard, the last proprietary governor of North Carolina; and Samuel Swann, who in 1731 allegedly committed an assault in Edenton. Swann's son, Samuel Jr., who was an assembly leader in his own right, was charged thirty years later with assaulting a Pasquotank County sheriff. Thomas Polk, in 1764, even led a band of rioters in Mecklenburg County against local land surveyors.

The public rectitude of many leaders was no more savory than their turbulent dispositions. Quite a few were involved in the various instances of government malfeasance that surfaced from time to time in the colony. Edward Moseley and Samuel Swann, for instance, participated in the mammoth "blank patent" frauds of the late 1720s, when over four hundred thousand acres of prime land fell into the hands of a few government officials. Edmond Porter, in his capacity as vice-admiralty judge, not only ran a corrupt court but also was charged with beating a prisoner and with attempting to enslave a free Black named Peter Vantrump. During the 1740s Thomas Hunter embezzled public funds that were originally earmarked for a prison and warehouse in Pasquotank County. In later years several leaders were accused of corruption by Governor Arthur Dobbs, notably the assembly's two treasurers, John Starkey and Thomas Barker, charged with embezzling public taxes. Dobbs's allegations were borne out by a later investigation, and the Regulators, beginning in the late 1760s, pointed to similar abuses on both the provincial and the local levels. Among their chief nemeses were a handful of leading representatives: Samuel

Benton, John Frohock, John Dunn, and Edmund Fanning, the last-named allegedly the kingpin of backcountry corruption. Popular discontent arose slightly earlier from the extortionate dealings of Francis Corbin. As resident agent for the Granville proprietary, Corbin and his deputies—among them Richard Caswell, Jr., himself a leader—extorted excessive fees from scores of expectant settlers. In 1764 Robert Jones, Jr., was accused of obstruction of justice and attempted rape. Still two other leaders, Andrew Knox and William Williams, were hauled into superior court on charges of simple theft.

One of the most distinctive features of eighteenth-century North Carolina was the near endemic strife afflicting its public realm. Up until the late colonial period, the commonweal periodically fell victim to the self-interested priorities of competing factions. Whereas harmony and responsibility normally characterized the political world of provincial America, Carolina politics revolved around conflicting private, group, and regional interests, resulting at times in social discord and the complete breakdown of civil institutions. North Carolinians, according to the Cape Fear planter, James Murray, were ever "broiling and squabbling over public affairs." Land conflicts in the 1730s, the north-south clash of the succeeding decade, the problems of the Granville District, and attempts by Governor Dobbs to root out corruption in the assembly in the late 1750s and early 1760s, as well as the Regulator riots in later years, all highlighted the degree to which North Carolina deviated from many of its sister colonies. "In this Country . . . ," complained Josiah Martin, "there prevails a proneness to contention without example."[14]

North Carolina's political turbulence arose from several sources. Some were basically external in nature, such as the inept policies pursued by the colony's royal governors. None of these men, from George Burrington to Josiah Martin, had the necessary expertise to execute London's instructions, which in themselves could pose formidable difficulties. North Carolina's rapid territorial and demographic growth also created severe strains. The opening of new areas of settlement and the influx of new groups with high expectations, as in the Cape Fear and the backcountry, had politically destabilizing consequences, especially because the colony did not enjoy a commensurable rate of economic growth.

Of related importance was the role North Carolina's elite played in provincial affairs. Though lesser men exercised an occasional influence in the public arena, the colony's upper class generally determined the course of politics. During the mid-1700s, members of this ruling group aggressively contested with each other over land as well as local and regional supremacy. Besides repulsing efforts by several governors to rid the government of corruption, they remained indifferent to the impassioned protests of the Regulators that governing authorities be more attentive to the needs of their constituents.

If the assembly's hierarchy offers an accurate profile of provincial leadership, of which there seem few grounds for doubt, North Carolina's elite was in a comparatively early stage of development. In contrast to political leaders in most other colonies, this was still very much an emergent elite—less wealthy, less educated, and predominantly non-native. Nearly every province, from Massachusetts to South Carolina, could, by midcentury, boast a ruling group distinguished by its economic power, internal cohesion, and relative political sophistication. North Carolina's experience more accurately resembled the early years of its sister colonies, when the economic ambitions of the first several generations frequently kept public life in turmoil. In Carolina, leaders continued to view politics not as a public trust but as an opportunity to advance personal and group interests. Still striving to achieve economic eminence, most leading men could simply not afford to entertain an altruistic ethic of public service. William Byrd II thought "all the officers there . . . as hungry as hawks" who "make a prey of every poor creature that falls into their pounces."[15] As newcomers to the colony, many leaders also lacked the strong sense of community identity characteristic of a more mature elite. Nor did their first-generation status permit the emergence of a wide network of family relations that could have muted political factionalism. Then, too, political leaders could not always command the deference of others. Given the lackluster social profile of these men, individuals outside of government were all the more likely to contest their claim to authority.

Not until after the American Revolution did North Carolina produce an elite comparable to those of its sister provinces in wealth, cohesion, and nativity. Ironically, with increasing popular participation in the public arena, many sections of the United States by that time were beginning to experience a decline in traditional patterns of deferential politics. But whatever direction later political leaders were able to exert, their predecessors had registered a significant impact. The character of Carolina's colonial elite meant that public affairs would be anything but tranquil during the mid-eighteenth century. Political strife still plagued North Carolina, partly because the social bases of political leadership, which normally insured a stable public world in colonial America, remained in a nascent stage of development.

RICHARD WATERHOUSE

Merchants, Planters, and Lawyers: Political Leadership in South Carolina, 1721–1775

<hr />

INSPIRED BY Sir Lewis Namier, historians of British political culture in the eighteenth century have examined closely the institutions of government, especially the membership of the House of Commons, in order to lay bare the complex pattern of political values and ideas in that era.[1] They have agreed that in part it was the success of the constitutional settlement of 1689 in securing long-term political harmony that caused the main political groups to accept the Whig principles upon which that settlement was based.[2] These historians have succeeded in blending political and social history, their systematic prosopographical studies of the membership of the eighteenth-century House of Commons always seeking to demonstrate how the composition of that body was determined by the nature of political values and structures.

Historians of the political culture of eighteenth-century South Carolina have adopted a more piecemeal approach. On the one hand, Gene Sirmans and Jack Greene have comprehensively described the main political events in the colony before 1763 and Robert Weir has carefully reconstructed the political value structure which shaped the local elite's response to such events.[3] On the other hand, Walter Edgar and his assistants have compiled detailed information on the membership of South Carolina's colonial assembly.[4] What I have sought to do in this study is to discuss the colony's evolving political culture during the period of royal government within the context of the interrelationship between legal institutions, political values, and assembly membership.

In eighteenth-century England, electorates consisted both of boroughs (of which there were six types) and counties, a standard franchise requirement applying to elections for the latter, franchise conditions for the former varying widely. This complex and irregular electoral system, patterned on traditions reaching back into the Middle Ages, was not easily transferred to a newly founded colony. At first, the Carolinians partially adopted this English model, designating counties as electorates. But because the compact nature of settlement made county-size electorates too large, in 1716 the assembly adopted another familiar example, that of Barbados, and passed legislation establishing the parishes as electorates.[5] Although the proprietors disallowed both this act and a similar one passed in 1719, the colonists simply ignored the proprietors' instructions and continued to hold elections using the new boundaries. The 1721 Elections Act, passed after the overthrow of the proprietors and accepted by the Crown, reaffirmed these boundaries, and the basic regulations governing the operation of the colony's electoral system remained virtually unchanged from 1721 until the end of the colonial period.[6] The assembly occasionally tinkered with the laws governing voting and office-holding qualifications, the conduct of elections, and the length of its own term, but in each case the proposed changes were disallowed by the English authorities.

By the 1721 electoral act, any adult white male owning at least fifty acres of land or paying a minimum of twenty shillings current money per annum in provincial taxes was eligible to vote in assembly elections.[7] Because the Crown continued to grant a fifty-acre headright to all applicants, and the provincial government to levy a twenty-shilling provincial tax on all adult white males, these voting requirements were hardly restrictive—in fact, all white men were qualified to vote.[8] Though in 1745, and again in 1759, the assembly passed acts raising these qualifications, both acts were disallowed by the Crown.[9] The 1721 act also required that those elected to the assembly own either a minimum of five hundred acres and ten slaves; or houses, buildings, and town lots to the value of one thousand pounds currency. Three times during the colonial period, attempts were made to raise these qualifications, but on each occasion they were rejected either by the assembly itself or by the Crown.[10] However, the assembly's endeavors to raise voting and office-holding qualifications reflected the growing prosperity of the colony's inhabitants. In effect, they were attempts to maintain, rather than to raise, economic standards for office holding.

The 1745 act, which raised both voting and assembly membership qualifications, also provided for annual elections, but the frequency of such elections quickly proved inconvenient, and the assembly passed an amending statute in 1748 providing for elections every two years. When the Crown disallowed these acts, the triennial provisions in the 1721 law were automatically restored.[11]

Under the provisions of the act of 1721, eleven parishes elected a total of thirty-six representatives to the assembly: five from St. Philip's Charles Town and thirty-one from the county parishes. As the colony's population increased and moved into more remote coastal and hinterland areas, new parishes were carved from old, or, in the case of the further hinterland, new parishes were located where none had existed before. By 1775, there were twenty-one parishes electing a total of forty-eight representatives: six from the two Charles Town parishes (St. Philip's and St. Michael's) and forty-two from the country. Yet in the very last years of the colonial period, the assembly failed in its attempts to extend the electoral system to the newly settled areas. After 1767 the Privy Council adopted a policy of disallowing all acts that increased the membership size of colonial legislatures; and in compliance with that policy, disallowed the 1767 South Carolina acts providing for the establishment of St. Luke's and All Saints'.[12] The assembly only secured the passage of the 1768 acts establishing St. Mathew's and St. David's by taking one representative each from two of the low country parishes and apportioning them to the new hinterland ones.[13]

Before 1716, when members of the assembly represented counties, elections for all counties were held in Charles Town and supervised by the sheriff; but when parish boundaries became electoral boundaries, parish officials—the churchwardens—became responsible for the conduct of elections. It was their responsibility to give notice of elections, and, on election day, to record the names of the voters and to count the votes after the poll had closed. They also attended the first two sitting-days of each new assembly, to inform the house of the names of those elected and of any irregularities in the conduct of the poll.[14]

Neither at the local nor the central level were South Carolina's institutions of government exact replicas of England's.[15] Not only did the colonists select only those institutions and offices which suited their needs, but they often utilized them for purposes different from those they served in England. Because property qualifications required for assemblymen and for voters were so modest, the South Carolinian system of government allowed for a wider degree of participation than existed in England. Originally this was only accidentally the case, restrictive English franchise laws having become permissive in a colony where freehold property was almost universal among whites. But what began as unintentional became essential, as Carolina's political leaders, seeking to ensure political harmony, maintained an inclusive political structure.

Merchants, planters, lawyers, and physicians constituted the elite of mid-eighteenth-century South Carolina. It was these men who sought to pursue and uphold in the New World the political, cultural, and social values of their English inheritance. This elite based its cultural and social habits on an exaggerated imitation of the standards proclaimed by the contemporary English gentry.[16] However, as with the contemporary Virginia gentry, its members drew their political assumptions from what J. G. A. Pocock has called "the country ideology"—a complex of ideas, rooted in seventeenth-century English puritanism, which received only limited acceptance in eighteenth-century England but was widely disseminated in the American colonies.[17]

Because they were strongly influenced by this ideology, the Carolinians distrusted human nature and deeply admired the British Constitution, whose system of checks and balances prevented tyranny and protected "liberty and property."[18] They maintained that they possessed all the traditional rights of Englishmen, rights which no royal instructions could take away, and that the local assembly was an exact constitutional replica of the English House of Commons. This claim was clearly articulated by the Speaker of the House, John Lloyd, in 1733 and would be repeated by succeeding generations.[19] "This Colony was settled by English subjects—by a People from England herself," declared William Henry Drayton in 1774, "a people who brought over with them . . . the invaluable rights of Englishmen."[20]

The Carolinians assigned a crucial constitutional role to the assembly, for it served as a counterbalance against tyranny and corruption. It followed that the assembly should consist of the colony's most eminent, talented, and respected citizens—men who were virtuous and disinterested, and who placed the colony's interests ahead of personal ambition. Of course they were also expected to be men of property, for wealth was not only a sign of talent but also a guarantee of independence.[21] Precisely because they were conceived to lack independence, placemen—even wealthy ones—were considered unfit to sit in the assembly, and the assembly twice voted to exclude them from membership, though in each case the attempt was blocked.[22]

Country ideology stressed the importance of the legislature as a bulwark of a liberty constantly threatened by an executive that sought power at its expense. In part because they accepted this view, Carolinians placed great emphasis on the need to maintain harmony and order in the social and political structure: the good of the whole community always took precedence over individual interests. "Private Interest" declared the Charles Town merchant Henry Laurens, "must not be set in competition with public good." [23]

In the later colonial period, spokesmen for the elite confidently proclaimed that the practice of politics in South Carolina closely approximated these ideals. Yet in the proprietary period, before such ideas were formulated or articulated, economic self-interest was a more important determinant of political behavior. Before the emergence of a rice-producing plantation economy in the early eighteenth century, most settlers made modest profits raising cattle and hogs for the Caribbean market. Only trade with the Indians for deerskins offered the opportunities for large profits, and such opportunities were open only to the few. Until 1691 the Governor's Council consisted of men nominated by the proprietors, together with seven elected by the General Assembly. Because the council exercised legal authority over the Indian trade, whoever controlled the assembly ultimately also controlled the trade. To ensure their continued trade monopoly, the wealthy planter-councillors ruthlessly manipulated elections to the assembly, boasting in 1685 "They can with a bole of punch get who they would chosen to ye grand Councell." [24] After 1691, however, the proprietors chose to nominate all council appointees, while in 1707 the assembly assumed legal control of the Indian trade from the Council. In the early eighteenth century, newly arrived merchants from England broke the planter-councillors' monopoly of the trade. These developments effectively put an end to attempts by the Indian-traders to unfairly influence the outcome of elections.

Gradually, with the emergence of a more stable economy, the politics of self-interest and manipulation gave way to the politics of lack of interest. Because few elections were now contested, the resort to malpractice was unnecessary. In any event, the elections acts of 1716, 1719, and 1721, which provided for decentralization of the election process, made large-scale manipulation impossible.

The decline of interest in politics was reflected in the fact that after 1720 a relatively high proportion of those elected to the assembly declined to take their seats. The nadir of interest was reached in the late 1740s when the assemblies of 1747 and 1749 were dissolved because they failed to obtain a quorum. [25] Illegal election procedures were still practiced, but they now resulted from the churchwarden's negligence,

TABLE 1
Elected members refusing to serve, 1721–1775

Period	Percentage of total	Period	Percentage of total
1721–30	17	1751–60	30
1731–40	30	1761–70	20
1741–50	37	1771–75	6

not from attempts at election fixing. In 1725, in St. James's Santee parish, for example, the churchwardens failed to hold an election at all, while in 1742, in St. Paul's, they opened the poll for only one day, instead of the two required by law.[26] The voters were hardly more enthusiastic. It was common in many country parishes at this time for the churchwardens to cast the only votes.[27]

The decline of interest in politics followed the disappearance of contentious issues and the establishment of political, economic, religious, and social harmony in the colony. The reintroduction of the bounty on tar, the replacement of an incompetent proprietary government with a stronger royal one, the procurement of peace with the Indians, the stabilization of the rate of exchange between sterling and local currency, and the Crown's decision to allow the export of rice directly to southern Europe produced a prosperous plantation economy and a period of economic growth that lasted, with temporary interruptions, from the mid-1730s until the Revolution. In the 1720s, bitter conflict did erupt in the assembly between merchants and planters, as the latter sought to relieve their indebtedness to the former by using their majority to secure the large-scale emission of paper currency. However, the new prosperity alleviated the planters' indebtedness, and, from the mid-1730s, they no longer insisted upon this measure.[28] Indeed, the economic interests of merchants and planters became increasingly congruent. Merchants invested their surplus capital in land and slaves, while planters invested in coastal vessels and country stores. Familial ties reinforced economic ones as marriages between merchant and planter families became commonplace.

Political harmony in the colony was linked, too, to the emergence by 1740 of a relatively large and clearly defined elite. It was virtually impossible now for a single small group to monopolize political power. Moreover, because the voters were just as much committed to the precepts of deference as were their contemporaries in other colonies, they were less likely to choose men of inferior economic standing, whose

TABLE 2

Inventories of assemblymen, 1721–1775

(N = 286)

Value of estate £ (sterling)	Number of estates	Percentage	Cumulative percentage
1–500	23	8.04	—
501–1,000	28	9.79	17.83
1,001–2,000	63	22.03	39.86
2,001–3,000	45	15.73	55.59
3,001–4,000	22	7.69	63.28
4,001–5,000	27	9.44	72.72
5,001–10,000	46	16.08	88.80
10,001–20,000	23	8.04	96.84
20,001–60,000	9	3.15	99.99

economic interests might have led them, as members of the assembly, to oppose the policies of the representatives of the very wealthy planters and merchants.

But threats to the colony's security reappeared in the late 1730s with the outbreak of King George's War and the Stono rebellion—the only large-scale slave revolt experienced by the colony. If the prospects of a Spanish invasion diminished in the wake of a series of British military victories, the continued importation of slaves only heightened fears of further slave revolts. This sense of panic persisted through the remainder of the colonial period and was reflected in attempts to restrict, and even prohibit, further importation of slaves; in the introduction of laws limiting the movement of blacks; and in the vicious punishments meted out to those blacks who committed even minor crimes.[29] The presence of "70,000 intestine enemies," strengthened the Carolinians' determination to maintain political harmony: faction was potentially fatal.[30]

By the 1740s, then, a series of factors had produced in fact the political harmony for which the colonists' political philosophy called. Sirmans has argued that, with the disappearance of contentious issues in the 1730s, representatives of the wealthier planter families refused altogether to sit in the assembly.[31] If this were the case it reflected a curious irony, for it meant that just as they were turning the theory of harmony into practice, they were abandoning another cherished political principle—that government was the prerogative and duty of independent men of property. In fact, the wealthy planters did not neglect their duty. Seventy-nine percent of all inventories made between 1736 and 1775 were valued at £1,000 sterling or less while only 9 percent were

TABLE 3

Assemblymen owning estates valued at £2,000 sterling or
more, 1721–1775

(percent)

Period of assembly membership	Percentage
1721–30	30.25
1731–40	30.26
1741–50	44.71
1751–60	62.50
1761–75	100.00

estimated at more than £2,000 sterling.[32] Inventories are extant for 286 of the 470 men who were members of the Assembly between 1721 and 1776. Of these, 60 percent were appraised at more than £2,000 sterling, and only 17 percent at £1,000 sterling or less. Throughout the period between 1721 and 1776, richer and richer men were elected to the assembly.

Of the 172 men who were elected to the assembly but declined to qualify themselves by taking the oath on the Bible, 126 (73 percent) did later take both the oath and their seats in that body. Of the 46 men who consistently refused to take the oath, some were dissenters, who declined for reasons of conscience.[33] Other dissenters had no scruples about taking the oath, and many identifiable nonconformists sat in the assembly in this period.

Such evidence suggests that many Carolinians, in refusing to qualify themselves as members of the assembly, were not altogether abandoning their political responsibilities, but merely indicating their unwillingness to serve for more than a few terms. That they adopted such an attitude was hardly surprising. Unlike their counterparts in Virginia and North Carolina, members of the South Carolina assembly were not paid. Yet their legislature was probably the hardest-working in British North America, often meeting for eight months of the year. Despite frequent adjournments during the planting and harvest seasons, the inconveniences involved in membership—especially for the planters—were very considerable.[34]

Wealthy Carolinians, particularly planters, were less committed than were Virginians to the notion that public service was the hallmark of the man of virtue and the mark of a gentleman. Lieutenant Governor Bull commended the unselfish spirit of those elected to office in declining payment for their services but also noted that "this laudable spirit is attended with its inconveniences, for when a man receives no compensation for his service, there is a tenderness and reluctance shewn to call him to account for his neglect of duty, whereby the public often receives detriment."[35] Still, the South Carolina elite was no less committed than the Virginia gentry to the notion that it was their duty, as independent men of property, to serve in the assembly. The simple fact was that there was a sufficient number of wealthy men in the colony to ensure, despite a rapid membership turnover, that they maintained control of the assembly.

In the 1750s the Carolinians began to display a renewed interest in politics, an interest which was more widely based than it had been in the proprietary period. Political behavior was no longer determined by an almost exclusive preoccupation with economic self-aggrandizement. In part, this simply reflected an inevitable maturing process: the elite had come of age. Yet two factors hastened that maturation. In the first place, the rapid settlement of the back country in the 1750s created a new set of political problems. Not only did the back country lack schools, churches, roads, and an effective system of law enforcement, but, because the Crown had disallowed the laws establishing electorates in the western hinterland, it was unrepresented in the legislature—the westerners had no mechanism for airing their political grievances. In seeking redress, many of them determined to vote in the low country electorates, even though they had to travel as far as 150 miles to do so. Here was one section of the electorate that was no longer politically apathetic, and, in some parishes, at least, the churchwardens now found themselves busy on election day.[36]

But it was not only the back country which displayed renewed interest in politics. After 1755 many Carolinians began to distrust British imperial policies, interpreting them as a threat to the colony's political and economic interests. As the crisis deepened in the 1760s, so did the elite's sense of its political responsibilities, for the "Properties and Liberties of Thousands—even of Thousands yet unborn" were now at risk.[37] Once again elections were bitterly contested. Henry Laurens condemned his fellow merchant, Christopher Gadsden, for holding a "Grand Barbecue" to win votes, but, at the same time, took care to provide free drinks at Dillon's tavern for his own supporters.[38] The low-country voters, too, displayed a renewed political interest. In the 1768 election, for example, 630 votes were cast in the Charles Town electorates of St. Philip's and St. Michael's, a turnout which the local press claimed was unprecedented. By the last years of the colonial period, then, both the electors and their representatives, in acting with greater political zeal, adhered more closely to the political values to which they had always paid nominal heed.

Throughout the period of royal government, the local elite also sought to ensure that its commitment to the principle of separation of the executive and legislative branches of government was carried out in practice. Although the Crown twice rejected laws passed by the assembly providing for the exclusion of placemen from the legislature, practice secured what the law could not. Less than 2 percent of those elected to the assembly in this period were professional placemen, while a further 2 percent were merchants, planters, or lawyers who also held office under the Crown. This reflected, on the one hand, the Carolinians' commitment to country ideology and, on the other, the simple fact that there were in any case few placemen in the colony. The Crown appointed nine placemen, the Admiralty and commissioners of customs three and six respectively.[39] Still, despite such limited executive patronage, it was a measure of the elite's concern over possible "executive tyranny" that the assembly constantly sought to impose legislative restraints on the patronage system. No Crown official was ever granted a permanent salary from colonial revenues and twice the assembly passed laws regulating the fees charged by royal officials.[40]

Between 1721 and 1776, Carolina's elite strove to ensure that the practice of politics in the colony adhered to the body of ideas that the English dissenters had first articulated in the late seventeenth century. In some areas they were successful, for, in the whole period between 1721 and 1776, wealthy and independent men of property dominated assembly membership while placemen were largely excluded. At the same time, the assembly always acted as if it were an exact colonial replica of the English House of Commons—citing English parliamentary precedents to defend and extend its rights and privileges.[41] If the establishment of political harmony came only in the late 1730s and the elite began to display real political zeal only from the late 1750s, by 1760 political theory and practice in the colony were in harmony, and its destiny was in the hands of a powerful and newly self-confident ruling class.

A large majority of those elected to the assembly between 1721 and 1775 were planters.[42] Even though their numerical superiority declined somewhat from the late 1740s, they remained the largest group in every assembly in this period. The proportion of merchants, lawyers, and physicians elected to the Assembly was much higher than their proportion of the total population. This was true for the whole period in the case of the merchants and for the years after 1750 in that of the lawyers and physicians. In a white population of approximately forty-five thousand in 1770, there were only about two hundred mer-

TABLE 4
Professions of assemblymen, 1721–1775 (All sessions combined)
(percent)

Profession	Percentage	Profession	Percentage
Merchants	19.57	Lawyer-Officeholders[a]	1.06
Merchant-Officeholders[a]	0.21	Physicians	4.47
Planters	65.32	Artisans	0.64
Planter-Officeholders[a]	0.21	Indian-traders	1.28
Placemen	1.49	Others	1.06
Lawyers	4.68		

NOTE: Only those elected assemblymen who took their seats are included in this and the following tables.
[a] Listed in these categories are men who held office under the Crown but whose prime source of income was from trade, planting, or law.

chants and even fewer lawyers—perhaps thirty.[43] Only thirty-seven physicians can be identified as practicing in the colony in the whole period between 1670 and 1776; at any given time they made up only a tiny percentage of the population.[44] However, because of their high trade profits, the merchants were a disproportionately large section of the elite and, therefore, were not so overrepresented in the assembly.

Most assemblymen were planters and most of them were second-generation, or later, Carolinians.[45] Sixty-one percent of those who sat in the assembly in this period were descended from families that had arrived in the colony before 1700. A much higher proportion of merchant-, lawyer-, and physician-assemblymen were first-generation settlers.

The number of first-generation members of the legislature declined steadily after 1750, in part because, as the number of native-born Carolinians who became merchants, lawyers, and physicians gradually increased, a higher proportion of later-generation representatives of these groups was elected to the assembly.[46] Also, as tensions increased between the British authorities and the colonies in the 1760s, the Carolinians became suspicious of newly arrived merchants, fearing the ties of economic interest and loyalty that bound them to England. During the Stamp Act crisis, the colonists called for the election of "natives" to the assembly, and, after the imposition of Non-Importation, they denounced the newly arrived merchants as "strangers," concerned with their own, and not the colony's, interests.[47] Though the merchants observed Non-Importation and became, in some instances, leaders of the resistance, suspicion remained, and the number of first-generation merchants elected to the assembly continued to diminish. Only men born in the colony, Carolinians insisted, "Men whose ALL centre in this Colony," were now qualified to direct its affairs.[48]

TABLE 5

Professions of assemblymen by session, 1721–1773

(percent)

Assembly	Merchants	Merchant-officeholders	Planters	Planter-officeholders	Placemen	Lawyers	Lawyer-officeholders	Physicians	Artisans	Indian traders	Other
1721	10.00	—	80.00	—	—	10.00	—	—	—	—	—
1725	23.08	—	64.10	—	2.56	2.56	2.56	—	2.56	2.56	—
1728(1)	22.85	—	65.71	—	—	—	2.86	2.86	—	5.71	—
1728(2)	21.43	—	71.43	—	—	—	—	—	—	7.14	—
1728(3)	No quorum										
1729(1)	31.03	—	55.17	—	—	—	—	3.45	3.45	6.90	—
1729(2)	13.89	—	66.67	—	2.78	5.56	2.78	2.78	2.78	2.78	—
1730	22.22	—	62.96	—	3.70	—	—	—	3.70	7.41	—
1731	18.18	—	68.18	—	2.27	6.82	—	—	2.27	2.27	—
1733	20.00	—	70.00	—	2.50	5.00	—	—	2.50	—	—
1736	25.00	—	60.42	—	—	4.17	4.17	2.08	2.08	2.08	—
1739	26.09	—	58.70	—	2.17	4.35	2.17	4.35	2.08	—	—
1742	26.09	—	60.87	—	4.35	4.35	2.17	2.17	2.17	—	—
1745	27.50	2.50	60.00	2.50	—	2.50	—	2.50	2.50	—	—
1746	28.57	—	66.67	—	—	—	—	4.76	—	—	—
1747	No quorum										
1748	35.90	—	53.85	—	—	2.56	—	7.69	—	—	—
1748/9	No quorum										
1749	26.67	—	55.56	—	—	2.22	2.22	8.89	—	2.22	2.22
1751	33.33	2.22	44.44	—	—	8.89	—	4.44	4.44	2.22	—
1754	24.49	—	51.02	—	2.04	12.24	2.04	6.12	—	—	2.04
1757	29.41	—	54.90	—	—	13.73	—	1.96	—	—	—
1760	32.26	—	41.94	—	—	12.90	—	12.90	—	—	—
1761	29.79	—	53.19	—	—	8.51	2.13	6.38	—	—	—
1762(1)	29.17	—	45.83	—	2.08	14.58	—	8.33	—	—	—
1762(2)	26.00	—	50.00	—	—	16.00	—	8.00	—	—	—
1765	28.85	—	48.08	—	—	13.46	—	7.69	—	—	1.92
1768[a]	26.92	—	53.85	—	—	11.54	—	7.69	—	—	—
1769	29.09	—	50.91	—	—	10.91	—	7.27	1.82	—	—
1772(1)[a]	23.53	—	50.00	—	—	23.53	—	2.94	—	—	—
1772(2)	25.00	—	55.00	—	—	17.50	—	2.50	—	—	—
1773(1)[a]	21.43	—	53.57	—	—	17.86	—	7.14	—	—	—
1773(2)	24.49	—	57.14	—	—	12.24	—	6.12	—	—	—

[a] Assembly met for only a few days, many members not arriving in time to qualify.

TABLE 6

Professions of Carolinians owning estates valued at £1,000 or more, 1736–1775
(percent)

Profession	Percentage	Profession	Percentage
Planters	78.20	Artisans	1.62
Merchants	10.46	Clergymen	0.76
Widows/Spinsters	6.69	Lawyers	0.33
Physicians	1.94		

NOTE: Data taken from the 927 inventories valued at £1,000 (sterling) or more made during this period.

The old and well-to-do planter families were most strongly entrenched politically in the early-settled and wealthy parishes of St.
Andrew's, St. John's Berkeley, St. James' Goose Creek, St. Thomas
and St. Dennis, St. George's, and St. Stephen's. In each of these parishes, representatives of these families constituted a majority of those
elected and served more than half of the total terms for that parish.[49]
Such families were also strongly represented in the parishes of St. Bar-
tholomew's, St. James' Santee and St. John's Colleton—all in early-
settled areas—where they either constituted a majority of the total
assembly membership elected for the parish, or were elected for a majority of the total terms served for that parish. Finally, those elected to
represent these early-settled parishes came from families which were
not merely long-established and usually wealthy, but which also possessed a continuing tradition of electing representatives to the assembly. St. George's, St. Andrew's, St. Stephen's, St. James' Santee, and
St. John's Berkeley, especially, elected a high proportion of representatives whose fathers, brothers, and/or sons also served in the assembly.

Naturally, the merchants' electoral strongholds were the two Charles
Town parishes, St. Philip's and St. Michael's. These electorates sent to
the assembly a higher percentage of merchants and a lower percentage
of planters than any of the others. They also returned the highest number of first-generation assemblymen.

Some parishes, essentially old planter-family strongholds, elected
merchants to represent them, and occasionally these merchants were
first-generation settlers. These included St. Thomas and St. Dennis,
St. John's Colleton, and St. James' Goose Creek. However, merchants
were elected in even greater numbers to represent electorates further
removed from Charles Town, electorates which the old planter-families
did not dominate. Such electorates were of two types. First, they included the parishes of St. Helena's, Prince George's, Prince Frederick's,
and Prince William's, encompassing areas of the low country which,
although early settled, remained sparsely populated until well into the

TABLE 7

First-generation assemblymen, by profession, 1721–1773

(percent)

Assembly	Merchants	Merchant-officeholders	Planters	Planter-officeholders	Placemen	Lawyers	Lawyer-officeholders	Physicians	Artisans	Indian traders	Other
1721	100.00	—	44.00	—	—	100.00	—	—	—	—	—
1725	55.56	—	32.00	—	100.00	100.00	—	—	—	—	—
1728(1)	37.50	—	—	—	—	—	—	—	—	—	—
1728(2)	50.00	—	15.00	—	—	—	—	100.00	—	50.00	—
1728(3)	No quorum										
1729(1)	55.56	—	18.75	—	100.00	—	—	100.00	100.00	50.00	—
1729(2)	60.00	—	29.17	—	100.00	50.00	—	100.00	100.00	100.00	—
1730	83.33	—	23.53	—	100.00	—	—	—	100.00	50.00	—
1731	50.00	—	16.67	—	100.00	66.67	—	—	—	—	—
1733	50.00	—	10.71	—	—	50.00	—	—	—	—	—
1736	58.33	—	6.90	—	—	50.00	—	—	—	—	—
1739	50.00	—	7.69	—	100.00	50.00	—	—	—	—	—
1742	58.33	—	2.17	—	100.00	100.00	—	50.00	—	—	—
1745	45.45	2.50	4.17	2.50	—	100.00	—	100.00	—	—	—
1746	25.00	—	10.71	—	100.00	100.00	—	50.00	—	—	—
1747	No quorum										
1748	28.57	—	9.52	—	—	100.00	—	33.33	—	—	100.00
1748/9	No quorum										
1749	58.33	—	20.00	—	—	100.00	—	75.00	—	100.00	—
1751	40.00	2.22	10.00	—	100.00	75.00	—	50.00	50.00	100.00	—
1754	41.67	—	12.00	—	—	50.00	—	66.67	—	—	100.00
1757	33.33	—	7.41	—	—	42.86	—	100.00	—	—	—
1760	60.00	—	7.69	—	—	50.00	—	75.00	—	—	—
1761	35.71	—	8.00	—	100.00	50.00	—	100.00	—	—	—
1762(1)	35.71	—	9.09	—	100.00	28.57	—	75.00	—	—	—
1762(2)	38.46	—	8.00	—	—	25.00	—	75.00	—	—	—
1765	33.33	—	12.00	—	—	14.29	—	75.00	—	—	100.00
1768	57.14	—	—	—	—	33.33	—	100.00	100.00	—	—
1769	37.50	—	7.14	—	—	16.67	—	75.00	—	—	—
1772(1)	—	—	2.94	—	—	12.50	—	—	—	—	—
1772(2)	30.00	—	2.50	—	—	14.29	—	100.00	—	—	—
1773(1)	—	—	—	—	—	—	—	—	—	—	—
1773(2)	—	—	—	—	—	—	—	50.00	—	—	—

TABLE 8
Nativity to colony of assemblymen, 1721–1776
(percent)

Assembly	First generation	Second generation	Third generation	Fourth generation	Later[a] generation	Unknown generation
1721	55.00	37.50	—	—	—	7.50
1725	41.03	41.03	—	—	7.69	10.26
1728(1)	17.14	48.57	—	—	8.57	25.71
1728(2)	25.00	32.14	—	—	14.29	28.57
1728(3)		No quorum				
1729(1)	37.93	31.03	—	—	10.34	20.69
1729(2)	41.67	16.67	—	—	8.33	33.33
1730	44.44	25.93	—	—	11.11	18.52
1731	29.55	34.09	—	—	11.36	25.00
1733	22.50	52.50	2.50	—	7.50	15.00
1736	25.00	39.58	8.33	—	8.33	18.75
1739	26.09	47.83	4.35	—	4.35	17.39
1742	30.43	39.13	10.87	—	10.87	8.70
1745	20.00	50.00	15.00	—	2.50	12.50
1746	16.67	47.62	9.52	—	9.52	16.67
1747		No quorum				
1748	20.51	46.15	17.95	—	5.13	10.26
1748/9		No quorum				
1749	42.22	31.11	6.67	—	8.89	11.11
1751	35.56	33.33	17.78	—	2.22	11.11
1754	32.65	32.65	24.49	—	4.08	6.12
1757	21.57	43.14	25.49	—	3.92	5.88
1760	38.71	19.35	25.81	—	12.90	3.23
1761	25.53	29.79	36.17	—	8.51	—
1762(1)	27.08	33.33	18.75	2.08	12.50	6.25
1762(2)	24.00	38.00	14.00	2.00	12.00	10.00
1765	23.08	26.92	30.77	5.77	3.85	9.62
1768	26.92	30.77	26.92	3.85	7.69	3.85
1769	23.64	21.82	41.82	1.82	5.45	5.45
1772(1)	5.88	26.47	52.94	2.94	11.76	—
1772(2)	15.00	20.00	45.00	7.50	12.50	—
1773(1)	3.57	28.57	50.00	10.71	7.14	—
1773(2)	14.29	26.53	38.78	8.16	10.20	2.04

[a]Can only be identified as later than first generation.

colonial period. Second were the parishes of St. David's, St. Mathew's, St. Mark's, St. Luke's, St. Peter's, and All Saints', which were located on the very periphery of settlement—the first three in the back country, the latter three on the coast—and which remained essentially unsettled until the last twenty or so years of royal government.

Despite the virtual merchant monopoly of representation for Charles Town, some placemen, office holders, artisans, physicians, and, especially, lawyers were elected for St. Philip's and St. Michael's. More

TABLE 9
Election to the assembly of descendants of pre-1700 settlers
(percent)

Parish	Representatives descended from pre-1700 settlers	Total terms served by descendants of pre-1700 settlers
St. Philip's and St. Michael's	37.50	37.91
St. Paul's	38.30	48.96
Christchurch	25.00	15.38
St. John's Berkeley	72.97	73.81
St. James' Goose Creek	52.83	59.85
St. George's	65.52	68.25
St. Andrew's	77.78	79.55
St. James' Santee	53.57	43.40
St. Thomas'	55.26	59.30
St. Bartholomew's	53.45	42.34
St. Helena's	26.79	18.28
Prince George's	32.35	42.37
St. Stephen's	100.00	100.00
St. John's Colleton	62.16	47.83
Prince Frederick's	30.77	34.29
Prince William's	52.17	46.67
St. David's	17.86	17.86

TABLE 10
The wealth of the assemblymen, 1721–1776
(percent)

Parish	Average value of estate (£ sterling)	Average slaveholdings	Assemblymen with extant inventories (%)
St. Philip's and St. Michael's	8883	79	39
St. Paul's	4910	106	32
Christchurch	2009	37	38
St. John's Berkeley	5299	84	35
St. James' Goose Creek	6737	107	47
St. George's	8691	137	59
St. Andrew's	4208	93	36
St. James' Santee	4209	80	43
St. Thomas and St. Dennis	4101	71	50
St. Bartholomew	3605	76	45
St. Helena's	3216	73	43
Prince George's	2713	66	50
St. Stephen's	—	—	14
St. John's Colleton	4468	56	59
Prince Frederick's	2153	37	42
Prince William's	5045	104	26

TABLE 11

Family relationships among assemblymen, 1721–1775

(percent)

Parish	Assemblymen with close relatives also elected to assembly (%)	Parish	Assemblymen with close relatives also elected to assembly (%)
St. Philip's and St. Michael's	50	St. Thomas'	55
St. Paul's	55	St. Bartholomew's	45
Christchurch	25	St. Helena's	41
St. John's Berkeley	59	Prince George's	50
St. James' Goose Creek	49	St. Stephen's	71
St. George's	76	St. John's Colleton	43
St. Andrew's	72	Prince Frederick's	46
St. James' Santee	61	Prince William's	57
			29

NOTE: "Close relatives" here includes fathers, brothers, and sons.

often, however, men in these categories secured election for the country parishes, even though most were Charles Town residents. The old low-country parish of Christchurch sent more lawyers to the assembly than did any other parish, and more physicians than any electorate except Prince Frederick's. Christchurch was not a political stronghold of the old and wealthy planter families because of its inferior soil and general poverty.[50] Both the lawyers and physicians were also elected to represent the more distant parishes, particularly Prince Frederick's, St. Helena's, and the even more geographically peripheral electorates. Because of the competition from the merchants, and perhaps because the more politically aware Charles Town voters were unlikely to vote for them, the placemen, too, were obliged to seek election for the more distant parishes.

This indicates, of course, that unlike their counterparts in the northern colonies, South Carolina's freeholders had no scruples about electing to the assembly men who were not resident in the parishes which they represented. This casual attitude was probably encouraged by the fact that in order to avoid contracting the malaria which was endemic to the low country, and to enjoy the social pleasures for which the capital was famous, most of the wealthy low-country planters lived for much of each year in Charles Town. In a sense, almost all representatives (except those elected for St. Philip's and St. Michael's) were nonresident. However, the inhabitants of the electorates most remote

TABLE 12

Professions of assemblymen by parish, 1721–1775
(percent)

Parish	Merchants	Merchant-officeholders	Planters	Planter-officeholders	Placemen	Lawyers	Lawyer-officeholders	Physicians	Artisans	Indian-traders	Other
St. Philip's and St. Michael's	76.79	—	3.57	—	3.57	8.93	3.57	1.79	1.79	—	—
St. Paul's	12.77	2.13	74.47	—	—	6.38	—	4.26	—	—	—
Christchurch	4.17	—	54.17	—	—	20.83	4.17	8.33	4.17	—	4.17
St. John's Berkeley	5.41	—	94.59	—	—	—	—	—	—	—	—
St. James' Goose Creek	18.87	—	66.04	—	—	1.89	—	3.77	3.77	5.66	—
St. George's	6.90	—	82.76	—	—	3.45	—	3.45	—	—	—
St. Andrew's	16.67	—	69.44	—	—	5.56	3.45	2.78	2.78	—	—
St. James' Santee	14.29	—	75.00	—	—	—	—	7.14	—	3.57	2.78
St. Thomas'	28.95	—	63.16	—	—	2.63	—	2.63	—	—	—
St. Bartholomew's	6.90	—	81.03	1.72	—	1.72	—	6.90	2.63	—	—
St. Helena's	30.36	—	44.64	1.79	8.93	8.93	—	1.79	1.72	1.79	—
Prince George's	23.53	—	70.59	—	—	2.94	—	—	—	2.94	1.79
St. Stephen's	—	—	100.00	—	—	—	—	—	—	—	—
St. John's Colleton	24.32	—	59.46	—	—	8.11	—	5.41	—	—	—
Prince Frederick's	19.23	—	53.85	—	—	3.85	7.69	15.38	—	—	2.70
Prince William's	43.48	—	39.13	—	—	4.35	4.35	8.70	—	—	—
St. David's[a] ⎫ St. Mathew's ⎪ St. Peter's ⎬ St. Mark's ⎪ St. Luke's ⎪ All Saints' ⎭	17.86	—	53.58	—	3.57	10.71	—	10.71	3.57	—	—

[a]These six newly settled parishes are grouped together because each had had only a very few assemblymen by 1775. Listing the percentages by individual parishes might be misleading, so an average is given.

TABLE 13
Residency patterns of assemblymen, 1721–1775
(percent)

Parish	Resident of parish for which elected	Charles Town resident	Resident of other country parish
St. Philip's and St. Michael's	96.43	—	3.57
St. George's	82.76	6.90	10.34
St. John's Berkeley	75.68	2.70	21.62
St. Stephen's	71.43	—	28.57
St. Mathew's	66.66	33.34	—
St. Andrew's	69.44	22.22	8.34
Prince George's	64.71	17.65	17.64
St. James' Goose Creek	64.15	18.87	16.98
Christchurch	62.50	33.33	4.17
St. Paul's	59.57	21.28	19.15
St. David's	50.00	—	50.00
St. Luke's	50.00	50.00	—
St. Bartholomew's	48.28	10.34	41.38
St. Thomas'	47.37	36.84	15.79
St. James' Santee	42.86	28.57	28.57
St. John's Colleton	40.54	48.65	10.81
Prince Frederick's	30.77	38.46	30.77
St. Helena's	26.79	44.64	28.57
St. Mark's	22.22	11.11	66.67
Prince William's	17.39	43.48	39.13
St. Peter's	10.00	70.00	20.00
All Saints'	—	—	—

TABLE 14
First-generation assemblymen by parish
(percent)

Parish	First-generation Assemblymen	Parish	First-generation Assemblymen
St. Philip's and St. Michael's	48.21	Prince George's	29.41
St. Paul's	25.53	St. Stephen's	0.00
Christchurch	29.17	St. John's Colleton	24.32
St. John's Berkeley	18.92	Prince Frederick's	30.77
St. James' Goose Creek	20.75	Prince William's	26.09
St. George's	13.79	St. David's	
St. Andrew's	11.11	St. Mathew's	
St. James' Santee	28.57	St. Peter's	
St. Thomas'	26.32	St. Mark's	35.71
St. Bartholomew's	24.14	St. Luke's	
St. Helena's	42.86	All Saints'	

TABLE 15

Professions of assembly leaders, 1721–1775

(percent)

Profession	First-rank leaders	Second-rank leaders	Profession	First-rank leaders	Second-rank leaders
Merchants	43.28	30.14	Lawyer-Officeholders	4.48	—
Merchant-Officeholders	1.49	—	Physicians	1.49	5.48
Planters	25.37	53.42	Artisans	—	2.74
Placemen	4.48	—	Indian-traders	1.49	1.37
Lawyers	17.91	5.48	Others	—	—

from Charles Town were the most willing to elect nonresident assemblymen because, compared to the parishes near Charles Town, fewer wealthy men—that is, those considered most suitable to sit in the assembly—lived in the more remote areas. The Charlestonians were to some extent filling a vacuum. At the same time, the comparatively few wealthy men who lived in these parishes were more reluctant to accept election than were men of similar standing in the low-country parishes adjacent to Charles Town. For the former, such service involved a great deal more expense and time.[51] The result was that a high proportion of those elected to represent the more remote parishes were merchants, office holders, placemen, lawyers, and physicians, who, although they owned land in these parishes, did not live in them.

The planters remained the largest group elected to the assembly throughout the period of royal government. Moreover, the old, wealthy planter families maintained their strong electoral base in some of the early-settled parishes. On the other hand, Charles Town residents, particularly the merchants and, to a lesser extent, the lawyers and physicians, were well represented. Not only did they monopolize representation from the metropolis but significant numbers of them were elected by the country parishes. In this way Charles Town extended its political influence into the hinterland.

If the majority of those elected to the legislature were planters, the largest number of those classified by Jack P. Greene as leaders of the first rank were merchants and lawyers. In Virginia, by contrast, planters dominated both membership and leadership.[52] Although planters were in a majority amongst Greene's second-rank leaders, merchants were strongly represented here also. Not only were the merchants, law-

yers, and even physicians elected to the assembly in ratios disproportionate to their numbers in the whole community, but in the assembly
itself they constituted a higher proportion of leadership than membership.

An analysis of leadership trends reveals some important developments. It becomes clear that placemen were excluded altogether from
assembly leadership after 1750, a fact that reflected the rising influence
of country ideology and the growing independence of the assembly
(tables 16 and 17). Second, planters played a decreasingly important
role as assembly leaders, particularly at the first-rank level. Third,
while the merchants remained politically powerful throughout the period, they were steadily replaced as first-rank leaders, in the 1760s and
1770s, by the lawyers. The latter were, for the most part, the sons of
successful local planters and merchants, who were dispatched by their
families to England to be educated at the Inns of Court. Their assumption of first-rank leadership, with that of the native-born merchants,
meant the end of leadership domination by first-generation merchants
(see table 17). Fourth, Charles Town's political dominance is reflected
both in the fact that the majority of assembly leaders were Charles
Town residents and by the increasing percentage of representatives
elected by St. Philip's and St. Michael's who were first-rank leaders.[53]
And, finally, those leaders of both the first and second rank who were
planters were drawn from the old planter families. Next to St. Philip's
and St. Michael's it was the parishes in which the old planter families
were politically dominant—St. Andrew's, St. George's, St. James'
Goose Creek—which elected the highest number of leaders of both
ranks. The planters' declining political influence is reflected in the de-
creasing number of assembly leaders elected by these parishes in the
later years (table 18).

How do we account for the large share of political leadership provided by the merchants, lawyers, and, at the second level, the physicians? There is one simple explanation. Because they lived in Charles
Town, it was easier for these men regularly to attend the assembly
when it was in session—and constant attendance was certainly a prereq-
uisite for leadership. But the fact that these men were able to provide
leadership does not explain why they chose to do so. Gene Sirmans has
argued that, because law was the profession chosen by young men who
lacked family influence, the lawyers regarded assembly service as a
means of social and economic advancement.[54] However true this was
of the earlier period, in the last years of the colonial era the lawyer-
leaders in the Assembly were members of some of the colony's most
prestigious and influential families—the Pinckneys, Rutledges, and

TABLE 16
Changes in leadership patterns: Professions, 1721–1775
(percent)

Rank and profession	1721–30	1731–40	1741–50	1751–60	1761–70	1771–75
First-rank leaders:						
Merchants	31.25	35.29	50.00	66.67	47.37	27.27
Merchant-Officeholders	—	—	—	4.17	—	—
Planters	37.50	29.41	22.22	8.33	21.05	9.09
Placemen	18.75	11.76	5.56	—	—	—
Lawyers	6.25	17.65	11.11	16.67	21.05	63.64
Lawyer-Officeholders	—	5.88	5.56	4.17	5.26	—
Physicians	—	—	5.56	—	5.26	—
Artisans	—	—	—	—	—	—
Indian-traders	6.25	—	—	—	—	—
Other	—	—	—	—	—	—
Second-rank leaders:						
Merchants	18.75	26.32	36.84	18.18	38.89	40.00
Merchant-Officeholders	—	—	—	—	—	—
Planters	81.25	63.16	47.37	45.45	33.33	40.00
Placemen	—	—	—	—	—	—
Lawyers	—	5.26	5.26	9.09	5.56	10.00
Lawyer-Officeholders	—	—	—	9.09	5.56	—
Physicians	—	—	5.26	18.18	11.11	10.00
Artisans	—	5.26	—	—	5.56	—
Indian-traders	—	—	5.26	—	—	—
Other	—	—	—	—	—	—

TABLE 17
Changes in leadership patterns: Nativity, 1721–1775
(percent)

Rank and period	First generation	Second generation	Third generation	Fourth generation	Later generation	Unknown generation
First-rank leaders:						
1721–30	62.50	25.00	6.25	—	6.25	—
1731–40	76.47	11.76	—	—	—	11.76
1741–50	61.11	27.78	11.11	—	—	—
1751–60	54.17	37.50	8.33	—	—	—
1761–70	26.32	47.37	26.32	—	—	—
1771–75	27.27	27.27	45.45	—	—	—
Second-rank leaders:						
1721–30	62.50	25.00	—	—	—	12.50
1731–40	26.32	42.11	—	—	5.26	26.32
1741–50	36.84	36.84	5.26	—	5.26	15.72
1751–60	45.45	55.55	—	—	—	—
1761–70	47.06	17.65	11.76	—	17.65	5.88
1771–75	40.00	10.00	30.00	10.00	10.00	—

TABLE 18

Parishes represented by assembly leaders, 1721–1775

(percent)

Rank and parish	1721–30	1731–40	1741–50	1751–60	1761–70	1771–76
First-rank leaders:						
St. Philip's and						
St. Michael's	50.00	47.06	61.11	79.17	78.95	81.82
St. Helena's	6.25	—	—	—	—	—
St. John's Berkeley	12.50	—	—	—	—	—
St. James' Goose Creek	18.75	11.76	5.56	4.17	5.26	—
St. Andrew's	6.25	11.76	5.56	—	—	—
St. George's	6.25	5.88	5.56	4.17	5.26	—
Christchurch	—	11.76	16.67	4.17	—	—
Prince George's	—	—	—	8.33	5.26	9.09
St. Paul's	—	—	5.56	—	5.26	9.09
St. James' Santee	—	11.76	—	—	—	—
Second-rank leaders:						
St. Philip's and						
St. Michael's	18.75	42.11	47.37	54.55	44.44	30.00
St. Helena's	6.25	5.26	5.26	9.09	—	10.00
St. John's Berkeley	6.25	10.53	5.26	—	5.56	—
St. James' Goose Creek	25.00	10.53	10.53	18.18	5.56	—
St. Andrew's	—	10.53	15.79	9.09	11.11	40.00
St. George's	12.50	5.26	5.26	—	5.56	10.00
Christchurch	12.50	—	—	—	5.56	—
Prince George's	—	—	—	—	—	—
St. Paul's	12.50	10.53	5.26	—	5.56	—
St. James' Santee	—	—	—	—	5.56	—
St. Thomas' and Dennis'	6.25	—	—	—	—	—
St. Bartholomew's	—	5.26	—	9.09	5.56	—
St. John's Colleton	—	—	5.26	—	—	—
St. Mark's	—	—	—	—	5.56	10.00

Manigaults. Still, until these latter years the status of the legal profession in the colony remained low and the competition for business fierce, so that only a few reaped rich rewards from their practices.[55] For the lawyers, then, and perhaps also for the physicians, whose profession too was held in low esteem, public service, in the form of assembly leadership, was a means of raising their own status and that of their professions to a level compatible with the social status of their eminent families. Also, for the lawyers, assembly leadership was an important means of advertising their qualities as orators and their knowledge of the law, thereby securing advantage in a competitive business. Perhaps old Gabriel Manigault was concerned both with maintaining the family status and promoting his son's career when, upon young Peter Manigault's return from the Inns of Court, he transferred land in St. Thomas' and St. Dennis' Parish to Peter, "in order to qualify and entitle the said Peter Manigault to take his seat in the Commons House of Assembly."[56]

Perhaps because so many of them were first-generation settlers, Charles Town's merchants may have assumed leadership roles in the assembly as a technique for ensuring social acceptance. Yet many merchants who were descended from old and eminent local families were also assembly leaders. The profession of trade was held in high regard throughout the period; no stigma was attached to it. More than any other factor, wealth was the crucial criterion of social acceptance, and those who provided assembly leadership were wealthier men than those who sat in the assembly as a whole. In other words, whatever roles the merchant-leaders played in the assembly, their social status was, in any case, largely assured.

The merchants may have assumed assembly leadership in part because they were concerned to protect their economic interests. Both in 1723 and again in 1736 the planters used their majorities to pass bills providing for the emission of paper money on a large scale, bills that favored the indebted planters at the expense of their merchant creditors. Merchants and planters had reached an accord on this issue by 1740, but another remained. Throughout the colonial period, the merchants objected to the provincial tax laws, on the grounds that they required Charles Town's residents to pay a disproportionately large share of the public charges. Petitions protesting this discrimination were presented to the council in 1744, and to the assembly in 1770.[57] The merchants themselves were aware that the needs of trade did not always coincide with those of agriculture. In a 1741 by-election for St. Philip's, for example, the voters were urged to elect a merchant, for "those who are immediately and actively engag'd and continue to engage in Trade . . . ought to be better Judges of the Concerns of it . . . than those who are unskill'd in the Practice."[58]

Nevertheless, the economic issues that divided merchants and planters after 1740 were of relatively minor importance and caused only slight political friction. If the merchants assumed positions of political leadership as a means of protecting their economic interests, their concern was with a potential rather than an actual threat. Of much greater importance in motivating the merchants, and the lawyers and physicians too, was the fact that they were imbued with a deeper sense of their political obligations as independent men of property than were the planters. Since many merchants were recent arrivals, and all of them corresponded regularly with their English counterparts in London, Bristol and Liverpool, they were more exposed to upper-class

TABLE 19
Inventories of assembly leaders, 1721–1775
(N = 59)

Value of Estate (£ sterling)	Number of leaders	Percentage of leaders	Cumulative percentage
1–500	5	8.47	—
501–1,000	5	8.47	16.94
1,001–2,000	9	15.25	32.19
2,001–3,000	6	10.17	42.36
3,001–4,000	6	10.17	52.53
4,001–5,000	5	8.47	61.00
5,001–10,000	15	25.42	86.42
10,001–20,000	4	6.78	93.20
20,001–60,000	4	6.78	99.98

SOURCE: These figures are based on the extant inventories of leaders of both the first and second ranks.

English values. The lawyers and physicians, of course, had rubbed shoulders with the English gentry at Oxford, Cambridge, Edinburgh, and the Inns of Court. As a result, these men were keenly aware not only of their political, but of their social and cultural, responsibilities as colonial counterparts of the English gentry. In 1748 it was the merchants who formed the colony's most important, influential, and prestigious society, the Library Society; and it was they, together with the merchants and physicians, who continued to dominate its membership. The concern of some Carolinians, merchants in particular, to provide both cultural and political leadership is reflected in the fact that of the thirty-eight classified by Greene as leaders of the first rank in the assembly from 1748 to 1770, twenty-five (66 percent)—including thirteen merchants, five lawyers, four planters, two physicians, and one placeman—were members of the Library Society.[59]

The merchants' dominance of political leadership, together with the increasingly important role assumed by the lawyers in the last years of royal government, were to be of considerable importance in shaping the Carolinian response to the events leading to Revolution. The lawyers' training at the Inns of Court prepared them to mount a confident colonial defense based on the principles of common law.[60] The experiences of these men in England had made them realize, too, that they were outsiders. They had compared the two societies and found that Carolina was not a transplanted England. That discovery prepared them for their later opposition to Great Britain.[61] Because of their greater contact with England, these merchants and lawyers were also more fully exposed to country ideology, which was to give a particular intensity to their responses as assembly leaders to the changed British policies. These new policies, particularly the stricter enforcement of the Navigation Acts, affected the merchants' interests more directly than those of the planters, for whom the issues were, at first, of a constitutional and somewhat abstract nature. Henry Laurens was more concerned by the threat to "liberty and property" posed by the Stamp Act mobs than by the act itself, but the actions of "wicked and Ignorant Officers" who illegally confiscated his ships and cargoes turned Laurens into a supporter of the rights of the colonies.[62] Because they were surrounded by an "intestine enemy," the black majority, and because, at first, British policies represented only a potential threat to their traditional "rights and privileges," the planters were inclined to caution. But political leadership had passed to the merchants and lawyers, guaranteeing that, from the beginning, the South Carolina House of Assembly would insist upon a determined and stern colonial defense.

Throughout the period of royal government, South Carolina's elite succeeded in maintaining a responsible, responsive and inclusive political system. The legal restrictions on the franchise and assembly membership were certainly liberal by eighteenth-century standards, and, because wealth was the essential criterion for assembly membership, men were usually not, as they would be in the nineteenth century, denied the right of political involvement because they practiced trade, law, or medicine.[63] Yet some men were excluded from assembly membership because of their professions. Placemen were distrusted for ideological reasons, and fewer and fewer of them served in the legislature in the later years of the colonial period. Further, although a significant number of wealthy tradesmen lived in Charles Town, very few artisans were elected to the assembly in this period, which may reflect the elite's development of a sense of social distance between itself and the mechanics. Still, it was a remarkably open political system, because the property qualifications required of voters and assembly members were modest. As new areas were opened to settlement, the assembly sought to incorporate them into this system, and if it partly failed in this regard, that was because of the obstructive tactics of the British Crown.

The local elite had failed to reproduce the English social system and found themselves instead inhabiting an isolated outpost, surrounded by only quasi-assimilated slaves. The fear which this situation created in the collective mind of the elite drove them to establish and maintain social and political harmony in the colony. One important means of achieving that harmony was to establish a comprehensive political system, albeit one over which they, as members of, and leaders in, the assembly, maintained tight control. Though they failed, in their own terms, to establish a "successful" social system, they produced, in response to that failure, a political system that, again in their own terms, fulfilled all their expectations.

THOMAS WENDEL

At the Pinnacle of Elective Success:
The Speaker of the House in
Colonial America

———————•◉•———————

FROM THE PERIOD of the Glorious Revolution to 1775, 275 men held
the position of Speaker of the House in the thirteen lower assemblies of
colonial America.[1] With the exception of the two corporate colonies
and Massachusetts, the speakership was the highest elective office in
America. In Rhode Island and Connecticut, both the court of assistants and the governorship were elective offices. The same prevailed
in Massachusetts until the 1691 Charter, which, though leaving the
court of assistants an elective body, made the governorship a Crown
appointment. But, if in three of the thirteen colonies higher office was
open to elective politics, the speakership in the other ten represented
the pinnacle of elective success.[2]

The Speaker wielded considerable authority as the embodiment of
the dignity of the legislature. But his position in the colonies was more
than ceremonial. Cut off from the executive function by the institutions of royal prerogative, the colonial legislatures developed no such
quasi-executive institutions as the ministry, which in England had
evolved slowly under the three Georges.[3] In England, the speakership
remained chiefly presidential, as other members of Parliament assumed the great offices of government. No such assumption took place
in America. The speakership, therefore, emerged as a position of extraordinary political leadership.[4]

Elected by the members of the assembly, the Speaker was usually
the head of the dominant faction in the legislature. From the chair, he

173

not only did the will of the majority faction but also frequently led in the formation of that will.[5] Colonial speakers came more to resemble their descendants after the Revolution than they did their contemporary English counterparts.[6] Arthur Onslow may not have achieved the high ideal of the nonpartisan Speaker, nor, certainly, did either of his immediate successors, but he hardly compares, as a partisan politician, with Edward Mosely of North Carolina; Adolph Philipse of New York; John Kinsey, Jr., of Pennsylvania; James Otis, Sr., of Massachusetts; or dozens of other men who filled the chairs of the thirteen colonial assemblies.[7] Not all of the colonial Speakers exercised the kind of power and leadership of these men, but in every colony the speakership was more often than not a highly politicized office, frequently filled by the leading politicians of the provinces.

What sort of men were they? Were there regional differences among them? Did they differ in profile from colony to colony and over time? Of the 275 speakers under study, can we make generalizations that tell us something of power and status in colonial America? To answer these questions, the writer, with the help of researchers in several historical societies, gathered biographical data on each of the men who held the office.[8] The data fell under thirteen categories. An explanation and analysis of each follows their listing. Some concluding remarks follow category thirteen. The categories are as follows:

1. Years of service
2. Previous years of assembly service
3. Other offices held
4. Age
5. Wealth
6. Social status
7. Residence
8. National origin
9. Occupation
10. Religion
11. Education
12. World view
13. Party

The number of years during any part of which an individual held the office of Speaker. The length of assembly sessions differed widely from colony to colony. In the royal colonies, the governors had the power to call, to prorogue, and to dissolve their assemblies. Royal Massachusetts was something of a special case, for, in addition, the Charter of 1691 specified an annually elected assembly, a carry-over from her original corporate charter. In the eighteenth century, the two proprietary colonies differed: Maryland followed the royal pattern (after her return to proprietary governance in 1715), while Pennsylvania, under the Charter of Privileges, held annual assemblies. The two corporate colonies' assemblies met semiannually. Though a particular assembly session might be quite short, the title of Speaker remained with an in-

TABLE 1

Average years of service

Colony	Years	Colony	Years
Virginia	7.4	New Jersey	4.0
New York	7.3	North Carolina	3.6
Maryland	5.9	Delaware	3.1
Pennsylvania	5.6	Georgia	3.0
New Hampshire	5.1	Rhode Island	2.6
Massachusetts	5.0	Connecticut	2.1
South Carolina	4.3		

dividual so long as he exercised that office during that assembly. For this reason and for purposes of comparison between colonies through time, duration in office has been treated as indicated above. The same reasoning applies to the following category.[9]

For the 275 speakers, tenure of office varies from twenty-eight years (John Robinson, Jr.) to one year (26 percent of the total). The average for the entire period is 3.8 years. Speakers who served during the year 1700 averaged 5.5 years in office; in 1725, 7.6 years; and in 1750, 11.3 years. A breakdown by colony is given in Table 1.

The number of years during which an individual served as an elected assemblyman previous to attaining the chair. The operative word here is "elected." Important as the position of clerk was, this category includes only those years during which an individual actually represented his county, parish, town, incorporated borough, or other electoral district.[10] In some cases, for instance, Benjamin Arnold and Benjamin Bartin of Rhode Island, men served as assistants previous to their speakerships. Although the assistants were a part of the legislature, I have counted only those years of membership in the lower house.

The previous years of service for five (2 percent) of the 275 speakers were not ascertained. All of these were in Delaware (24 percent of Delaware's twenty-one speakers) before 1739, after which Delaware's legislative records are available.

With the exception of the pre-1739 Delawarians, then, the average number of years of Assembly service previous to an individual's elevation to the chair is 6.1 years. Speakers serving in 1700 averaged 2.3 years previous service; in 1725, 6.6 years; 1750, 8.5 years; and 1775, 8.3 years. The average number of years previous service is low for some colonies because more of their Speakers had no previous service. The case of Rhode Island is not as different as it appears: thirty-four

TABLE 2
Speakers without previous assembly service

Colony	Total number of Speakers	Speakers with no previous assembly service (%)
Georgia	9	44 (4)
New Hampshire	23	39 (9)
North Carolina	14	29 (4)
New Jersey	18	28 (5)
Virginia	12	25 (3)
South Carolina	25	20 (5)
New York	12	17 (2)
Rhode Island	45	13 (6)
Delaware	21	5 (1)
Massachusetts	24	8 (2)
Pennsylvania	18	6 (1)
Connecticut	36	0 (0)
Maryland	18	0 (0)

NOTE: Figures in parentheses are Ns for each colony.

of her forty-five Speakers, or 76 percent had previously served less than five years. By comparison, only three of Maryland's eighteen Speakers (17 percent) had previously served less than five years.

Other offices held: colony-wide, local, or both. Among innumerable colony-wide offices would be provincial secretary; surveyor general; receiver general; attorney general; treasurer; councilman; colonial agent (as in the case of Peyton Randolph); the chief justiceship, or membership on a court with colony-wide jurisdiction; and senior militia officers named, as in Connecticut, by the legislature or, more usually, by the governor. Local offices include the many town and county positions, such as selectman, alderman, town councilman, the various surveyors, commissioners, lower militia officers, sheriff, coroner, and vestryman. Justices of the peace—though named, as in Virginia, by

TABLE 3

Additional offices of 260 Speakers

Colony-wide		Local		Both		None	
N	%	N	%	N	%	N	%
64	25	57	22	121	46	18	7

the governor, or as in Connecticut by the Legislature and governor—
had local jurisdiction and are therefore considered local offices.

Of the 275 Speakers, the offices of 15 (5 percent) of them were not
ascertained. Nine of these unknowns are in Rhode Island (20 percent
of Rhode Island's 45 Speakers), 2 in New Hampshire (9 percent), and 4
in Delaware (19 percent).

Of the remaining 260 Speakers, the vast majority—185 (71 percent)—held colony-wide, or both colony-wide and local, offices before
becoming Speakers. Of the 75 remaining, 57 (76 percent) held local
offices; of these, New England supplied 30.

One of the eighteen men who held no previous office, William
Donning was elected Speaker of the South Carolina Commons House
of Assembly in 1731, the year of his arrival in the colony. In Pennsylvania, although the proprietors courted Benjamin Franklin and John
Kinsey, Jr., with office, antiproprietary speakers Edward Biddle and
Joseph Galloway appear to have held no office other than their assembly seats. Kinsey monopolized offices in Pennsylvania, his major residence, rather than in New Jersey, where his legal activities in that
colony's endemic land squabbles brought him election to the assembly
and the speakership.[11] William Trent, like Kinsey, active in Pennsylvania and New Jersey, devoted his major activities to the former colony.

In Rhode Island, six of the thirty-six Speakers about whose offices
information was obtained appear not to have been officeholders before
their assumption of the chair. These included the recent immigrant
and Baptist minister Jonathan Sprague of Providence, John Rogers,
Benjamin Newberry, Benedict Arnold, and the Wanton brothers, John
and William, who as young men started their political careers as assemblymen from Newport. The Wantons, of course, would later each
assume the colony-wide post of governor.[12]

Age of an individual when he first became Speaker. In some cases,
those of John Fenwick and Thomas Smith for example, approximate
birthdates, as given in such a work as the *Biographical Directory of the*

South Carolina House of Representatives, have been used. In other cases, Speakers' ages cannot be estimated. There are fifty-nine such cases, 21 percent of the total. Thirteen of these, 52 percent of her twenty-five speakers, are in South Carolina. The ages of seven of Georgia's nine Speakers (78%), five of North Carolina's fourteen (36%), eight of New Hampshire's twenty-three (35%), ten of Delaware's twenty-one (48%), four of Rhode Island's forty-five (9%), four of New York's twelve (33%), three of New Jersey's eighteen (17%), and one or two Speakers in the remaining colonies were not ascertained. Of the 21 percent of the Speakers whose ages were not obtained, South Carolina is responsible for 5 percent of the total; Delaware, 4 percent, New Hampshire, 3 percent; Georgia, 3 percent with smaller contributions by the other colonies. Clearly, generalizations about the Speakers' ages in South Carolina, Georgia, or Delaware are not tenable, and they are tenuous at best in North Carolina and New Hampshire. Overall, however, the 216 Speakers whose ages are known (78% of the total) are sufficiently distributed among the several colonies to allow tentative generalizations.

Over the whole period, the average age of the 216 Speakers whose ages were ascertained was 47. At the extremes, 6 of the Speakers were in their seventies and 7 in their twenties, or 3 percent for each age. Average age varied little among regions. New England's Speakers averaged 49 years; the South's, 42; and the Speakers of the Middle Colonies, 48. By colony, the average age of New Hampshire's speakers was highest: 52; South Carolina's, the lowest: 38.

Wealth: wealthy, well-to-do, moderate, poor in relation to a Speaker's locality at the time of his Speakership. Comparative wealth, then, is estimated strictly in terms of a particular place at a particular time. An Elisha Williams of Connecticut, wealthy in relation to the Wethersfield community of 1740, is not comparable in actual wealth to his Virginia contemporary, John Robinson, Jr., a planter and large landholder. Both, however, are wealthy, for purposes of the present study.

Landholding throughout the colonies is one important measure of wealth. For the southern region, number of slaves is another significant indicator. Slave ownership in South Carolina, for example, "constitutes the most accurate index or guide to wealth in the colonial period."[13] The South Carolina *Biographical Directory* gives the slave ownership of nine Speakers; their average holding is 116 slaves, whereas the average for the 373 legislators for whom slaveholding was ascertained is 92. Speakers for whom slave ownership is not given include such men as Peter Manigault, the wealthiest individual in

TABLE 4
Average age by colony

Colony	Average age	Colony	Average age
New Hampshire	52	Delaware	48
New Jersey	51	Connecticut	46
Pennsylvania	50	Georgia	43
Maryland	50	Virginia	41
Massachusetts	48	North Carolina	38
Rhode Island	48	South Carolina	38
New York	48		

Alice Hanson Jones's statistical study, *Wealth of a Nation to Be*; the wealthy lawyer Charles Pinckney; the wealthy sea captain-buccaneering trader William Rhett; and Benjamin Smith, "one of the wealthiest and most prominent of Charleston's merchant bankers." [14]

The *Biographical Dictionary of the Maryland Legislature, 1635– 1789*, volume 1, supplies the total estate values at death of Maryland's legislators, as well as wealth during an individual's lifetime. For example, at the time of his first election to the assembly, Kenelm Cheseldyne had something over 3,800 acres. William Dent's total estate value was over 3,000 pounds, and he held 6,000 acres, in contrast to the moderately wealthy merchant Robert Bradley, who appears to have held "at least 100 acres" at the time of his first election and who bequeathed 870 acres to his son before his death.

The *Dictionary of North Carolina Biography* supplies literary as well as statistical evidence as to wealth. John Baptiste Ashe, for example, with 5,000 acres, had a "considerable estate." The *Abstract of North Carolina Wills*, edited by J. Bryan Grimes (Raleigh, 1910) also contains information on the immensely wealthy Edward Moseley and on John Porter's estate. Likewise, *Abstracts of Wills and Other Records, Currituck and Dare Counties, North Carolina, 1663–1850*, Gordon C. Jones, compiler (Philadelphia, 1958), contains evidence of Richard Sanderson's wealth. The *Colonial Records of North Carolina*, edited by William Saunders, give William Downing's landholdings as 1,466 acres, on which he paid an annual quitrent of 25 pounds. Swanns, Moseleys, and Harveys made up the Albemarle Sound area's local aristocracy, the Moores and Ashes being among the dominant Pamlico families. [15]

Virginia's twelve Speakers included a Beverly, Harrison, Ludwell, Robinson, and Carter, and three Randolphs. Daniel McCarty emerged from his father's bankruptcy to political prominence and to at least

moderate wealth. John Holloway, likewise "a new man," seems to have
been unsuccessful in a hectic pursuit of wealth, having, in the words of
Sir John Randolph, "turned Projector and ruined himself." [16]

The Crown grant series for Georgia (particularly Pat Bryant, ed.,
*English Crown Grants in Christ Church Parish in Georgia, 1755–
1775* [Atlanta, 1973]) notes the large grants allotted to Grey Elliott,
Lewis Johnson, and Noble Wimberly Jones. The *Dictionary of American Biography* supplies information concerning Archibald Bulloch.

Turning to the Middle Colonies, New York's Speakers, including
Adolph Philipse; Lewis Morris, Jr.; two Nicolls; and two Livingstons;
like Virginia's, comprised a roster of the colony's mercantile and landed
wealth. New Jersey inventories are available in William A. Whitehead,
et al., eds., *Archives of the State of New Jersey . . .* (Newark, 1880–
1928), vols. 23 and 33. Based on these lists, Thomas L. Purvis calcu-
lates that 93 percent of New Jersey's assemblymen elected after 1737
were in the wealthiest tenth of the population. Assembly leaders were
in the top 2 percent. The median value of all probated inventories
was approximately 175 pounds. Speaker Fretwell left 1,125 pounds;
Thomas Gardiner, 930 pounds; and William Trent, 1100 pounds, including nine Negro and two Indian slaves. [17]

As for Pennsylvania, Gary Nash ranks such as Dickinson, Lloyd,
Yeates, Norris, and Langhorne among Pennsylvania's wealthy men.
Later individuals, including the second Norris, Hamilton, Galloway,
Franklin, and Fox were of near or equal stature. [18] Delawarians include
Thomas Noxon, owner of 3,000 acres and one of the colony's finest
mansions; John Vining, whose estate was valued at over 1,908 pounds
and who owned seventeen slaves; Jehu Curtis, "a leading citizen
of New Castle"; wealthy landholder William Clark; and Thomas Mc-
Kean, owner of more than 2,000 acres. [19]

According to Alice Hanson Jones, of the three regions, New England was the poorest in aggregate physical wealth. Excluding slaves,
"the wealth of the South, at 60.9 pounds per white head, is 63 percent
greater than that of New England." [20] New England's Speakers, by and
large, reflect this division. They tend also to fall into a pattern described by Edward Cook, Jr.: Cook writes, "The data suggest that the
richest men lived in towns where the centralizing influence of commercial and political activities was strongest, and that leading men
from towns where political and economic activities were more lo-
calized were of more modest means." [21]

The probate of New Hampshire's Meshech Weare's estate, for example, lists an inventory valued at over 953 pounds, which puts him
near the richest 1 percent of New England's probated population of

1774.[22] The Weares, three of whom were Speakers, were a leading family of Hampton, as were the Gilmans of Exeter (two Speakers). Pickerings, Penhallows, Waldrons, Wiggins, all belonged, as David Van Deventer points out, among New Hampshire's economic elite.[23]

Connecticut and Rhode Island likewise sent their wealthiest men to the assemblies: Burrs, Pitkins, Huntingtons, Sillimans, Talcotts, and Wadsworths, and others for Connecticut; Greenes, Willetts, Hopkins, Coddingtons, Cranstons, Arnolds for Rhode Island. Boston's commercial elite shared the Massachusetts speakership with leading men of the towns, such as James Otis of Barnstable and John Quincy of Braintree.[24]

Of the 275 Speakers, the economic positions of 35 (13%) were not determined. Five of these are Georgia Speakers (56% of that colony's total), 5 are in Massachusetts (21%), 9 in Delaware (43%), 4 in Connecticut (11%), 6 in Rhode Island (31%), 3 in North Carolina (21%), and 1 and 2 in New Hampshire and Pennsylvania respectively. With the exception of Georgia, Delaware, and Rhode Island, it is possible to make useful generalizations based on the known economic standing of the remaining 240 Speakers distributed rather evenly over the other ten colonies.

Of these, 212 were either wealthy or well-to-do in terms of their period and locale. Though the line between "wealthy" and "well-to-do" is hardly absolute, some 91 Speakers appear to fall in the latter class, 122 in the former. Only 27 (11 percent) may be labeled moderately wealthy; none was poor. A distinct difference emerges between the New England colonies on the one hand and the Middle and Southern colonies on the other, as the following table indicates.

A breakdown by colonies of those Speakers whose wealth was ascertained indicates that all eleven of North Carolina's Speakers and four of Georgia's were in the wealthy category. In fact, in all of the colonies except Connecticut and Rhode Island, over 90 percent of the Speakers were either wealthy or well-to-do.

Social Status: prominent, not prominent. Wealth in colonial America was the chief bestower of status within the community. "The indigenous class structure," writes Jackson Turner Main, "was based upon property rather than inherited status. When a new prestige order was created, it corresponded closely with economic classes." The rule of wealth is invariable as it applies to the second generation and beyond. The nouveaux riches may not achieve prestige commensurate with their possessions. Generalizing from his Virginia findings, Main comments that "it was rare for any parvenu to achieve eminence

TABLE 5
Economic status by region

Region	Wealthy		Well-to-do		Moderate		Poor	
	N	%	N	%	N	%	N	%
New England	31	28	59	53	22	19	0	0
Middle Colonies	42	72	14	25	2	3	0	0
Southern Colonies	49	70	18	26	3	4	0	0

among the landholders."[25] His family would "arrive," however, with the acceptance of his son into the ruling class.

The descendants of early settlers, town proprietors in New England, and beneficiaries of proprietary and crown grants inherited social status with their wealth. The Pitkin, Burr, and Huntington families of the Connecticut towns of Hartford, Fairfield, and Norwich provide striking testimony regarding inherited status. The Burrs and Huntingtons were founders of their towns; the first Pitkin married into one of Hartford's proprietary families. These families alone provided six of Connecticut's Speakers.[26]

As the above example indicates, one could marry status as well as inherit it.[27] Numerous literary sources, including genealogies and biographies, provide evidence concerning the Speakers' family connections. An example of a parvenu who made it through marriage is South Carolina's Rawlins Lowndes. His marriage into the Elliott family gave him the status to which his great abilities alone may not have carried him.[28] Benjamin Franklin is perhaps the best example of one whose abilities and achievements were yet insufficient to place him within the charmed circle of Philadelphia society. His common-law marriage to Deborah Read could hardly have enhanced his social status.[29]

Of the 275 Speakers, the social positions of 20 (7 percent) were not ascertained. Eight of these are Delaware Speakers (38% of the Delaware total). Four are in Massachusetts (17%), three in Rhode Island (7%), three in North Carolina (21%), and two in Georgia (22%). With the exception of Delaware, then, useful generalizations can be made on the basis of the 255 Speakers whose status is known.

Of these, the overwhelming majority enjoyed prominent social status by the time they took the chair. Of 255 ascertained cases, 207 (81%) were socially prominent. Forty-seven (18%) lesser individuals managed to gain the speakership. These range from South Carolina's Job Howe, who according to a political opponent had been a "linkboy

TABLE 6
Economic status by colony

Colony	Wealthy		Well-to-do		Moderate	
	N	%	N	%	N	%
North Carolina	11	100	0	0	0	0
Georgia	4	100	0	0	0	0
Delaware	10	83	2	17	0	0
South Carolina	18	72	6	24	1	4
New Jersey	12	72	5	28	0	0
Pennsylvania	11	69	4	25	1	6
New York	8	67	3	25	1	8
Maryland	11	61	6	33	1	6
New Hampshire	10	46	11	50	1	4
Virginia	5	42	6	50	1	8
Massachusetts	8	42	10	53	1	5
Rhode Island	8	20	17	44	14	36
Connecticut	5	16	21	66	6	18

and barber in London," to the formidable upstart Benjamin Franklin of Pennsylvania.[30] South Carolina's ratio of nonprominent to prominent Speakers, in fact, was slightly higher than the average: one to three as against one to four (6 of her 25 Speakers). Most of the nonprominent Speakers appear quite early in her history; other than Howe, they include such men as Jonathan Amory, born in 1654, the son of a Bristol merchant; and James Risbee, about whose background little is known.[31]

Connecticut, Pennsylvania, and Delaware likewise have higher ratios of nonprominent to prominent Speakers than the average, as the following table makes clear. Finally, in looking at a cross-section of the Speakers on particular dates, it appears that the ratio of prominent to nonprominent, though dropping slightly from 1700 to 1725, rises towards the end of the period. Making due allowance for the fact that in one year there are, of course, very few Speakers, the data are nonetheless suggestive.

Residence: urban or rural. For purposes of this study, the term "urban" applies to the major seaboard cities, as well as to those other communities which in function and population density contrast with the farm or plantation. "Urbanization," writes Eric E. Lampard, "is conceived as a societal process resulting in the formation of cities."[32] Such a process can be traced almost from the first settlements. James T. Lemon's description of the early towns of southeastern Pennsylvania

TABLE 7

Social status by colony

Colony	Total number of Speakers	Socially prominent		Not prominent	
		N	%	N	%
New Jersey	18	17	94	1	6
New Hampshire	23	21	91	2	9
New York	12	11	92	1	8
Maryland	18	16	89	2	11
Georgia	7	6	86	1	14
Massachusetts	20	17	85	3	15
Rhode Island	42	35	83	7	17
Virginia	12	10	83	2	17
North Carolina	11	9	82	2	18
Delaware	13	10	77	3	23
South Carolina	25	19	76	6	24
Connecticut	36	25	69	11	31
Pennsylvania	18	12	67	6	33

and adjacent Delaware is applicable to much of colonial America: "In these urban places," Lemon writes, "farmers and other rural folk traded with merchants, shopkeepers and craftsmen, transacted their public business, and interacted socially with one another. Town dwellers provided some of the key connecting links with the outside world."[33]

In New Hampshire, for example, I have considered Portsmouth, Exeter, Kingston, and Hampton as urban communities. In Connecticut such communities include New London, Hartford, New Haven, Milford, Middletown, and Norwich. Though almost one-half of Massachusetts' Speakers came from urban Boston, others represented urban communities such as Salem and Cambridge. Rhode Island urban centers include Providence, Newport, Bristol, and Portsmouth. The city of Philadelphia provided most of Pennsylvania's Speakers. Likewise, the city of New York dominated the speakership in that colony, while men such as William Nicoll II lived on their estates in Suffolk, Westchester, or other adjacent counties. I have considered New Castle, Dover, and Lewes as urban centers in Delaware.

Urban centers were far fewer in the five Southern colonies. In Maryland, for example, although Robert Ungle was a merchant in the town of Oxford, Talbott County on the eastern shore was, of course, a predominantly rural area. Virginia's Speakers were mainly rural, though Sir John and Peyton Randolph resided for the most part at Williamsburg. Each derived his principal income and reputation from

TABLE 8
Social status in selected years

Year	Socially prominent		Not prominent	
	N	%	N	%
1700	8	89	1	11
1725	11	79	3	21
1750	10	83	2	17
1775	11	92	1	8

nonrural pursuits. With the exception of John Hodgson of Edenton in Chowan County, I have considered the other Speakers in North Carolina to be rural. Edward Mosely, likewise a Chowan County attorney, was a planter and according to Governor Burrington, "the great land-jobber of this Countrey."[34] Men such as John Harvey and Samuel Swann, attorneys who speculated in land and had mercantile interests, were also planters whose primary residence was rural.

Charleston, South Carolina, was the most distinctively urban center of the several Southern colonies. Men like Jonathan Amory, John Fenwick, and Thomas Hepworth were Charleston merchants and lawyers. Other Speakers were merchant-planters who divided their activities between their estates and their governmental and mercantile pursuits in the city. Thomas Broughton of Mullberry Plantation and William Donning of Woodbury and Weston Hall are among South Carolina's seven Speakers whose principal residence may be said to be rural.

Several Speakers of the Georgia Assembly, like their South Carolina counterparts, divided their interests between their plantations and the capital city. Such men as Archibald Bulloch, William Little, and Grey Elliott appear to have had their principal residence in Savannah; they have therefore been listed in the urban category.

Of the 275 Speakers, the residences of 10 (4%) were not ascertained. Seven of these are in Delaware (33% of Delaware's total), 3 (33%) in Georgia. Rural residence predominated among the 265 Speakers whose residence could be judged. One hundred forty-three (54%) of the Speakers were rural; 121 (46%) were urban. In those colonies with major urban centers, those centers accounted for a high percentage of Speakers, as the table shows.

A breakdown by colony reflects the influence of these major urban centers. In this connection, although South Carolina's Speakers and other leading men had several residences, Charleston nevertheless appears to be the seat of eighteen of her Speakers' principal activities.

TABLE 9
Speakers from dominant urban centers

Urban center	Speakers from urban center	Total Speakers from colony
Portsmouth	12	23
Newport	14	45
Boston	10	24
New York	5	12
Philadelphia	10	18
Charleston	18	25

The residency of the Speakers appears to be increasingly urban through the century. The figures are at best only suggestive due to the small number of Speakers in any single year.

National origin: the country, or other English colony, from which a Speaker emigrated. If he was native to his colony, the nationality of his forebears.

The striking fact about the national origins of the 272 Speakers whose origins were determined is the difference between the New England colonies and the other nine. Overall, 153 Speakers (56%) were English and native to the colonies. But in New England, 84% were native colonial English. All of Connecticut's Speakers were native colonial English, 96% of Massachusetts's Speakers (22 of 23; the one non-native was an emigrant from England); 75% of Rhode Island's (33 of 44; 9 others were English, though not native Rhode Islanders); and 70% of New Hampshire's Speakers were native English.

In the Middle Colonies, only eighteen of the total sixty-eight Speakers (27%) were English and native to their colonies. In the South, the figure is 37%, or twenty-nine out of seventy-eight speakers. Both of these regions show far higher proportions of emigrants from England or other English colonies than is the case for New England.

The rest are a scattering of Welsh (one), colonial Swedish (one), colonial French (one), immigrant Scotch-Irish (two), other Irish (three), Dutch (three), and German (one).

New York had the highest number of Speakers whose background was other than English: five out of twelve (42%). They were: John Cruger, German; Abraham Gouvernour and Adolphus Philipse, both of Dutch background; James Graham, a Scot; and David Jones, Irish. New Jersey followed, with five of eighteen (28%) non-English Speakers: Andrew Johnstone, John Johnstone, Thomas Gordon, Cortland

TABLE 10
Residency by colony

Colony	Urban		Rural	
	N	%	N	%
Delaware	10	56	8	44
South Carolina	18	72	7	28
Georgia	4	67	2	33
Pennsylvania	10	56	8	44
New Jersey	10	56	8	44
Rhode Island	24	53	21	47
New Hampshire	12	52	11	48
Massachusetts	12	50	12	50
New York	6	50	6	50
Connecticut	13	36	23	64
Virginia	2	17	10	83
North Carolina	1	7	13	93
Maryland	0	0	18	100

Skinner, and William Trent—all Scots. Delaware is next with four of twenty (20%): James Coutts, John French, Andrew Hamilton—all Scottish, and Thomas McKean, Scotch-Irish. Four (22%) of Pennsylvania's Speakers were non-English: two Scots, Andrew Hamilton and William Trent; John Morton, who was of Swedish background; and a Welshman, David Lloyd. South Carolina's three non-English Speakers (12%) were the Scots James Michie and George Logan and the Scotch-Irish Andrew Rutledge.

Finally, to complete the roster of non-English Speakers, there were in Rhode Island Benjamin Barton and Daniel Ayrault, Jr., of Dutch and French background respectively; in Virginia, Daniel McCarty, and in North Carolina, John Campbell, both of whom were Irish.

Occupation. Typically in the Southern colonies, a Speaker would be involved in several occupations. In such cases, I have listed what appear to have been his chief sources of income. The same principle is followed for the other colonies where an involvement in several occupations was not uncommon. The occupations of thirty-eight (14%) of the Speakers were not ascertained. Seven of these are from Massachusetts (29% of Massachusetts's 24 Speakers), three from Delaware (14%), six from Connecticut (17%), fourteen from Rhode Island (31%), two from North Carolina (14%), four from Georgia (44%), and one each from New Hampshire and Pennsylvania.

An occupational profile of the Speakers is complicated by the fact

TABLE 11

Residency in selected years

	Urban		Rural	
Year	N	%	N	%
1700	3	33	9	67
1725	5	36	9	64
1750	8	61	5	39
1775	7	58	5	42

TABLE 12

Speakers of English national origin, New England

	Conn.		Mass.		N.H.		R.I.	
Origin	N	%	N	%	N	%	N	%
Native English	36	100	22	96	16	70	33	75
Non-native English	0	0	1	4	6	26	9	20
TOTAL	36	100	23	100	22	96	42	95

TABLE 13

Speakers of English national origin, Middle Colonies

	N.Y.		N.J.		Pa.		Del.	
Origin	N	%	N	%	N	%	N	%
Native English	3	25	7	39	4	22	4	20
Non-native English	4	33	6	33	10	56	12	60
TOTAL	7	58	13	72	14	78	16	80

TABLE 14

Speakers of English national origin, Southern Colonies

	Md.		Va.		S.C.		N.C.		Ga.	
Origin	N	%	N	%	N	%	N	%	N	%
Native English	11	61	7	58	7	28	4	27	0	0
Non-native English	6	33	4	33	15	60	9	64	9	100
TOTAL	17	94	11	91	22	88	13	91	9	100

TABLE 15
Occupations of Speakers

Occupation	Total Speakers		Multi-occupation		Sole occupation	
	N	%	N	%	N	%
Attorney	71	30	32	14	39	16
Large landowner	43	18	23	10	20	8
Planter	55	23	44	19	11	5
Farmer	18	7	7	3	11	5
Merchant	83	35	45	19	38	16
Artisan	5	2	0	0	5	2
Minister	4	2	3	1	1	1
Manufacturer	8	3	4	2	4	2
Doctor	12	5	2	1	10	4
Surveyor	6	2	2	1	4	2
Other professional[a]	15	6	11	5	4	2
Miscellaneous	14	6	8	3	6	3

[a] In this and the following tables, "Other professional" includes occupations such as gentleman, pharmacist, professor, and school headmaster.

that, of the 237 individuals whose occupations are known, eighty-five (36%) had more than one occupation. Speakers frequently combined two or more such pursuits as land speculation, planting, trade, and the law. John Robinson, Jr., of Virginia; attorney, planter, merchant, and organizer of two western land ventures (the Loyal Land Company and the Greenbrier Company) is an archetypal example.

Table 15 indicates the number of Speakers over the whole period found in each occupational category. Because of the overlapping occupations, the first column adds up to more than the 237 known Speakers. It is noteworthy that 30% of the Speakers were lawyers, 35% merchants. Thirty-eight, or not quite half of the merchants, appear not to have combined their mercantile interests with other interests.

The average number of occupations per Speaker is higher for the South (1.8 occupations per Speaker) than for the Middle Colonies (1.3) or New England (1.2). Forty-one (61%) of the South's Speakers were planters, eleven of them to the practical exclusion of other pursuits; but most were also merchants, lawyers, or both.

In this connection, the category "miscellaneous" clearly implies multi-occupations. There are not so many of these hard-to-categorize Speakers as seriously to influence the above tables. "Miscellaneous" is reserved for such entrepreneurs as the publisher, printer, and paper dealer, Benjamin Franklin; or New Jersey's Charles Read, who pursued iron manufacturing, farming, and a legal career. Pennsylvania's David

TABLE 16
Occupations by region: New England
(N = 100)

Occupation	Total Speakers		Multi-occupation		Sole occupation	
	N	%	N	%	N	%
Attorney	16	16	7	7	9	9
Large landowner	12	12	2	2	10	10
Planter	0	0	0	0	0	0
Farmer	11	11	3	3	8	8
Merchant	36	36	9	9	27	27
Artisan	5	5	0	0	5	5
Minister	4	4	3	3	1	1
Manufacturer	7	7	3	3	4	4
Doctor	7	7	0	0	7	7
Surveyor	6	6	2	2	4	4
Other professional	12	12	8	8	—	4
Miscellaneous	5	5	1	1	4	4

Lloyd was principally an attorney, but he was also a land speculator and landlord, with varied business interests. Rhode Island's Wanton brothers seem to have been involved in every facet of Newport's economic activities. Finally, South Carolina's Robert Hume combined a legal career in Charleston with complex business dealings chiefly having to do with land speculation. Hume's mixing of business and politics ultimately led to scandal and his political demise.

As for single-occupation Speakers, it may be noteworthy that there are fewer in the South (30% of her seventy-two Speakers) than in the Middle Colonies (75%), or in New England (83%). None of the South's merchants, for example, was a merchant only. The highest percentage of attorneys—single- or multi-occupational Speakers—is in the Middle Colonies: twenty-nine of her sixty-five Speakers (45%).

A look at the Speakers' occupations by quarter-century cross-sections —keeping in mind that one Speaker could have more than one occupation—shows a marked increase in the number of attorney-Speakers. Other categories, such as merchants and planters, appear to have held steady throughout the colonial period.

A significant number of Speakers were clearly entrepreneurial types, men who generally sought out the ways to wealth available to them. It seems clear that men on the make, rather than philosopher-kings, dominated the several Chairs of England's American colonies.

Religion. The religions of forty-nine (18%) of the Speakers were not ascertained. Seven of these are in New Hampshire (30% of New Hamp-

TABLE 17
Occupations by region: Middle Colonies
(N = 65)

Occupation	Total Speakers		Multi-occupation		Sole-occupation	
	N	%	N	%	N	%
Attorney	29	45	8	12	21	32
Large landholder	22	34	12	18	10	15
Planter	0	0	0	0	0	0
Farmer	7	11	4	6	3	5
Merchant	17	26	6	9	11	17
Artisan	1	1	0	0	1	1
Manufacturer	1	1	1	1	0	0
Doctor	2	3	1	1	1	1
Surveyor	0	0	0	0	0	0
Other professional	1	1	1	1	0	0
Miscellaneous	4	6	2	3	2	3

TABLE 18
Occupations by region: Southern Colonies
(N = 72)

Occupation	Total Speakers		Multi-occupation		Sole occupation	
	N	%	N	%	N	%
Attorney	26	36	17	24	9	12
Large landholder	9	13	9	13	0	0
Planter	55	76	44	61	11	15
Farmer	0	0	0	0	0	0
Merchant	30	41	30	42	0	0
Artisan	0	0	0	0	0	0
Manufacturer	0	0	0	0	0	0
Doctor	3	4	1	1	2	3
Surveyor	0	0	0	0	0	0
Other professional	2	3	2	3	0	0
Miscellaneous	5	7	5	7	0	0

TABLE 19
Occupations in selected years

Year	Total Speakers	Attorneys		Merchants		Planters	
		N	%	N	%	N	%
1700	8	2	25	3	38	3	38
1725	12	5	42	4	33	3	25
1750	12	9	75	3	25	3	25
1775	12	6	50	4	33	3	25

TABLE 20
Religion by region

Religion	New England N	New England %	Middle Colonies N	Middle Colonies %	Southern Colonies N	Southern Colonies %
Anglican	11	11	26	42	61	93
Presbyterian	1	1	8	14	2	3
Congregational	66	66	—	—	1	2
Dutch Reformed	—	—	3	5	—	—
Quaker	10	10	21	36	1	2
Baptist	12	12	—	—	—	—
Free Thought	—	—	2	3	—	—

shire's twenty-three Speakers), three in Massachusetts (12%), six in Delaware (29%), sixteen in Rhode Island (36%), three in New York (25%), six in Georgia (67%), one each in Connecticut and Maryland, and two each in the Carolinas and Virginia.

Of the 226 Speakers whose religion is known, 98 (43%) were Anglicans. Congregationalism was the second most numerous denomination with 61 votaries, 30% of the whole. The Speakers' religious preferences, however, varied markedly by region, as indicated in table 20.

As for individual colonies, Massachusetts's Speakers were 100% Congregational; Virginia's, 100% Anglican. Of the New England colonies, Rhode Island shows the broadest mix: 24% Anglican, 35% Quaker, and 41% Baptist. Rhode Island, not surprisingly, is the only colony in which Baptists obtained the speakership.

Education: formal training, college or university; formal training, pre-college; self-educated. The educational background of the Speakers was the most difficult to derive of all the categories. All the Speakers were literate; probably most were self-educated, yet firm evidence is lacking. Jackson Turner Main's observations with regard to the Revolutionary-generation assemblymen would be even more appropriate for the earlier period. "Presumably," Main writes, "almost all of the legislators could read and write and had acquired a minimal education. The sources seldom reveal much about the educational background of the Revolutionary generation, because most men learned at home. The records do identify college men, and in addition they sometimes indicate when one had received a superior education without attending college."[35] I have included attendance at the Inns of Court as "superior education" on a par with college or university training.

Although I found no information on 187 of the 275 Speakers (68%), the evidence concerning the remaining 88 seems significant. Because of

TABLE 21
Religion by colony

	New England							
	N.H.		Mass.		Conn.		R.I.	
Religion	N	%	N	%	N	%	N	%
Anglican	4'	25	0	0	0	0	7	24
Presbyterian	0	0	0	0	1	3	0	0
Congregational	12	75	21	100	34	97	0	0
Dutch Reformed	0	0	0	0	0	0	0	0
Quaker	0	0	0	0	0	0	10	35
Baptist	0	0	0	0	0	0	12	41
Free Thought	0	0	0	0	0	0	0	0

	Middle Colonies							
	N.J.		Pa.		Del.		N.Y.	
	N	%	N	%	N	%	N	%
Anglican	8	44	5	28	10	67	3	33
Presbyterian	3	18	0	0	2	13	3	33
Congregational	0	0	0	0	0	0	0	0
Dutch Reformed	0	0	0	0	0	0	3	33
Quaker	7	41	11	61	3	20	0	0
Baptist	0	0	0	0	0	0	0	0
Free Thought	0	0	2	11	0	0	0	0

	Southern Colonies									
	S.C.		N.C.		Ga.		Md.		Va.	
	N	%	N	%	N	%	N	%	N	%
Anglican	21	91	11	92	3	10	15	88	10	100
Presbyterian	0	0	0	9	0	0	2	12	0	0
Congregational	1	9	0	9	0	0	0	0	0	0
Dutch Reformed	0	0	0	9	0	0	0	0	0	0
Quaker	0	0	1	8	0	0	0	0	0	0
Baptist	0	0	0	0	0	0	0	0	0	0
Free Thought	0	0	0	0	0	0	0	0	0	0

the high number of unknowns in this category, a tabular summary may
be appropriate (table 22).

Of the entire group of 275 Speakers, 52 (19%) had some formal education at the college or university level or at one of the Inns of Court.
Fourteen (5%) had formal precollegiate training. Evidence exists that
21 (8%) were self-educated; in fact, probably 75% of them were self-
educated.

Of the thirty-nine New England Speakers whose educational back-

TABLE 22
Speakers of unknown educational background

Colony	Number of Speakers	Education unknown	Percentage	Colony	Number of Speakers	Education unknown	Percentage
Rhode Island	45	40	89	Delaware	21	13	62
New Hampshire	23	18	78	Maryland	18	15	83
Connecticut	36	21	58	Virginia	12	5	42
Massachusetts	24	9	37	North Carolina	14	12	86
New York	12	8	67	South Carolina	25	20	80
New Jersey	18	11	61	Georgia	9	8	89
Pennsylvania	18	7	39				

ground was discovered, 79% attended a college or university—in most cases, Harvard. The educational background of thirty of the Middle Colonies' sixty-nine Speakers was ascertained. Thirty-eight percent of these had higher education; 21% formal training, precollege; and 41% were self-educated. The education of only eighteen of the South's seventy-eight Speakers could be discovered. Nine of these had college training, which, as above, probably indicates the total number of college-trained Speakers in that area. Five had precollege formal education, and four were self-educated.

It seems clear that New England had the highest percentage of college-educated Speakers, assuming that those Speakers whose education is in the "unknown" category were not college graduates. Any other conclusions must be conjectural, for instance, that the Middle Colonies were next in percentage of college-educated Speakers and the southern region, last.

The number and percentage of Speakers with formal education in individual colonies is shown in table 23, which assumes that none of the unknowns attended formal educational institutions.

World View: "localist" versus "cosmopolitan." These terms are drawn from Jackson Turner Main's *Political Parties Before the Constitution*, cited above. A cosmopolitan displays breadth of intellectual interests through ownership of a library, authorship, extensive travel and correspondence, scientific curiosity, or the like. A localist lacks these interests and experiences. An effort was made to differentiate between men for whom no evidence is available and those who can, with reasonable certitude, be judged localists.

Of the ninety-two unknowns (33% of the total), the majority were undoubtedly localist. Eleven of the ninety-two are in New Hampshire

TABLE 23
Education by colony

Colony	Formal education	% of Speakers	Colony	Formal education	% of Speakers
Massachusetts	14	58	Pennsylvania	4	22
Virginia	5	42	Maryland	3	17
Connecticut	12	33	South Carolina	4	16
New Jersey	6	33	North Carolina	2	14
New York	3	25	Rhode Island	3	7
Delaware	5	24	Georgia	0	0
New Hampshire	5	22			

(48% of the New Hampshire Speakers), fourteen in Massachusetts (58%), ten in Delaware (48%), sixteen in Connecticut (44%), eleven in South Carolina (44%), nine in North Carolina (64%), and seven in Georgia (78%). The remaining three are one each in Pennsylvania, Maryland, and New Jersey.

Overall, 109 (60%) of the Speakers whose world view could be judged were localists. Because cosmopolitan Speakers would be the more identifiable, the probability is that most of the ninety-two Speakers whose world view was not ascertained were also localists. On that assumption, we have posited some 77% of the total 275 Speakers as localists. Seventy-four (27%) were cosmopolitan in outlook.

A breakdown by regions, again assuming the unknowns to be localists, indicates that both the Middle Colonies (34%) and the southern colonies (33%) had a higher percentage of cosmopolitan speakers than the New England colonies (19%) [table 24]. The differences are accentuated when the unknowns are subtracted (tables 25 and 26).

Party: "imperial" versus "local." A speaker described as "imperial" served the interests of the Crown or proprietor. "Local" refers to the Speaker's support of assembly demands contrary to the wishes of royal or proprietary authority. Such a Speaker would strive to further local interests—the freedom to cut New Hampshire's white pines, the issuance of paper money in Pennsylvania and other colonies, tobacco inspection laws in Virginia and Maryland—as against the commercial interests of the mother country, interests which governors, councils, and other agents of the royal or proprietary prerogative were supposed to protect.[36]

Because of the formal nature of the Assembly journals, a Speaker's political stance is extremely difficult to document, even though the

TABLE 24
World view by region

Region	N	Localist		Cosmopolitan		
		N	%	N	%	(Unknown)
New England	128	104	81	24	19	(47)
Middle Colonies	69	45	65	24	35	(17)
Southern Colonies	78	52	67	26	33	(28)

NOTE: Those of unknown world view are tabulated as localists.

TABLE 25
World view by region, revised

Region	N	Localist		Cosmopolitan	
		N	%	N	%
New England	81	57	70	24	30
Middle Colonies	52	28	54	24	46
Southern Colonies	50	24	48	26	52

NOTE: Those of unknown world view have been excluded.

TABLE 26
Cosmopolitans by colony

Colony	N	%	Colony	N	%	Colony	N	%
N.C.	4	80	Ga.	1	50	Pa.	5	29
S.C.	11	78	N.J.	9	53	R.I.	11	28
Va.	8	75	N.Y.	3	43	Conn.	3	15
Del.	7	64	N.H	4	33	Md.	2	12
Mass.	6	60						

office itself is usually prima facie evidence of his power within the prevailing majority faction. As in the case of world view, however, it seemed best not to categorize on the basis of such presumptive evidence. Sixty-one (22% of the whole) have unknown party affiliation. Twenty-three of these, or more than one-third, are in Connecticut (64% of Connecticut's thirty-six Speakers), though the majority, given Connecticut's corporate charter, must have been local in party sentiment. Seven are in Massachusetts (29%), six in Delaware (29%), nine in Rhode Island (20%), three in Georgia (33%), and the other thirteen were fairly evenly

TABLE 27
Party by region

Party	New England		Middle Colonies		Southern Colonies	
	N	%	N	%	N	%
Imperial	12	14	32	52	20	30
Local	74	86	30	48	46	70

divided: three in Virginia and New Hampshire, two in Maryland, South Carolina, and North Carolina, and one in New York.

Sixty-four (30%) of the 214 Speakers whose party was judged appear as imperial. One hundred fifty (70%) were local. The regional breakdown indicates that New England had the highest percentage of locally oriented Speakers, the South next, while the Speakers of the Middle Colonies were about evenly divided between imperialists and localists.

Of the individual colonies, New Hampshire and the two corporate colonies have the highest percentage of local-party Speakers. Proprietary Pennsylvania and Delaware, and, to a lesser extent, proprietary Maryland, have a high percentage of Speakers in the proprietary interest.

Based upon the available data, the following picture of the typical colonial Speaker emerges. He is wealthy or well-to-do, about forty-seven years old, from a socially prominent family, and a veteran of other important offices. He is of English origin, more likely native to his colony than not. He would probably be a Church of England man, though his religion would vary from colony to colony.

Most of the Speakers appear to have been provincial in their outlook. Their residence was more likely rural than urban, though urban centers, considering their small populations, appear to have had a disproportionate influence in producing Speakers for the lower houses of assembly.

The Speakers, furthermore, tended to represent local rather than Crown or proprietary interests. This is not to say, however, that the typical Speaker was necessarily a strong partisan in politics. The chair, it is true, was generally captured by the more aggressive assemblymen, though in some cases Speakers were chosen less for their leadership abilities than because they represented a compromise in a bitterly divided Assembly. A case in point was the choice by the Pennsylvania Assembly of the seventy-eight-year-old John Wright, picked because Israel Pemberton, the leader of the pacifist faction, was too divisive a figure.[37]

TABLE 28
Party by colony

Colony	Imperial		Local		Colony	Imperial		Local	
	N	%	N	%		N	%	N	%
New Jersey	11	61	7	39	South Carolina	7	30	16	70
Pennsylvania	10	56	8	44	New York	3	27	8	73
Delaware	8	53	7	47	New Hampshire	3	15	17	85
Massachusetts	7	41	10	59	Virginia	1	11	8	89
Maryland	6	37	10	63	Connecticut	1	8	35	97
North Carolina	4	33	8	67	Rhode Island	1	3	35	97
Georgia	2	33	4	67					

As for occupation, the typical Speaker would be involved in agriculture, trade, the law, or some combination of these. Probably self-educated, and definitely literate, a Speaker would have served some six years in his assembly before being chosen by his colleagues. Like his tenure in office, his previous assembly service would lengthen as the colonial period drew to a close.

Such is a composite portrait of the colonial Speakers. The portrait is made up, however, of sometimes striking differences among regions and between colonies with regard to many of the categories.

Regional differences are particularly apparent with regard to religion and national origin. The typical southern Speaker was Anglican, and an immigrant from England or another English colony, whereas his New England counterpart was Congregational and native to his colony. Quakerism and Anglicanism predominated among Speakers from the Middle Colonies, who represented the greatest variation in national origins of the three regions.

As for wealth, the typical southern- or middle-colony Speaker was in the highest category; the typical New England Speaker was merely well-to-do. The situation is reversed with regard to education. The typical New England Speaker was a college graduate; his Middle-Colony or southern counterpart was more likely self-educated.

Another significant regional contrast concerns the category of occupations. Here, the typical southern Speaker was more likely to combine mercantile and planting activities, whereas his New England colleague pursued one career, usually trade, single-mindedly. In the Middle Colonies, there were also fewer multi-occupation Speakers, the law claiming more of them than in the other two regions. As for age, both the Middle-Colony Speaker and his New England counterpart hovered around forty-nine at the time of their election; at age forty-two, the typical southern Speaker was a comparative youngster.

TABLE 29

Summary: Typical Speaker by region

Characteristics	New England	Middle Colonies	Southern Colonies
Years of service	3.7	5.0	4.8
Previous years in Assembly	6.1	5.9	4.4
Held other offices	36.7%	42.6%	56.4%
Age	48.5	49.2	42.0
Wealth	Well-to-do	Wealthy	Wealthy
Social status	Prominent	Prominent	Prominent
Residence	Rural	Urban	Rural
National origin	Native English	Colonial English	Colonial English
Occupation	Merchant	Attorney	Merchant-Planter
Religion	Congregational	Anglican	Anglican
Education	Formal	Self-educated	Self-educated
World view	Localist	Localist	Localist
Party	Local	Imperial	Local

Revealing as regional differences may be, variations among individual colonies are even more significant. Within one region, such variations may be quite wide. Speakers in Connecticut and Rhode Island, for example, served in the chair fewer years than their colleagues in Massachusetts and New Hampshire. Two factors help explain this difference among the New England colonies: first, the corporate colonies' system of semiannual elections and second, the fairly consistent movement of their Speakers into the upper house.

On the other hand, there is a wide divergence between the two corporate colonies themselves with regard to a Speaker's years of assembly service previous to his obtaining the chair: 10.9 years for Connecticut, 3.1 years for Rhode Island. Connecticut Speakers fall well below Speakers in New Hampshire and Massachusetts in terms of wealth and social status. Such contrasts may be at least partially explained by institutional differences between royal and corporate colonies, and, perhaps more significantly, by the fact that a smaller percentage of Connecticut's Speakers represented urban communities than was the case in Massachusetts, Rhode Island, and New Hampshire.

There may also be some correlation between urban residence and world view. The dominance of Charleston as the residence of South Carolina's Speakers may help explain the high percentage of cosmopolitans who obtained the chair in the Commons House of Assembly.

Religious differences are as significant within, as among, the three regions. Congregationalism dominated both Massachusetts and Connecticut; Rhode Island Speakers, on the other hand, show great diversity in religious predilections; they included Quakers, Baptists, and Anglicans. New Hampshire was predominantly Congregational, but Anglicanism claimed one-fourth of her Speakers.

Of the religiously heterogeneous Middle Colonies, Delaware Speakers stand out as predominantly Anglican; those from Pennsylvania as predominantly Quaker. New York's Speakers were evenly divided among Anglicanism, Presbyterianism, and the Dutch Reformed Church. Only in the southern region was there religious homogeneity. Yet in the matter of the Speakers' national origin, the southern region shows significant variation—between Maryland, for example, with 61% native Speakers, and North Carolina, with only 27%. Such a difference may suggest something of the relative maturity of the two societies and their political institutions. It is noteworthy in this connection that of all the colonies Maryland's Speakers had the longest previous Assembly service, 11.2 years, North Carolina's Speakers only averaging 3.3 years. Maryland's Speakers also served twice the number of years in office as did North Carolina's. Finally, Maryland's Speakers were on the average fifty years old when they attained the chair, while North Carolina's averaged thirty-eight.

Such contrasts suggest that, for the study of political leadership in colonial America, differences between colonies may be more significant than regional differences. An exclusive look at the latter, in fact, may obscure the vivid chiaroscuro that was America's political landscape before the Revolution.

Nevertheless, some common themes do emerge among the thirteen colonies. The colonial Speakers throughout the period were generally men of wealth, standing, and ability. They were leaders in their local communities as well as on the colony-wide stage. They were men of broad and usually long political experience, and they commanded the respect of their legislatures as well as of their constituents, who generally returned them to office. Such men often went on to higher office, including, in the corporate colonies, the governorship.

During the course of the eighteenth century, such characteristics became even more marked. The office of Speaker of the House may frequently have represented the popular side of local and imperial issues, but its incumbents were anything but populists. Though there were exceptions—a few ordinary men who obtained the chair through extraordinary ability and timely seizure of opportunity—the Speakers by and large represented the colonial elite. The suffrage may have been fairly widespread throughout the period, but the colonial chair fails to fit the democratic model of colonial politics. It was a time when the dignity of the person coincided with the dignity of the office.

The colonial speakership is evidence of the workings of the politics of deference in prerevolutionary America. Only well after the Revolution would this popular office also become a democratic one. Then, not only within the states but also on the national scene, for which the colonial speakership provided a foundation, the democratic potential of the office was in fact fulfilled.

INTERCOLONIAL
LEADERSHIP

JESSICA KROSS

"Patronage Most Ardently Sought": The New York Council, 1665–1775

ON APRIL 5, 1756, New Yorkers learned the sad news:

To the unspeakable loss of his family and the public, on Friday evening last died the Honorable James Alexander, Esq.: in the sixty-fifth year of his age.

A gentleman in his disposition, generous, courteous and humane, delicate in his sense of honor, steadfast in friendship, of strict probity, temperate in his diet, and in business indefatigable. The relations of husband, father and master, he sustained with the highest reputation. In these parts of the world few men surpassed him either in the natural sagacity and strength of his intellectual powers or in his literary acquirements. In the mathematical sciences his researchs were very great. He was also eminent in his profession of the law; and equally distinguished in public affairs. He had the honor to serve the king in several important offices, and was a wise and faithful Councillor to his Majesty for the Provinces of New York and New Jersey. Always true to the interest of his country, well knowing that the rights of the Crown are the bulwark of the liberties of the people; that the liberties of the people are the safety and honor of the Crown, and that a just temperament of both in the administration of government constitutes the health of the political body. His zeal for the defence of the public against the common enemy, led him to Council when he was not sufficiently recovered from the gout. From thence, he brought those mortal symptoms that closed his days, within about a week. His remains are to be interred this evening, in his family vault.[1]

James Alexander's obituary served two purposes. First, it told New Yorkers that one of their own had died. Second, it reaffirmed values, noting the virtues that colonial society deemed important and worth emulating. Alexander's strengths were both private and public. He was a gentleman of manners and kindness, honorable, trustworthy, honest, temperate, and hard-working. He served his King in many capacities, the most important being his seat on the royal council. There, and out of doors, he understood and helped maintain the balance between the Crown and the people, safeguarding both. Indeed, Alexander was the intelligence behind John Peter Zenger's *New-York Weekly Journal*, and the author of *A Brief Narrative of the Case and Tryal of John Peter Zenger*, "the most widely known source of libertarian thought in America during the eighteenth century." He died in public service, leaving a sickbed prematurely because duty called. What more could King or province ask of any man?[2]

Although obituaries can overstate a person's worth, they did not do so in this case. There was even more to James Alexander's public career than noted so briefly. *The New-York Weekly Mercury* identified Alexander's seat on the council as the apex of that career. Alluded to first in the designation "Honourable," this trust was mentioned twice more. No other office was specifically identified, although Alexander was recorder and surveyor general of New Jersey; deputy secretary, attorney general, and general assemblyman in New York. To the reading public of 1756, this particular seat summed up a noted man's achievements, and in a larger sense, articulated his status and his power.[3]

Historians, many of whom have discussed James Alexander, have had surprisingly little to say about the council. Indeed, it might be termed the forgotten branch of colonial government. Institutional studies such as Edgar A. Werner's *Civil List and Constitutional History of the Colony and State of New York* told what the council did, but always within the framework of the rising power of the general assembly. This theme, in fact, permeated all work on New York politics. Carl Becker, in his prodigiously influential study, *The History of Political Parties in the Province of New York, 1760–1776*, felt no need to mention the council at all.[4]

More recently, Douglas Greenberg, in his 1979 historiographic essay on New York, describes the interpretive trend toward pluralism and the instability it could foster. He concludes that Middle Colony politics were inherently unstable because "their societies were more complex, their elite groups more fragmented, and their institutions less completely legitimized by smooth, long-term operation and a shared fund of political culture and experience." This judgment overlooks the council's long history, and, as it turns out, relatively long individual tenures, but it reflects Greenberg's sources, which discuss governors, assemblys and Anglo-American politics but not councils. Perhaps

Nicholas Varga, in a fine and neglected unpublished dissertation, unwittingly lays out the paradox. Even as late as the 1770s, "when presumably all astute politicians should have known that 'real' power resided in the Assembly, the title of 'Councillor' was sought by men who later would be Whigs as well as Tories." Yet, Varga concludes, some 240 pages later, that the council was dulled by the 1750s, and by the early 1760s, "the Council had become a relatively withered limb in New York's government and politics."[5]

If historians' concerns, as reflected in their writing, are correct, why did James Alexander, by all accounts one of New York's most astute politicians, accept a council seat, and, even more to the point, fight to retain that seat once lost, finally giving up a place in the assembly to sit on the council? Maybe we need to look at the council again, concentrating not upon its fights with the assembly over revenue bills, or its support of the royal prerogative, but upon its functions, its rewards, and the men who held its seats.

In the evolution of colonial government, councils which gave their advice and consent often preceded elected assemblies. Indeed, in most of the earlier colonies, such as Virginia, Plymouth, Massachusetts Bay and New Netherland, the first government was a governor and council; assemblies came later. New York's experience with government by governor and council lasted longer than most. From 1665 to 1673, ten men, chosen by the governor, comprised the council. They were the administration. From 1673 to 1691, the number of councillors fluctuated. With the restoration of provincial government in 1691, the council was fixed at twelve members, where it would remain until Independence. It was then joined by a general assembly.[6]

The Council occupied a position similar in some ways to the House of Lords and the Privy Council. It was in fact neither. Nicholas Varga suggests that New Yorkers thought of government in terms of mayor, aldermen and assistants rather than King, lords and commons. Without lifetime tenure or hereditary claimants, the council was not "another distinct state or rank of people," as the assembly reminded it in 1711. However, assembly aside, it did more than just advise the governor. As the upper house, the council approved of bills. This role was somewhat compromised before 1735 when governors sat in on the legislative deliberations of the council. The Board of Trade forbade this practice, explaining to the King that it was "inconsistent with the tenor and intention of Your Majesty's Commission and Instructions."[7]

The independence of the second branch of government fit into contemporary theories about checks and balances of power in two ways.

Councillors were supposedly among the first men of the province. This necessitated an independent income. In 1702, for example, the Earl of Nottingham nominated Colonel Jeremiah Bass and Daniel Cox to the council. This recommendation was pointedly turned down, the Lords of Trade icily noting that "Councils should be men who have great estates and we do not hear of any estates that either Mr. Bass or Mr. Cox has in that Province." Why must men have wealth? So that they would not be tempted to put their own business before the public good. As early as 1711, Robert Hunter told the Lords of Trade that Chief Justice Roger Mompesson was "in such necessitous circumstances that it wants a virtue more than human to guard him against the temptation of corruption." In 1746 George Clinton wrote to the Duke of Newcastle, asking that His Majesty remove Daniel Horsmanden, he being "of no estate in the country and much in debt whereby he may be too much exposed to temptations, when the secrets of the Council are (at this time) of great importance." As any good student of country ideology knew, a necessitous man was a dependent man, one thus incapable of independent judgment.[8]

Not only was the council supposed to be economically secure, but its functions were also meant to be a check upon both the governor and the assembly. About 1745, Cadwallader Colden, a councillor himself and an avowed defender of the prerogative, wrote a treatise on the balance of power in government. In it he argued that colonial government was "in imitation of the King, Lords and Commons so far as the very great odds in circumstances will admit." Each branch limited the other. The council would never permit a governor to strengthen his power at the expense of the people, since that would jeopardize the liberty of the councillors' children. The big danger, Colden felt, lay in the pretensions of the General Assembly. Governors agreed. In 1774, Governor Tryon, in his closing speech to the council, thanked them for their support, but chided them for refusing to act as a buffer between him and the assembly. They should not pass bills that they then advised him to veto. This criticism prodded William Smith, Jr., to note the delicate position of the council. On the one hand, if the council "were considered as bound legislatively acting by instructions we should lose weight with the people and be perhaps rendered insignificant and our negative despised. That on the other hand if we went into a perfect independency as the Lords in Parliament we could by joining the Assembly render the Governor odious or contemptible."[9]

In its legislative capacity, the council passed or vetoed bills. However, the council also advised the governor, thereby acting as a privy council. Royal instructions limited the activities a governor could undertake by himself. The 1692 commission of Governor Benjamin Fletcher defined his council's role. They must advise and consent to summoning the assembly, and establishing and constituting courts. Most important, both their advice and consent was necessary for granting lands; spending money under the governor's warrant; and erecting fairs, markets and ports. The council's advice only was necessary for establishing quitrents, raising forts and castles, encouraging trade and the conversion of Negroes and Indians, and erecting public work houses. An additional discretionary clause authorized the governor, with the advice and consent of the council, to do whatever was necessary for the "advantage and security of our said Province." These instructions would remain the same throughout the colonial period.[10]

Finally, the council acted with the governor as a court for correction of errors and appeals. This appellate jurisdiction seems to have evoked little correspondence, perhaps because most of the cases which appeared before it could be appealed to England.[11]

Officially, the council was an upper house, a privy council which advised and consented, and a court. Less official, but possibly more powerful, were the councillors' informal roles as local advisors to foreign-born governors and as bankers to both governors and the province. Governors often arrived as strangers with little knowledge of the province's problems. In 1766, for example, Governor Henry Moore noted that Lieutenant Governor Cadwallader Colden had departed New York City right after Moore arrived. Moore complained to Secretary Conway, "I am left entirely to myself without the least personal knowledge of a single member of the council or any other person in office and without a possibility of getting a proper information of things as they then were." Knowledge was power, as councillors well knew, and their knowledge could mean the difference between a successful administration and an impotent one.[12]

In addition to inside advice governors needed money, sometimes for their own expenses, often for provincial affairs. Historians have recognized this need, especially in the early period. As Sung Bok Kim notes, "The Governor's council was not merely an executive, legislative, and judicial branch of government. It functioned also as a private lending agency from which the Governor could borrow money to carry out his responsibilities. Because the Councillors extended loans or rendered themselves as security for loans from others, the New York government avoided bankruptcy, and the colony was spared from ruin." Robert Livingston loaned money in the form of victuals for Governor Thomas Dongan in 1687 and 1688. In 1692, Governor Fletcher wrote to Mr. William Blathwayt, "I found the revenue much indebted, several sums of money taken upon the personal credit of the Councillors at 10 percent interest." In 1696, with the French threatening New York's borders, Stephen Van Cortlandt, Nicholas Bayard, Frederick Philipse, Gabriel Minvielle, and Caleb Heathcote each pledged £1,200 of their personal credit towards raising a fighting force. In 1701, Abraham DePeyster and Thomas Weaver did the same. Even as late as 1751 old patterns persisted, as Cadwallader Colden wrote to Governor Clinton that the double garrison at Oswego was left stranded until William Johnson advanced the money "by which a very large sum became due him for the Province." [13]

The council's legislative, executive, judicial and advisory roles were sufficient to make it a powerful body. The council, however, held still other attractions. Certainly, a council seat bestowed prestige, or legitimization of worth. It was the highest colonial office, other than those of governor and lieutenant governor, and was granted by the King upon the recommendation of the Board of Trade. Ideally, it meant recognition both at home and abroad, even though, in fact, favor and connection played a large part in gaining access to a seat.

Councillors enjoyed certain privileges. They were protected from lawsuits. When they held conferences with the assembly, the latter house always stood when a councillor entered. And when a member of the council died he usually received an obituary in the New York papers. This enhanced status was sought even by those presumably beyond such things. Sir Peter Warren, for example, said that he wanted the position because it gave him "rank above the commoner sort" and enabled his wife, the American-born Susannah DeLancey, precedence at balls and other social occasions. [14]

A council seat also brought more tangible rewards. First, it enabled men to benefit both legally and illegally from selective enforcement of the trade laws. Second, it placed them in a position to influence the governor's distribution of patronage. Third, and most important, the council controlled the distribution of New York's unclaimed lands. As William Smith, Jr., noted, "in the grant of all patents the Governor is bound to consult with them, and regularly they cannot pass the Seal without their advice." [15]

The vested interest that merchants had in flouting the Navigation Acts was well known to both governors and Whitehall. Smuggling and abetting piracy were of course easier with friends in high places. At least five councillors—Frederick and Adolphus Philipse, Samuel Staats, William Nicolls, and Nicholas Bayard—were accused of violating the trade acts, and Nicolls, with Governor Fletcher, was charged with actually aiding pirates. Lord Bellomont, intent on eradicating these excesses, noted his difficulties to the Lords of Trade by reporting that, "I shall have but small assistance from the Gentlemen of his Majesty's Council because they are most of them merchants, and several of themselves the persons concerned in the breach of these laws." New York City merchants were hardly the sole offenders. In Albany an illegal trade was carried out with the French and the Indians.[16]

The merchants benefited not only from their private trade but from government contracts. At least twenty-five members of the council, or 42 percent of the merchants on it, supplied the government with goods. Contracts were awarded during the four colonial wars and when circumstances required supplying materials to large numbers of people. In the seventeenth century, some of the most lucrative and most disgraceful transactions saw governors and contractors connive to defraud the men of the four independent companies stationed in New York by inflating prices and overstating the number of men actually provisioned. Because repayment from London could take forever, and was subject to political as well as atmospheric winds, contractors like Robert Livingston not only received interest on their unpaid balances, but, to quote Lawrence Leder, "other benefits in turn." Livingston received land, offices, and further contracts. The maintenance of the four companies gradually passed from the American contractors to the governors and then to the London merchants. During this last period, they subcontracted to their American correspondents, who included William Alexander and the firm of DeLancey and Watts.[17]

Contracts and trade brought immediate monetary rewards, once the bills were paid, but New Yorkers also realized longer term benefits from patronage. Everybody knew that a council seat helped establish a career for one's children. George Clarke, secretary of the province, was able to procure that extremely influential and lucrative position for his son. Indeed, between the two of them, they held the post for over seventy years. Cadwallader Colden, with a large family and modest estate by contemporary standards, used his influence to place his offspring. With wartime profits imminent in 1746, he recommended his son to the governor as commissary for provisions: "This as I take it will be more profitable than a Captain's commission as it usually has a good salary annexed to it but the commission cannot be made certain til the General arrive because perhaps he may have the nomination but though it should be so the Governor's interest with Captain Rutherford [another councillor] and my own may obtain it if he do not bring one with him."

Son Alexander Colden became surveyor general in place of his father. In 1749 the senior Colden asked that Governor Clinton grant his son John the office of storekeeper at the fort at Albany; in the next year, he requested that John be appointed clerk of the peace and of the Court of Common Pleas for Albany. In 1769 Colden gave the office of private secretary and Surrogate of the Prerogative Court to his son David— a post which was reclaimed shortly by the better-connected George Clarke—and in 1774 he tried to award him the surveyor generalship, Alexander having died. Archibald Kennedy's son was destined for the military, Governor Clinton reminding Henry Clinton that "you must push with all your might for young Kennedy to succeed to the first vacancy you being sensible what interest his father has, that must not be disobliged nor is it possible for me to carry any points here if I have not the liberty from home of obliging my friends."[18]

Council seats put New Yorkers in the front line for patronage both for themselves and their clients. Sir William Johnson reminded Lieutenant Governor Colden: "You were pleased to assure me, that, I should be acquainted whenever there was a new Commission of the Peace to be made out, and that my recommendation should have a due weight." Indeed, the patron-client relationship which access to contracts, offices, and lands made possible was yet another source of power to councillors. As the anthropologist Eric Wolf has shown, by placing others in their debt, patrons create obligations which may be repaid in many coins including favors and votes. Moreover, the whole nature of the relationship reinforces the superordinate position of the patron in the eyes of the client, other patrons and the society at large.[19]

Perhaps more important to New Yorkers than war contracts or offices was land. The two were hardly exclusive. At least fifty-nine members of the council, or 63 percent, tried to obtain land grants of some sort. This process began early and ended late. It was accompanied by fraud, scandal, and blatant disregard for instructions from England. Many cases are well known. With Governor Dongan's connivance, Robert Livingston turned a small grant into 160,000 acres. Stephanus Van Cortlandt received 86,000 acres; Adolphus Philipse 205,000 acres; Nicholas Bayard 24 square miles in Albany County; and William "Tangier" Smith 50 square miles in Suffolk County.[20]

More interesting than these early grants are the later ones. The Lords of Trade, realizing that engrossing such large amounts of land undermined the King's potential revenue and led to Indian problems, tried to limit the amount of acreage any one person might patent. In 1753 their article 56, on Governor Sir Danvers Osborne's instructions, placed a one-thousand-acre limit on land grants. These measures failed, as dummy partnerships and outright bribery of governors caused lands to be given away throughout the period. With the end of the

Seven Years' War and the settlement of boundary disputes with Massachusetts, Connecticut, and New Jersey, new opportunities for speculation opened up in New York, Vermont, New Hampshire, and the upper Connecticut River. Whitehall expressly forbade granting these lands. In 1761 additional instructions to Governor Monckton prohibited land grants in Indian territories. In 1767 and 1769 land grants in New Hampshire and on Lake Champlain were placed off-limits. However, even though specifically forbidden by instructions to grant these territories, Governors Tryon and Dunsmore, and Lieutenant Governor Colden did make grants, sometimes to themselves. William Smith, Jr., who chronicled much of this self-serving behavior, said of Lord Dunsmore, "I observed to his Lordship before them all, that the 50,000 acres lately granted to himself were prohibited by this instruction, but I suppose he will nevertheless put the Seal to the Patent." John Watts, no friend of Cadwallader Colden, noted sarcastically to General Monckton, "The old Gentleman affects much to appear very profound at Home, grant him that indulgence, and one other, of *granting lands* and you have the man." While not giving lands to himself, Colden helped his family by including David; Cadwallader, Jr.; and Alice among the patentees of Virgin Hill, Vermont; and Jane, John, and Richard Nicolls Colden among the grantees of Kersborough, Vermont.[21]

The council, which of course had to pass all land grants, went along with the governors as an interested party. Indeed, in 1773 Tryon "promised to give the council 100,000 acres without fees" for their compliance. To the Earl of Dartmouth he ingenuously explained that the good name of the government was at stake, since men already had put up the monies for their claims and relied henceforth on "the honor and justice" of the government to receive their letters patent. The temptation to misconduct was too strong, and the tension it produced is beautifully documented by William Smith, Jr. An intelligent and sensitive man, he was caught between obedience and greed. Writing in 1774 to Philip Schuyler, he mused that Colden, contrary to instructions, was granting land in the New Hampshire district. At eighteen pence per acre, "I intend to sport away about £1,000 as I suppose it will be the last chance. . . . I shall buy lands that I opposed the grant of— Is there any thing wrong in this?—Have I not discharged my duty when I voted against a petition in which I was myself concerned."[22]

Patronage, contracts, and lands all remained a potential source of fortune right to the eve of the Revolution, and given these sources of power and wealth, a council seat remained a plum worth having. The dependence of governors, especially later governors, on the council,

further insured that councillors would have their say. Sir Henry Moore
sadly noted to Secretary Conway that the Stamp Act would be dis-
obeyed in New York: "You will perceive by the minutes of the council
here enclosed, that I am not to be supported in the execution of the
Act, and that their apprehensions of future disturbances have influenced all the opinions they have given me on this occasion. In consequence of their resolutions, I am obliged to suspend a power which I
am not able to exert without their assistance."

Scholars have concentrated on the "rise" of the assembly and thereby
have implied a "fall" of the council. However, as long as governors
needed local allies of "estate and abilities" and as long as those allies
obtained position, power and pelf from their council seats, they would
maintain the desirability and authority of that house.[23]

New York's most important and most ambitious men vied for council seats, jockeying for that honor both abroad and at home. Lewis
Morris, Jr., having been removed from the council in 1729, was still
seeking reinstatement in 1752. In 1766 Sir Henry Moore and William
Smith, Jr., hatched plans by which William Smith, Sr., and William
Alexander, Lord Stirling, would resign, thus freeing two seats for the
younger Smith and for Robert Livingston. As late as 1774 (at a time
when South Carolina's elite would not consider taking a council seat)
Lieutenant Governor Cadwallader Colden wrote to the Earl of Dartmouth that Sir John Johnson had asked to be appointed in his deceased
father's place. "I could not reject such a request from the son of my
old and much esteemed friend," Colden explained, in passing on the
request.[24]

Governors played the largest role in recommending prospective
councillors. They did this through temporary appointments and recommendations to the Lords of Trade. These suggestions were just that,
however. As the lords petulantly told Clinton, "the Board have always
a proper regard to such recommendations, but they do not apprehend
themselves to be confined by the Governor's recommendations if any
other person shall appear to them properly qualified to discharge this
trust." Others could propose councilmen. Powerful friends and relatives in England helped, as did business associates. In a letter to Peter
Collinson, Cadwallader Colden's friend, fellow botanist, and London
agent, the Earl of Halifax insisted that he would have been glad to
oblige both Collinson and Colden by appointing Colden's son to the
council, but a new governor was to be appointed, and, first, he might
need that slot to "oblige some Gentleman of the greatest consequence
to him with a seat;" second, the new chief justice should probably have

a seat; and, third, "I have been very strongly solicited by my relation Col. Fitzroy, who married Lt. Governor DeLancey's niece, and by others to make his eldest son, who inherits his estate, a councillor of New York." Sir Henry Moore confided to William Smith, Jr., that former governor Monckton and "Elliot the collectors friend" had tried to get Smith appointed but they failed. He went on to say that he had seen the list in England and "that will not do[,] a parcel of people . . . who are named by merchants who know nothing of the matter . . . who have no other merit than having dealt well by their correspondents in trade and utterly unfit for the great ends of government."[25]

If those whose qualities consisted solely of a good credit rating were "utterly unfit for the great ends of government," what were the qualities required? Royal instructions were general, not specific. Councillors should "be men of estate and abilities and not necessitous people or much in debt, and . . . persons well affected to our government." Governors and their critics had more to say, often in complaints, etched in acid, to the Lords of Trade, English patrons or local partners-in-crime.[26]

Letters of recommendation told the Lords of Trade what governors thought requisite and what they hoped would appeal to the board. In 1695, Governor Fletcher recommended Mr. Caleb Heathcote, remarking that he "has been very serviceable and forward upon all occasions." What Fletcher really meant was that Heathcote would use his wealth and influence to help underwrite and support the government. Lord Cornbury asked, as did others, for "what vacancies are first to be filled with persons inhabiting this City; because very often I find it difficult to get five together, so many of them living at a distance." Governor Hunter, in his unsuccessful petition for Mr. David Jamison in 1716, noted that Jamison's apparent liabilities, which included both his youthful conversion to a pacifistic religious sect—"sweet singers," as Hunter called them, who would ban all books but the Bible—and his later fathering of an illegitimate child, were far outweighed by his positive qualities. Jamison had attended college in Scotland, taught school in America, mastered the law, and acquired considerable wealth. He was also responsible for legally establishing the Church of England, noted Hunter, who concluded, "He is the greatest man I ever knew, and I think of the most unblemished life and conversation of any of his rank in these parts." In a most fateful recommendation, Governor Montgomerie nominated James DeLancey, at twenty-six one of the youngest members of the Board: "He is every way well qualified for the post, his father is an eminent merchant, and he his eldest son." Montgomerie omitted to note DeLancey's years of study at Cambridge or his admission to the Inner Temple. His father's wealth and political connections in the lower house were enough.[27]

Special skills also played a part in seating the council. A good knowledge of the English language helped. In 1699 Bellomont complained of his inability to find good people: "Those that are honest of the Dutch, being formerly kept out of employment and business are very ignorant, and can neither speak nor write proper English." As late as 1729, Lewis Morris, Jr., complained, with some exaggeration, that Rip Van Dam and Abraham Van Horne "never were perfect masters of the English tongue, nor never will be." At least one slot was held by somebody who could negotiate with the Indians. Peter Schuyler, Philip Livingston, and Sir William Johnson fulfilled this role. Perhaps George Clinton's brief in favor of reinstating James Alexander sums up most of these strands: "As he has one of the best estates in the country has been long conversant in public affairs and is one of the most skilled lawyers among us, no man could be of more use to His Majesty's service."[28]

Excluding those who only served when the normal government of New York was suspended during the Dominion of New England, or during the Lieutenant-governorship of Jacob Leisler—or those like Sir Peter Warren and George Clarke, Jr., who never took the oath of office in New York—ninety-two men sat on the New York Council between 1665 and 1776. Their wealth, so crucial a variable, is one of the hardest to measure. Some, even among the earliest councillors, were wealthy. Cornelius Steenwyck, who came to New Amsterdam in 1651 as mate on a trading vessel, already was well off by 1653. By 1664, the year of the English conquest, he was the wealthiest and most important merchant in New York. A New York City resident, he also owned a home in Albany, so that he could qualify for the fur trade. He purchased the manor of Fordham as well, which he bequeathed to the Dutch Reformed Church. Others, like Thomas Topping, were men of more moderate means. Topping left an estate which, including lands, was valued at £703. Lucas Santen, a receiver general of New York who was removed for malfeasance, might have distributed his gains in his lifetime. His will suggests little wherewithal, the bequests totalling £150, and £10 to his landlord for a mourning ring.[29]

The pattern of placing wealthy, middling, and even skilled but necessitous men on the council continued. In contrast to the independently wealthy Caleb Heathcotes, James DeLanceys, and Philip Livingstons, there were also the Daniel Horsmandens and Benjamin Pratts. Pratt, appointed chief justice and councillor in 1761, was pitifully honest about his circumstances. Writing to Lieutenant Governor Colden he said, "What little I have in the world consists in a real estate for which I can neither find purchasers nor tenants without sinking one half the value . . . and in a personal estate all out in many debts, chiefly small, and many doubtful. . . . I have not a fortune that will support me in running risks, or maintain me." He died in December, 1763, leaving as little as he had when he came to the council.[30]

Benjamin Pratt did not "make it." But many on the council were self-made entrepreneurs who had achieved at least some position by the time they were appointed. Perhaps Robert Livingston's is the best known of New York's success stories. Born in Scotland in 1654, he came to New York with his father's good name, a few contacts, and nothing else. He parlayed his knowledge of Dutch, his business sense, and his single-minded pursuit of wealth into an advantageous marriage, a mercantile fortune, and 160,000 acres in upper New York. He died one of the wealthiest men in the province.[31]

James Alexander, another Scotsman, had good connections but apparently few financial resources when he arrived from Scotland in 1715. Born into a cadet branch of the Earls of Stirling, he enjoyed the patronage of the Duke of Argyll. In Scotland, Alexander received a fine education in mathematics, including at least some time at Glasgow University, and legal training in London. A freethinker and youthful Jacobite, he ran into problems at home and was appointed surveyor general of New Jersey. He was admitted to both the New Jersey and New York bars and held a number of public offices. Alexander, like Livingston, made a good marriage which tied him into New York's international mercantile community. His wife, the widow Maria Sprat Provoost, daughter of a Scots father and a DePeyster mother, inherited her husband's business, which she managed with notable skill. Alexander also tended to business and acquired lands in both New Jersey and New York.[32]

James Alexander left no surviving will, but in 1756, the year of his death, Maria Alexander did. Her first bequest of £5,000 to her son John Provoost established her wealth. She then went on to dispose of silk clothing, gold, jewels, sixteen crimson damask chairs, crimson damask window curtains, eighteen green bottomed chairs with green window curtains, and twelve yellow bottomed chairs and five pairs of yellow window curtains, among numerous other items. The scale of this home establishment seems thoroughly in keeping with a fortune which Lewis Morris estimated at £100,000.[33]

New Yorkers reaching the council, while not as wealthy as James Alexander, were, like him, usually vigorous men in the prime of their lives. Unlike the seventeenth-century Chesapeake, but probably much like New England, New Yorkers chose leaders who were approaching middle age. The average age of New York's seventeenth-century councilmen was 41.7 years when first appointed to the Board. In Maryland, this was about the age a man could expect to die. The eighteenth century saw New York leaders' ages increase slightly. The average age of the thirty-four men who first sat in the eighteenth century was 43.4 years. For the total of fifty-two councillors for whom age is known, the mean was 42.7 years. Presumably, as life in the Chesapeake proved less precarious, the age of its officeholders would increase. In New England, where the best data emerges at the town level, the pattern is the same. Townsmen first chose selectmen who were in their early forties.[34]

By the time a man reached forty, his talents and his potential were well known. Usually he was married and had a growing family. This set of responsibilities, along with the economic roots they sank into New York soil, gave councillors weight and maturity, as well as a commitment to the province. Those few councillors chosen much younger than forty compensated for their lack of years through other qualities which further demonstrate what leaders needed. Four men reached the board before they turned thirty. Lewis Morris, Jr.; James DeLancey; and James Jauncey, Jr., all had wealth and, perhaps more important, an active, vigorous parent in the General Assembly. Caleb Heathcote, newly arrived from England, had an independent fortune, brothers who traded to New York, and a cousin—George—already established as a New York merchant. His brother, Gilbert, was lord mayor of London, a valuable ally.[35]

Councillors reached the board in the prime of their lives and there they often stayed, giving New York's council a continuity never experienced by the executive and perhaps only partially shared by the General Assembly. Whereas New York's colonial governors only averaged 3.5 years in office—ranging from the two days of Sir Danvers Osborne, who committed suicide, to the ten years and one month of George Clinton—councillors served an average of 9.9 years, from less than a year for Thomas Johnson to the thirty-five years of Daniel Horsmanden and Archibald Kennedy. (Cadwallader Colden, who served for fifty-five years, has been excluded from these calculations because his term artificially inflates the average.) This lengthy tenure was shared by most of the colonial councils, at least in the late eighteenth century. James Kirby Martin found that 152 councillors seated on the eve of the Revolution averaged 11.8 years in office, a tenure which was higher than that for governors, lieutenant governors, attorney generals and associate justices. Only secretaries of the province spent more years in office.[36]

Tenure might have been even longer but for mortality and the accidents of history. Twenty-four New York councillors died in office, and ten more died within a year of leaving office. Twelve were still sitting in 1776 when normal royal government ceased. Thus, one-half of New York's councillors stayed on the board as long as possible. Stability, measured by longevity on the council, increased during the eighteenth century. The thirty-nine men who were seated before 1700 averaged 8.2 years on the council. Thirty of the thirty-nine who served less than six years did so before 1710. The fifty-two men, excluding Colden, who first sat after 1700 averaged 11.3 years on the board.

Long tenures lent stability to the province in a number of different ways. First, a long tenure gave councillors a sense of the office. They learned its power and its vocabulary. They learned how it ran, what it had to offer, and what its limits were. As the anthropologists Robert J. Maxwell and Philip Silverman point out, there is a high correlation between deference to age and control of information. Long years on the board allowed councilmen to amass knowledge of interest to governors, the elite, and themselves. Second, long years on the board permitted these men to get used to one another. They "settled in" and could work as a team. Third, the years in office themselves lent gravity and respect to men as they aged. Arriving on the council in their forties, they became political elders, physically as well as experientially.[37]

The long overall average span on the council suggests stability throughout New York's history. Unfortunately, average figures obscure significant trends within the time period. New York's council was more stable at some times than at others. Instability can be seen through two related patterns, the holding of broken tenures and suspension from the council. The number of years a man spent on the council was calculated by adding up all the years he sat. However, twenty men sat more than once. Of these, fifteen sat twice, four held three different terms, and John Youngs sat four different times. Anthony Brockholles, second in command to Governor Edmund Andros, left his council seat in 1679 and was reappointed in 1683. From 1686 to 1710, excluding the Dominion of New England and Leisler's lieutenant-governorship, sixteen men left the council or were suspended and were later reinstated. After 1710, with the arrival of Governor Robert Hunter, only three men sat twice—James Alexander, James DeLancey, and Daniel Horsmanden. Alexander and Horsmanden were suspended. Clearly, measured by broken tenures, the years 1686 to 1710 were the greatest periods of turmoil in New York politics.

Closely related to broken tenures were suspensions. Twenty-two men, or 24 percent of the council, were suspended. Nine of those suspended were later reinstated. Before 1686, only one councillor,

William Dyre, was removed from the council. The charge against him was treason, but the real issue was collecting taxes on commerce, and the move was far more political than patriotic. Other suspensions would follow the same pattern. From 1686 to 1710 fourteen councillors were suspended, two by Governor Dongan, six by Governor Bellomont, and six by Lord Cornbury.[38]

Some suspensions were for cause, and others were obviously political; however, the two are not mutually exclusive categories. In 1698 Governor Bellomont charged that John Lawrence was superannuated and suspended him. Lawrence was already eighty, and he died the next year. Bellomont, however, was one of two royal governors given to wholesale suspension of councillors. William Nicolls, William Pinhorn, Chidley Brooke, Nicholas Bayard, and Frederick Philipse all lost their seats as Bellomont, an avowed Leislerian partisan, tried to sweep out the opposition. Lord Cornbury played the same game a few years later. William Lawrence, a nephew of John's, and apparently a genuinely unpleasant character, was suspended for brawls and riots. Cornbury then also tried to pack the council, by ridding it of Leislerians. He suspended William Atwood, Thomas Weaver, Abraham DePeyster, Samuel Staats, and Robert Walters. The fact that William Lawrence had married the daughter of Samuel Edsall, one of Leisler's key lieutenants, suggests that his suspension was based on more than his uncivil behavior.[39]

Cornbury's purge would be the last. Sporadic suspensions took place in 1721, 1729, 1735, and 1747 but each was under a different chief executive. Governor Clinton, had he been stronger, might have done more. He did rid himself of Daniel Horsmanden and Stephen Bayard, charging both with faction, but his real adversary, James DeLancey, was far too firmly entrenched, both at home and abroad. Clinton, in fact, wanted the Lords of Trade to do his dirty work for him. Maintaining that DeLancey, Horsmanden, Joseph Murray, Stephen Bayard, and Philip Livingston all were part of a cabal, he further accused Livingston of trading with the French and supporting Indian neutrality. The lords should suspend him, "as he is a dangerous person to be employed under government and indeed I have the like reasons to complain of the rest of the Council herein mentioned." The lords declined, as would the secretary of state, who wrote to Cadwallader Colden, then eyeing DeLancey's position as lieutenant governor, that "it was thought that a step of this sort would create discord and dissention, and therefore it was judged impolitic and unsafe to suffer it to be taken."[40]

Governor Clinton's problems with his board suggest a shift in the balance of power within New York's government. After all, Bellomont and Cornbury—both peers, it might be noted—felt little compunction about purging the council. Even William Cosby, hard pressed by enemies, only rid himself of James Alexander. Other governors were also obviously weaker, although the reasons for this are unclear. Cosby lost the respect of Cadwallader Colden, at least, because "he became more familiar with the people and invited many of low rank to dine with him such as had never pretended or expected so much respect." Some of this invective, generated in hindsight, might have been prompted by sour grapes. More to the point was Governor Clinton's sense of social ostracism. Instead of setting the tone for New York society, he was manipulated by it. Writing bitterly to Colden about the DeLanceys in 1753, he noted that "a whole family in town related to you has never been once nigh Mrs. Clinton since she came to town nor had the good manners as to send to know how my child did that has been ill above this three months."[41]

Governors were wary of alienating councilmen, and with good reason. Their wealth and political connections, and perhaps their knowledge and ability, had placed them on the council in the first place. Moreover, these were men who knew how to carry out tasks and get what they wanted. They worked for a living. The overwhelming majority, 60 or 65 percent, were merchants. This was true throughout the period. Twenty-five merchants sat before 1700 and thirty-five sat afterwards. Twenty lawyers occupied council seats, four before 1700 and sixteen later. The greatest number of attorneys, nine, or 31 percent of those appointed, were seated between 1700 and 1735. Between 1735 and 1776, of twenty-five men seated, seven, or 28 percent, were lawyers. Four men were doctors.[42]

The large number of merchants on the New York Council, through their overseas trading partners, gave that board entrée into English politics. Among other consequences, this alliance established a communication network that allowed councillors, as well as governors, to know what English concerns were. Just as elders might, the merchants controlled information which allowed them to plan their domestic strategies and use what leverage they had to influence British policy.

The relatively small number of lawyers appointed after 1735 seems surprising given the affinity of lawyers for politics and the professionalization of the bar in the latter eighteenth century. However, one must look at not only the number of lawyers, but the lengthening of tenures in the 1700s and the distribution of those tenures over time. Before 1705 eight lawyers sat on New York's council, but most of their tenures were short. Indeed, in 1692 and 1702, perhaps as many as three lawyers sat, a high number considering their distribution in the general population. These numbers bespeak a conscious effort on the Crown's part to professionalize the board and, as we shall discuss later, represent an attempt to seat placemen. This attempt failed but the Board of Trade tried to keep at least one trained legal advisor on the council.

After 1721, there were always two lawyers seated and at times many more. In 1755–1756 and 1759–1760, as many as five men of the bar might have sat on the Board, and in 1733–1736, 1742–1747, and 1752–1763, four councilmen were lawyers, although one—Philip Livingston of Albany (1725–1749)—was chiefly a landowner and merchant. After 1763, no more than three lawyers sat, two remaining after 1771. Their heyday was 1725 to 1771, when their numbers included James Alexander, James DeLancey, William Smith, and William Smith, Jr.; all accounted by contemporaries as able and shrewd men. When William Smith, Jr., advised Governor Moore in 1768 to appoint more lawyers to the council, he was less commenting on the current composition of the board, which contained Daniel Horsmanden and Joseph Reade, besides himself, than communicating the desire to see his friends John Morin Scott and Robert Livingston seated.[43]

The increasing importance of lawyers in the council was closely related to the burgeoning complexity of New York life, a development which both Milton Klein and Michael Kammen discuss for the eighteenth century. Life was becoming more compartmentalized, or more specialized, calling for specialists who could offer particular skills. Lawyers dealt with both mercantile and land questions. They also helped untrained governors try the cases which came before the chancery court and decide cases of error in suits which came before the governor and council acting as a court.[44]

Lawyers and merchants, the most numerous groups on the council, both tended to cluster in New York City. Of the eighty-eight men whose residences as councillors can be determined, sixty-three, or 72 percent, lived in New York City, another five residing in easily accessible surrounding areas, like Kings County or Staten Island. Only seven lived in Albany, but there seemed to be a slot reserved for someone from that city. Five men lived in Westchester.[45]

The overwhelming number of New York men on the board gave the city protection and privileges. Before 1673, this special relationship was institutionalized, in that New York mayors were chosen from the council, and provincial councillors and city aldermen tended to be the same men. After 1673, the offices became more independent. For the whole group of ninety-two men, twenty-nine—or 32 percent—also had held municipal office as mayors or aldermen in New York or Albany, but twenty-one of the twenty-nine first sat before 1700. Even without the overlapping of personnel, the city's friends in high places protected their own interests. In 1680 the council awarded New York the wheat bolting monopoly and in 1684 made the city the sole port of entry. While both of these privileges were later lost, the council rebuffed attempts by the assembly to assess unduly high taxes on the city. As late as 1775, a close relationship remained between the council and city politics. In explaining why an amended swine control bill was withheld from the assembly, the council "answered that they had a request from the city members that if we stood upon the amendment it might be such as would hurt them in the ensuing election."[46]

Given that the largest number of councillors lived close to or within the city, the governors' oft-professed inability to obtain a quorum needs further scrutiny. These complaints began with Governor Dongan in 1687. In 1695 Governor Fletcher noted that, with Joseph Dudley and William Pinhorn removed for nonresidence, some of the council being superannuated, "some living remote in the country and some others taken up in their private vocations," he might not have a quorum. His solution was to call Caleb Heathcote to the council. Fletcher's twelve-man council of 1695—including Pinhorn, suspended in 1692 for living in New Jersey but later, as a New York resident, restored—had only three men who lived outside New York City (William "Tangier" Smith, Thomas Willett, and Peter Schuyler). More to the point was his notice of "private vocations." These men were highly ambitious, and could hardly spend day after day in council meetings, a point noted by Dongan. Ironically, Caleb Heathcote, brought in to give Fletcher another city man, chose to live in Westchester.[47]

Cornbury, in 1708; Hunter, in 1715; Lieutenant Governor Clarke, in 1741; and Moore, in 1767, said much the same thing as Fletcher had. However, the problem of a quorum was not geographic. Governors could refuse to call certain councillors, such as Lewis Morris, Jr., Rip Van Dam, or James Alexander. Periodically, councillors could choose for political reasons to stay away, as did James Alexander, William Smith, Jr., John Watts, and Henry Cruger. Or councillors could decide there was no reason for them to attend. Colden, who did live miles away, wrote in 1745 that there were enough councillors in New York City able to attend without additional expense. Those in the country should be excused. Mr. Livingston, he pointed out, had not attended the last session, and besides, "I suppose that the business of the Council is little else besides formality because we have no parties or disputes among us." He asked if he and Livingston could alternate sessions. Sir William Johnson ceased anywhere near regular attendance in 1753 even though he remained on the council until his death in 1774.[48]

Just as people could absent themselves, they could also choose to come to the council. Apparently a full seating was unusual, especially when the council sat in its capacity as privy council. In 1747 Cadwallader Colden was unpleasantly surprised to see a full council seated. Obviously called on purpose, it then proceeded to defend itself and to attack a report he had published.[49]

The governors attempted to pack the council with those living close by, and, given New York City's preeminence in the colony, they had little trouble. Attempts to put those more dependent on the crown, that is, placemen, on the board, fared less well. Historians have been misled by the complaints of governors and their suggestions to the Lords of Trade. Beverly McAnear, for example, accused Governor Cosby and Lieutenant Governor Clarke of filling the board with placemen, while Stanley Katz notes that, "Even in this small body, a few places were taken up by professional officers of the Crown [who could be counted on to support the governor anyway] and by English members who never came to America." Katz was undoubtedly thinking of George Clarke, Jr., and Sir Peter Warren, but these are the only two examples of councillors living in England. Only fifteen of ninety-two, or 16 percent, can be positively identified as placemen; two more were possibly so. Even if Thomas Lovelace (1671–1673) and Wolfgang Romer (1702–1708) were placemen, the total would be only 18 percent. And the fifteen certain dependents on the Crown are spread oddly over time. Five first sat before 1700, five between 1700 and 1705, and five between 1706 and 1763. As Jackson Turner Main recognized, no placeman sat after 1763. The largest cluster occurs between 1700 and 1706, when the Lords of Trade tried to professionalize the civil service by sending over William Atwood, Thomas Weaver, John Bridges, Sampson Shelton Broughton, and Roger Mompesson, all of whom had a formal legal education. Indeed, such a constellation of professionally trained lawyers would never appear again. Perhaps more important, this effort failed. Atwood and Weaver fled the colony in disgrace in 1702, and Bridges and Broughton died by 1705.[50]

The last fifty years of the colonial period saw three placemen: Archibald Kennedy (1726–1761), who was receiver general and took his seat a full sixteen years after he migrated to New York; Captain John Rutherford (1745–1759), a captain of one of the independent companies, whose appointment brought bitter yelps of betrayal from the governor whose placeman he was supposed to be (and who, ironically, would be well served by him); and Benjamin Pratt of Boston (1762–

1763), a genuine dependent, who sat but one year. Of these men, only Kennedy would live in New York City and regularly attend the council, and he was at least partly Americanized. His second wife, Mary Walter Schuyler, was one of the local aristocracy, and he died in America, fifty-three years after leaving England.[51]

Placemen depended on salaried offices. Some of the council who were not necessarily placemen also held crown-controlled positions. Two were surveyor generals; nine, customs' collectors; fifteen, receiver generals; five, attorney generals; and twenty sat on the Supreme Court. No position guaranteed a seat on the council, but receiver generals, commissioners, judges of the Admiralty Court, and members of the Supreme Court usually were so appointed. The Lords of Trade, in commenting on Governor Monckton's instructions, noted that his council consisted of eleven men who sat previously and Benjamin Pratt, "[he] having been lately Chief Justice to New York, . . . it being usual in all your Majesty's plantations to give the Chief Justice a seat at that Board." In fact, some chief justices, for example Lewis Morris, never sat on the council, and New York's most famous ones, James DeLancey and Daniel Horsmanden, were councillors before they became chief justices. Governors would have preferred to have such slots. Lieutenant Governor Clarke noted in 1738, "I think it highly necessary that such of the King's officers as held the most considerable posts should be preferred to seats at that Board, and I have found the want of them more than once in matters that concern the Government." However, the Lords realized early on the necessity of both rewarding the locals and giving them responsibility. In 1715, they approved of Governor Hunter granting the chief justiceship to Lewis Morris, saying,

We must take leave to observe that it is for his Majesty's service that persons in the plantations who shall distinguish themselves in His Majesty's interest and for the good of the government, be rewarded with such places as are in the disposal of the Governors there. If this method were observed it would be an encouragement to gentlemen to exert themselves for the public good, and would strengthen the governors in the execution of the trust reposed in them, whereas we apprehend, the contrary method will not fail of producing a contrary effect.[52]

Councilmen were most likely to be New York City merchants who might also have some other office. They were not so likely to have sat in the assembly. Only twenty-one, or 23 percent of those on the council, were elected to the assembly. Ten men who were on both were appointed to the council before 1700. The other eleven came afterwards, four of them falling into the first ten years of the eighteenth century. While the council and the assembly undoubtedly drew from the same larger pool of people, they did not draw exactly the same people. The pattern is far more complex. Seven men moved from the assembly to the council. Six men, including James Alexander, served assembly terms between council terms, marking time as it were, until the political climate changed, and higher office would be theirs again. Eight men moved from the council to the assembly. Of these, four served in the council in the seventeenth century, and three of the eight had been suspended. All of the eight served on the council before 1730. Council membership apparently was not a reward for faithful service in the assembly, nor did those who sensed the winds of power and opportunity, as the assembly supposedly gained power in the eighteenth century, bolt from the upper house. Perhaps the most remarkable were James Alexander and John Watts—and perhaps a few others—who held both council and assembly seats simultaneously. Elected in 1737, Alexander was permitted to sit, as long as he refrained from acting on the council. Lewis Morris, Jr., was the last councillor to move from the council to the assembly. Suspended in 1729, he tried to regain that seat in 1752. In the meantime, as his second choice, he sat in the assembly from the borough of Westchester.[53]

Lewis Morris, Jr., was a native American, and so were many of his colleagues, the pattern of nativity among officeholders further arguing against a board filled with late arrivals who were creatures of the Crown. Of the sixty-four councillors for whom place of birth is available, twenty-four, or 38 percent, were born in New York or New Netherland, while another five were born in other American colonies. Nineteen came from England, seven from Scotland, four from Holland, three from Ireland, and two from elsewhere. Some distinct patterns emerge over time. Almost all, sixteen of nineteen, or 84 percent of the English-born, were appointed by 1705. All of the Dutch were appointed before 1690, as were a Welshman and a Frenchman. The Scots were appointed between 1685 and 1745, the Irish between 1740 and 1775.

New York, it seems, increasingly appealed to those in the secondary, or more provincial, centers of the British Isles. Perhaps their opportunities were limited by prejudices in England against both the Scots and the Scots-Irish. Their talents, so much harder to find in America, would gain them place in New York and the other American colonies.

Those born in New York span the entire period. Twelve were seated before 1705 and thirteen afterward. This distribution, so unlike that in the Chesapeake, suggests that a native-born elite emerged early. It did not prevail through becoming more numerous as mortality changed, but through its consistent longevity, which left little room for newcomers to exploit. Governor Moore, speaking in 1767, saw this quite clearly. Complaining that judges' salaries were too small, and that only the independently wealthy could afford the position, he said, "The persons of most independence here are the descendents of the first settlers of the country; and are generally related to all the best families in the Province." He might have added that upwardly mobile newcomers like James Alexander would marry into these same families. [54]

Men lived long enough to sire children, to guide those children to adulthood, and to provide for them the offices and lands which council seats made possible. Age of death is available for fifty-one councillors; it averaged sixty-five years. Twenty-three men lived past sixty-five, and eighteen past seventy. Longevity was unrelated to time appointed. Ten of those who lived to be sixty-five were appointed before 1700, fourteen were appointed in the seventy-six years afterward. Of the three men who died before their late forties, one was appointed in 1692, one in 1702, and the third in 1775. Long lives, of course, aided stability. These men would carry the history of the province and its peculiarities with them. [55]

James Alexander died "in the sixty-fifth year of his age." Wealthy, literate and talented, he had served on New York's council a total of twenty-two years. His first term ended with his suspension by William Cosby in 1737, due to his opposition to that governor's attempts to accrue more power than his predecessors. Restored in 1750—the long wait a result of his name having been inadvertently left out of Governor Clinton's instructions—, he remained on the Board until his death. [56]

For colonial New Yorkers like James Alexander a seat on the council was the premier political office. This paper, by concentrating on the council's functions, rewards, and personnel, has suggested why New Yorkers would wish to have a place on the Board and described those who won those coveted slots. In a short essay, certain relationships necessarily have been stressed and other questions slighted. New York's government was a system. Governor, General Assembly, and council had to work together and depend upon one another for the system to work. While governors depended upon councilmen, councilmen also depended upon governors. Governors did have power, and even the weakest of them exercised it.

The council, as Nicholas Varga recognized, served to stabilize New York government. How it did this institutionally needs to be carefully

TABLE 1
The New York Council from 1665 to 1775

Name	Birth	Death	Total years on Council
1. Alexander, James	1691	1756	22
2. Alexander, William	1726	1783	6
3. Apthorpe, Charles Ward	—	—	12
4. Atwood, William	1652	1709	1
5. Axtell, William	—	1794	5
6. Barbarie, John	—	1727	22
7. Baxter, Jervais	—	—	3
8. Bayard, Nicholas	1644	1707	10
9. Bayard, Stephen	—	—	2
10. Beekman, Gerardus	1653	1723	22
11. Bridges, John	1667	1704	2
12. Brockholles, Anthony	—	—	10
13. Brooke, Chidley	—	—	9
14. Broughton, Sampson Shelton	1652	1705	2
15. Byerly, Thomas	—	1726	14
16. Chambers, John	1699	1764	11
17. Clarke, George	1676	1759	20
18. Colden, Cadwallader	1688	1776	55
19. Cruger, Henry	1707	1780	5
20. Cruger, John Harris	—	—	3
21. Darvall, William	—	—	4
22. Delancey, James	1703	1760	24
23. DeLancey, Oliver	1718	1785	16
24. De La Noy, Peter	—	—	2
25. Delaval, Thomas	—	—	6
26. Depeyster, Abraham	1657	1728	17
27. Dyre, William	—	—	7
28. Graham, James	—	1701	5
29. Harison, Francis	—	—	15
30. Heathcote, Caleb	1666	1721	23
31. Holland, Edward	—	1756	7
32. Horsmanden, Daniel	1694	1778	35
33. Jauncey, James, Jr.	1747	1777	2
34. Johnson, Thomas	1656	1693	1
35. Johnson, Sir William	1715	1774	23
36. Johnston, John	—	—	5
37. Kennedy, Archibald	1685	1763	35
38. Lane, Henry	—	1742	9
39. Lawrence, John	1618	1699	13
40. Lawrence, William	—	1719	5
41. Ling, Mathew	—	1704	2
42. Livingston, Philip	1686	1749	25
43. Livingston, Robert	1654	1728	2
44. Lovelace, Thomas	—	—	2
45. Martin, Josiah	—	—	3
46. Mompesson, Roger	1662	1716	10
47. Minvielle, Gabriel	—	—	7

TABLE 1 *(continued)*
The New York Council from 1665 to 1775

Name	Birth	Death	Total years on Council
48. Moore, John	—	1749	4
49. Morris, Lewis	—	1691	2
50. Morris, Lewis, Jr.	1698	1762	8
51. Morris, Roger	1717	1794	12
52. Murray, Joseph	1694	1757	13
53. Needham, Robert	—	—	2
54. Nicolls, Mathias	1626	1687	13
55. Nicolls, William	1657	1723	7
56. Palmer, John	—	—	4
57. Peartree, William	1642	1714	2
58. Philipse, Adolph	1665	1749	16
59. Philipse, Frederick	1627	1702	6
60. Pinhorn, William	1650	1719	6
61. Pratt, Benjamin	1709	1763	2
62. Provoost, David, Jr.	1670	1724	3
63. Provoost, William	—	—	9
64. Reade, Joseph	1692	1771	7
65. Romer, Wolfgang	—	—	6
66. Rutherford, John	—	1758	13
67. Santen, Lucas	—	1692	3
68. Schuyler, Peter	1657	1724	28
69. Smith, William "Tangier"	1655	1705	13
70. Smith, William	1697	1769	14
71. Smith, William, Jr.	1728	1793	9
72. Spraag, John	—	—	3
73. Staats, Samuel	—	1715	11
74. Steenwyck, Cornelius	—	1684	3
75. Topping, Thomas	—	—	1
76. Van Cortlandt, Philip	1683	1746	16
77. Van Cortlandt, Stephen	1643	1700	17
78. Van Dam, Rip	1660	1749	33
79. Van Horne, Abraham	—	1741	18
80. Van Renssalaer, Killian	1663	1719	15
81. Van Ruyven, Cornelius	—	—	4
82. Wallace, Hugh	—	—	7
83. Walters, Robert	1660	1731	25
84. Walton, William	1705	1768	10
85. Watts, John	1715	1789	18
86. Weaver, Thomas	1642	1705	2
87. Wenham, Thomas	—	1709	6
88. White, Henry	1737	1786	7
89. Whitefield, Ralph	—	—	2
90. Willet, Thomas	1610	1674	7
91. Willet, Thomas	—	1724	6
92. Youngs, John	1623	1698	10

charted, by analyzing the minutes of the council in both its administrative and legislative capacities. How many and what bills did it veto?
How many and what bills did it pass and the Governor veto? How many
and what bills were eventually overturned by the Privy Council? [57]

It is currently fashionable to focus on New York's instability, but how
can one measure this? Governors sometimes had to wait for their salaries, but did government grind to a halt? As Jack Greene has suggested,
after 1710, with the exception of the controversies surrounding Governor William Cosby and the devolution of government after his death,
New York ran rather smoothly. Laws were passed, and most of the bills
were paid. Groups contested for power and patronage, but they did this
within boundaries which permitted the orderly exercise of control. If
the contest took place within the assembly, where turnover was faster
and the locals exercised more leverage, then what was the relationship
between the assembly and the council? Did they really have the same
interests, or, if not, were the most important assemblymen—those
equivalent to Robert Zemsky's power brokers in Massachusetts—indistinguishable from the councilmen? [58]

The preponderance of New York City merchants and lawyers also
raises questions about the council's relationship to the assembly. Given
the rural character of the assembly, was its fight to win power from the
council related to a rural-urban, merchant-farmer conflict of interests,
or even of values? Again, which men, both in the assembly and in the
council, were really powerful, and who or what did they represent?

There are also social considerations which this paper raises but
leaves unanalyzed. Bernard Bailyn called the eighteenth-century Virginia aristocracy "one great tangled cousinry." He then went on to note
that in the eighteenth century the council lost its superiority and had to
exercise its authority through alignments with burgesses, "alignments
made easier as well as more necessary by the crisscrossing network of
kinship that united the two houses." As most students of New York
have recognized, New York's aristocracy was also one great tangled
cousinry. However, the kinship network—alluded to above—that
linked council and assembly remains unexplored. When did it begin?
What were the kinship ties? Who was placed where and under what
circumstances? Were some channeled into the council while others
were directed toward the assembly? [59]

New York contained an inbreeding core-elite, but this elite was ethnically and religiously diverse. Robert Ritchie says that the first English
government under Richard Nicolls excluded the Dutch. Governor
Edmund Andros brought the Dutch merchants into government, thereby alienating the English. Every historian recognizes that Leisler's Re-

bellion had ethnic conflict as one of its roots, a conflict that stayed near the surface until Robert Hunter's administration. Thereafter, ethnic differences among the elite, who always set the social boundaries and initiated changing mores, diminished. Dutch names remained, but these men often had English mothers and attended Trinity Church. When did the elite begin to intermarry? When did the "Dutch" embrace the King's religion? When did ethnicity no longer matter in the acquisition of power? Foreign-born councillors ceased to be English-born; instead they came from Scotland and Ireland. Did Scotsmen and the Scots-Irish also sit in the assembly? Into what families did they prefer to marry? Is there, in fact, a "Scots-Dutch" connection, as Henry Noble MacCracken suggests? [60]

Power and status in colonial New York were achieved, not ascribed. Men fought for both, trying in the process to gain enough wealth to give their children a head start in the race which every generation ran. Seats on the council confirmed status and placed councilmen in a position to acquire the wealth and patronage which in turn granted power and confirmed status. As such, a council seat was "the patronage most ardently sought" [61] and most tenaciously held throughout the colonial period. It was the council that bridged the uncertain and often short-lived administrations of colonial governors and the council that met in its executive capacity when assemblies were prorogued or dismissed. We need to look at it more closely, not only listening to what contemporaries said, but also watching what they did as they desperately tried to serve the King, the province and themselves.

THOMAS L. PURVIS

A Beleaguered Elite:
The New Jersey Council, 1702–1776

AS HIS MAJESTY'S royal councillors returned home from the legislative session adjourned on October 23, 1751, all must have reflected upon the unmistakable evidence of their collective inability to command respect and exert leadership in New Jersey. Within the past year, the assembly had demanded Thomas Leonard's dismissal as a person unfit for public service,[1] and a Monmouth County grand jury had indicted Lewis Morris Ashfield for public intoxication on the Sabbath, damning the King's laws, and assaulting a constable.[2] In the previous year, freeholders from Somerset and Middlesex counties had presented strong evidence to the legislature that Robert Hunter Morris had improperly vacated a jury verdict as a favor to a business associate, while sitting as chief justice.[3] Whether accurate or not, the allegations against these three councillors were widely believed, and, more important, they reflected on the other eight.

Andrew Johnston and his fellow East Jersey proprietors leaving the session must have felt chagrined at the seeming impunity with which squatters cut valuable timber on their lands, dispossessed their grantees and tenants on disputed lots, and broke open jails to release friends awaiting trial for these offenses. Even more shocking must have been the apparent unconcern of the colony's freeholders to their predicament, and the assembly's repeated refusals to enact the stern measures they demanded. Johnston had little reason to suspect that anything more than his property might be threatened in 1751, but within two years he would discover himself face-to-face with a menacing crowd trying to block his eviction of a squatter family.[4] Royal councillors were not supposed to find themselves in such situations.

In addition to accusations of personal misconduct and bitter conflicts over land titles, other problems tarnished the image of the governor's appointed advisors in the mid-eighteenth century. Hundreds of West Jersey residents signed petitions in 1751 and the following year protesting that their division was being denied its rightful share of half the council seats, a clear violation of the concessions which had established New Jersey as a royal colony in 1702.[5] The fact that only three of the twelve councillors sitting in 1752 resided in western counties constituted prima facie evidence to western politicians that East Jersey interests enjoyed unwarranted influence in the government at their own expense. A more irritating problem than this divisional imbalance was the governors' common practice of appointing nonresidents to the upper house and permitting members to retain their seats after leaving the colony. The proportion of nonresidents had decreased considerably by 1751, but even though only one absentee member held office in that year, his presence still undermined the house's credibility by making it appear that the province's interests were being subordinated to benefit outsiders.

The councillors of the early 1750s were clearly a beleaguered elite, on the defensive and with little prospect of quickly regaining the public's respect. Historians have long emphasized the controversy surrounding New Jersey's upper house; they have written as if the unrepresentative character of its members' backgrounds was a constant source of friction in eighteenth-century politics, and have even suggested that restricted access to the council fostered the rise of revolutionary sentiment after 1763.[6] Given the importance traditionally accorded to the council's role in public affairs, it is regrettable that no detailed study has yet examined the social origins of this group to determine why they should have sparked such widespread resentment.

The need for such information becomes apparent when the scope of the upper house's role in government is considered. The councillors functioned as the governor's closest political advisors, especially before 1738, when the chief executive and upper house deliberated together during assembly sessions. They reviewed legislation passed by the lower house, returned bills with amendments for the representatives' consideration, and occasionally blocked measures sought by the assembly by withholding their assent. They, furthermore, controlled the distribution of every civil and military commission in the province, from the lowliest ensign of militia to the judges of common pleas, and refused to allow the governors any independent role in the allocation of patronage. These extensive powers made the councillors formidable opponents, even during periods of widespread popular antipathy like the early 1750s.

Despite the prominence of this exclusive group, little is still known of the members' socioeconomic backgrounds regarding wealth, economic interests, education, religious affiliation, ancestry, and family connections. This essay will examine the relationship between social status and political power by, first, summarizing these characteristics for all sixty-nine men who sat on the council from 1702 to 1776[7] and then inquiring into three general questions concerning the upper house's influence upon provincial politics. Why did council members encounter such individual and collective hostility as that confronting them at midcentury? Did the upper house's composition remain static, or change in significant ways, during the eighteenth century? And finally, did the members ever succeed in gaining widespread acceptance and respect from the citizens and from the lesser gentry in the legislature?

The Privy Council allowed each governor to control access to New Jersey's upper house through his power of nomination, but it provided no explicit guidance on who should be recommended. "In the choice & Nomination of the Members of Our said Council," royal instructions routinely ordered, "you are to always take care that they be men of good Life and well affected to Our Government, of Good Estates & Abilities & not necessitous people."[8] So loose were these guidelines that many governors took the extraordinary step of naming nonresidents to the council. Even without specific directions, however, governors invariably chose men from certain backgrounds, and so recruited the council from a highly exclusive group of wealthy individuals who came from an increasingly interrelated circle of families.

Governors could not have known the exact state of their nominees' personal finances, but they did succeed in identifying men of "Good Estates." Councillors nominated between 1702 and 1737 were exceptionally affluent by that period's standards, and those appointed after then were even more wealthy. During the years from 1700 to 1737, when half of all decedents in New Jersey left inventories worth no more than £100 proclamation money, and only 5 percent left personal property worth at least £600, the median value of inventories or bequests made by councillors was £620.[9] At a time when candidates for the lower house of the General Assembly were required to own one thousand acres, the typical councillor possessed more than twice that amount, twenty-two hundred acres.

Councillors serving during the second half of the royal period were even wealthier than their predecessors. Half of all inventories probated in New Jersey during the 1760s were less than £175, but the median value of bequests or inventories in the wills of councillors who died after 1737 was £3,000, an amount exceeded by fewer than 1 percent of all decedents.[10] Landholdings in New Jersey declined steadily during the eighteenth century, until thirty percent of all adult males were landless and the typical farmer owned about eighty acres by the 1770s, but acreage held by councillors increased. Councillors appointed after 1737 owned a median of twenty-seven hundred acres, approximately one quarter more than was held by men nominated before 1738. During the eighteenth century, every third councillor owned over four thousand acres, every fourth over five thousand, and every seventh over ten thousand. The councillors' total wealth far exceeded that of the average Jersey colonist. By the 1770s, the typical resident of the province was probably worth between £350 and £400 proclamation money in real and personal property.[11] Most councillors possessed total estates worth approximately £5,000 to £7,500, an amount equal to the property held by the wealthiest one percent of the Delaware Valley.[12] Two-thirds of all councillors stood among the wealthiest 2 percent of the population. Few ranked below the wealthiest 5 percent, and most were probably considerably more affluent, but the full extent of their property cannot be ascertained because of insufficient documentation. The wealth of the councillors is impressive even when compared to other elite groups, like the gentry sitting in the assembly, only 38 percent of whom ranked among the wealthiest 2 percent.[13]

Most councillors engaged in commerce or the law, occupations which conferred high status and offered great opportunities for pecuniary gain in early America. Planters composed the largest portion of the upper house before 1738, furnishing slightly less than half the members; after that date, only one man in eight occupied himself primarily in agriculture. The proportion of merchants remained constant during the royal period at approximately one-third, a substantial representation for this profession in a colony with no truly populous urban centers or large ports. Few lawyers appeared in the upper house before 1738, but afterwards they composed the largest occupational group, providing two of every five members. Merchants and lawyers together comprised three-fourths of all councillors in the latter half of the royal period.

The council also included a small number of placemen, individuals primarily dependent on such positions of profit as provincial secretary, lieutenant governor, or surveyor general of customs. Most took office before 1738 and served less than six years, about half the usual tenure of members. None of the placemen was especially wealthy, although some positions yielded substantial incomes, including the secretaryship, estimated to be worth £450 current money (approximately £300 sterling) yearly.[14] Placemen rarely contributed any substantial amount of talent or effort to public affairs, the major exception being the able Chief Justice Frederick Smyth who served from 1764 to the Revolution.[15]

Councillors frequently had supplemental sources of income. Many men in professional occupations preferred to reside on country estates worked by slaves or indentured servants. For example, when the absentee councillor John Stevens returned to New Jersey in 1771 after several years spent in New York as a merchant, he established himself on an estate in Hunterdon County in a manner more befitting an English country gentleman than a man of commerce. Charles Read practiced law, speculated in real estate, engaged in mercantile ventures, established a number of forges, and managed a plantation where he conducted agricultural experiments enthusiastically.[16] One-quarter of the councillors appointed after 1737 owned, or had investments in, mines or iron forges. The primary occupations of the councillors became increasingly more professional during the eighteenth century, but they often pursued several avocations simultaneously, helping to make the planter-merchant-land speculator a feature of New Jersey's economic life, just as in the Chesapeake.[17]

The colony's landed proprietors comprised a majority of the upper house's members. These were the individuals entitled to participate in the land divisions of the East Jersey Board of Proprietors or the West Jersey Council of Proprietors, along with any close relatives liable to inherit shares at a future date. The first proprietors of both divisions purchased their titles from Lord John Berkeley and Sir George Carteret. The number of investors providing financial backing for the separate colonies of East and West Jersey proliferated as shares were divided into smaller units and sold. Many shareholders settled in the provinces, where they became planters, merchants, and land speculators. Many resident proprietors seized the opportunity to preempt the most valuable tracts and profited enormously, usually at the expense of their less aggressive or more trusting associates. Fifty-two percent of all councillors were proprietors—approximately half coming from each division—and another 9 percent were their relatives. The upper house was not an exclusively proprietary body, but three-fifths of its personnel did possess a direct interest or familial connection with either group.

East Jersey proprietors exercised far more influence than those in the western division during most of the eighteenth century. Few eastern proprietors gained admittance to the council in the first dozen years of the royal period, and even as late as 1715 they numbered only four of

TABLE 1

Economic status of councillors

Status[b]	1702–1737[a]		1738–1776		Total 1702–1776	
	% of councillors	N	% of councillors	N	% of councillors	N
Wealthiest 2%	55.2	21	80.6	25	66.6	46
Wealthiest 5%	18.5	7	13.0	4	16.0	11
Wealthiest 10%	10.5	4	6.4	2	8.7	6
Unknown	15.8	6	—	—	8.7	6

[a]Councillors were placed in either period according to their date of appointment.

[b]The criteria used for assigning wealth levels are as follows: When only an inventory or bequests are available from a will, for anyone taking office after 1737, a value of £2,000 placed one in the top 2%, £1,500 in the top 5%, and £800 in the top 10%. (See n. 10. The distribution of inventory values for New Jersey approximates the table of distribution in Jackson Turner Main, The Social Structure of Revolutionary America [Princeton, N.J., 1965], 113, n. 115.) When only land ownership is available, for those appointed after 1737, 800 acres (which only 1% owned), 400 acres (which only 2% owned), and 250 acres were used to assign individuals to the 2%, 5%, and 10% levels. (Acreage estimates are based on tax lists for 6,641 ratables for 15 townships containing about 20% of the 1770 population.) For those individuals appointed before 1738, twice as much land was required for inclusion in the respective rankings, to allow for the general reduction in landholdings that occurred in the 1700s in the province. For those seated before 1738, an inventory value of £1,000, £500, and £300 assigned a man to the top 2%, 5%, and 10% categories. (See n. 9.) Anyone who was appointed before 1738 and died after that date was required to meet the higher standards of the later period for his ranking.

the ten members.[18] They first became a majority in 1718 and continued to provide at least half the personnel for the next forty-four years, with the exception of the decade from 1733 to 1743. Their representation declined to approximately 40 percent after 1762 and remained at that level until the Revolution. Eastern proprietors were a majority of the upper house for almost half the royal period, and often maintained working control in other years by forging alliances with various individuals.

Whether they were proprietors, placemen, or planters, the councillors' occupations and economic resources generated exceptionally large incomes, especially when compared with the £16 estimated to be the annual earnings of the typical Jersey farmer.[19] Peter Sonmans sold at least 43,000 acres between 1703 and 1734, for a total of £10,895, providing him with an average yearly income of £351. James Alexander disposed of 11,000 acres between 1721 and 1754, but, by selling at better prices than Sonmans, he obtained £6,562, almost £200 per year. Daniel Coxe, who practiced law before the Revolution, earned perhaps £400 a year. Chief Justice Frederick Smyth received compensation as a loyalist for £500 in official income lost as a result of his allegiance to the crown. John Stevens had £8,000 lent out at 6 percent interest in 1778, which would have netted him £480. Neverthe-

TABLE 2
Occupations of councillors

	1702–1737[a]		1738–1776		Total 1702–1776	
	% of councillors	N	% of councillors	N	% of councillors	N
Merchants	34.2	13	32.2	10	33.3	23
Planters	47.5	18	13.0	4	32.0	22
Lawyers	8.0	3	42.0	13	23.1	16
Placemen	10.5	4	6.4	2	8.6	6
Doctors	—	—	6.4	2	3.0	2

[a]Councillors were placed in each period according to the date of their appointment to office.

less, economic success was not guaranteed. Charles Read, whose official income was probably £600 in the 1740s, had to leave New Jersey furtively while trying to restore solvency to his finances and died in North Carolina as a country storekeeper.[20] William Alexander's land speculations left his credit greatly overextended by 1772 and forced him to resort to the disreputable expedient of a lottery.[21]

Two exceptionally significant advantages councillors derived from their wealth were the opportunity to attain a superior education and the leisure time necessary to pursue cultural activities. Eight of the sixty-nine councillors attended American or European colleges, and four others received formal education below the college level in England. Five councillors belonged to the American Philosophical Society. Nine involved themselves in the founding of colleges in the Middle Colonies, serving as trustees or other corporation officers. Samuel Smith wrote the first history of the province. During the last eight years of royal rule, between one-quarter and one-third of the members were college graduates. The proportion of college-educated councillors in New Jersey at that time approached that of the best educated upper house in colonial America, Massachusetts, where two-fifths of the pre-Revolutionary members were college men.[22] The collective learning and cultural sophistication of the councillors was impressive, especially considering that only 4 of the 256 assemblymen sitting between 1703 and 1776 are known to have attended college (including two later named to the upper house).

Despite the undeniable wealth of the New Jersey upper house, its personnel were less opulent than corresponding elites elsewhere. The typical New Jersey councillor possessed twenty-five hundred acres, far below the seventy-seven hundred acres possessed by South Carolina

TABLE 3

East and West Jersey proprietors on council

	East Jersey proprietors	West Jersey proprietors	Other members		East Jersey proprietors	West Jersey proprietors	Other members
1702–4	1	4	6	1740	3	4	4
1705	0	5	7	1741	4	3	3
1706	0	4	8	1742	3	3	3
1707	1	4	7	1743	4	3	3
1708	2	3	7	1744	4	2	1
1709–12	2	4	5	1745–47	6	3	2
1713–14	3	3	4	1748–50	6	3	3
1715	4	3	3	1751–56	8	3	1
1716	4	4	2	1757	7	2	1
1717	4	5	1	1758–61	7	1	4
1718–19	6	3	1	1762	7	0	4
1720–21	6	4	2	1763	5	1	5
1722	7	3	2	1764–67	5	1	6
1723–26	6	3	2	1768	4	1	6
1727–32	6	3	3	1769–76	5	1	6
1733–34	4	3	4				
1735–39	3	3	3				

councillors or the ten thousand acres held by members of Virginia's upper house.[23] The median inventory of councillors who died after 1737 was £3,000 proclamation (£2,000 sterling), a figure easily dwarfed by the average inventory of South Carolina councillors, £9,022 sterling; or that of pre-Revolutionary New York councillors, £10,000 proclamation (£6,000 sterling).[24] The councillor-elite closest to New Jersey's in wealth was probably that of North Carolina. Members of the North Carolina upper house held approximately two thousand acres, about five hundred less than their New Jersey counterparts.[25]

Virtually no men with great fortunes sat on the New Jersey Council, the main exceptions being nonresidents from New York. In 1745, Governor Lewis Morris estimated the fortune of James Alexander, a New Yorker, to be £100,000, and that of John Schuyler, a Bergen County resident, to be £65,000.[26] Morris, a former councillor who had lived in New York during most of his service, probably possessed an estate equal to or exceeding Alexander's. James Alexander's son William, who served on both the New York and New Jersey councils, also may have been worth about £100,000 in the 1760s.[27] Otherwise, few councillors could rank with the wealthiest men in Anglo-America. Those whose total worth exceeded £25,000 proclamation included Daniel Coxe, who filed a loyalist's claim for £41,000 sterling; Andrew Johnston, who purchased 61,000 acres for £20,000 proclamation in

TABLE 4
Religious affiliation of councillors

	1702–1737		1738–1776		Total 1702–1776	
	%	N	%	N	%	N
Anglican[a]	65.8	25	61.3	19	63.8	44
Quaker	18.4	7	16.1	5	17.4	12
Presbyterian	5.3	2	19.4	6	11.6	8
Dutch Reformed	7.9	3	3.2	1	5.8	4
Baptist	2.6	1	0	0	1.4	1

[a]Three Anglicans sitting before 1737 had been Quakers prior to the Keithian Schism.

1750; and John Stevens, a former New York merchant who had £8,000 proclamation lent out in 1778.[28] Wealth existed among the New Jersey councillors, but not such great wealth as in Virginia, South Carolina, Pennsylvania, or New York.

The backgrounds of the councillors were distinguished by more than their wealth, for members of the upper house derived from groups unrepresentative of the colony in several ways. The smallest, but reputedly most affluent, religious denomination in the province dominated the council. Anglicans numbered about 8 percent of the colony, but furnished 64 percent of all councillors.

Quakers also had a reputation for economic success, and they provided the second largest portion of councillors. The Quakers' contribution approximately equalled their share of the colony's population, 16 percent. This figure was nevertheless well below what their actual political influence should have merited, since Friends provided 37 percent of all assemblymen and 39 percent of the lower house's leaders.[29] No governor except Lewis Morris ever admitted to excluding Quakers from political influence, but it is clear that professing the inner light was a liability which excluded many otherwise qualified men from consideration in every administration except that of Jonathan Belcher, who was heavily indebted to prominent English Friends for his appointment as chief executive.[30]

No other religious bodies enjoyed representation on the council proportional to their percentage of the colony's white population. Presbyterians composed one-fifth of the members appointed after 1737, far less than their one-third share of the colony's population. Only five of the sixty-nine councillors were Baptist or Dutch Reformed, although almost one-quarter of the province worshipped in those churches.

As would be expected from their religious backgrounds, most coun-

TABLE 5
Ancestry of councillors

	Percentage of councillors	Percentage in N.J. population in 1790
English	68.1 (47)	50.6
Welsh	4.3 (3)	3.6
Scottish	17.4 (12)	3.4
Dutch	5.8 (4)	20.1
Irish[a]	3.0 (2)	4.1
French	1.4 (1)	3.8

SOURCE: The estimate of each national stock's percentage of the colony's population is taken from Thomas L. Purvis, "The European Origins of New Jersey's Eighteenth-Century Population," *New Jersey History*, vol. C (1982), 24.
NOTE: Only descent in the male line was considered in calculating the above figures.
[a] Irish category includes Anglo-Irish families who settled in Ireland after 1600.

cillors were of British ancestry. Sixty-eight percent were of English descent alone, compared to 51 percent of all white residents. Seventeen percent were Scottish in origin, a figure five times that group's size in the colony; the majority of these men were East Jersey proprietors, often called "Scottish proprietors," and most were Anglicans. While the recent arrival of most Scotch-Irish and Germans (who together included over 13 percent of the colony's white population) essentially explains their absence from the upper house, it is surprising that the numerous, long settled, and prosperous Dutch would number only four of the sixty-nine members, although seven additional men could claim kinship with Dutch families through marriage or common descent.

The immediate places from which their families had migrated varied more than the preceding figures indicate, since almost half moved to New Jersey from other American provinces rather than Europe. One-third of all the councillors' male ancestors came directly from England, one-quarter from New York, and one-ninth from Scotland. Approximately one-sixth emigrated from the three colonies of Massachusetts (7.2%), Pennsylvania (5.8%), and Barbados (4.4%). Seven percent were nonresidents who never lived in New Jersey.[31]

A highly advantageous factor for the accumulation of property and the establishment of political dynasties was the early arrival of many councillors' families in New Jersey. The paternal ancestors of 19 percent of those seated after 1737 had settled in the colony by 1679, 45 percent immigrated by 1699, and 61 percent were resident by 1719. Most of the councillors who migrated later were affluent sons of prominent families in neighboring provinces who brought wealth and social status with them, rather than upwardly mobile, self-made men; frequently they were related to members of New Jersey's upper house.

Because many newly arrived immigrants and residents of neighboring colonies gained appointment to the council—after which they normally held office for life—non-natives of New Jersey remained a majority of the upper house until shortly before the Revolution. Prior to 1740, it was usual for more than 80 percent of sitting councillors to have been born outside the province. The proportion of Jersey-born councillors increased steadily, but over half continued to be non-natives until 1764. Even in 1776, four of the eleven members had been born outside the colony. Although many of the non-natives were residents of exceptionally long duration, it is striking that the council lagged a full generation in the appearance of a creole elite behind the assembly, where native-born representatives overwhelmingly gained election, after 1738.[32]

The social standing of the councillors' forebears who settled in New Jersey was generally high, despite a few skeletons in some ancestral closets. Thomas Leonard was fortunate that few individuals knew the circumstances behind his family's removal to New Jersey from Massachusetts, his grandfather having absconded from Rowley to avoid prosecution for debts in 1674; his grandmother being notorious for seating herself in a chair from which she could comfortably shout obscene comments to men as they bathed in the nude; and several uncles having been indicted on a number of morals offenses, including a habit of parading naked wherever they were most likely to catch the eye of the local townswomen.[33]

Most other families were considerably more respectable. James Alexander was so closely related to the family holding the earldom of Stirling in Scotland that his son William sued in a British court to have himself declared the rightful heir to the title in the 1750s. Archibald Home was eligible to succeed to a baronetcy in England, but he died prematurely and it devolved on his younger brother. John Anderson's father was the lord provost of Glasgow, and had been that city's leading investor in the Darien Company. The ancestors of Thomas Gordon, Andrew Johnston, and John Johnston served in the Scottish Parliament, and the grandfather of Peter Sonmans in the Diet of the United Provinces. Roger Mompesson came from the English landed gentry and had sat in the English House of Commons. Such men as these were a small proportion of the upper house, but the ancestors of most appear to have been accounted gentlemen upon arriving in New Jersey.

Family status, early arrival, and personal wealth all played an important role in producing a highly exclusive elite composed of increasingly interrelated families. Forty-six percent were related to councillors who sat in the proprietary or royal governments before their own service began. The degree of interrelatedness among councillors increased steadily throughout the eighteenth century. Thirty-seven percent of those appointed before 1738 were related to former members, compared to sixty-one percent taking office after that date.[34]

Extending the range of family ties to include both houses of the General Assembly reveals a range of kinship that is even more impressive. Two-thirds of the upper house were related to at least one former member of the council or assembly. Most of these connections were consanguineous and close. Nineteen of the sixty-nine members were the sons of former councillors or assemblymen, another fourteen were sons-in-law, and an additional three were grandsons. Five of every six men appointed after 1737 were related to at least one other member of either house upon the commencement of their service. Eight of the twenty-four unconnected councillors were nonresidents who lived in New York or Philadelphia during all or part of their service; all the remaining men were the first of their families to reside in New Jersey, most having lived there fifteen years or less. Councillors who lacked ties of kinship with politically prominent New Jersey families upon assuming office rarely succeeded in establishing a base for their children or in-laws to follow them. Only six of the twenty-four unconnected members left descendants who later served in either the council or assembly.

Especially close connections existed between councillors and the individuals who became assembly leaders.[35] Both groups came from similar backgrounds—in many cases, from the same families. One-quarter of the councillors served as leaders in the lower house. Fifty-seven percent of all legislative leaders came from Burlington or Middlesex counties, compared with 52 percent of all councillors. Members of proprietary families likewise furnished 60 percent of the council and of the lower house's leaders. Forty-four percent of the assembly leaders serving after 1722 were related to royal councillors, as were five of the seven Speakers elected after 1740.

New Jersey councillors were also well connected to elite families in New York and Pennsylvania, and occasionally in other provinces. Forty-five percent of all married members of the upper house had fathers-in-law residing in another colony; for the years after 1737,

TABLE 6

Councillors related to other New Jersey councillors or
assemblymen upon appointment to seat

Number of relations	1702–1737		1738–1776		Total 1702–1776	
	%	N	%	N	%	N
1	28.9	11	25.8	8	25.7	19
2	13.2	5	9.7	3	11.6	8
3–4	7.9	3	19.3	6	13.0	9
5–6	0.0	0	6.5	2	3.0	2
7+	0.0	0	22.5	7	10.1	7
TOTAL	50.0	19	83.8	26	65.2	45

NOTE: Only those relationships that existed when a councillor first entered the upper house were counted; subsequent relationships, gained when new members joined, were excluded. The relevant kinship ties were: all connections based on common descent, son-in-law, brother-in-law, nephew-by-marriage. Connections with assemblymen or councillors in other colonies were not included.

61 percent did. Twenty-eight percent of married councillors were the sons-in-law of assemblymen, councillors, or governors from other provinces; during the years between 1738 and the Revolution, 40 percent of all councillors had fathers-in-law holding such offices outside New Jersey. These relationships were significant in enabling a relatively large number of councillors to play an active role in the public life of other colonies. Eleven of the sixty-nine members of New Jersey's upper house served as councillors, assemblymen, or deputy governors elsewhere in North America. Close ties of kinship did not usually link the gentry of different provinces in eighteenth-century America; it is most likely that the counciliar families of New Jersey were better related with other colonial elites than any similar group on the mainland.[36]

The councillors' backgrounds marked them as a highly exclusive group by contemporary American standards. They overwhelmingly derived from the eight percent of whites who worshipped in the Church of England, in particular from the most prosperous communicants. The great majority possessed extensive estates that ranked them among the wealthiest two percent of the province. They were well educated and many showed significant evidence of cultural sophistication. Sixty percent were landed proprietors or their relatives, the individuals who had dominated the colony's history since the 1670s and who still controlled access to all unpatented land in the province. They derived from families with a tradition of public service in both houses of the legislature, and many held high office in neighboring colonies.

Why then did a group which possessed the wealth, education, and

distinguished family backgrounds necessary to meet the standards expected of gentlemen in high office encounter the widespread hostility
described in the introduction? Every account of New Jersey's colonial
past has emphasized the assembly's frequent refusals to cooperate with
the upper house on matters of public policy and the smoldering resentment felt by many private citizens against individual members who
were proprietors. The council's ability to exert leadership and command respect reached its nadir in the early 1750s; at that time, the
issues of nonresidency and eastern domination drew widespread criticism from the lower house and western politicians, outbreaks of collective violence in several counties challenged the private interests of the
majority who were proprietors, and the publicity surrounding the irre-
sponsible actions of several prominent members seriously damaged the
upper house's public stature.

It is remarkable how quickly this situation changed. The councillors
of midcentury were clearly an embattled elite, whose private reputations and collective image undermined their ability to lead. Only
twenty-five years later, the successors of this beleaguered group discovered themselves on the verge of being drafted to lead the Revolutionary
movement. A dramatic reversal in popular estimation obviously occurred between these two events.

That reversal was the most significant long-term development in
provincial politics during the royal period, yet it has been ignored by
historians. The remainder of this article will examine the developments which enabled the upper house to gain widespread popular acceptance by the time of the Revolution. The three most important
factors contributing to the cessation of controversy were the decrease in
nonresidency, the reduction of tensions involving proprietary land
claims, and the improved quality of appointments after 1755.

New Jersey was the only colony where significant numbers of councillors lived outside the province during all or part of their tenure.
Nonresidency seriously damaged the upper house's image, by encouraging a belief that certain members were not attending adequately to
the public business because their own interests were not directly involved. Colonists were also apprehensive about the ability of outsiders
to make knowledgeable decisions concerning the colony's affairs, especially the nomination of persons to hold important civil or military
positions. Furthermore, every seat in the upper house held by the in-
habitant of another province created inevitable resentment among the
colony's elite, as it deprived an eligible New Jersey politician of a powerful, prestigious office. Nonresidency consequently became a highly
visible issue, detracting considerably from the council's reputation.

A significant portion of the upper house lived outside New Jersey.

Thirteen of the sixty-nine members (19 percent) were inhabitants of other colonies while holding office, and six of them never established homes in New Jersey. Ten of the thirty-eight men appointed before 1738 were absentee members, many of them continuing to hold office for long periods. From 1723 to 1737, between one-quarter and one-third of the council lived in New York or Philadelphia. Nonresidency was so pervasive prior to 1772 that only during the years 1745, 1746, 1747, and 1757 did all councillors live in New Jersey.

Resentment over this situation flared up several times, producing public protests against the evident subordination of local welfare to outside interests. As early as 1733, the assembly noted that the non-attendance of several councillors from New York obstructed the province's affairs, and it resolved unanimously that all members of the upper house should live in New Jersey.[37] Eleven years later, the representatives complained, "There is not nor hath not for several Years past been, as the Committee can be informed, more than six or seven Persons of his Majesty's Council residing in this colony at any one time."[38] The assembly again felt obliged to address the problem in 1751 and 1752, in response to petitions signed by hundreds of West Jersey freeholders who expressed outrage that nonresidents and eastern politicians were holding council seats that rightfully belonged to men from their division.[39]

The problem of nonresidency quickly receded from public prominence after the protests of 1751 and 1752. Following the latter date, governors named only two inhabitants of other colonies to the council—John Stevens and William Alexander, both of whom were closely connected to the province. Stevens was a New Jersey native who had sat in the assembly, and Alexander possessed large tracts of land upon which he soon settled. Only during the last five years of the royal period, however, did all members of the upper house live in New Jersey.

The elimination of nonresidency ultimately proceeded from factors unrelated to public opinion. Prior to the 1760s, talented members of New Jersey's first families frequently relocated in neighboring provinces to seek greater economic, political, or marital opportunities, thus reducing the pool of qualified candidates from which councillors could be nominated. New York's and Philadelphia's more promising prospects appealed to New Jersey councillors, especially to merchants who wished to escape the limitations of the colony's small population and satellite economy. The reversal of this trend in the 1760s was of vital importance to the eventual acceptance of the conciliar elite. Councillors John Smith and John Stevens, two wealthy merchants who had moved to Philadelphia and New York, returned to New Jersey at approximately this time. A number of wealthy, educated, and prominent individuals from other provinces also established their homes in New Jersey during these years, including William Livingston, John Witherspoon, James Kinsey, William Alexander, and Francis Hopkinson. The last two served as councillors, and all became prominent in public life.[40] Able men of unusual ability from other colonies were now moving to New Jersey, and the province's native elite was demonstrating an increased disposition to remain permanently in the colony. Under these circumstances, absenteeism on the council ended, and the willingness of all councillors to sever ties of residence with other provinces dispelled doubts that they saw their personal interests to be different from those of New Jersey.

A second major factor undermining the ability of councillors to command respect by midcentury was the steady increase in tensions surrounding claims by members who were proprietors to vast tracts of land. These controversies were highly inflammatory; they culminated in a series of public disturbances between 1745 and 1754. Proprietors comprised half the upper house at that time, and their actions ensured that the council would be closely associated in the public mind with the measures which helped spark the violence.

Problems surrounding disputed land titles had unsettled the province since the 1670s, and by 1745 the amount of land embroiled in litigation had swelled to perhaps a half million acres in six of the colony's ten counties. A seemingly interminable stream of court battles originated from several large patents granted in the 1660s, and most remained unresolved by 1745. A more serious cause of alienation was the failure of proprietors in both divisions to provide an efficient system of land registration. Eastern and western proprietors alike lost deeds, authorized overlapping surveys, and failed to record important transactions. Several prominent proprietors exploited this situation by filing ejectment suits against individuals holding deeds given by speculative rivals. Councillors Peter Sonmans, Robert Hunter Morris, and John Coxe all repudiated deeds signed by themselves and attempted to force landowners to repurchase their property at prices far higher than had been originally paid. Such suits made many honest freeholders feel insecure about their property and were a source of great outrage in both divisions.[41]

Failure to guarantee firm title and the renunciation of signed deeds brought almost universal condemnation upon the proprietors. One critic of their inclination to sue for the invalidation of deeds on the basis of technical defects in the original conveyances described them as they must have seemed to many Jersey farmers threatened by eviction actions. "It has always been supposed that a *just* and *honest* Purchase of, and from those who had Right and Property would secure the same unto the Purchaser, and it has always done so and been so Accounted of, save, in these Parts, and among such *Creatures* as the *Proprietors.*"[42]

It became impossible not to associate the grievances arising from this situation with the council. Proprietors on the East Jersey board and the council coordinated the simultaneous presentation of petitions to the Privy Council demanding royal intervention when public disorders broke out after 1745; they even composed a joint memorial from both bodies on one occasion, indicating that they saw no distinction between private concerns and their public duties as councillors.[43] Such obviously self-interested use of their official position as councillors by the proprietary majority made the upper house appear to be little more than an extension of the East Jersey Board of Proprietors. As the perception grew that this was indeed the case, the councillors lost much of their credibility and ability to exercise leadership.

It was during this period that relations between the upper and lower houses of the General Assembly reached their nadir. The assembly repeatedly rejected measures demanded by the council to punish rioters and prevent crowds from releasing prisoners from jail. The representatives refused to cooperate with the councillors in part because their draconian recommendations seemed out of proportion to the offenses committed, which rarely resulted in serious damage or injury. The lower house's unwillingness to cooperate with the upper also stemmed from what assembly leader Richard Smith described as "the general Outcry or dislike to those called the Proprietors." "The People wod not pay any Money to support their Schemes," Smith said, in defense of the lower house's refusal to appropriate expenditures for guarding the jails. He insisted that "it would but have been setting the Country by the Ears for [th]e Legislature to have attempted the raising of Money for that service."[44]

Few public disturbances directed against proprietary interests occurred after 1750, none for sixteen years after 1754. The absence of violence and the increased willingness of all parties to explore possibilities for a negotiated settlement steadily reduced tensions over land tenure. As the property disputes receded from their former prominence and the colony's military role in the Seven Years' War dominated politics, controversies over disputed titles ceased to be a serious issue affecting the council's public standing.

These problems also became much less closely associated with the upper house as later governors redressed the imbalance of East Jersey proprietors, whose actions had stirred most of the popular discontent before 1754. Eastern proprietors were strongly represented in the upper house until 1762, but they ceased to be a majority after that year. The strong connection in the public mind between the council and the East Jersey Board of Proprietors afterwards became increasingly unrealistic and finally irrelevant.

The consequences of these changes can be seen by comparing the assembly's reaction to the incidents occurring during the climax of antiproprietary agrarian unrest from 1745 to 1754 with its response to a more limited outburst of discontent in 1770. The representatives had condemned the violence that occurred at midcentury, but, mindful of public resentment against the proprietors, they showed little urgency in taking steps to deter future disturbances. They repeatedly rebuffed the council's proposals for restoring order, and they indicated obliquely on several occasions that provocations by the proprietors had played a major role in sparking the outbursts.[45]

The assembly sitting in 1770 showed neither hesitation nor ambivalence when, after Newark magistrates roughly arrested several leaders of a large crowd protesting a recent award of 13,500 acres to the proprietors, several outbuildings belonging to the chief legal counsel for the East Jersey proprietors, David Ogden, were burned.[46] David Ogden had been a leading proprietary spokesman since the 1740s, when he assisted in preparing the ejectment suits that had precipitated much of the violence of that time. The assemblymen sitting then had demonstrated little interest in aiding Ogden or his proprietary associates when the latter sought measures which would prevent trespassers from cutting valuable timber on their lands or restrain crowds from disturbing the peace with impunity. The representatives of 1770 showed themselves to be of an entirely different stripe, ready to align themselves unmistakably on the councillor's side against the land claimants whose titles had just been forfeited. Only three days after the governor opened the yearly session with his address, the representatives passed strongly worded resolutions calling for the arrest of the arsonists who had destroyed Ogden's property, directing the governor to offer a £25-reward for information leading to their apprehension, and praising the Newark magistrates for dispersing the antiproprietary crowd.[47] The resolutions were noteworthy for their firm support of a councillor long known as a leading proprietary spokesman, especially since the house failed to consider evidence that the magistrates had overreacted by ordering a peaceful crowd to disperse, precipitously arresting its leaders with undue force, and imposing excessive fines on the group's spokesmen, to make examples of them.[48]

The assembly's actions supporting David Ogden and the Newark magistrates demonstrate that by 1770 proprietary land claims against small landholders had ceased to be a political issue adversely affecting the council's public image or its ability to gain support from the lower house. Many of the suits had fallen into abeyance, and most others seemed likely to be resolved impartially through arbitration. Consequently, public opinion no longer inhibited the assembly from taking stands favorable to proprietors in the upper house. The representatives were, if anything, too hasty and uncritical in interpreting the events in Newark to the proprietors' advantage. It is remarkable how quickly the tensions associated with the colony's tangled land controversies diminished. Within the short span of sixteen years, grievances that had sparked heated exchanges between both houses of the legislature, generated outright violence in half the province's counties, and brought the council itself into general disrepute no longer poisoned relations between both houses of the General Assembly or seriously detracted from the councillors' reputation among the general population.

The final circumstance contributing to the rising esteem enjoyed by councillors after midcentury was the improved quality of appointments by the governors. The eventual elimination of nonresidency and the reduced number of eastern proprietors gave the council an appearance of being more representative of the colony in general. These changes eliminated a major liability undercutting the upper house's prestige— the fear that outsiders or narrow groups would make important decisions based upon self-interest rather than the public good. Governors also appointed more Quakers and other West Jersey residents, and so eliminated another source of dissatisfaction and anger, dating from the 1730s, among politicians in that district.[49]

The councillors named after 1755 were more capable of commanding respect than many of their predecessors, whose involvement in several well-publicized incidents had seriously damaged the upper house's reputation. Fenwick Lyell had assaulted and beat an assemblyman in 1730. The assembly voted to make Thomas Leonard liable for prosecution for negligence as a loan-office commissioner in 1739, and it demanded his dismissal from council in 1751 for irresponsibly having named an unqualified and corrupt man to be sheriff of Somerset County. A grand jury in Monmouth County indicted Lewis Morris Ashfield in the same year for public intoxication on the Sabbath and assaulting a constable. Robert Hunter was believed to have misused his office as chief justice to set aside a jury verdict as a favor to a fellow proprietor.[50]

Many of the councillors holding office at midcentury gave evidence of being significantly less public-spirited than corresponding elites elsewhere, particularly when compared to the sense of noblesse oblige shown by many of Virginia's first families.[51] Robert Lettice Hooper neglected to pay the fees necessary to qualify as a councillor for several years after his nomination was confirmed.[52] John Schuyler, a talented and wealthy aristocrat, vacated his seat in 1739 because it interfered with his business affairs. John Wills, Cornelius Van Horne, and David Provoost all resigned voluntarily shortly after Schuyler did.[53] David Ogden, a wealthy lawyer and a Yale graduate, only accepted office after specifying, "I shall Rely on the Goodness of the Council to Excuse my attendance when it would too much interfere with my Interests & Business."[54] Public-spiritedness declined to its lowest point in the 1740s, when Governor Lewis Morris wrote to the Lords of Trade:

[It] is with difficulty I can get above three or foure Councillors together at any other time than at a sessions: Every such meeting being Expensive to them besides the inconvenience of being called from their habitations and Private affaires; and should I suspend any for not attending, the Case would be the same in others named to that place, Could they be prevailed on to accept of it, w'ch very few that are but tollerably fit for it are willing to do;—it being a sort of tax on them to serve the publick at their owne Expense besides neglect of their business.[55]

In contrast, the personal conduct of the men holding office by the late 1760s was notably free of scandal. The only councillor of these years who fell into disrepute was Stephen Skinner, and even then the controversy over his loss of treasury funds was slow to develop and entirely limited to his own reputation.[56] The collective backgrounds and personal achievements of the eleven councillors sitting in 1776 recommended virtually all of them for high office. They were, without exception, wealthy and socially prominent. Four were college graduates, and two others were trustees of colleges. At a time when military service was admired as an indicator of private virtue, three had served as officers on campaigns against the French. Two members whose close kinship connections with the elites of New York and Pennsylvania could have enabled them to build prestigious careers in those provinces, William Alexander and Francis Hopkinson, had chosen to settle in New Jersey rather than hold office as nonresidents. In Alexander's case, this decision had cost him his seat on the New York council, a sacrifice highly appreciated in New Jersey as proof of his willingness to make the colony's interests his own.

A suggestive indication of the manner and bearing of these men is given in the obituary of Frederick Smyth:

He was born of a respectable family, in the county of Norfolk, in Old England; and came to this country about the year 1765; from which time, till the

Revolution, he filled the station of Chief Justice with fidelity to the old government, yet without making one personal enemy in the new. Judge Smyth, accordingly (to the credit of the Patriots of '76 be it spoken) never met with harsh usage for his unshaken loyalty; and was permitted to reside in the Government House, at Amboy, as long as he chose, after he had been superceded in office. . . .

Mr. Smyth was a true Gentleman of the Old School—in habit easy—in temper affable—in manner ceremoniously polite. His memory having been richly stored with the literary and historical anecdotes of a half a century, was an unfailing source of instructive, or amusing conversation, and he continued to welcome his friends, and to make himself agreeable to visitors of every age, to the last day of his long protracted life.[57]

If most other councillors holding office with Frederick Smyth also met the standards expected of a "gentleman of the old school," the prestige enjoyed by the conciliar elite immediately prior to the Revolution becomes more understandable. Personal demeanor and social status were finally intersecting to produce a body of men capable of commanding the respect so often denied in the past.

The most impressive evidence that the upper house's personnel had gained public acceptance by the 1770s was the effort made by New Jersey Whigs to give the most important leadership positions in the new government to royal councillors. The Whigs hoped to cap the Revolutionary movement with leaders from the conciliar families, so that their social status would provide respectability to the American cause. They considered the accession of William Alexander, a second-generation councillor and East Jersey proprietor popularly called Lord Stirling, to be a vindication of their cause, and they made him the province's highest-ranking military officer. "The Jerseys appear spirited," Eliphalet Dyer wrote Samuel Adams in early 1776, "Animated principally by Ld. Stirling."[58] It was indeed Alexander who brought the King's authority to an end by ordering the last royal governor to be placed under house arrest. Two councillors, Robert Stockton and Francis Hopkinson, led the New Jersey delegation to the Second Continental Congress and signed the Declaration of Independence. The state assembly divided evenly between Stockton and William Livingston in the first gubernatorial election, but then elected Livingston on the second ballot, very likely because Councillor John Stevens, a relative of Livingston, purposefully misled the legislators into believing that Stockton would prefer to head the Supreme Court. The legislature then offered Stockton the chief-justiceship, which he seems to have refused in anger at having been denied the governorship by

Stevens.[59] Stevens sat for six years after 1776 as the Revolutionary council's vice-president—in effect the state's second-ranking officer, since the governor was president—and chaired the convention that ratified the Constitution. Francis Hopkinson served, after Independence, in the legislature and on the Supreme Court. The Whigs also offered East Jersey proprietor Cortlandt Skinner, closely connected to the council through his brother Stephen and brother-in-law James Parker, the choice of any military or civil post he desired in the new government, in return for his talents and social prestige; they considered his refusal a major disappointment.[60] By the end of 1776, former royal councillors had, among them, cast two of the colony's five votes for independence, assumed command of the Revolutionary militia, declined the opportunity to become chief justice, held the second-highest position in the government, and lost the election for governor by the narrowest of margins. Every important post in the new government was either theirs or had been within their grasp.

The Revolution did not begin as a social upheaval. There was no attempt to supplant the authority of the councillors, in fact, the opposite was the case. The old conciliar elite's position nevertheless declined greatly after 1776. Individual members continued to be important, but the new government's highest positions increasingly had to be filled by men of less distinguished backgrounds as the decisions of individuals to enter military service on either side, to become loyalists and seek the safety of British lines, or to profess neutrality decreased the number of candidates for the new state council who could have met the old standards for membership in the upper house.[61] Most members of the council declined to commit themselves to the patriots' cause, or, more commonly, equivocated. Whether they did so for reasons of conscience, ideology, or self-interest is less important than the ultimate result of their actions, for they committed political suicide.

Whatever effects proceeded from the Revolutionary movement in New Jersey, its cause was not resentment against the exclusive group that sat in the upper house. This circumstance highlights one of the most important facts concerning the evolution of politics in colonial New Jersey: without a doubt, the conciliar elite had legitimated its claim to power by the 1770s. Had it not done so, the imperial crisis over the limits of Parliamentary authority would certainly have been used as a pretext for removing its members from the center of power.

It was the ironic fate of most New Jersey councillors to have to drop the reins of power just when they seemed to have gained a firm grasp. After struggling for acceptance and respectability during most of the eighteenth century, the upper house's members largely failed to seize the opportunity offered by the Revolution to establish themselves at the center of power. This result was not foreordained. In colonies like Virginia and South Carolina, where the Whig movement originated among the conciliar families, members of these families continued to have as much political influence after the war as before.[62] New Jersey diverged from their experience only because so many members of the conciliar elite discredited themselves by holding aloof from the patriotic cause. The failure of most councillors to take the vigorous actions expected by the Whigs sealed their fortunes, for it forced men from less distinguished backgrounds to discover for the first time that they could govern themselves as well as, or better than, their predecessors.

GRACE L. CHICKERING

Founders of an Oligarchy:
The Virginia Council, 1692–1722

———————◆———————

THE WORLD OF political leadership has never been very large: it has always been commanded by a few, who must rely upon a well-ensconced
ruling class at the provincial level for its support. Not until the last decade of the seventeenth century could the colony of Virginia boast of
men and families of such political, economic, and social status at all
levels of leadership.[1] At the apex of the political structure were "the
elite," members of the governors' councils of Virginia. By 1692 these
men of great wealth, first-generation Virginians who had emigrated to
Virginia after the colony's privation period had ended, had produced
sons who were to inherit not only their estates but their reputations and
offices as well. For three decades, from 1692 to 1722, they and their
families, as the colony's landed gentry, claimed political authority and
social eminence at all levels of government and society in tidewater
Virginia.

   Unlike most of their predecessors, members of the governors' councils after 1692 had come to Virginia not as frontiersmen, but as men of
substantial families long associated in London circles with either business or government connections in Virginia. Within several decades
these Virginians, through purchase or inheritance of a developed property interest or through a propitious marriage, succeeded in subduing
or absorbing the leadership of an older generation. William Byrd I
emigrated to Virginia about 1670 as heir to the Stegg properties
through his mother's family, whose claim dates back to the early days
of the Virginia Company. Westover had passed through many hands,
including those of De la Warr, before passing, with improvements,

255

to Byrd. Some of Robert (King) Carter's lands, acquired through inheritance from his father John Carter, can be traced in ownership
and probably cultivation to as early as 1628. Philip Ludwell I acquired
the plantation of Green Spring upon his marriage to Lady Berkeley
after Governor Berkeley's death. The fortunes of Lewis Burwell I were
inherited from his father Edward Burwell through early subscriptions
to the Virginia Company and cultivated lands from his stepfather
Wingate. Edward Digges, who emigrated in 1650, inherited original
investments of Sir Dudley Digges and two of his brothers in the Virginia Company. The Wormleys and the Scarboroughs had survived as
struggling planters of the first generation.[2]

All members of the Governor's Councils, these men qualified for
their offices under the provisions of Royal Instructions to Colonial
Governors regarding appointees of the council "as men of estates and
abilities and not necessitous people or much in debt. . . ."[3] Appointed
for life,[4] councillors assumed the highest office in the colony. Appointment came via London with royal approval. They served in all three
capacities of government. In the executive branch of government they
were the cabinet, or the governor's advisors. Writing at the turn of the
century when the Byrds, the Ludwells, the Harrisons, the Carters, and
James Blair were at loggerheads with Governor Francis Nicholson, historian Robert Beverley maintained that the "Gentlemen of the Council"
were to be "a restraint upon him (the Governor) if he should exceed the
bounds of his Commission: They are able to do this, by having each of
them an equal Vote with the Governor, in most things of Consequence
Viz. In calling Assemblies. In disposing of Publick Revenue, and inspecting the accounts thereof. . . . In making Grants and passing all
the Patents for Land."[5] The council also nominated and, together with
the governor, placed and displaced all persons in lucrative public offices. In the legislative capacity, the council comprised the 'upper
house' and had the right of veto on all laws. Both Nicholson and Governor Alexander Spotswood complained that, when the council acted
in its legislative capacity, councillors voted as Virginians to protect Virginia's constitution and their own interests "to the prejudice of the
Crown and the interests of Great Britain."[6] In the judicial capacity, the
council, together with the governor, was the supreme court of the
land. Spotswood complained that, in the courts (including county
courts headed by justices of the peace, from which cases were referred
to the higher court), "if a suit be brought against any member of the
great families to the Supreme Court of Justice there would not be one
amongst them who will rule on it."[7]

Hence, by the last decade of the seventeenth century, members of the governors' councils were in a position to thwart policies of the Crown or the Crown's royal governors when the two were in conflict with their vested interest in the colony. Between 1692 and 1722 events in England and abroad led indirectly to continual conflict between councillors and governors.

During most of these thirty years, England was involved in a life-and-death struggle with the *bête noire* of Europe, Louis XIV. The time was critical for the North American colonies. It was a period in which the English reassessed their position in relation to the colonies, founded the Board of Trade, and attempted to reform colonial land and tax policies to protect England's commercial interests against France and its allies. The role of enforcing old regulations and implementing new ones fell to the governors of England's royal colonies. The struggle that ensued between the governors and members of the council in Virginia arose over a conflict of interests between the mercantile policy of the Crown, represented by the Royal Governor, and the elite of colonial Virginia. The conflict resulted in the recall or removal of governors Edmund Andros, Francis Nicholson, and Alexander Spotswood.

This study is essentially an attempt to delineate the extent of the economic, political, and social power of the elite of colonial Virginia during this period. The three decades selected represent the period in which councillors were at the height of their power and in which they founded the most distinguished eighteenth-century oligarchy in the colonies.

As has been indicated before, elevation to such a station of political influence was, by the last decade of the seventeenth century, the consequence of enormous wealth. Virginia was an agricultural society, one whose economy, until well into the eighteenth century, was built on tobacco. Tobacco was the Virginians' medium of exchange at home and in England. It followed, then, that its largest producers were the holders of the greatest tracts of productive land and, by the first two decades of the eighteenth century, the owners of the greatest number of slaves.

The disparity in wealth between the elite and the freeholder or tenant farmer in early eighteenth-century Virginia is starkly drawn in the contrast between the Byrds of Virginia and the fifty-acre freeholder described by a traveler in the colony. In 1726 William Byrd II of Westover wrote to Charles, Earl of Orrery, describing his domestic estate:

Like one of the patriarchs I have my flocks and my herds, my bond-men and bond-women, and every soart of trade amongst my own servants, so that I live in a kind of independence on everyone but providence. However this soart of life is without expense, yet it is attended with a great deal of trouble. I must take care to keep all my people to their duty, to set all springs in motion and to make every one draw his equal share to carry the machine forward. But then 'tis an amusement in this silent country and a continual exercise of our patience and economy.[8]

By contrast, Louis Michel, a Swiss Frenchman from Berne, visiting several of his countrymen who had settled in Virginia at the end of the seventeenth century (two years before Michel's visit) wrote:

About 300 dollars are necessary in order to set up a man properly, namely to enable him to buy two slaves, with whom in two years a beautiful farm can be cleared, because the trees are far apart. Afterwards the settlers must be provided with cattle, a horse, costing at the usual price 1 lb., a cow with a calf 50 shillings, a mare (?) 10 shillings, Furniture and clothes, together with tools and provisions for a year, must also be on hand. It is indeed possible to begin with less and succeed, but then three or four years pass before one gets into a good condition.[9]

Families of wealth and influence in Virginia, as in most societies, were linked by marriage ties. For example, William Fitzhugh II of Stafford County, who was a member of the council from 1711 until his death in 1714, was the son of William Fitzhugh I, a London draper's son. Lawyer, planter, businessman, burgess, politician, and speculator, Fitzhugh arrived in Virginia between 1670 and 1671. Having come with sufficient funds, and having married soon after into an established Virginia family, the elder Fitzhugh's beginnings were propitious. His rise to wealth and influence were meteoric and, before his death in 1701, he had amassed a land fortune totalling approximately 56,245 acres in Westmoreland and Stafford counties. His property included 43 slaves and 900 indentured servants. Fitzhugh's pretensions, like many of Virginia's elite, extended to having large pieces of silver in his household marked with the Fitzhugh coat of arms. He lived in the main plantation house, which had 13 rooms. The plantation estate included, in addition, other "houses for use well furnished with brick Chimneys, four good Cellars, a Dairy, Dovecoat, Stable, Barn, Hen house Kitchen & all other conveniencys." His son William Fitzhugh II, prior to being appointed to the council, had served as clerk, justice and high sheriff of Stafford County and had been elected to the House of Burgesses in 1700, 1701, and 1702. He married one of the elite, Ann Lee, daughter of Councillor Richard Lee II of Mt. Pleasant, Westmoreland County, who served the council from 1676 until his death in 1717.[10]

One of the most influential of Virginia's elite families during this period was the Ludwell family. Councillor Philip Ludwell I of Rich Neck and Green Spring, James City County, was born in England and came to Virginia about the same time as the elder Fitzhugh. In 1674/ 1675 he was appointed to the governor's council, where he served until retirement in 1704. His son, Philip Ludwell II of Greenspring, re- membered by American colonial historians of the period as Governor Nicholson's nemesis, was appointed to the governor's council in 1702, after having served as burgess from James City County, and remained on the council until his death in 1727. Although there is no extant description of the lands of the Ludwell family, the inventory of the estate of Philip Ludwell of Green Spring or Rich Neck, James City County, who had served in the governor's council for three genera- tions—the son of Councillor Philip Ludwell II and the last male heir of the Ludwells to bear the name—reflects the same proportionate wealth as that held by the Fitzhughs. The inventory lists nine separate properties, including Green Spring, Rich Neck, and Hott Water, all three of which were large plantations on the north side of the James River. A fourth property, Scotland, was probably at the present Scotland Wharf, opposite. Besides these, the Ludwell estate included Cloverton, Pinewood Meadow, Mill Quarter, Archers Hope, and New Quarter.[11]

The inventory lists a total of 242 slaves—a separate list under the property to which they were attached—334 head of cattle, 213 sheep, 210 pigs, and 27 horses. Furniture is specified as "Walnut" or "Ma- hogany" and bed quilts are "silk." Table service includes 7½ dozen china plates, 58 wine glasses, and 2 dozen ivory knives and forks. Stores include 12 dozen Irish hose and 22 yards of "Rushia Linen." That the plantations were to a large degree self-sustaining is suggested by inventory items such as "Shoe Maker's Tools," "Wheel Wrights Tools," and a "Chest of Carpenters Tools."[12]

The Ludwells were persons of influence both in England and Vir- ginia. Philip Ludwell I was the grandson of James Cottington, nephew of Lord Cottington of Somerset, England. In Virginia the first Ludwell was able to marry off children and grandchildren to other influential families of the colony. His son and heir, Councillor Philip Ludwell II, married Hannah Harrison, daughter of Councillor Benjamin Harrison. Daughter Jane married Councillor Daniel Parke II. Granddaughter Lucy married Burgess, later Councillor, William Byrd II and grand- daughter Frances married Councillor John Custis. To further compli- cate the web of marriage alliances and influence among the elite, the Ludwells were related through marriage to James Blair, the Scottish commissary who was also the founder and president of the College of William and Mary and a member of the governors' councils from 1688 until his death in 1743. Blair married Sarah Harrison, daughter of Benjamin, and Councillor Robert (King) Carter's daughter Anne was married to Burgess Benjamin Harrison of Berkeley, son of Councillor Benjamin Harrison I.[13]

Of similar vintage was Robert (King) Carter of Corotoman, Lancaster County, councillor from 1699 until his death in 1732. "King" Carter was the son of John Carter, mentioned before, also of Corotoman, who had been both a member of the House of Burgesses and a member of the governors' councils before his son. Like the Ludwells, King Carter was by blood and marriage related to a number of councillors' families. Carter's first wife was Judith Armistead, daughter of Councillor John Armistead. Carter's daughter married Councillor Mann Page, and his son John married Elizabeth Hill, daughter of Councillor Edward Hill. Carter's daughter Anne, already mentioned above, was married to Benjamin Harrison II, son of Councillor Benjamin Harrison.[14] King Carter's will indicates that he owned an estimated 300,000 acres of land in nine different counties at the time of his death.[15]

A sampling of surviving wills of other members of the governors' councils during the period reveals that Councillor Nathaniel Harrison, son of Councillor Benjamin Harrison, owned land in five different counties and an acre of land in Williamsburg, and Mann Page owned land in nine different counties, 700 acres of which were in Williamsburg.[16] According to Bassett, William Byrd I owned at the time of his death 26,231 acres of land.[17] Acreage is not estimated in some wills. Nathaniel Bacon, for example, left the plantation at King's Creek and other lands in Hampton and Bruton parishes in York County, lands in Isle of Wight, Nansemond, and New Kent counties;[18] and, similarly, Edmund Berkeley refers in his will to 8,198 acres in King William County, lands including Barn Elms in Middlesex, lands in Gloucester, and lands in King and Queens counties, acreage unspecified.[19]

In spite of Hugh Jones's observation that the timber houses of the common planter were "neater than the farm houses are generally in England"[20] vast discrepancies in style of life existed between the very rich and the ordinary farmer, between the successful farmer and the poor farmer. A representative successful farmer was one John Brooke, who died in 1729. The inventory of his estate reveals that he was a man of modest means compared with the Fitzhughs, the Ludwells, the Carters, and other families of their class. John Brooke owned four slaves, sixteen head of cattle, and one horse. Obviously he had both aspirations and pretensions. The inventory included "four Suits of new Sagathy Cloaths, a New Wigg, pictures and prints, nine Silver Spoons,

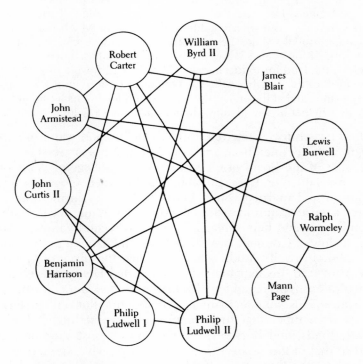

FIG. 1 Family connections among leading men of the council, 1692–1722
Lines represent relationship by marriage, except in the case of the Ludwells,
where blood ties are obvious.

1 Silver Teapot and 2 Silver Tankards." Unsettled accounts due the estate totalled "about 25 £."[21] Still more modest was the estate of one Samuell Barkhead, who died in 1720. His name was not distinguished by the sequence "Gent," nor did he own slaves. His total estate, land and house discounted, was valued at £16 16s. 6d., the most valuable single item in the inventory being his livestock which comprised "five head of cattle and 14 young hoggs." He ate from pewter plates, and there is no mention of silver in the inventory.[22]

There is record of at least one other type of settlement in tidewater Virginia in the early 1700s attesting to the social and economic differences between the elite and other members of the farming population. Louis Michel wrote of one of his countrymen who had settled in Virginia two years before:

We were surprised at the good condition they had reached in so short a time. Especially one of them, born at Neuenstatt, was well provided with horse, cattle and grain. They are the last settlers on this side of the Mattabany [Mattaponey] . . . But their condition of settlement which they had made with Major Borell (Major Lewis Burwell of "Carter's Creek", Gloucester county, and "King's Creek", York county), did not suit us. There were to plant and clean the land for fourteen years. They in return were to give him one third of the cattle, together with 100 pounds of tobacco annually, repay the money loaned and at the end of the above mentioned years he should be free to decide whether he would allow them to stay there any longer or not.[23]

The Lewis Burwell referred to in Michel's report was a member of the governor's council from 1702 until his death in 1710. He was also a member of the Board of Governors of the College of William and Mary and father of Lucy Burwell, who spurned Governor Francis Nicholson and married young Edmund Berkeley, a member of the council from 1713 until 1718. Lewis Burwell was married to Nathaniel Bacon's niece and heir, Abigail Smith. His second wife was Martha Cole, widow of Councillor William Cole and daughter of Councillor John Lear. Burwell's brother James married the niece of Councillor John Armistead; his daughter Martha married Henry Armistead, the councillor's son; his daughter Elizabeth married Councillor Benjamin Harrison; and his daughter Joanna married Councillor William Bassett.[24]

If we remember that there were very few Fitzhughs, Ludwells, Carters, Byrds, and Burwells, the position of most Virginians being closer to that of the Brookes or the Barkheads, what emerges is a pattern not unlike that of the English countryside, dominated by the landed gentry. Surveyor General of the Customs for the American colonies after Edward Randolph, Colonel Robert Quary writes in 1703, "The people . . . take little leisure to busy themselves about matters of state. . . . But in every River of this Province there are men in number from ten to thirty, who by trade and industry have gotten very competent estates. Those gentlemen take care to supply the poorer sort with goods and necessaries, and are sure to keep them always in their debt, and consequently dependent on them. Out of this number are Chosen her Majesties Council, the Assembly, the Justices, and Officers of the Government."[25] Hugh Jones wrote, "At the Capitol (Williamsburg), at publick times, may be seen a great number of handsom, well-dressed, compleat gentlemen. . . . They live in the same neat manner, dress after the same modes, and behave themselves exactly as the gentry in London: most families of any note having a coach, chariot, berlin or chaise."[26]

Virginia, by the turn of the seventeenth century, was a deferential

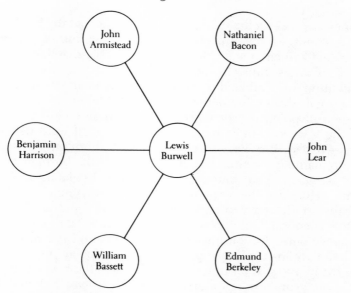

FIG. 2 Lewis Burwell's connections with other councillors' families during his membership in the council

society, the wealth and land—the source of power and status—being in the hands of a relative few. In some cases landed wealth meant virtual political control of an entire area or county. The Fitzhughs, for example, held unprecedented wealth in Stafford and Westmoreland counties. Records reveal that they were also the political power of Stafford County. Although William Fitzhugh I was never appointed to the council, he was an agent for the Fairfaxes, who were Proprietors of the Northern Neck. Two brothers of Councillor William Fitzhugh II, Henry and George, succeeded him as burgesses from the county, while brother Thomas was clerk of Stafford County.[27]

The power of such families was not confined to the locale in which they lived. William Fitzhugh I was a lawyer and probably a tobacco agent for the surrounding planters, as was his son Henry. The younger William Fitzhugh was related through marriage to the Corbins, who held considerable influence in the House of Burgesses, and to council president Edmund Jenings of York County, who had blood and marriage ties to Henry Compton, Bishop of London, and to a Lord Mayor of London. The point is that these men of prominence and their families exercised enormous local power, its reverberations sometimes heard in the counting houses, tea houses, and councils of state in England. The fact that Councillor Edmund Jenings simultaneously had the ear of members of the ruling class in England and the Fitzhughs of Stafford County is not surprising. And what was true of Jenings was also true of Councillor and Commissary James Blair, and of the Byrds, Ludwells, Carters, Burwells, and Harrisons.

In addition to wealth and political influence, members of the governor's councils during the period had vested interests in Virginia and were men of political experience. Between 1692 and 1722, twenty-six of the total forty-three members of the council were native Virginians—that is, they were second-generation, born on Virginia soil. Of the remaining seventeen council members, the birthplace of two cannot be determined, fourteen were born in England, and one in Scotland. However, the proportion of native-born Virginians changed drastically in the six-year-period between 1692 and 1698. Of the twenty-five councillors appointed between 1698 and 1722, twenty were native-born, the birthplace of one is unknown, and only four were definitely born in England. Of those four, Robert Quary, who was appointed in 1702, is an unusual case; he held the position of councillor, more in an honorary than in an active capacity, in four different colonies at the same time. Doctor William Cooke of Williamsburg, who arrived from London and was promptly appointed in 1712, was an "old schoolfellow" of William Byrd II at the Inns of Court in London.[28]

In addition to the significant fact that eighty percent of the councillors appointed between 1698 and 1722 were second-generation Virginians, it can be determined that twelve of the councillors in the thirty years under scrutiny succeeded fathers who were councillors before them. Peter Beverley, William Byrd II, Robert (King) Carter, John Custis II, Cole Digges, Nathaniel Harrison, Edward Hill II, Philip Ludwell II, Mann Page, Matthew Page, Daniel Parke II, and John Robinson were all sons of councillors.[29]

Of vast importance is the fact that of the total of forty-three councillors, twenty-seven had served as members of the House of Burgesses prior to their appointment to the council. At least fifteen councillors— probably more—served as justices of the peace in their respective counties. A few, including Robert Carter, were successively members of their parish vestries, clerks of the county courts, or sheriffs. Such evidence suggests that the filtering process for positions of the highest leadership, so ably examined by Charles Sydnor several decades ago, applied not only to the burgesses in "Washington's Virginia," but to the councillors, and as early as the last decade of the seventeenth century.[30]

Sydnor maintained that members of the House of Burgesses in the eighteenth century had been schooled for the responsibility of representing and legislating for their constituents. He points to the fact that,

TABLE 1
Offices held by councillors at various times

Councillor	Sheriff	Justice	Burgess	Naval officer	Escheator	Other offices
John Armistead		*	*			
Nathaniel Bacon			*			*
William Bassett	*	X	X			X
Edmund Berkeley						
Peter Beverley						*
James Blair						*
Lewis Burwell						*
William Byrd I			*		X	X
William Byrd II			*		X	X
Robert Carter		*	X			X
William Churchill		*	*			
William Cocke						*
William Cole				*		*
John Custis I						
John Custis II	*	X	X	X	X	
Cole Digges			*			
Dudley Digges			*			*
Henry Duke	X	*	X			
William Fitzhugh	*	*	*			
Benjamin Harrison	*	*	*			*
Nathaniel Harrison		*	*	*		*
Henry Hartwell			X			X
Edward Hill II			*			*
Edward Jenings				*		*
Richard Johnson		*				
John Lear			*			*
Richard Lee II			*	*		
John Lewis I						
John Lightfoot					*	
Philip Ludwell I						*
Philip Ludwell II			*			*
Mann Page						
Matthew Page					*	*
Daniel Parke II			*	*	*	*
Robert Porteus						
Robert Quary						
Christopher Robinson			*			*
John Robinson			*			*
Charles Scarborough		*	*	*		
John Smith		*	*			
Henry Whiting		*	*			*
Christopher Wormeley	*	*		*		
Ralph Wormeley			*	*		

NOTE: * indicates the office was held prior to the assumption of a council seat. x indicates the office was held concurrently or prior to the assumption of a council seat.

prior to electing a burgess to the House, voters had the opportunity to assess him and his capabilities as vestryman, sheriff, and probably as local justice of the peace. All three offices involved aspects of the law-making process, as well as law enforcement. Most members of the House of Burgesses were landholders of some wealth and were obligated to uphold reputations as responsible leaders of society and the community, if they expected the votes of the franchised. This test might be applied equally to men who were selected for appointment to the governors' councils between 1692 and 1722.[31]

Council members exercised power through other offices they held. While a burgess, King Carter became agent for the Fairfaxes, a position he continued to hold later as councillor, and maintained until his death. William Bassett, Lewis Burwell, William Byrd II, John Lear, both Ludwells, Matthew Page, Daniel Parke II, John Robinson, Charles Scarborough, and Ralph Wormeley were members of the Board of Governors of the College of William and Mary during the years that its president, James Blair, exercised considerable influence on the Bishop of London against Virginia governors Andros, Nicholson, and Spotswood. One can scarcely ignore this association in considering the political conflict between councils and governors. By and large, councillors were, concurrenty, members of the vestries of their respective parishes and thus able to wield considerable local influence in both matters of state and religion. Most were also colonels, majors, or captains in the militia and were usually addressed throughout society by their rank.

Furthermore, members of a number of councillors' families served in the local political and judicial process at the same time that their relatives served in the council. The Armistead-Blair-Burwell-Byrd-Carter-Custis-Harrison-Ludwell connections through blood and marriage also extended to the Pages and the Wormeleys, as well as to the Corbins and the Grymeses, who, during the period, were members of the House of Burgesses and families of considerable local importance. Gawin Corbin, burgess from Middlesex County, married the sister of Richard Lee of the council.

The outlook of most council members in this period was, consequently, the product of intimate knowledge of the entire political life of Virginia. It is little wonder if they regarded themselves better appraised of, and more closely attached to, the customs, habits, and traditions of Virginians—as well as to their needs and preferences—than a governor whose lack of first-hand knowledge made him almost unfit to command those who were appointed to advise him.

As men of political, economic, and social distinction, the venerable members of the governors' councils were also favored with positions which might enhance their holdings. They were frequently appointed, for example, to the post of naval officer and collector of the revenues for the various districts although some who were concurrently naval officers and collectors of the revenues farmed out their role of collector for a percentage of the fees collected. Such a post carried with it a considerable remuneration. Naval officers received "large Fees upon the entering and clearing of all Ships and Vessels. . . . ten per Cent. for all Money's receiv'd both on the two Shillings per Hogshead, Fort Duties, Skins and Furs, and also on the New Imposts on Servants and Liquors."[32] Collectors' fees included fifteen shillings for every foreign-built vessel less than twenty tons arriving in the waters of their respective districts, thirty shillings and sixpence for every foreign-built one of more than twenty tons, and ten shillings and sixpence for ships built in Virginia. "They were also authorized to charge two shillings and sixpence for every license to trade issued to a sea captain, and the like amount for every bond given by him on the same occasion."[33] In addition, collectors were paid a salary "out of the Treasury of England, of Forty pounds, Sixty pounds, or an Hundred pounds according to their several districts . . . and have moreover Salaries of 20 per Cent. on all the Duties they collec."[34] Among council members from 1692 to 1722, John Custis I, John Custis II, Edmund Jenings, Richard Lee, John Lightfoot, Matthew Page, Daniel Parke II, Charles Scarborough, Christopher Wormeley, and Ralph Wormeley were holders of these offices awarded by the commissioners of customs in England.[35]

The secretary of the colony was remunerated from fees which are estimated at "70,000 £ Tobacco per year" as well as "other Perquisites" which "proceed out of the acknowledgements pay'd him annually by the County Clerks." The "other Perquisites" were valued at 40,000 £ of tobacco a year, "and Cask."[36] Councillors Philip Ludwell I, Christopher Robinson, Ralph Wormeley, Edmund Jenings, and William Cocke held this office.[37]

The office of auditor carried with it a salary of seven-and-one-half percent "of all the publick Money." In addition it included "the Quit Rents, the money arising by the two Shillings per Hogshead, Fort Duties, the Fines and Forfeitures, and the Profits of Escheats."[38] Councillors Nathaniel Bacon, William Byrd I, Dudley Digges, and Philip Ludwell II, and Peter Beverley and John Grymes, burgess for Middlesex County, held the office in succession during the period.[39]

By the second generation, men of such wealth, by and large acquainted with the offices of government at the lower levels, were included on the council. Though they were English by heritage, their

TABLE 2
Offices held concurrently with the office of councillor

Councillor	Collector and/or naval officer	Escheator	Secretary	Treasurer	Auditor General	Receiver General	Governor of Wm.&M.	Proprietor	Surveyor General
John Armistead									
Nathaniel Bacon					X				
William Bassett							X		
Edmund Berkeley									
Peter Beverley					X				X
James Blair									
Lewis Burwell							X		
William Byrd I		X			X	X			
William Byrd II		X				X	X		
Robert (King) Carter					X			X	
William Churchill									
William Cocke			X						
William Cole	X		X						
John Custis I									
John Custis II	X	X							
Cole Digges									
Dudley Digges					X				
Henry Duke									
William Fitzhugh II									
Benjamin Harrison									
Nathaniel Harrison	X				X				
Henry Hartwell							X		
Edward Hill II	X			X					
Edward Jenings	X		X			X			
Richard Johnson									
John Lear							X		
Richard Lee II	X								
John Lewis I									
John Lightfoot		X							
Philip Ludwell I			X				X		
Philip Ludwell II						X	X		
Mann Page									
Matthew Page		X					X		
Daniel Parke II	X	X					X		
Robert Porteus									
Robert Quary									X
Christopher Robinson			X						
John Robinson									X
Charles Scarborough	X						X		
John Smith									
Henry Whiting				X					
Christopher Wormeley	X								
Ralph Wormeley	X		X				X		

economic and political power base in the colony had become the most significant factor in Virginia society. English forces might touch the colonies through the governor, the Board of Trade, and the Royal Instructions, but day-to-day events controlled the existing structure at the local levels. And one cannot escape the fact that the roles of vestrymen, sheriff, and justice of the peace in the administration of justice were frequently connected to the roles not only of burgesses but also of members of the council. Face to face with royal governors and English policy, as well as English attitudes, second-generation members of elite families during this period demonstrated that they had strong ties to the new continent. The administration of all levels of government—in spite of, or because of, English policy—was carried out by the leading families of Virginia. While Edward Randolph could complain of violations of the laws regarding customs collections in the colony, for instance, the English could do little about it if those who had authority over both collections and rulings in the Courts of Admiralty were controlled by people who rejected English mercantile policy.[40]

After 1692, although they were committed, to a great extent, to the interests of the province, as coinciding with their fortunes, these men found that there were limitations upon their powers. For example, the political fortunes of individuals who dominated the Privy Council in England reverberated to the colonies and directly affected Virginians seeking office under the Crown. Some members of the council had close connections in London with influential members of both clergy and aristocracy. Influential individuals in London frequently nominated their candidates for colonial offices. Sometimes these nominations were carried through the Board of Trade, sometimes they were not. On 21 June 1711 the bishop of London wrote the commissioners for trade and plantations upon the death of Councillors Dudley Digges and William Churchill to recommend Edward Hill, "a sober good man and having one of the best Plantations in the colony" to fill one of these vacancies. Although he was the son of former councillor Edward Hill II, the nominee was not appointed to the post.[41]

The complicated route to council membership is revealed in the minutes of the council for 8 and 9 February 1704 concerning the nomination of John Lewis. Appointees evidently needed not only the approval of the governor and members of the council but the advocacy of a higher power. The precedent for Lewis's case was that of John Lightfoot, who was appointed in 1692. Nicholson, governor at the time of the debate, reminded John Lightfoot

that it was through his Excell[en]cys means that he the s[ai]d Coll Lightfoot was of the Councill, & admitted afterwards when Sir Edm[un]d Andros denyed him and that if it had been left to the Councill here to name him, he would never have been named in that station. And Coll Lightfoot owned to his Excell[en]cy did recommend him to Sr Ed[mu]nd Andros, from my Lord Pembroke.

Upon w[hi]ch his Excell[en]cy was pleased to say that he owned himself Extraordinarily obliged to the Earl of Pembroke beyond His Hopes or Deserts.[42]

William Bassett of Eltham—who was appointed to the council in 1702, resigned, and later applied to fill a vacancy—was reappointed in 1712 but not to his former place on the board. In order to achieve that appointment Bassett wrote to Philip Ludwell I, then in England:

I showed you Mr Perry's Lett[e]rs where in he writt of the interest he was making w[i]th the Councill, of Trade for me to take place in the Councill of Virg'a as before; and that he hopes to Effect it, I have lately Received a Letter from him in w[hi]ch he tells me . . . that he singly & w[i]th Collo Blakston, & gott Collo Blakston to speak to the Lord Orkney, & he did speak to the Board relating to me & they seemed to be resolved not to be concern'd in my affair at all, what reason may be in the way he knows not, but they seem not willing to do anything, & that he must have my farther advice, having done the utmost w[i]th the Councill of Trade, & can gett noe manner of answer from them, save if not answer'd he may goe to the Queen & she may doe what she pleases. That is what Mr. Perry writes me, what favour I desire of you is, that if it lyes in your way before the Councill of Trade, you will doe me Justice to take of what reflections has been lay'd on me that Board. I am apt to thinke, if their Lord Ship's had not been misinformed to my prejudice they would never have been soe harsh in their answer,—I am not conscious of any crime that I ever committed, & I should have been better sattysfyd, if I had not been put into the Councill, y[ou]r to have it in this manner.[43]

Like Bassett, Spotswood, who had convinced the former councillor to again take his place on the council, attributed opposition to Bassett's restoration to his former seniority position to the opposition of former president of the council, and acting governor after the death of Governor Nott, Edmund Jenings. This opposition was, in all probability, connected to political interests and maneuverings behind the scenes.[44] According to Leonidas Dodson, Jenings relied upon the favor of the Duchess of Marlborough.[45] Bassett's fate may well have been decided by the vicissitudes of English politics.

Not only did such factors influence the appointment of members of the council, but they affected appointment to places of profit and prestige. William Byrd II, seeking the governorship of Virginia through friends in London prior to Spotswood's appointment, was rejected in spite of the fact that he was a close friend of John Perceval (Baron

Perceval, created Earl of Egmont in 1733), and of Sir Robert Southwell (President of the Royal Society of London, 1690–1695) and, after Sir Robert's death, of other members of the Southwell family. An entry in William Byrd's secret diary for 31 March 1710 mentions: "I met Mr. Bland, who brought me several letters from England and among the rest two from Colonel Blakiston who had endeavored to procure the government of Virginia for me at the price of £1,000 of my Lady Orkney and that my Lord [agreed] but the Duke of Marlborough declared that no one but soldiers should have the government of a plantation, so I was disappointed. God's will be done."[46] At this time the Board of Trade was under the control of the military in England. On 23 July 1710 Alexander Spotswood received the appointment sought by Byrd.

At about the same time Philip Ludwell II sought Nathaniel Blakiston's assistance in acquiring the office of auditor general. A letter addressed to Ludwell from the colonial agent vividly portrays the methods employed for conducting such business. Blakiston says:

Before Mr. Blathwayt determined who he would give it Mr. Perry came to me before we went the second time and communicated another letter from you in which you suggested to him that Coll. Digges allowed _____ Ct and you £500 to be admitted. I frankly told Mr. Perry I would be your opponent rather than y[ou]r advocate to consent you should part w[i]th any such sume upon soe precarious a foundation as Upon Mr. Blathwayt's Life, and many other contingent accidents, besides the cause will not heare it, but Mr. Perry seemed to think rather than you should loose it to offer a 100 or 200 of Pounds. I told him I did not doubt but we should worke it for you on better terms, for Mr. Blath: has for a late piece of friendship I have done assured me he would be ready to do any Services he could.[47]

Nor were such decisions totally unconnected to the course of events in England. On 8 August 1710 Stephen Fouace, one of the first trustees of William and Mary College, and afterwards of Sutton, Middlesex, in England, wrote to Philip Ludwell II from England. The letter suggested that Ludwell had contacted him to intervene for him in some matter, possibly the same matter mentioned by Nathaniel Blakiston. Fouace reports: "The change of ministers already made and the further change w[hi]ch is feared will render your business more difficult. My Lord Sunderland was much depended upon but he is turned out and my Lord Dartmouth in his place. . . . The animosities Betwixt Whigs & Tories are rais'd to a vast Degree and beyond all imagination, and of Such pernicious consequences that it is though the French K. expecting great advantages from them hath broken off the negotiations of Peace w[hi]ch is much wanted and desired every where."[48]

Many examples of the workings of "the reason the Springs act," to quote Nathaniel Blakiston, are present.[49] Nor is influence peddling in the acquisition of office of some estate unique to this period. Long before the turn of the seventeenth century there is evidence of the same process. Of William Byrd I, Bassett says that he tried several schemes "to make money through his political connections." The third was his attempt to get "the office of auditor, which was in fact, the office of colonial treasurer." Bassett says, "It was held at that time by Nathaniel Bacon, uncle of the revolutionary leader, but he was old and quite willing to give up the office." Byrd went to London and through the use of certain means interested Blathwayt on his behalf, and he received the appointment on 4 December 1687.[50]

In 1687 Burgess William Fitzhugh wrote his brother, Captain Henry Fitzhugh, then in England, regarding the possibilities of a lucrative future if he moved to Virginia. He outlined the value of a number of positions, including "Commander of one of the King's Ships, that gives attendance here . . . , Keeper of the Broad Seal of this Country . . . ," and "farmer of the Virginia Duty," i.e., "Two shillings p. hogshead" etc. But he advises his brother to use "caution to inform yourself of My Lord Howard's interest (Lord Howard of Effingham, governor of Virginia) and friends at court before you may embark upon any of them, for all my proposals are branches lopped from the tree of his Interest, except that of being Commander of the King's Ships, therefore it cannot be to my advantage to publish from whom you receive this information."[51]

So the personal fortunes, as well as the political influence, of the members of the council were not unaffected by their ties with the mother country. In addition to the impact of British political maneuverings on the appointees or would-be appointees of the Crown, members of the General Court, as advisors to the governor and as the upper house of the legislature, had loyalties not only to benefactors, but to those who supported them in the political, economic, and social life of the colonies. When these interests were in conflict and the struggle for power or for equity was at stake, the councillors frequently found themselves in the middle. From 1692 until 1722 councillors increasingly found this to be the case.

Entrenched as they and their families were in colonial government at both the upper and local levels, Virginia's elite regarded land and tax reforms implemented during these decades as a threat to their vital interests. Leading Virginians saw little relationship between the fate of fortifications in Albany, New York, and their own protection, and they saw the loss of their tobacco markets in France, Spain, Sweden, Poland, and Russia during war with the French as a threat to their own economic survival.[52] To administer and execute policies regarding the tobacco trade, taxation, and land reform, the Crown sent three successive royal governors—Andros, Nicholson, and Spotswood—who seemed from the outset to be temperamentally unsuited to cope with Virginia's elite.

The experience of all three governors prior to their Virginia appointment was limited to commanding men or administering territories under military domination. The authority vested in military command rests, and has always rested, solely on the inviolability of the chain of command and the authority of the office.[53] Andros, governor from 1692 to 1698 after a long military career, carried with him to Virginia the dubious reputation of governor of the "Dominion of New England," from which he was deposed and arrested in 1689 soon after news of England's Bloodless Revolution reached Massachusetts. His successor, Nicholson, who was governor from 1698 to 1705, had not only been Andros's deputy in New York under the "Dominion" during Leisler's Rebellion, but also had had a long military career. He had governed the Moors in Morocco, and in New York he had preached that "the Scabbord of a Redcoat should quickly signify as much as the Commission of a Justice of the Peace."[54] He then served as Lieutenant Governor of Virginia, during which time he ingratiated himself not only to the council but also to James Blair, president of the college. As Governor of Maryland from 1692 to 1698, he threatened his opposition that he would hang them "with Magna Charta about their necks."[55] Spotswood, governor from 1710 to 1722, a man of less blemished reputation, from an old Scottish family, had served under Marlborough in the War of the Spanish Succession and was wounded at Blenheim.

Members of the governors' councils had come to think, because of their influence and privilege, education, wealth, and experience, that, in the words of Robert Quary, "they almost stand upon equal terms with the Honorable the House of Lords."[56] Increasingly during these three decades visitors to the colony were able to distinguish the ruling class from the fifty-acre freeholder who held the franchise, the indentured servant, the tenant farmer, and the black slave population.[57] On the other hand, a military governor, without a retinue of redcoats, could do little to distinguish himself if the entrenched ruling class at the top of the pyramidal social structure refused him their support and used their influential contacts in London to undermine his position.

Andros resigned in 1698, following the Lambeth Palace Conference in England where James Blair presented evidence against him alleging gross financial misconduct in the construction of William and Mary College. Blair's correspondents were John Locke, founder of the Board of Trade, and Henry Compton, Bishop of London.[58] Nicholson was recalled in 1705, after being charged by many of the council with conduct unbefitting the office of governor. Differences with the council, surfacing over Nicholson's unsuccessful pursuit of Lucy Burwell, magnified into a scandal which for a time shook all of Virginia's ruling families and the entire political structure of the colony, and became the subject for gossip in England's ruling circles.[59] Spotswood, the most able of the three, met the same fate when he attempted to implement land, tax, and court reforms in the colony. His complaints, like those of his predecessor, were against the entrenched elite of the colony. He wrote that "that powerful knot of relations in the Council," by virtue of their position in the Council and Courts, "have gained a mighty influence over the Legislature, and the people begin to strive more for their good graces than for those of a Governor." He added that if one member of the family of relatives was touched, the others began to swarm like a nest of wasps.[60]

By 1722 an English policy of laissez-faire toward the colonies had been initiated under Walpole. Spotswood was removed. England had been at peace for almost a decade. Virginia's tidewater aristocracy was entrenched. Under the flexible and conciliatory governorships of Hugh Drysdale and his successor William Gooch, the colony expanded westward over the Alleghenies to the Blue Ridge Mountains, forming new counties beyond the tidewater. The council retired into little more than a ceremonial body. Power passed to the burgesses, accommodating the extension of the elite to the frontier as the young of established families intermarried with those of a new generation of successful colonists. Not again until the French and Indian War in 1754 were Virginia's planter-elite threatened. At that time, more than four decades had elapsed since Spotswood's removal—decades in which new generations of the elite schooled themselves in the art of self-government. By the time the Stamp Act was passed, Virginia's early eighteenth-century tidewater oligarchy had been absorbed or replaced by new leadership. With the onset of Revolution, it was this new class of influence and wealth that led the way.

NOTES

Notes

"Ambitious of Honor and Places": The Magistracy of Hampshire County, Massachusetts, 1692–1760

[1] Hendrik Hartog, "The Public Law of a County Court: Judicial Government in Eighteenth-Century Massachusetts," *American Journal of Legal History*, XX (1976), 232–239; David Thomas Konig, *Law and Society in Puritan Massachusetts: Essex County, 1629–1692* (Chapel Hill, N.C., 1979); William E. Nelson, *Americanization of the Common Law: The Impact of Legal Change on Massachusetts Society, 1760–1830* (Cambridge, Mass., 1975); Evelyn Belz Russel, "An Overview of the Criminal Justice System of Hampshire County, 1677–1728," *Historical Journal of Western Massachusetts*, V (1977), 13–20; Yasu Kawashima, "Jurisdiction of the Colonial Courts over the Indians in Massachusetts, 1688–1763," *New England Quarterly*, XLII (1969), 532–550; Paul D. Marsella, "The Court of General Sessions of the Peace in the Eighteenth Century," *Essex Institute Historical Collections*, (1981), 105–118. Gregory H. Nobles's *Divisions Throughout the Whole: Social Politics and Society in Hampshire County, Massachusetts, 1740–1775* (Cambridge, 1983) was published after I completed this essay.

[2] For some of the most important statements on New England elites see James A. Henretta, "The Morphology of New England Society in the Eighteenth Century," *Journal of Interdisciplinary History*, II (1971), 143–149; David Grayson Allen, "The Zuckerman Thesis and the Process of Legal Rationalization in Provincial Massachusetts," *William and Mary Quarterly*, 3d Ser., XXIX (1972), 443–454, hereafter cited as *WMQ*; Robert Zemsky, *Merchants, Farmers, and River Gods: An Essay on Eighteenth-Century American Politics* (Boston, 1971); Bruce C. Daniels, *The Connecticut Town: Growth and Development, 1635–1790* (Middletown, Conn., 1979); Edward M. Cook, Jr., *The Fathers of the Towns: Leadership and Community Structure in Eighteenth-Century New England* (Baltimore, 1976); Michael Zuckerman, *Peaceable Kingdoms: New England Towns in the Eighteenth Century* (New York, 1970).

[3] In Hampshire the elective offices of treasurer and of registrar of deeds invariably belonged to one man and almost invariably to one of the appointive court clerks; for the sake of simplicity they will not be mentioned again. For institutions of eighteenth-century county government, see Snell, "The County Magistracy in Eighteenth-Century Massachusetts, 1692–1750" (Ph.D. diss., Princeton Univ., 1970).

[4] Snell, "County Magistracy," 112–155.

[5] John Adams to Abigail Adams, 30 June 1774, in L. H. Butterfield, ed., *Adams Family Correspondence* (Cambridge, Mass., 1963–   ), I, 116.

[6] William Douglass to Cadwallader Colden 20 Nov. 1727 and 4 Dec. 1727, Massachusetts Historical Society *Collections*, 4th Ser., II, 176–178 hereafter cited as MHS *Coll.*.

[7] Cotton Mather, *The Deplorable State of New England* (Boston, 1709), reprinted, MHS *Coll.*, 5th Ser., VI, 118.

[8] Good sources on the wars in the Connecticut Valley of Massachusetts include George Sheldon, *A History of Deerfield, Massachusetts* (Deerfield, Mass., 1895–

1896); Sylvester Judd, *A History of Hadley* (Northampton, Mass., 1863; reprinted Somersworth, N. H., 1976); Nathaniel Bartlett Sylvester, "History of the Connecticut Valley in Massachusetts," in Louis H. Everts, *History of the Connecticut Valley in Massachusetts*, 3 vols. (Philadelphia, 1879), I, 9–162.

[9] William H. Whitmore, *The Massachusetts Civil List for the Colonial and Provincial Periods, 1630–1774* (Boston, 1889), 91–94, 139–140, lists most Hampshire officials; names of minor officials, like clerks, appear in Hampshire County Court Records, office of the clerk of court, Northampton, Mass.; office of the clerk of court, Springfield, Mass.; and vol. U, Registry of Deeds, Springfield, Mass. The special justices of the court of common pleas listed in Whitmore, *Civil List*, 93, were appointed temporarily to replace justices who were involved with a case the inferior court was to hear; they sat only for the individual cases for which they were appointed. Information on military titles is from Sheldon, *Deerfield*; Judd, *Hadley*; and material scattered through Abner C. Goodell and Ellis Ames, eds., *The Acts and Resolves, Public and Private, of the Province of Massachusetts Bay*, 21 vols. (Boston, 1869–1922), and the sources of biographical data listed in note 10, below.

[10] For the tables that follow, names of representatives were taken from *Acts and Resolves*, VII–IX, and *Journal of the House of Representatives of Massachusetts* (44 vols. to date, Boston, 1919–   ), I–XXXVII. Information on incorporation of towns: Robert T. Swan, ed., *Thirteenth Report on the Custody and Condition of the Public Records of Parishes, Towns, Counties, and Parishes* (Boston, 1901), 43–44. Principal sources for genealogical data: Franklin Bowditch Dexter, *Biographical Sketches of the Graduates of Yale College, 1701–1745* (New York, 1885); Benjamin W. Dwight, *The History of the Descendants of John Dwight of Dedham, Mass.*, 2 vols. (New York, 1874); Alphaeus C. Hodges, "Yale Graduates in Western Massachusetts," New Haven Colony Historical Society *Papers*, IV (1888), 253–298; Judd, *Hadley*; Joseph Charles Pynchon and W. F. Adams, *Record of the Pynchon Family in England and America* (Springfield, Mass., 1898); Sheldon, *Deerfield*; John Langdon Sibley and Clifford K. Shipton, *Biographical Sketches of Graduates of Harvard University* (Cambridge and Boston, 1873–   ); Joseph H. Smith, ed., *Colonial Justice in Western Massachusetts, 1639–1702: The Pynchon Court Record* (Cambridge, 1961); Charles Stoddard and Elijah W. Stoddard, *Anthony Stoddard of Boston, Mass., and His Descendants: A Genealogy* (New York, 1865); Henry W. Taft, "Judicial History of Berkshire," Berkshire Historical Society *Collections*, I (1892), 87–115; J. H. Temple and George Sheldon, *History of the Town of Northfield, Massachusetts* (Albany, 1875); Francis Bacon Trowbridge, *The Ashley Genealogy: A History of the Descendants of Robert Ashley of Springfield, Massachusetts* (New Haven, 1896); James Russell Trumbull, *History of Northampton, Massachusetts, from its Settlement in 1654*, 2 vols. (Northampton, 1898); Harrison Williams, *The Life, Ancestors, and Descendants of Robert Williams of Roxbury* (Washington, D.C., 1934).

[11] *House Journals*, VI, 458–459; XVII, 256–258; XVIII, 47–48, 185–186, XXVII, 195, 224; XVIII, 28; XXX, 18, 153; XXXI, 38, 152–153, 182; XXXII, 60, 116. I have excluded the vote recorded in vol. XXX, 260, because only one Hampshire delegate voted on each side of the issue; at least five voted on each of the other issues. The particular votes discussed can be found in *House Journals* XVIII, 47–48, 185–86; XXX, 153.

[12] Zemsky, *Merchants, Farmers, and River Gods*, 32–34, 317; John Pynchon to William Phips, 2 Jan. 1692/93, Massachusetts Archives, Boston, III, 51; Jonathan Belcher to John Stoddard, 15 Apr. 1734 and 25 Feb. 1734/35, Belcher Letter Books, Massachusetts Historical Society, for quotations; for other examples, Belcher Letter

Books, 31 Mar. 1732, 27 Aug. 1733, 10 Apr. 1734, 22 July 1740, 30 Mar. 1741, 18 Aug. 1741; William Shirley to John Stoddard, 2 June 1744, *Shirley Correspondence*, I, 127–128; Elisha Jones to William Williams, 13 July 1766, William Williams Collection, Berkshire Athenaeum, Pittsfield, Mass; "Dignitaries of 1759," *New England Historical and Genealogical Register*, XI (1857), 79, hereafter cited as NEHGR; Robert J. Taylor, *Western Massachusetts in the Revolution* (Providence, R.I., 1954), 11–26.

[13] The following discussion is based on these town records: Deerfield Town Records, Pocumtuck Valley Memorial Association, Deerfield, Mass; Francis Olcott Allen, ed., *The History of Enfield, Connecticut*, 3 vols. (Lancaster, Pa., 1900) [Enfield was part of Hampshire until 1749]; Hadley Town Records, office of the town clerk, Hadley, Mass.; Hatfield Town Records, office of the town clerk, Hatfield, Mass.; Northampton Town Records, office of the city clerk, Northampton, Mass.; Temple and Sheldon, *Northfield*; Henry Burt, ed., *The First Century of the History of Springfield: The Official Records, 1636–1736*, 2 vols. (Springfield, Mass., 1898); Springfield Town Records, office of the city clerk, Springfield, Mass; Hezekiah S. Sheldon, ed., *Documentary History of Suffield in the Colony and Province of the Massachusetts Bay, 1660–1749* (Springfield, Mass., 1879); Sunderland Town Records, office of the town clerk, Sunderland, Mass.; Westfield Town Records, office of the town clerk, Westfield, Mass. A number of the manuscript records are available on microfilm at the Forbes Library of Northampton, Massachusetts, and I am grateful to Mr. Stanley Greenberg of that library for his assistance.

[14] Cook, *Fathers of the Towns*, 23–62, 95–118.

[15] See town sources cited in note 13.

[16] Whitmore, *Civil List*, 91–94, 139–140; Hampshire Court Records, *passim*.

[17] Smith, *Colonial Justice in Western Massachusetts*, 1–59; Stephen Chandler Innes, "A Patriarchal Society: Economic Dependency and Social Order in Springfield, Massachusetts, 1636–1703" (Ph.D. diss., Northwestern University, 1977); Pynchon and Adams, *Pynchon Family*; William Pynchon Account Book, 1720–1743, Forbes Library, Northampton, Mass.

[18] Daniel W. Wells and Reuben F. Wells, *History of Hatfield, Massachusetts* (Springfield, 1910), 105–115, 431–433; Judd, *Hadley*, pt. 1, 26, 48–55, 202–206, 278–284, pt. 2, 108–109; Hampshire Probate Records, office of the registrar of probate, Northampton, Mass., V, 161–162, VI, 11–12; Hampshire Probate Files, office of the registrar of probate, Northampton, Mass., 110:51–52; *Harvard Graduates*, IV, 416–417, V, 289; *Yale Graduates*, I, 393, 417.

[19] Probate Record, I, 199; Probate Files, 69:35, 36; *Harvard Graduates*, II, 445–446, V, 483; *Yale Graduates*, I, 709–711; Trumbull, *Northampton*, I, 109–111, II, 79–82; Hawley Papers and Account Books, Forbes Library, Northampton, Mass; David Wilton Account Book, Forbes Library.

[20] Judd, *Hadley*, pt. 2, 111–114; Probate Records, I, 262–263, IV 106–110, V, 72; Probate Files, 117:10, 25; *Harvard Graduates*, V, 441–444; *Yale Graduates*, II, 153; Andrew Raymond, "A New England Colonial Family: Four Generations of the Porters of Hadley, Massachusetts," *NEHGR*, CXXIX (1975), 198–220.

[21] Benjamin Dwight, *John Dwight*, I, 109–119, 131–134, 271–272, II, 620–623; *Yale Graduates*, I, 246–247, 558–559, 757–778; Probate Records, V, 115–117, 145; Probates Files, 51:16, 25, 40, 48.

[22] T. H. Breen, *Puritans and Adventurers: Change and Persistence in Early America* (New York, 1980), 81–105; Judd, *Hadley*, pt. 1, 71, 95–96, 353–354, 368; Wilton Acct. Bk.; Sheldon, *Deerfield*, I, 81–178, 220–264; Karen J. Friedmann, "Victualling Colonial Boston," *Agricultural History*, XLVII (1973), 195–196. Probate Records, I,

163–220, depicts wartime devastation in Hampshire County; Superior Court Records, office of the clerk of courts, Boston, vol. for 1733–1736, 5, 6, and Hampshire Court Records, II, III, contain data on the nature of the livestock trade.

[23] Perry Miller, "Solomon Stoddard," *Harvard Theological Review*, XXXIV (1941), 277–320; Ralph J. Hoffman, *Solomon Stoddard* (Boston, 1978); Paul R. Lucas, *Valley of Discord: Church and Society Along the Connecticut River, 1636–1725* (Hanover, N.H., 1976), 146–187; *Harvard Graduates*, V, 96–118; Probate Files, 142:53; Patricia J. Tracy, *Jonathan Edwards, Pastor: Religion and Society in Eighteenth-Century Northampton* (New York, 1980), 20–50.

[24] Williams, *Robert Williams*, 89–102; *Harvard Graduates*, III, 249–260, 263–265, V, 471–474, 588–598, VI, 25–35, VIII, 301–333, 638–657; *Yale Graduates*, I, 321, 695–696, II, 69; Sheldon, *Deerfield*, I, 458–467, II, pt. 2, 376–383; Wyllis E. Wright, *Colonial Ephraim Williams: A Documentary Life* (Pittsfield, Mass., 1970); Probate Records, V, 44, 51, 63; Williams Papers, Pocumtuck Valley Memorial Association, Deerfield, Mass., # 11, 91; William L. Welch, Jr., "River God: The Public Life of Israel Williams, 1709–1788" (Ph.D. diss., University of Maine, 1975).

[25] Probate Files, 142:53; Probate Records, V, 44, 51, 63, Williams Papers, # 11, 91; Stoddard, *Stoddard Genealogy*, 1–10; Dwight, *John Dwight*, 1033–1035; Sheldon, *Deerfield*, II, pt. 2, 376–384.

[26] Benjamin Dwight, *John Dwight*, 109, 271, 620–623, 1033–1035; Sheldon, *Deerfield*, II, pt. 2, 376–384; *Yale Graduates*, I, 405; Trowbridge, *Ashley Genealogy*, 23–30; Wells and Wells, *Hatfield*, 431–432.

[27] Mary Catherine Foster, "Hampshire County, Massachusetts: A Covenant Society in Transition, 1729–1754" (Ph.D. diss., University of Michigan, 1967) is an excellent study of ecclesiastical affairs in Hampshire for the period, although Foster exaggerates the degree to which dissent disrupted society. An important source for the period is Stephen Williams, Diary, Longmeadow Public Library, Longmeadow, Mass. B. B. Edwards, "Complete List of the Congregational Ministers in the Old County of Hampshire, Ms.," *American Quarterly Register*, X (1837–1838) is riddled with errors but remains useful. Detail on incumbencies is drawn from those sources, *Harvard Graduates*, and *Yale Graduates*.

[28] Family ties also existed between justices' families and clerical families in towns where the principal Hampshire families were not present, for instance, Sunderland and Northfield. See Temple and Sheldon, *Northfield*, 443; Smith, *Sunderland*, 437.

[29] Perry Miller, *Jonathan Edwards* (Delta edition, New York, 1967), 210–229; Foster, "Hampshire County," 257–290; C. C. Goen, *Revivalism and Separatism in New England, 1740–1800: Strict Congregationalists and Separate Baptists in the Great Awakening* (New Haven, Conn., 1962), 85–86, 101–103, 254–255. Towns with dissenting churches can be identified from the maps in *ibid.*, facing 114, 256. Two Hampshire Baptist churches predated the Great Awakening, those at West Springfield and at Brimfield; Goen did not notice the Brimfield example. Isaac Backus, *A History of New England, With Particular Reference to the Baptists*, 2 vols. (Newton, Mass., 1871), II, 467; Edward Upham, Ministerial Record, American Antiquarian Society, Worcester, Mass.; *Harvard Graduates*, IX, 443–446; Town of Brimfield, *Historical Celebration* (Springfield, Mass., 1879), 134–135; Harold Field Worthley, *An Inventory of the Records of the Particular (Congregational) Churches of Massachusetts Gathered 1620–1805* (Cambridge, Mass., 1970), 667. I have not considered the two pre-Awakening Baptist churches in my argument in the text. The one at Brimfield supports my argument; the West Springfield church possibly does not.

[30] Zemsky, *Merchants, Farmers, and River Gods*, 99–128; Michael C. Batinski,

"Jonathan Belcher of Massachusetts, 1682–1741" (Ph.D. diss., Northwestern University, 1969); *Harvard Graduates*, IV, 434–450.

[31] *Harvard Graduates*, IV, 142–143; Mass. Archives, LXX, 89, 195.

[32] Partridge's career can be pursued in *Acts and Resolves*, IX, X, and in MHS *Coll.*, 6th Ser., III. Whitmore, *Civil List*, 139–140.

[33] Harvard Graduates, V, 96–118, VIII, 301–333; Taylor, *Western Massachusetts*, 11–26.

[34] Compare Taylor, *Western Massachusetts*, 22–26.

[35] This paragraph and table 5 are based on Hodges, "Yale Graduates in Western Massachusetts"; *Yale Graduates*; *Harvard Graduates*; Sunderland Town Records, 128; and Temple and Sheldon, *Northfield*, 441–443. Harvard graduates have been traced through the geographical index in *Harvard Graduates*, through checking schoolmasters' names against the collegiate biographies, and through references in town histories. The exceptional college graduate was Josiah Pierce (Harvard, 1735).

[36] *Harvard Graduates*, IV, 142–443, V, 96–118; *Yale Graduates*, I, 709–711, 757–758.

[37] *Yale Graduates*, I, 453–454; *Harvard Graduates*, VIII, 69–74; Temple and Sheldon, *Northfield*, 364–365, 443; Sunderland Town Records, 128.

[38] Judd, *Hadley*, 443; Sheldon, *Suffield, passim*; Westfield Town Records; Burt, *Springfield*, II, 593–594; Taft, "Judicial History of Berkshire," 91–92; Brimfield, *Historical Celebration*, 287, 353–355, 451; Probate Files, 41:52.

[39] Sheldon, *Deerfield*, II, pt. 2, 376–385; Burt, *Springfield*; Springfield Town Records; Hatfield Town Records; Hadley Town Records; Raymond, "New England Colonial Family."

[40] Snell, "County Magistracy," 112–154.

[41] See sources cited in note to table 6.

[42] Nathaniel B. Shurtleff, ed., *Records of the Governor and Company of the Massachusetts Bay in New England*, (5 vols. in 6, Boston, 1853–1854), IV, pt. 2, 542, 554; *Acts and Resolves*, IX, 397, 621, X, 47, 189–190, 569, XI, 177, 728, XII, 317–318, XXI, 834, 840.

[43] Sheldon, *Suffield*, 53–78; Allen, *Enfield*, I, 60–135; Temple and Sheldon, *Northfield*, 133–155; Sunderland Town Records, 4–25.

[44] Pelham Proprietors Records, 1738–1830, office of the town clerk, Pelham, Mass., 1–6; Pelham Town Records, office of the town clerk, Pelham, 1–19; Ware Town Records, 1742–1795, office of the town clerk, Ware, Mass., 1–2; Edward H. Gilbert, *Early Grants and Incorporation of the Town of Ware* (New York, 1891), 6–43; Catherine A. Archer *et al.*, eds., *A Bicentennial History of Becket* (Becket, Mass., 1964), 1–30; Lucy K. Cutler, *History of the Town of Bernardston* (Greenfield, Mass., 1902), 1–37; Perry, *Williamstown*, 267–268; Taylor, *Great Barrington*, 14–89; Smith, *Pittsfield*, 72–124; Ephraim Williams, to Jonathan Ashley, 2 May 1751, in Wright, ed., *Ephraim Williams*, 61–62. The correspondence printed in the last-mentioned work is an invaluable source for the techniques by which principal Hampshire families extended their power and status to the frontier.

[45] Whitmore, *Civil List*, 123, 152; Taft, "Judicial History of Berkshire"; Richard D. Birdsall, *Berkshire County: A Cultural History* (New Haven, Conn., 1959).

[46] T. B. Bottomore, *Elites and Society* (New York, 1964), 1–18; Reinhard Bendix and Seymour Martin Lipset, *Class, Status, and Power: Social Stratification in Comparative Perspective*, 2d ed. (New York, 1966), 210–219; W. G. Runciman, "Class, Status, and Power?" in J. A. Jackson, ed., *Social Stratification*, vol. I of *Sociological Studies* (Cambridge, 1968), 25–61.

Diversity and Democracy: Officeholding among Selectmen in Eighteenth-Century Connecticut

[1] Robert E. Brown, *Middle-Class Democracy and the Revolution in Massachusetts, 1691–1780* (Ithaca, N.Y., 1955).

[2] Among the most important recent books to comment directly on democracy in the colonial New England town are Edward Cook, Jr., *The Fathers of The Towns: Leadership and Community Structure in Eighteenth-Century New England* (Baltimore, 1976); Charles Grant, *Democracy in the Connecticut Frontier Town of Kent* (New York, 1961); Dirk Hoerder, *Society and Government 1760–1780: The Power Structure of Massachusetts Townships* (Berlin, 1972); Kenneth Lockridge, *A New England Town: The First Hundred Years* (New York, 1970); Robert Zemsky, *Merchants, Farmers, and River Gods: An Essay on Eighteenth-Century American Politics* (Boston, 1971); and Michael Zuckerman, *Peaceable Kingdoms: New England Towns in the Eighteenth Century* (New York, 1970). Among the important articles are Bruce C. Daniels, "Democracy and Oligarchy in Connecticut Towns: General Assembly Officeholding, 1701–1790," *Social Science Quarterly*, XXXVI (1975), 460–475; Bruce Steiner, "Anglican Officeholding in pre-Revolutionary Connecticut: The Parameters of New England Community," *William and Mary Quarterly* (*WMQ*), XXXI (1974), 369–405; and William Willingham, "Deference Democracy and Town Government in Windham, Connecticut, 1755 to 1786," *WMQ* XXX (1973), 401–421.

[3] For the political role of the selectmen, see Daniels, *The Connecticut Town: Growth and Development, 1635–1790* (Middletown, Conn., 1979), chap. 3.

[4] Men elected between 1701 and 1710, and between 1770 and 1780, were not excluded from the calculations for the four time periods, as they were from the overall analysis. This is because the overall analysis seeks absolute data on officeholding, but the comparative analysis of the four time periods seeks relative figures. For the latter purpose, the data must be made consistent for all four periods, and this can only be done by including all men elected. The average terms-per-man for each of these four twenty-year-periods will be less than in the overall analysis since many men served terms in more than one of the periods.

[5] The data from Rhode Island can be found in Daniels, "The 'Particular Courts' of Local Government: Town Councils in Eighteenth-Century Rhode Island," *Rhode Island History*, 41 (1982), 54–65. See Cook, *The Fathers of the Towns*, 54–55.

[6] Daniels, "Democracy and Oligarchy in Connecticut Towns," 464–465; and Daniels, "The Long-Lasting Men of Local Government: Town Clerks in Colonial Connecticut," *Bulletin of the Connecticut Historical Society*, 41 (1976), 90–96.

[7] Daniels, "Democracy and Oligarchy in Connecticut Towns," 464; Zuckerman, *Peaceable Kingdoms*, 276; Nicholas Henry, *Governing At the Grass Roots: State and Local Politics* (Englewood Cliffs, N.J., 1980), 219–220.

[8] See Philip Greven, Jr., *Four Generations: Population, Land, and Family in Colonial Andover, Massachusetts* (Ithaca, N.Y., 1970) for an analysis of the reluctance of young men to leave their hometowns. Daniels, "Democracy and Oligarchy in Connecticut Towns," 465.

[9] Daniels, *The Connecticut Town*, 47.

[10] See Robert Taylor, *Colonial Connecticut: A History* (New York, 1979), chap. 5; Gaspare John Saladino, "The Economic Revolution in Eighteenth-Century Connecticut" (Ph.D. diss., University of Wisconsin, 1964), iv; and Daniels, "Economic Development in Colonial and Revolutionary Connecticut: An Overview, *WMQ*, 37 (July, 1980), 429–450.

[11] The two most important discussions of the dislocation in Connecticut occasioned by the Great Awakening and the Revolution are Richard Bushman, *From Puritan to Yankee: Character and the Social Order in Connecticut, 1690–1765* (Cambridge, Mass., 1967), and Oscar Zeichner, *Connecticut's Years of Controversy, 1750–1776* (Williamsburg, 1949).

[12] See Bushman, *From Puritan to Yankee*, chaps. 12, 13.

[13] See Daniels, *The Connecticut Town*, chap. 6.

[14] Edward Cook, Jr., "Local Leadership and the Typology of New England Towns, 1700–1785," *Political Science Quarterly*, 96 (1971), 586–608.

The Development of Local Power Structures: Maryland's Lower Western Shore in the Early Colonial Period

Note: Analysis of inventories for the four lower western shore counties to 1705 and for St. Mary's County to 1775 has been funded by grants to the St. Mary's City Commission from the National Science Foundation (GS-32272) and the National Endowment for the Humanities (RO-6228-72-468, RO-10585-74-267, RS-23687-76-431). Charles County inventories, 1706–1720, were analyzed with an Arthur H. Cole Grant-in-Aid to the author from the Economic History Association.

Inventories and associated estate accounts are in the Maryland Hall of Records, Annapolis, Maryland. Analysis of inventories for the four lower western shore counties to 1705 and for St. Mary's County to 1775 was completed by the St. Mary's City Commission, and for Charles County, 1706–1720, by the author. Results may be consulted at the research office of the St. Mary's City Commission, Hall of Records, Annapolis.

[1] For Virginia, see Bernard Bailyn, "Politics and Social Structure in Virginia," in James Morton Smith, ed., *Seventeenth-Century America: Essays in Colonial History* (Chapel Hill, N.C., 1959), 90–115; David Alan Williams, "Political Alignments in Colonial Virginia, 1698–1750" (Ph.D. diss., Northwestern University, 1959); Martin Herbert Quitt, "Virginia House of Burgesses, 1660–1706: The Social, Educational and Economic Bases of Political Power" (Ph.D. diss., Washington University, 1970); Warren Martin Billings, "'Virginia's Deploured Condition,' 1660–1676: The Coming of Bacon's Rebellion" (Ph.D. diss., Northern Illinois University, 1968); Jack P. Greene, "Foundations of Political Power in the Virginia House of Burgesses, 1720–1776," *William and Mary Quarterly* (hereafter WMQ), 3rd ser., XVI (1959), 485–506; and John C. Rainbolt, "The Alteration in the Relationship between Leadership and Constituents in Virginia, 1660 to 1720," WMQ, 3rd ser., XXVII (1970), 411–434. Among relevant sources for Maryland, see Lois Green Carr and David William Jordan, *Maryland's Revolution of Government, 1689–1692* (St. Mary's City Commission Publication no. 1; Ithaca, N.Y., 1974); and David W. Jordan, "Political Stability and the Emergence of a Native Elite in Maryland," in Thad W. Tate and David L. Ammerman, eds., *The Chesapeake in the Seventeenth Century: Essays on Anglo-American Society* (Chapel Hill, N.C., 1979), 243–273.

[2] For evidence of early local stability, see Lois Green Carr, "County Government in Maryland, 1689–1709" (Ph.D. diss., Harvard University, 1968) and Carr and Jordan, *Maryland's Revolution of Government*. (For an opposing view, see Billings, "'Virginia's Deploured Condition.'") Descriptions of two tidewater Virginia county power structures include Williams, "Political Alignments in Colonial Virginia," chap. 3; and Gwenda Morgan, "The Hegemony of the Law: Richmond County, 1692–1776" (Ph.D. diss., Johns Hopkins University, 1980), chap. 2; these make little attempt to

integrate analysis of the power structure with the social and economic history of the locality. Richard R. Beeman's studies of an eighteenth-century Virginia frontier county demonstrate that the transition from leadership by hardened early "survivors" to gentry rule was neither swift nor sure. See *idem.*, "Social Change and Cultural Conflict in Virginia: Lunenburg County, 1746 to 1774," *WMQ*, 3rd ser., XXX (1978), 455–476; "The Creation of an Elite Ruling Tradition in the Virginia Southside: Lunenburg County as a Case Study," paper presented at the annual meeting of the Organization of American Historians, San Francisco, Calif., April 1980; and "Patterns of Community in the Southern Backcountry: An Ethnohistorical View of Lunenburg County, Virginia," paper presented at the 41st Conference of the Institute of Early American History and Culture at Millersville State College, Millersville, Pa., April, 1981.

[3] Russell R. Menard, "Economy and Society in Early Colonial Maryland" (Ph.D. diss., University of Iowa, 1974).

[4] Carr, "County Government in Maryland," chaps. 3, 4, 5, and 6.

[5] Menard, "Economy and Society," and *idem.*, "From Servant to Freeholder: Status Mobility and Property Accumulation in Seventeenth-Century Maryland," *WMQ*, 3rd ser., XXX (1973), 37–64.

[6] *Archives of Maryland*, William Hand Browne et al., eds., (72 vols.: Baltimore: Maryland Historical Society, 1883–) 61:87 (hereafter *Maryland Archives*).

[7] If studies of various colonial Chesapeake counties have demonstrated anything, it is that no one unit is typical of the region as a whole, or even of any given smaller subregion. Differing dates of settlement, soil quality, and position vis-à-vis major trade routes affected the rate of population growth, the kind and numbers of the labor force, and the rate of accumulation and distribution of wealth within the free population. Differing social origins and religious affiliations among the settlers in areas with similar endowments could produce very different local societies. Other chance factors—the location of the provincial capital, the routing of major roads, or the arrival of organized clusters of immigrants might also have long-lasting effects on a particular locality. Still, from the bewildering array of information available, one can begin to establish the range of possible experience and then to determine where a locality stood within this range, given constraints of time and physical and human resources. Whitman H. Ridgway, *Community Leadership in Maryland, 1790–1840: A Comparative Analysis of Power in Society* (Chapel Hill, N.C., 1979) demonstrates that great variety appeared in local power structures in the post-Revolutionary period, given differing circumstances and resources.

[8] Lorena S. Walsh, "Charles County, Maryland, 1658–1705: A Study of Chesapeake Social and Political Structure" (Ph.D. diss., Michigan State University, 1977), chaps. 1 and 2. I have subsequently revised county population estimates. Some of the results are reported in *idem.*, "Mobility, Persistence, and Opportunity in Charles County, Maryland, 1650–1720," paper presented at the annual meeting of the Social Science History Association, Bloomington, Ind., November, 1982.

[9] *Maryland Archives*, 25: 256–259; and Walsh, "Mobility, Persistence, and Opportunity."

[10] On the demography of early Maryland, see Lorena S. Walsh and Russell R. Menard, "Death in the Chesapeake: Two Life Tables for Men in Early Colonial Maryland," *Maryland Historical Magazine*, LXXIX (1974), 211–227; Russell R. Menard, "Immigration to the Chesapeake Colonies in the Seventeenth Century: A Review Essay," *ibid.*, LXVIII (1973), 323–329; *idem.*, "Immigrants and Their Increase: The Process of Population Growth in Early Colonial Maryland," in Aubrey C. Land, Lois Green Carr, and Edward C. Papenfuse, eds., *Law, Society, and Politics in Early Maryland* (Baltimore, 1977), 88–109; and Walsh, "Charles County."

[11] Vestrymen were not included in this group, since Anglican parishes were not organized in Maryland until 1692 and the vestry's role not well established for some year's thereafter. Biographies of officeholders were compiled from a variety of sources. Information on Charles County officers comes from my prosopographical study of that community. Comparative information for other lower western shore counties comes from a variety of sources. Biographies of Prince George's County officers are found in Carr, "County Government," appendix 2. Information on St. Mary's County leaders is available in career files of all seventeenth-century residents and of eighteenth-century decedents compiled by the St. Mary's City Commission, MSS, Hall of Records, Annapolis, Maryland. Information on officers of all counties serving before 1692 was compiled by Russell R. Menard and deposited at the Hall of Records (Menard File). Biographies of all members of the assembly were supplemented by reference to the files of the Maryland Legislative History Project, 1635–1789, Edward C. Papenfuse and David W. Jordan, principal investigators, MS, Hall of Records. Materials on legislators with surnames A through H are published in Edward C. Papenfuse, Alan F. Day, David W. Jordan, and Gregory A. Stiverson, eds., *A Biographical Dictionary of the Maryland Legislature, 1635–1789* (Baltimore, 1979), I: A–H. Thanks is due to all of the above for permission to use their unpublished materials.

[12] Carr, "County Government"; *idem.*, "The Foundations of Social Order: Local Government in Colonial Maryland," in Bruce C. Daniels, ed., *Town and County: Essays on the Structure of Local Government in the American Colonies* (Middletown, Conn., 1978), 71–110; and *idem.*, "Magistracy and Social Order in Seventeenth-Century Maryland," paper presented to the annual meeting of the Southern Historical Association, Atlanta, Ga., November, 1973.

[13] Carr, "County Government," chap. 6.

[14] *Ibid.*

[15] *Ibid.* and David W. Jordan, "Maryland's Privy Council, 1637–1715," in Land, Carr, and Papenfuse, eds., *Law, Society, and Politics*, 65–87.

[16] The county's early settlers included a higher proportion of free immigrants (41%) than were to be found among migrants to the colony as a whole.

[17] Walsh, "Charles County," chaps. 2, 4, and 7.

[18] *Ibid.*, chap. 6. The absence of men with traditional qualifications for ruling was a problem even at the provincial level. In 1666 Lord Baltimore contemplated having his councillors wear "habbits medals or otherwise," so that "some visible distinction or Distinctions might be drawn." *Maryland Archives* 15:16, cited in Jordan, "Maryland's Privy Council."

[19] Carr, "County Government," 623–636, demonstrates that appointments were made with an eye to providing a justice for each concentration of population. Cf. Williams, "Political Alignments in Colonial Virginia," chap. 3.

[20] Walsh, "Charles County," p. 341.

[21] The men were John Stone; Humphrey Warren, Senior; Benjamin Rozer; Thomas Matthews; and Gerrard Fowke.

[22] These were Edward Pye; John Courts, Junior; John Addison; and Thomas Burford.

[23] David W. Jordan discusses Charles Calvert's attempts to secure men of more established wealth and lineage for provincial offices as well. Still, in 1671, Calvert had "little comfort or satisfaction in the society" of most members of his council. "Maryland's Privy Council," pp. 72–74.

[24] Charles County Court and Land Records, MSS, Hall of Records, K#1, f. 87 (hereafter Charles County Court).

[25] Almost all of the leaders owned indentured servants at some point in their careers. About half of those taking office before 1680 also owned slaves, as did just under three-

quarters of those entering office thereafter. Most were small-scale slaveowners, the majority holding fewer than six slaves. The ten percent of the officers who owned twenty or more slaves were in a position to wield immense economic power.

[26] For the impact of the Revolution of 1689 on local government see Carr and Jordan, *Maryland's Revolution of Government*. About one-quarter of Charles County residents at the turn of the century were Catholics (*Maryland Archives* 25:258). Their exclusion from office had a marked effect on the social composition of minor local officeholders in Charles County. Jurors, constables, and overseers of the highways serving after 1689 were on the average much poorer than earlier local officers. Walsh, "Charles County," chap. 6.

[27] Walsh, "Charles County," chaps. 6 and 7; *idem.*, "Mobility, Persistence, and Opportunity." Natives at all wealth levels were much less likely to leave the county than were immigrants. On the altered *mentalité* of the native-born, see Carole Shammas, "English-Born and Creole Elites in Turn-of-the-Century Virginia," in Tate and Ammerman, eds., *The Chesapeake in the Seventeenth Century*, 274–296.

[28] David W. Jordan, "The Royal Period of Colonial Maryland, 1689–1715" (Ph.D. diss., Princeton University, 1966), chaps. 3 and 5; *idem.*, "Political Stability and the Emergence of a Native Elite."

[29] Only decedents with £200 or more in personal property were likely to own one or more slaves. Analysis of inventories for the four lower western shore counties to 1705 and for St. Mary's County to 1775 has been funded by grants to the St. Mary's City Commission from the National Science Foundation (GS-32272) and the National Endowment for the Humanities (RO-6228-72-468, RO-10585-74-267, RS-23687-76-431). Charles County inventories, 1706–1720, were analyzed with an Arthur H. Cole Grant-in-Aid to Lorena S. Walsh from the Economic History Association.

[30] Schoolmasters, who began appearing in the county after 1700, had little status whatsoever. Clerks, bookkeepers, and surveyors gained status only when they managed to acquire landed estates.

[31] Compare Kenneth A. Lockridge and Alan Kreider, "The Evolution of Massachusetts Town Government, 1640 to 1740," *WMQ*, 3rd Ser., XXIII (1966), 549–574 and Edward M. Cook, Jr., *The Fathers of the Towns: Leadership and Community Structure in Eighteenth-Century New England* (Baltimore, 1976). Similarly, Williams found almost no instances of major leaders in colonial Middlesex County, Virginia, first holding lesser offices ("Political Alignments in Colonial Virginia," chap. 3).

[32] Characteristics of minor local officers are discussed in Walsh, "Charles County," chap. 6. In Virginia, unlike Maryland, the position of county clerk was a major office of power.

[33] A mapping of communication networks of a number of seventeenth- and eighteenth-century St. Mary's County residents compiled for the St. Mary's City Commission clearly demonstrates this. Most settlers maintained frequent contacts only with persons living within about a two-mile radius of their homes, and seldom interacted with families more than five miles away. Merchant networks were much more extensive.

[34] Walsh, "Charles County," chap. 5. Innkeepers, especially those operating near the county courthouse, stood to gain substantial revenues from the entertainment of justices, jurors, and prisoners during meetings of the court. From the late 1670s, justices were required to suspend any innkeeping operations while they sat on the bench, because of a likely conflict of interest.

[35] There were, of course, no formal boundaries, but a study of communication patterns on the local level reveals the existence of a number of separate communities within each county (*Ibid.*).

[36] A similar situation prevailed throughout the colony. The mean number of years of service of all Maryland justices sitting in 1689 was 7.18 (Carr and Jordan, *Maryland's Revolution of Government*, 187, compiled from the Menard file).

[37] Lockridge and Kreider, "The Evolution of Massachusetts Town Government."

[38] The situation in the provincial government was similar. Between 1660 and 1689 only 15 out of a total of 175 provincial officeholders were of the second generation of their family to hold power, and only 1 was of the third generation. Jordan, "Political Stability and the Emergence of a Native Elite."

[39] Walsh, "'Till Death Us Do Part': Marriage and Family in Seventeenth-Century Maryland," in Tate and Ammerman, eds., *The Chesapeake in the Seventeenth Century*, 126–152.

[40] From an analysis of inventories for the four lower western shore counties to 1705 and for St. Mary's County to 1775. St. Mary's City Commission, Annapolis, Md.

[41] Carr, "County Government," 508–526.

[42] Many historians have maintained that county justices used their office for their own economic benefit. See, for example, Williams, "Political Alignments in Colonial Virginia," 343–345; Quitt, "Virginia House of Burgesses," chap. 5; and Edmund S. Morgan, *American Slavery, American Freedom: The Ordeal of Colonial Virginia* (New York, 1975), 201–211, 350–351. Neither Lois Carr nor I has found evidence of a general pattern of such abuses in the Maryland counties we have studied. (See Carr, "County Government," 468–480.) In order to prove or disprove this hypothesis, a number of questions require investigation; for example, how did justices distribute those economic perquisites (e.g., public works contracts, or town and mill sites) that they controlled? Did magistrates award swifter and more favorable rulings to members of the bench than to non-officeholders? How well developed was the concept of conflict of interest, and how broadly or narrowly was it applied?

[43] Carr, "County Government," 468–480. Men holding offices of profit in the colony are listed in Donnell M. Owings, *His Lordship's Patronage* (Studies in Maryland History, no. 1, Baltimore, 1953).

[44] A study measuring stability in the county by reconstructing censuses at fifteen-year intervals beginning in 1660 and ending in 1720 demonstrates that more than one-third of the white adult males present at the start of a fifteen-year interval would die within it, and another fifth would leave the county. Walsh, "Mobility, Persistence, and Opportunity."

[45] Walsh, "Charles County," chaps. 6 and 7.

[46] See especially Edmund S. Morgan, *American Slavery, American Freedom*.

[47] Walsh, "Charles County," chap. 6.

[48] Charles County Court, E#1, f. 138. Because Chesapeake neighborhoods had no established formal boundaries, their presence and functions become clear only when individuals' associations and interactions are examined in relation to local geography.

[49] For sources, see notes 11 and 29.

[50] Lois Carr's preliminary analysis of local power structures in other subregions of Maryland suggests that additional variations will indeed appear in other kinds of areas.

[51] Walsh, "Charles County," chap. 7; Jordan, "Political Stability and the Emergence of a Native Elite."

[52] For the number of resident Catholics, see *Maryland Archives* 25:258. The effect on minor local office was also pronounced. One St. Mary's County resident asserted he could not obtain a fair trial in his home county because "there are a great many freeholders in the said County who are Roman Catholicks and by being so disqualified . . . to be jury men." The implication was that it would be difficult to find enough

qualified jurors unrelated to the litigants in the case (Provincial Court Papers, St. Mary's County, *Richard Edelin's lessee* v. *John Edwards* (1743), MS, Hall of Records).

[53] The Carroll Papers, MSS 219, Maryland Historical Society, Baltimore, contain a series of documents relating to the career of justice and delegate Samuel Williamson and his relationship to his former master's family.

[54] Analysis of the consumer goods in the inventories of county officers shows that many leaders made little use of personal possessions to advertise their status. Beginning in the 1670s, some officers quickly adapted new fashions, dressing elegantly and furnishing their dwellings in a manner which clearly set their families off from most other county residents. Other leaders, equally wealthy, were content with the acquisition of ordinary comforts—feather mattresses, a few ceramics, some table linen, and perhaps a set of silver buttons were all that they aspired to. It may have been only when the elite came to share other characteristics than economic success that their personal possessions would serve to confirm their self-image and to reinforce a sense of group belonging.

[55] In 1708 Calvert County had only forty-eight Catholic residents (*Maryland Archives* 25:258). On the other hand, there were a number of Quakers in the county. How many men were disqualified because of their refusal to take oaths is uncertain. See David W. Jordan, "'God's Candle' Within Government: Quakers and Politics in Early Maryland," *WMQ*, 3rd Ser., XXXIX (1982), 628–654.

[56] Not surprisingly, at least one Prince George's County leader procured a private carriage at least a full twenty years before any St. Mary's County officer owned one. All lower western shore leaders were quite slow in taking up this form of ostentatious consumption, however. Just across the Potomac in Westmoreland County, Virginia, Justice William Fitzhugh had felt the need for a carriage for "present Recreation" in 1689, forty years earlier. *William Fitzhugh and His Chesapeake World, 1676–1701*, Richard Beale Davis, ed. (Chapel Hill, N.C., 1963), 258, 271.

[57] Bailyn, "Politics and Social Structure in Virginia," 106.

[58] Jordan, "Emergence of a Native Elite," 269.

[59] Jordan, "The Royal Period of Colonial Maryland," chaps. 4 and 5; Carr, "County Government," chap. 6.

[60] Ebenezer Cook, *The Sot-Weed Factor* (1708), reprinted in *Works of Ebenezer Cook, Gent.: Laureat of Maryland . . .* , Bernard C. Steiner, ed. (*Maryland Historical Society Fund Publication No. 36*); Baltimore, 1900. Cook may have been a resident of St. Mary's City in 1694 (*Maryland Archives* 19:75). He had traveled in Prince George's County and makes Calvert County the site of his famous court-day description. In 1718 he qualified as an attorney of the Charles County Court (Charles County Court, I#2, 42).

[61] Jordan, "Emergence of a Native Elite," 273.

Quaker Party and Proprietary Policies: The Dynamics of Politics in Pre-Revolutionary Pennsylvania, 1730–1775

[1] Among the more important of these monographs are Theodore Thayer, *Pennsylvania Politics and the Growth of Democracy, 1740–1776* (Harrisburg, Pa., 1953); William S. Hanna, *Benjamin Franklin and Pennsylvania Politics* (Stanford, Ca., 1964); James H. Hutson, *Pennsylvania Politics, 1746–1770: The Movement for Royal Government and its Consequences* (Princeton, N.J., 1972); Benjamin H. Newcomb, *Franklin and Galloway: A Political Partnership* (New Haven, Conn., 1972).

[2] The only study that focuses directly on the Quaker Party is Theodore Thayer's rather restrictive article "The Quaker Party in Pennsylvania, 1755–1765," *Penn-*

sylvania Magazine of History and Biography 71 (1947), 19–43 (hereafter cited as *PMHB*). The best treatment of proprietary affairs is William R. Shepherd, *History of Proprietary Government in Pennsylvania* (New York, 1896).

³Israel Pemberton, Jr., to John Fothergill, Nov. 17, 1755. Printed in Dietmar Rothermund, *The Layman's Progress: Religious and Political Experience in Colonial Pennsylvania, 1740–1770* (Philadelphia, 1961), 177–178; Minutes, Philadelphia Yearly Meeting, 1681–1746, 417, Quaker Collection, Friends' Library, Swarthmore College.

⁴For a description of county offices see Alan Tully, "*William Penn's Legacy: Politics and Social Structure in Provincial Pennsylvania, 1726–1755* (Baltimore and London, 1977), 103–121.

⁵The Quaker Party was also referred to as the "Assembly Party" and the "Old Ticket." All of these terms were in use from the 1740s through the mid-1770s.

⁶William Allen to John Penn, Nov. 17, 1739, Penn Papers, Official Correspondence, 3 (hereinafter cited as PPOC). Historical Society of Pennsylvania. Unless otherwise indicated, all manuscripts are located at this depository.

⁷Tully, *William Penn's Legacy*, 17–19. Hamilton married into a Quaker family and, although it seems he was an active member of no church or meeting, he was buried in Christ Church graveyard in Philadelphia. This would seem to make him a nominal Churchman. Note the error in *William Penn's Legacy*, 170 and 177, where I classified him as a Presbyterian.

⁸See the chapter in this volume by Richard A. Ryerson, "Portrait of a Colonial Oligarchy: The Quaker Elite in the Pennsylvania Assembly, 1729–1776"; as well as Tully, *William Penn's Legacy*, 170–173.

⁹On Kinsey, see Tully, *William Penn's Legacy*, 97–98; Thomas Wendel, "The Speaker of the House, Pennsylvania, 1701–1776," *PMHB*, 97 (1973), 3–21; Edwin B. Bronner, "The Disgrace of John Kinsey, Quaker Politician, 1739–1750," *PMHB*, 75 (1951), 400–415.

¹⁰For example, see Richard Peters to Thomas Penn, June 4 and June 6, 1743, Richard Peters Letterbook (hereinafter cited as RPLB).

¹¹William Allen to John Penn, March 27, 1741, PPOC 3.

¹²Gertrude MacKinney, ed., *Votes and Proceedings of the House of Representatives of the Province of Pennsylvania, Pennsylvania Archives*, 8th Ser. (Harrisburg, Penn., 1931–1935), 3:3519–3520; 4:3712–3713, 3718, 4021 (hereinafter cited as *Votes*).

¹³Historians have often emphasized the uncertainty of succession in Quaker Party leadership at this point, citing Richard Peters's comment that the issue was in doubt between Isaac Norris, Jr., and Israel Pemberton, Jr. If so, it was not long in doubt. When Acting Trustee James Morris died in early 1751, Isaac Norris quickly snatched this key patronage post for his brother Charles. Israel Pemberton, Jr., was defeated as an assembly candidate in the 1751 election after only one year of legislative experience. Assuming Pemberton did have political ambitions, it is clear he was no match for Norris (Richard Peters to Thomas Penn, July 13, 1750, PPOC 5).

¹⁴Christopher Wilson and John Hunt to Friends, Nov. 4, 1756, Miscellaneous Manuscripts, Quaker Collection, Friends Historical Library, Swarthmore College.

¹⁵Ryerson, "Portrait of a Colonial Oligarchy"; Richard Bauman, *For the Reputation of Truth: Politics, Religion, and Conflict among the Pennsylvania Quakers, 1750–1800* (Baltimore and London, 1971), 27, 103–107, 111–112, 145–147; Hermann Wellenreuther, *Glaube und Politik in Pennsylvania, 1681–1776. Die Wandlungen der Obrigkeitsdoktrin und des Peace Testimony der Quaker* (Cologne, 1972), 432–437; Wayne L. Bockelman and Owen S. Ireland, "The Internal Revolution in Pennsyl-

vania: An Ethnic-Religious Interpretation," *Pennsylvania History*, 41 (1974), 124–159 (hereinafter cited as *PH*); Richard A. Ryerson, *The Revolution Is Now Begun: The Radical Committees of Philadelphia, 1765–1776* (Philadelphia, 1978), 9–10, 13–15, 260–262.

[16] For recent efforts to deal with this theme, see the works cited in note 1.

[17] Richard Peters to Thomas Penn, Oct. 2, 1756, PPOC 8. On the continuation of Quaker political power through the 1750s, 1760s, and early 1770s, see note 15.

[18] James Pemberton to Samuel Fothergill, Nov. (?), 1756; James Pemberton to John Fothergill, Dec. 10, 1762 and March 3, 1764, Pemberton-Fothergill Manuscripts.

[19] The opposite, and dominant, interpretation has been to see the remains of the Quaker Party captured, reorganized, and used by Franklin and Galloway. This seems to me to have the tail wagging the dog for much too long a period. For the appropriate literature, see note 1.

[20] John Penn to Thomas Penn, Nov. 12, 1766, PPOC 10.

[21] Hutson, *Pennsylvania Politics*, 152–243.

[22] Bauman, *For the Reputation of Truth*, 77–101, 226.

[23] Israel Pemberton, Jr., to John Fothergill, April 6, 1758, Pemberton-Fothergill, vol. 34.

[24] James Pemberton to John Fothergill, Dec. 10, 1762, *ibid.* These nominal Friends were men who the strict Quakers would not claim but who among themselves and their political supporters were still considered Quakers. Many of these irregular or non-meeting attenders continued for some time as nominal Friends, because Quakers did not disown members for political involvement prior to the Revolution. Bauman, *For the Reputation of Truth*, 225–227.

[25] Richard Peters to Thomas Penn, Oct. 3, 1744, RPLB; James Logan to John Smith, Mar. 25, 1764, John Smith Manuscripts; John Drinker and Stephan Collins to Israel Pemberton, Jr., Sept. 25, 1766, Pemberton Papers.

[26] Quotation ("a public declaration . . .") in Samuel Fothergill to Israel Pemberton, Jr., April 8, 1742, Pemberton-Fothergill; Tully, *William Penn's Legacy*, 141–160.

[27] For a public expression of this sentiment, see the preamble to the 1755 Militia Act. James T. Mitchell and Henry Flanders, eds., *The Statutes at Large of Pennsylvania from 1682 to 1801* (Harrisburg, 1896–1915), 5, 197–201 (hereinafter cited as *Statutes at Large*).

[28] James Pemberton is the best example. After resigning from the assembly in 1756, Pemberton reentered politics in 1765, as he explained it, to "preserve unanimity" and keep an "envious Presbyterian [George Bryan] out." Six months earlier, he had complained that *not enough* Quakers were staying out of office (James Pemberton to John Fothergill, Dec. 18, 1765, March 7, 1764, Pemberton-Fothergill).

[29] For example, see Richard Peters to Proprietaries, Nov. 7, 1742, RPLB.

[30] For an example of this kind of thinking, see "Answer to Conrad Weiser's letter to the Germans," Sept. 29, 1741, PPOC 3.

[31] Over the years 1730 to 1776 Quaker Party support ebbed and flowed among different religious groups in different counties. There was no occasion that I know of, however, on which one religious group turned unanimously against the Quaker Party in all counties.

[32] Tully, *William Penn's Legacy*, 23–38; Newcomb, *Franklin and Galloway*, 61–62.

[33] *Statutes at Large*, 5, 448–455.

[34] James Hamilton to Thomas Penn, Feb. 22, 1750, PPOC 5; *Statutes at Large*, 5, 224–243, 320–344; Newcomb, *Franklin and Galloway*, 61–63.

[35] Richard Peters to Proprietaries, Nov. 17, 1742, RPLB.

[36] *Ibid.*, Richard Peters to Thomas Penn, June 5, 1742, RPLB; Conrad Weiser to Richard Peters, Oct. 2, 1755, Correspondence of Conrad Weiser; Minutes of Trustees General, Aug. 10, 1754, Rev. William Smith Papers, 6; "Answer to Conrad Weiser's letter to the Germans," Sept. 29, 1741, PPOC 3; *Votes*, 3, 2507.

[37] John Dickinson to Isaac Norris, Oct 24, 1764, Isaac Norris Letterbook 1756–1766 (hereinafter cited as INLB); William Logan to John Smith, March 25, 1764, John Smith Manuscripts; William Allen to Thomas Penn, Oct. 21, 1764, PPOC 9; Penn Manuscripts, Autograph Petitions, 66.

[38] *Votes*, 3, 2507.

[39] Charles Norris's appointment in 1751 indicates that Isaac, Jr. was consolidating his position as party leader. Charles was known to have more influence with his brother than any other politician. Edward Shippen to Edward Shippen, Jr., April 6, 1754, Edward Shippen Letterbooks, American Philosophical Society.

[40] Approximately £100 Pennsylvania Currency.

[41] *Votes*, 5, 3834.

[42] *Votes*, 4, 3519.

[43] *Votes*, 5, 3712, 3713, 3718, 4021, 4035.

[44] *Votes*, 3, 2197.

[45] John Smith to James Logan, Jr., Oct. 13, 1750, Correspondence of John Smith.

[46] Charles Norris to James Wright, Aug. 31, 1753, Norris Manuscripts, Miscellaneous, *PMHB* 22 (1898), 387–388.

[47] *Votes*, 3, 2411; 6, 5231–5232, 5252, 5288–5289.

[48] A complete roster of such posts may be compiled from the assembly *Votes* and the *Statutes at Large*.

[49] For examples of charges of patronage and corruption see Paul Veritt, *To My Friends in Pennsylvania . . .* (Philadelphia, 1738) and *Constant Trueman Advice to the Freeholders and Electors of Pennsylvania . . .* (Philadelphia, 1735).

[50] Tully, *William Penn's Legacy*, 7–15, 85–86.

[51] George Stevenson to Richard Peters, April 30, 1758, and May 15, 1758, *Pennsylvania Archives*, 1st Ser., 3 (hereinafter cited as PA); Isaac Norris to Robert Charles, June 20, 1755, INLB, 1719–1756; Report of Richard Peters and Lynford Lardner to the Provincial Council, Nov. 4, 1755, PPOC 7; Minutes, Warrington Monthly Meeting, 1747–1786, 62–68, Quaker Collection, Friends' Library, Swarthmore College. For related evidence from the northeast see Lewis Weiss to Timothy Horsefield, Aug. 1, 1763. Northampton County Papers, Miscellaneous Manuscripts, Bethlehem and Vicinity, 1741–1849.

[52] Conrad Weiser to Governor Morris, Oct. 19, 1755. Quoted in Morton L. Montgomery, *History of Berks County in Pennsylvania* (Philadelphia 1886), 123.

[53] Theodore Thayer, "The Friendly Association" *PMHB* 67 (1943), 356–376; Nicholas B. Wainwright, *George Croghan, Wilderness Diplomat* (Chapel Hill, N.C., 1959), 118–155, 162–163, 173, 178, 184–189.

[54] *Statutes at Large*, 5, 310–344.

[55] Bauman, *For the Reputation of Truth*, 77–101.

[56] Brooke Hindle, "The March of the Paxton Boys," WMQ, 3rd Ser., 3 (1946), 461–486; John R. Dunbar, ed., *The Paxton Papers* (The Hague, 1957).

[57] Susanna Wright to Isaac Whitlock, Jan. 16, 1764, Parrish Collection, Pemberton. It angered many western residents to have Philadelphia Quakers pronouncing arrogantly on Indian affairs when their lives were not at stake. Indeed the "sober sort" of Quakers were very chary of risks. The only one of this group I know of who lived in an exposed position was Peter Worral of Lancaster. Significantly enough, Worral chose to

move from Lancaster to Philadelphia and then to Burlington in 1756. Note, also, how swiftly Israel Pemberton, Jr., departed Philadelphia when the Paxton Boys marched on that city (James Pemberton to John Fothergill, March 7, 1764, Pemberton-Fothergill).

[58] John Penn to Thomas Penn, March 16, 1765, PPOC 10. Eleanor M. Webster, "Insurrection at Fort London in 1765: Rebellion or Preservation of Peace?" *The Western Pennsylvania Historical Magazine*, 42 (1964), 12ff. Stephen H. Cutcliff, "The Sideling Hill Affair: The Cumberland County Riot of 1765", *The Western Pennsylvania Historical Magazine*, 59 (1976), 39–45.

[59] For more information on the mechanics of underrepresentation, see Charles H. Lincoln, *The Revolutionary Movement in Pennsylvania, 1760–1776* (Philadelphia, 1901), 47, and Thayer, "The Quaker Party," 28–31.

[60] The best treatment of the Supreme Court issue is Edward O. Smith, "Thomas Penn, Chief Proprietor of Pennsylvania: A Study of his Public Governmental Activities" (Ph.D. diss., Lehigh University, 1966), 287–297.

[61] Samuel Purvience to James Burd, Sept. 10, 1764, Sept. 17, 1764, Sept. 20, 1765; Joseph Shippen to James Burd, Oct. 6, 1764; William Attlee to James Burd, Sept. 20, 1768, Sept. 26, 1768, Sept. 19, 1769; Edward Shippen to James Burd, Sept. 18, 1768; Jasper Yeates to James Burd, Sept. 17, 1769, Sept. 19, 1769, Shippen Family Papers; Jasper Yeates to James Burd, Sept. 20, 1773, Oct. 6, 1773; Samuel J. Attlee to James Burd, June 30, 1770, Burd-Shippen Papers, American Philosophical Society. For more information on Lancaster politics, see Alan Tully, "Ethnicity, Religion, and Politics in Early America," *PMHB* 107 (1983), 522–527.

[62] On the Penn family, see Tully, *William Penn's Legacy*, 4–15.

[63] John Penn to Thomas Penn, March 29, 1739, Hazard Family Papers; Remonstrance of several inhabitants of Chester County, March 7, 1733, Chester County Papers, 1684–1847, 95.

[64] Tully, *William Penn's Legacy*, 4–15.

[65] Thomas Penn to John and Richard Penn, August 16, 1738, Penn Manuscripts, Small Letterbook.

[66] *Votes*, 3, 2502, 2504–2505; John and Richard Penn to Thomas Penn, June 21, 1739; John, Thomas, and Richard Penn to Isaac Norris, Sr., Jan. 30, 1732. Thomas Penn Letterbook 1 (hereafter cited as TPLB).

[67] John Penn to Thomas Penn, May 1, 1738, TPLB, 1.

[68] *Statutes at Large*, 4, 344–359.

[69] Thomas Penn to Richard Peters, May 4, 1743, Penn Manuscripts, Saunders-Coates; Richard Peters to Thomas Penn, Nov. 23, 1743, RPLB.

[70] Records of Donnegal Presbytery, V-1. IB, 1736–1740, Sept. 4, 1739, Presbyterian Historical Society. See also Samuel Blunston to Thomas Penn, Feb. 20, 1738, Gratz Collection, Samuel Blunston; and Samuel Blunston to Proprietaries, Nov. 16, 1740, Lancaster County Miscellaneous Papers.

[71] Tully, *William Penn's Legacy*, 23–32.

[72] Richard Peters to Thomas Penn, Oct. 20, 1741, PPOC 3.

[73] Thomas Penn to John Penn, Jan. 14, 1736, P.A., 2nd Ser., 7.

[74] Tully, *William Penn's Legacy*, 28–38.

[75] Thomas Penn to Richard Peters, June 10, 1754, TPLB, 3.

[76] Thomas Penn to James Hamilton, July 31, 1749, Penn-Hamilton Correspondence.

[77] Hutson, *Pennsylvania Politics*, details the series of conflicts.

[78] On the care the governors had to take in choosing militia officers and the care these officers had to take with their men, see Conrad Weiser to James Burd, June 7, 1757, and Joseph Shippen to James Burd, June 7, 1757, Shippen Papers, Correspondence 2; and Richard Peters to Joseph Shippen, May 5, 1758, PA, 1st Ser., 3.

[79] Richard Peters to Thomas Penn, Jan. 30, 1751, Mar. 16, 1752, PPOC 5; Thomas Penn to Col. Thomas, Aug. 21, 1743, TPLB 2; Thomas Penn to James Hamilton, May 24, 1760, June 6, 1760, Penn-Hamilton Correspondence.

[80] *Pennsylvania Gazette*, March 30, 1738, Dec. 24, 1735; *Votes*, 3, 2506.

[81] James Hamilton to Thomas Penn, March 18, 1752, PPOC 5, Sept. 8, 1753, PPOC 6; Newcomb, *Franklin and Galloway*, 61–63.

[82] James Hamilton to Thomas Penn, Nov. 26, 1753, PPOC 6.

[83] John Penn to Thomas Penn, July 20, 1732, TPLB 1.

[84] The political intransigence of the assembly was mirrored by a popular intransigence in the payment of quitrents and purchase money. Richard Hockley to Thomas Penn, June 27, 1742, PPOC 3.

[85] Richard Peters to Proprietaries, July 12, 1750, PPOC 5.

[86] Thomas Penn to Richard Peters, Jan. 9, 1753, TPLB 3.

[87] Thomas Penn to Richard Peters, Aug. 22, 1743, Gratz Collection, Governors of Pennsylvania; Thomas Penn to Richard Hockley, Jan. 9, 1753, June 29, 1753, TPLB 3; Thomas Penn to James Hamilton, Nov. 15, 1760, Penn-Hamilton Correspondence.

[88] Richard Peters to Proprietaries, June 3, 1742, RPLB; Richard Peters to Thomas Penn, June 12, 1752, PPOC 5; Richard Peters to Proprietaries, Dec. 21, 1754, PPOC 6.

[89] Richard Hockley to Thomas Penn, March 31, 1759, PPOC 9. Proprietary agents were never very successful at collecting quitrents at the current exchange rate even though that obligation was stated in all post-1732 land patents. This was the reason Thomas Penn placed such heavy emphasis throughout the fifties and sixties on getting a clear statement in statute that landowners were legally bound to pay the equivalent of sterling. John Penn to Thomas Penn, Sept. 12, 1766, PPOC 10.

[90] Richard Peters to Thomas Penn, Oct. 4, 1752, PPOC 5.

[91] Jan. 24, 1757, PPOC 8, 223; Richard Hockley to Thomas Penn, Oct. 30, 1756, PPOC 8.

[92] Edmund Physick to Thomas Penn, April 2, 1757, PPOC 8.

[93] Richard Peters to Thomas Penn, June 1, 1756, PPOC 8.

[94] Hutson, *Pennsylvania Politics*, 6–123.

[95] Hannah, *Benjamin Franklin and Pennsylvania Politics*, 94–95.

[96] *Advice and Information to the Freeholders and Freemen of the Province of Pennsylvania* (Philadelphia, 1727).

[97] *Votes*, 6, 4887, 4930, 4971, 5039, 5216, 5220–5221.

[98] William Allen to Thomas Penn, Sept. 25, 1764, PPOC 9.

[99] William Allen to Dr. Chandler, Feb. 4, 1758, PPOC 9; Isaac Norris to Benjamin Franklin, Oct. 5, 1760, INLB, 1756–1766; *Votes*, 6, 4895.

[100] Hutson, *Pennsylvania Politics*, 110–113.

[101] Samuel Hazaard, ed., *Minutes of the Provincial Council of Pennsylvania* (Philadelphia and Harrisburg, 1852–1853), 8, 473 (hereafter cited as *CR*). Edmund Physick to Thomas Penn, Sept. 28, 1769, Penn-Physick Letterbook; Lamberton Scotch-Irish Collection, 41.

[102] Edmund Physick to Thomas Penn, Sept. 28, 1769, Penn-Physick Letterbook; James Tilghman to Thomas Penn, Aug. 14, 1766, Edmund Physick to Thomas Penn, June 11, 1770, PPOC 10.

[103] Petition of the Back Inhabitants, April 19, 1769, 18, Edmund Physick to Thomas Penn, Sept. 28, 1769, Penn-Physick Letterbook; *Votes*, 5, 3942–3943; 3986, 4041.

[104] Even during wartime, there was little friendliness for the proprietary men in Paxton. Rev. John Elder to Richard Peters, [July 30, 1757], PA, 1st Ser., vol. 3.

[105] William Smith to Thomas Penn, [?], 1755, PPOC 7; *CR* 8, 472–477, 479; Thomas Penn to John Penn, July 13, 1764, TPLB 8.

[106] Smith, "Thomas Penn," 484–539.

[107] For a similar view of the relationship between proprietary and Presbyterian frontiermen, see James K. Martin, "The Return of the Paxton Boys and the Historical State of the Pennsylvania Frontier, 1764–1774," *PH*, 38 (1971), 117–133.

[108] Newcomb, *Franklin and Galloway*, 78–124.

[109] Isaac Norris to Robert Charles, Oct. 5, 1755, INLB, 1719–1756.

[110] For example, see Richard Peters to Thomas Penn, Oct. 2, 1756, PPOC 8.

[111] The proprietary politicians were destroyed as an effective popular political group for fifteen years by their implication in the Philadelphia election riot of 1742. Despite that hard lesson, Samuel Purviance advised his Lancaster County friends prior to the 1765 election this way: "As soon as your ticket is agreed on let it be spread through the country that all of our party intend to come well armed to the election and that you intend if there's the least partiality in either sheriff, inspectors or managers of the election that you will thrash the sherrif, every inspector and Quaker and menonite to jelly. . . .

Have all our friends warned to put on a bold face . . . [and have] every man provided with as good shiely [shillelah] as if determined to put their threats in execution. . . . I see no danger in the scheme but that of a riot which would require great prudence to avoid" (Samuel Purviance, Jr., to James Burd, Sept. 20, 1765; Shippen Family Papers).

[112] Thomas Penn to John Penn, Dec. 14, 1765, Feb. 26, 1766, TPLB 8; Thomas Penn to John Penn, May 10, 1766, TPLB 9; Thomas Penn to William Peters, Aug. 10, 1764, TPLB 8.

[113] John B. Love, "The Colonial Surveyor in Pennsylvania" (Ph.D. diss., University of Pennsylvania, 1971), 184–246.

[114] What Thomas Penn did sanction was the *denial* of new commissions to those who strenuously criticized the proprietary during times of contention. The striking of John Wright in 1741 as chief magistrate of Lancaster County is one dramatic example of this. For others, see Thayer, *Growth of Democracy*, 105.

[115] John Penn to Thomas Penn, Dec. 15, 1765, PPOC 10. Proprietary placeman, William Peters, also made this argument (William Peters to Thomas Penn, June 4, 1764, PPOC 9).

[116] Perhaps the best example was the appointment of Thomas Smith, Provost William Smith's brother, to the clerk's and prothonotary's offices in Bedford County when it was created in 1771. See also John Penn to Thomas Penn, Oct. 14, 1765, PPOC 10.

[117] John Penn to Thomas Penn, June 16, 1764, PPOC 9.

[118] Joseph Shippen, Jr., to Edward Shippen, Sr., June 22, 1770, Shippen Family Papers.

[119] List of Justices, Berks, 1769, Miscellaneous County Papers, Philadelphia, Berks, Montgomery.

[120] John Penn to Thomas Penn, Dec. 15, 1765, Sept. 12, 1766, PPOC 10.

[121] Governor Denny to Proprietaries, June 20, 1757; Richard Peters to Joseph Shippen, May 5, 1758; Rev. John Elder to Governor Penn, Nov. 15, 1763; PA, 1st Ser.; Joseph Shippen to James Burd, June 7, 1757, Shippen Papers, Correspondence 2.

[122] John Armstrong to James Burd, Jan. 28, 1757, Shippen Papers, Correspondence 2.

[123] Richard Peters to Thomas Penn, Oct. 2, 1756, PPOC 8.

[124] William Allen to Thomas Penn, Oct. 12, 1768, PPOC 10.

[125] For example, see Governor Denny to Proprietaries, June 30, 1757, PA 1st Ser.; John Penn to Thomas Penn, Sept. 1, 1764, PPOC 9.

[126] William Allen to Thomas Penn, Nov. 12, 1766; James Tilghman to Thomas Penn, Jan. 30, 1773, Mar. 1, 1773, PPOC 10. On the Stump case, see G. S. Rowe,

"The Frederick Stump Affair, 1768, and its Challenge to Legal Historians of Early Pennsylvania", *PH*, 49 (1982), 259–288.

[127] James Tilghman to Thomas Penn, July 18, 1766, Aug. 14, 1766, PPOC 10.

[128] On the closing of ranks among Quaker Party and proprietary men, see Ryerson, *The Revolution Is Now Begun*, 7–24.

[129] Hutson, *Pennsylvania Politics*, 213, 236.

[130] It seems likely that the only political groups more organized than the Quaker Party in pre-Revolutionary America were those active in Rhode Island. I am indebted to Edward H. Cook, Jr., for information on Rhode Island. On Rhode Island politics in general, see David S. Lovejoy, *Rhode Island Politics and the American Revolution* (Providence, R.I., 1958).

[131] For the "court"/"county" distinction see J. G. H. Pocock, "Machiavelli, Harrington and English Ideologies in the Eighteenth Century," *WMQ*, 3rd Ser., 22 (1965), 565–583; "Virtue and Commerce in the Eighteenth Century," *Journal of Interdisciplinary History*, 3 (1972), 119–134; *The Machiavellian Moment: Florentine Political Thought and the Atlantic Republican Tradition* (Princeton, N.J., and London, 1975), 462–552. For the application of these categories to political organizations in the colonies, see Jack P. Greene, "Changing Interpretations of Early American Politics," in Ray Allen Billington, ed., *The Reinterpretation of Early American History* (San Marino, California, 1966; New York, 1968), 151–184; and John M. Murrin, "The Great Inversion, or Court versus Country: A comparison of the Revolution Settlements in England (1688–1721) and America (1776–1816)," in J. G. A. Pocock, ed., *Three British Revolutions: 1641, 1688, 1776* (Princeton, N.J., 1980), 368–453. For an interesting attempt to go beyond these categories, see Hermann Wellenreuther, "The Quest for Harmony in a Turbulent World: The Principle of 'Love and Unity' in Colonial Pennsylvania Politics," *PMHB* 107 (1983), 537–576.

Portrait of a Colonial Oligarchy: The Quaker Elite in the Pennsylvania Assembly, 1729–1776

[1] Charles P. Keith, *The Provincial Councillors of Pennsylvania, 1733–1776* (Philadelphia, 1883), 228.

[2] Frederick B. Tolles, *Meeting House and Counting House: The Quaker Merchants of Colonial Philadelphia, 1682–1763* (Chapel Hill, N.C., 1948), esp. chap. 10.

[3] John M. Murrin, "Anglicizing an American Colony: The Transformation of Provincial Massachusetts" (Ph.D. diss., Yale University, 1966); Robert M. Zemsky, *Merchants, Farmers, and River Gods, An Essay in Eighteenth-Century Politics* (Boston, 1971); Jack P. Greene, "Foundations of Political Power in the Virginia House of Burgesses, 1720–1776," *William and Mary Quarterly* (hereafter *WMQ*), 3rd Ser., 16 (1959), 485–506; Greene, *The Quest for Power: The Lower Houses of Assembly in the Southern Royal Colonies, 1689–1776* (Chapel Hill, N.C., 1963); Greene, "Political Mimesis: A Consideration of the Historical Roots of Legislative Behavior in the British Colonies in the Eighteenth Century," *American Historical Review* (hereafter *AHR*) 75 (1969–1970), 337–360; Greene, "The Growth of Political Stability: An Interpretation of Political Development in the Anglo-American Colonies, 1660–1760," in John Parker and Carol Urness, eds., *The American Revolution: A Heritage of Change* (Minneapolis, Minn., 1973), 26–52; and Bernard Bailyn, *The Origins of American Politics* (New York, 1968).

[4] See Jere Daniell, *Experiment in Republicanism: New Hampshire Politics and the American Revolution, 1741–1794* (Cambridge, Mass., 1970); Bernard Bailyn, *The Ordeal of Thomas Hutchinson* (Cambridge, Mass., 1974); Greene, "Changing Interpretations of Early American Politics," in Ray Allen Billington, ed., *The Reinterpreta-*

tion of Early American History (San Marino, Ca., 1966; New York, 1968), 151–184; and Richard Alan Ryerson, *The Revolution Is Now Begun: The Radical Committees of Philadelphia, 1765–1776* (Philadelphia, 1978), chaps. 1–2.

[5] In 1770 the British-American legislatures with the highest ratios of adult white males to legislators were: Virginia, 439:1; Maryland, 478:1; New Jersey, 910:1; New York, 1065:1; and Pennsylvania, 1301:1. See Jack P. Greene, "Legislative Turnover in British America, 1696 to 1775: A Quantitative Analysis," *WMQ*, 3rd Ser., 38 (July 1981), 442–463, table VII, p. 461. Throughout this essay, assembly sessions, which ran from October 15 to September 30 annually, will be designated, for brevity, by the year in which they began. Thus 1753/54 will be written "1753"; 1753/54–1759/60 will be written "1753–59"; and 1753/54, 1756/57, and 1759/60 will be written "1753, 1756, and 1759."

[6] Charles H. Lincoln, *The Revolutionary Movement in Pennsylvania, 1760–1776* (Philadelphia, 1901), 47.

[7] See Chester R. Young, "The Evolution of the Pennsylvania Assembly, 1682–1748," *Pennsylvania History* (hereafter *PH*), 35 (1968), 147–168; Alan Tully, *William Penn's Legacy: Politics and Social Structure in Provincial Pennsylvania, 1726–1755* (Baltimore, 1977), 82; and Greene, *Quest for Power*, 4.

[8] Tully, *William Penn's Legacy*, esp. chaps. 5–6, offers the fullest and most perceptive portrait of the Quaker oligarchy before the Seven Years' War, both at the local and the provincial level. On the Quakers' declining voting strength, see Tolles, *Meeting House*, 231–232; Tully, 54–55; and James T. Lemon, *The Best Poor Man's Country: A Geographical Study of Early Southeastern Pennsylvania* (Baltimore, 1972), 18–20. On Pennsylvanians as a passive, deferential electorate, see Tully, *William Penn's Legacy* 79–86, 91–94; Charles Sydnor, *Gentlemen Freeholders: Political Practices in Washington's Virginia* (Chapel Hill, N.C., 1952); and Richard Buel, Jr., "Democracy and the American Revolution: A Frame of Reference," *WMQ*, 3rd. Ser., 21 (1964), 165–190.

[9] Gary B. Nash, *Quakers and Politics, Pennsylvania, 1681–1726* (Princeton, N.J., 1968), esp. chap. 7.

[10] Tully, *William Penn's Legacy*, 83–84, 91.

[11] Tully, *William Penn's Legacy*, 85–86. This was particularly true of Lancaster County, which elected two or more Quakers to its four-man delegation every year from 1739 through 1767, except for 1763 (see Tully, 173).

[12] Tully, *William Penn's Legacy*, 82–86.

[13] The major contested elections after 1726 were those of 1740, 1742, 1754, 1764, 1765, 1770, and 1772, but, of these, only 1764 and 1772 resulted in a turnover of more than 25 percent. There were much higher turnovers through Quaker withdrawal in 1749 and 1756. See Tully, *William Penn's Legacy*, 89.

[14] Alan Tully, *William Penn's Legacy*, 83, 85–86, 91–92.

[15] The assembly first resolved to open its doors to the electorate, from time to time upon a motion and vote, in 1770; and first actually opened them in July 1774 (although it did not then debate any issues; note the quotation at the head of this essay). Later motions to open the House doors failed in March and October 1775. See J. R. Pole, *Political Representation in England and the Origins of the American Republic* (Berkeley, Ca., 1966), 278; Ryerson, *The Revolution Is Now Begun*, 60–61; and *Votes and Proceedings of the House of Representatives of the Province of Pennsylvania, 1682–1776*, ed. Gertrude MacKinney, in *Pennsylvania Archives*, 8th Series (Harrisburg, Pa., 1931–1935, hereafter *Votes and Proceedings*); 7:6589, and 8:7091, 7097, 7202–7203, and 7333.

[16] Note the quotation at the head of this essay; and see Tully, *William Penn's Legacy*, 95.

[17] On the assembly's powers and procedures, see Sister Joan de Lourdes Leonard, "The Organization and Procedure of the Pennsylvania Assembly, 1682–1776," in *Pennsylvania Magazine of History and Biography* (hereafter *PMHB*), 72 (1948), 215–239, 376–412. Jack Greene relates the Pennsylvania assembly's development to that of other colonial legislatures in *Quest for Power*, 4–7.

[18] The primary source for the following analysis of the assembly's committees is *Votes and Proceedings*. To construct the fullest picture of a legislative oligarchy, one ideally uses some form of roll-call analysis; unfortunately, the *Votes and Proceedings* contains only fifty-one roll calls for the entire period 1703–1776, and forty-nine of these fall in seven sessions: 1753, 1764–1765, and 1772–1775. These roll calls will be discussed briefly below.

[19] Greene, "Legislative Turnover," *WMQ*, 38 (1981), 446–447, compares the turnover rates, by decade, of all twenty-two British American colonies, and finds that the mean for Pennsylvania ranked fourth lowest among continental colonies in 1726–1735, second lowest in 1736–1745, and lowest after 1746; thereafter, only Barbados had a lower turnover. Bruce C. Daniels, in "Democracy and Oligarchy in Connecticut Towns: General Assembly Officeholding, 1701–1790," *Social Science Quarterly*, 56 (1975), 463, puts the problem of determining the existence of an oligarchy succinctly: "To one historian , . . . turnover rates of 50 percent may be indicative of a closed restrictive system, while another may feel this reveals an open system of opportunity for most." The level of turnover in Pennsylvania suggests that if oligarchy existed anywhere in British North America, it existed there.

[20] Tully, *William Penn's Legacy*, 95, 170–173. The view that most Quakers withdrew permanently from the assembly in 1756 began with contemporary Quaker commentators, was repeated by nineteenth-century Quaker historians, and appears prominently in Tolles, *Meeting House*, 26–28, and 234–235. Although this view is now widely accepted, it has recently been challenged effectively by Hermann Wellenreuther, *Glaube und Politik in Pennsylvania, 1681–1776: Die Wandlungen der Obrigkeitsdoktrin und des Peace Testimony der Quaker* (Cologne, 1972), 432–437; Wayne L. Bockelman and Owen S. Ireland, "The Internal Revolution in Pennsylvania: An Ethnic-Religious Interpretation," *PH*, 41 (1974), 125–159; and the present author in *The Revolution Is Now Begun*, chap. 1.

[21] See Tully, *William Penn's Legacy*, 95.

[22] In computing carry-over, veterancy, and seniority, a historian of the assembly encounters a methodological problem: how does one determine these measures for the years—here 1729, 1749, 1750, 1752, 1771, 1772, 1773, and 1775—in which new seats were added to the chamber? In this essay, I have chosen to follow a "minimum best case" rule, in effect arguing that my contentions rest upon quantitative measures that are at least as high—or as low—as those expressed in the essay's numbers. In the present instance, each measure has been computed upon the basis of all seats in the House. Other measuring strategies would alter these figures, but always by small margins.

[23] Thomas L. Purvis, "The New Jersey Assembly, 1722–1776," (Ph.D. diss., Johns Hopkins University, 1979), appendix I, pp. 255–312; and Purvis, "'High-Born, Long-Recorded Families': Social Origins of New Jersey Assemblymen, 1703–1776," *WMQ*, 3rd Ser., 37 (1980), 592–615, see esp. 601.

[24] This scholarship appears in Richard Bauman, *For the Reputation of Truth: Politics, Religion, and Conflict among the Pennsylvania Quakers 1750–1800* (Baltimore,

1971), 19, 27, 106, 111–112, 146; Wellenreuther, *Glaube und Politik*, 432–437; Bockelman and Ireland, "Internal Revolution," 127–142, 153–154, 157–159; Tully, *William Penn's Legacy*, 170–173; and Ryerson, *The Revolution Is Now Begun*, 9–10, 13, 14, 260–262. While there are disagreements among these scholars over the religious affiliation of certain legislators, particularly toward the end of the colonial era, the agreement among these lists and calculations is high.

[25] Quaker assemblymen were "numerically able" to dominate the House between 1761 and 1772 because they were never more than three members short of controlling one-half of the seats and because they came preponderantly from counties near Philadelphia, and thus could more easily attend sessions than their non-Quaker colleagues from the western and northern counties.

[26] For the initial appointments of standing committees, see *Votes and Proceedings*, 2:1218 (1716, audit), and 3:1992 (1729, minutes), 2120 (1730, correspondence), 2302 (1735, minutes), 2515 (1739, correspondence), and 2665 (1740, grievances). The establishment of these committees is discussed in Leonard, "Organization of the Assembly," *PMHB*, 72 (1948), 236–238. For comparisons with the systems of other colonial legislatures, see Greene, "Foundations of Political Power," *WMQ*, 3rd Ser., 16 (1959), 485–506; Greene, *Quest for Power*, 463–464; Zemsky, *Merchants, Farmers, and River Gods*, 13–16, 291–292; and George Edward Frakes, *Laboratory for Liberty: The South Carolina Legislative Committee System, 1719–1776* (Lexington, Ky., 1970), esp. chap. 2.

[27] In this essay, I have considered every group of assemblymen appointed by the Speaker to a specific task, exclusive of the four standing committees already described, as an ad hoc committee, with two exceptions: groups of trustees, appointed for terms of years or for unlimited terms; and the delegations sent to the governor each October to announce the chamber's choice of a Speaker and its readiness to do business.

[28] Joseph Fox, the most active of the six men named here who served under Galloway, left the House after the 1771 session. Had he served in the 1772 and 1773 sessions, the contrast between the three activists and three backbenchers would likely have been greater.

[29] See especially Tolles, *Meeting House*; and Tully, *William Penn's Legacy*, although Tully is careful to note (p. 96) that seniority was not, in several cases, a factor in determining legislative leadership.

[30] Greene, "Legislative Turnover," *WMQ*, 3rd Ser., 38 (1981), 449–451.

[31] Zemsky, *Merchants, Farmers, and River Gods*, 30–31, 294–295.

[32] The statistical correlation used here is Pearson's r. The seniority and ad hoc committee service have been correlated for every member except for the Speaker who, by tradition, assigned himself to few ad hoc committees. A Pearson's r correlation is said to be significant when the probability of a correlation of that degree is highly unlikely to occur in any random distribution. For the number of assemblymen involved here, ranging from 29 in the 1730s to 39 in 1774, Pearson's r levels of ca. .220 to .245 will occur randomly in less than 20% of all correlations, so their significance is 80%; the higher Pearson's r here (.245) corresponds to the lower number of assemblymen (29). At 90%, the levels are ca. .260 to .311; at 95%, ca. .310 to .367; and at 99%, ca. .400 to .471. The negative correlations of the years 1750–1755 are due in part to the fact that Isaac Norris awarded several ad hoc seats to new members from the newly created western counties. As these members acquired seniority in the 1760s, however, the correlation between seniority and committee activity did not climb to statistically significant levels. The %s of variation explained are derived by squaring the Pearson's rs.

[33] See Tully, *William Penn's Legacy*, 174–176. The tax data needed to determine relative wealth are broken or scattered for all counties except Chester, where Tully

found that thirty-two of the forty assemblymen sitting between 1729 and 1755 were in the top 10 percent of assessed taxpayers, making a significant correlation between legislative wealth and committee activity impossible.

[34] Joseph Galloway seems to have fallen away from the Society of Friends in his youth, along with his parents. In 1753 he was married to Grace Growden, daughter of the Bucks County political magnate—and disowned Quaker—Lawrence Growden, by the Anglican cleric and provincial secretary Richard Peters, who would later be a political enemy. Galloway never renounced this infraction of the Quaker marriage discipline, despite the probable ill effect that his wife feared a marriage before "a priest" would have upon his public career. In February 1760, Galloway and his wife were listed on the last, additional page of the Philadelphia Monthly Meeting's membership roll of 1759–1760, but they were not listed on two subsequent rolls made in the 1770s (on film, Friends Historical Library, Swarthmore College). It would appear that Galloway behaved as a Friend, and worshipped with Friends, but was considered to be a marginal member, at best. See Bruce R. Lively, "Toward 1756: The Political Genesis of Joseph Galloway," *PH*, 45 (1978): 117–138, esp. pp. 124–126.

[35] See Tully, *William Penn's Legacy*, 23–24, 28–30, 32–34, 39.

[36] Bauman, *For the Reputation of Truth*, especially chaps. 4–7, and appendix 2.

[37] For the data on the Quaker meeting activity of the assemblymen, I am indebted to Jean Ruth Soderlund, whose forthcoming book, *Quakers and Slavery: A Divided Spirit* (Princeton, N.J.), surveys the several hundred New Jersey and Pennsylvania representatives to the Philadelphia Yearly Meeting over nearly a century and discusses the political, economic, and social activities of these Friends.

[38] The roll calls appear in *Votes and Proceedings*, 3:2483 (1738/39); 5:3690, 3692–94, 3701–2, 3726–28 (1753/54); 6:5234 (1760/61); 7:5682–84, 5687, 5690–91 (1764/65); 7:5791 (1765/66); 8:6913, 6918, 6946, 6950, 6955, 6962, 6985–86, 7019 (1772/73); 8:7047–48, 7052–53, 7056 (1773/74); and 8:7165, 7174, 7203, 7212 (1774/75).

[39] A full portrait of the assembly will be essential for a better understanding of eighteenth-century Pennsylvania politics. Three kinds of studies needed for such an understanding now exist: the narrative histories and biographies of proprietors, imperial officials, governors, councillors, Assembly Speakers and key lawmakers written over the last century; Alan Tully's detailed analysis of the structure of politics at both the local and provincial levels in *William Penn's Legacy* (although this only covers the period up to the Quaker withdrawal of 1756); and the analysis of quantifiable measures of legislative leadership presented in this essay. Two other necessary studies are lacking: a comprehensive survey of the rhetoric and dialogue of political culture, as expressed both in the public press and in private letters; and a close analysis of the several hundred petitions, bills, and laws that will show more fully just what the Pennsylvania assembly did and did not do in the fifty years before the Revolution.

[40] See Tully, *William Penn's Legacy*, 3–24, on Hamilton and Pennsylvania politics in the 1730s, and 17–19, for a characterization of the man. Tully briefly discusses the geographic pattern of committee seat distribution under Hamilton, Kinsey, and Norris on p. 96.

[41] See Tully, 23–41, on politics in the 1740s, and 97–98, for a vivid portrait of Kinsey.

[42] On Norris's relationship to Kinsey, see Tully, p. 98.

[43] See particularly James H. Hutson, *Pennsylvania Politics 1746–1770: The Movement for Royal Government and Its Consequences* (Princeton, N.J., 1972), chaps. 3 and 4. Other treatments of Galloway, his mentor Franklin, and their political careers in the 1750s and 1760s are Theodore Thayer, *Pennsylvania Politics and the Growth*

of Democracy, 1740–1776 (Harrisburg, Pa., 1953); William S. Hanna, *Benjamin Franklin and Pennsylvania Politics* (Stanford, Ca., 1964); Brooke Hindle, "The March of the Paxton Boys," *WMQ*, 3rd Ser., 3 (1946), 461–486; and Benjamin H. Newcomb, *Franklin and Galloway, A Political Partnership* (New Haven, Conn., 1972).

[44] See note 14 above.

[45] See Tully, "The Quaker Party in Pre-Revolutionary Politics," above, on the alienation from their government of Pennsylvanians living in frontier areas near Virginia and Connecticut settlements.

[46] It is worth pointing out here that both Alan Tully, in "The Quaker Party in Pre-Revolutionary Politics," in the present collection, and the present author, using quite different methodologies, have independently arrived at the conclusion that because the Quaker Party had reached the end point in its geographic extension in the 1750s, it would have faced an unavoidable loss of power within an expanding assembly and province in the 1770s, even without an intervening Revolutionary crisis.

[47] See note 15 above.

[48] For the fourteen roll calls taken between January 1773 and January 1774, see the citations in note 38, and compare the cleavages in these votes with the very different cleavages in twenty-one roll calls taken in 1754, cited in the same note.

[49] For a detailed narrative of the confrontation between the Quaker Party and the Revolutionary movement in the summer of 1774, see Ryerson, *The Revolution Is Now Begun*, chap. 3.

[50] For a detailed narrative of the final months of the Quaker party, see Ryerson, *The Revolution Is Now Begun*, chaps. 3, 5 to 7, and 9. For a full statement of my view of the ensuing decade of political strife, see Ryerson, "Republican Theory and Partisan Reality: Toward a New View of Pennsylvania's Constitutionalist Party," in Peter J. Albert and Ronald Hoffman, eds., *Sovereign States in an Age of Uncertainty* (Charlottesville, 1982), 95–133.

"Hungry as Hawks": The Social Bases of Political Leadership in Colonial North Carolina, 1729–1776

[1] For these trends see, for example, Richard D. Brown, *Revolutionary Politics in Massachusetts: The Boston Committee of Correspondence and the Towns, 1772–1774* (New York, 1976), 1–16; Jack P. Greene, "The Growth of Political Stability: An Interpretation of Political Development in the Anglo-American Colonies, 1660–1760," in John Parker and Carol Urness, eds., *The American Revolution: A Heritage of Change* (Minneapolis, Minn., 1975), 26–52, and "Society, Ideology, and Politics: An Analysis of the Political Culture of Mid-Eighteenth-Century Virginia," in Richard M. Jellison, ed., *Society, Freedom, and Conscience: The American Revolution in Virginia, Massachusetts, and New York* (New York, 1976), 14–76; David W. Jordan, "Political Stability and the Emergence of a Native Elite in Maryland," in Thad W. Tate and David L. Ammerman, eds., *The Chesapeake in the Seventeenth Century: Essays on Anglo-American Society* (Chapel Hill, N.C., 1979), 243–273; John M. Murrin, "Political Development," in Jack P. Greene and J. R. Pole, eds., *Colonial British America: Essays in the New History of the Early Modern Era* (Baltimore, 1984), 435–441; Gary B. Nash, *Quakers and Politics: Pennsylvania, 1681–1726* (Princeton, N.J., 1968); Alan Tully, *William Penn's Legacy: Politics and Social Structure in Provincial Pennsylvania, 1726–1755* (Baltimore, 1977); Robert M. Weir, "'The Harmony We Were Famous For': An Interpretation of Pre-Revolutionary South Carolina Politics," *William and Mary Quarterly* (hereafter *WMQ*), 3rd Ser., 26 (1969), 473–501; and Robert Zemsky, *Merchants, Farmers, and River Gods: An Essay on Eighteenth-Century American Politics* (Boston, 1971).

[2] See Florence Cook, "Procedure in the North Carolina Colonial Assembly, 1731–1770," *North Carolina Historical Review*, 8 (1931), 276–282. The seventy-three were compiled from a more extensive list of North Carolina assembly leaders in Jack P. Greene's *The Quest for Power: The Lower Houses of Assembly in the Southern Royal Colonies, 1689–1776* (Chapel Hill, N.C., 1963), 489–492. See pp. 463–464 in *ibid.* for the manner in which they were selected on the basis of committee assignments.

[3] Jack P. Greene, "Foundations of Political Power in the Virginia House of Burgesses, 1720–1776," *WMQ*, 3rd Ser., 16 (1959), 485–506.

[4] Information about North Carolina's assembly leaders came from a wide variety of sources. For a detailed discussion of these, see Ekirch, *"Poor Carolina": Politics and Society in Colonial North Carolina, 1729–1776* (Chapel Hill, N.C., 1981), 286–288.

[5] Gabriel Johnston to Thomas Hill, April 6, 1750, Colonial Office 5/296, 308, Public Record Office, London (microfilm, Library of Congress, Washington, D.C.).

[6] William Tryon, "A View of the Polity of the Province of North Carolina, in the Year 1767," in William L. Saunders et al., eds., *The Colonial and State Records of North Carolina*, 30 vols. (Raleigh, Winston, Goldsboro, and Charlotte, N.C., 1886–1914), VII, 489.

[7] Burrington to Board of Trade, Jan. 1, 1773, Saunders et. al., eds., *N.C. Colonial and State Records*, III, 432; Ekirch, *"Poor Carolina,"* 24–25.

[8] Ekirch, *"Poor Carolina,"* 11, 22–23, 226.

[9] Greene, "Foundations of Power," *WMQ*, 3rd Ser., 16 (1959), 487.

[10] Louis B. Wright, ed., *The Prose Works of William Byrd of Westover: Narratives of a Colonial Virginian* (Cambridge, Mass., 1966), 54.

[11] See Harry Roy Merrens, *Colonial North Carolina in the Eighteenth Century* (Chapel Hill, N.C., 1964), 53–74.

[12] The Virginia calculation is based on Greene's list of leaders in "Foundations of Power," *WMQ*, 3rd Ser., 16 (1959), 493–502.

[13] Thomas C. Parramore, "The Saga of 'The Bear,' and the 'Evil Genius,'" *Bulletin of the History of Medicine*, 42 (1968), 321–331; [Henry McCulloh] to Board of Trade, [1749], Saunders et al., eds., *N.C. Colonial and State Records*, IV, 1216.

[14] Murray to Anne and Jean Bennet, Aug. 4, 1760, Letter Book, 1760–1761, James Murray Collection, Massachusetts Historical Society, Boston; Martin to Lord Hillsborough, March 1, 1772, Saunders et al., eds., *N.C. Colonial and State Records*, IX, 254. For a discussion of politics in eighteenth-century North Carolina, see Ekirch, *"Poor Carolina."* I do not mean to suggest that North Carolina was entirely alone in its factious brand of eighteenth-century politics. New York, also, was renowned for a contentious political system, as Patricia Bonomi has described in her study *A Factious People: Politics and Society in Colonial New York* (New York, 1971). On the other hand, it is significant that disputes in New York did not normally produce the same sort of civil breakdown, violence, uncompromising intransigence, and unbridled opportunism characteristic of North Carolina's public world. New York's political processes remained more noteworthy for restraint than for recklessness.

[15] Byrd to Johann Rudolph Ochs, July 15, 1736, in Marion Tinling, ed., *The Correspondence of the Three William Byrds of Westover, Virginia, 1684–1776* (Charlottesville, Va., 1977), II, 491.

Merchants, Planters, and Lawyers: Political Culture and Leadership in South Carolina, 1721–1775

[1] Sir Lewis Namier, *The Structure of Politics at the Accession of George III*, 2 vols. (London, 1929); *England in the Age of the American Revolution* (London, 1930); Sir Lewis Namier and John Brooke, *The House of Commons, 1754–1790: Introductory*

Survey (London and New York, 1964); Romney Sedgewick, *The Commons, 1715–1754.* 2 vols. (London, 1970).

²Jack P. Greene, "'The Plunge of Lemmings': A Consideration of Recent Writings on British Politics and the American Revolution," *South Atlantic Quarterly,* 67 (1968), 141–177. Not all historians agree that there was consensus on matters of political principle in mid-eighteenth century England. See Herbert Butterfield, "Some Reflections on the Early Years of George III's Reign", *Journal of British Studies,* IV (1965), 78–101, J. C. D. Clark, "The Decline of Party, 1740–1760," *The English Historical Review,* 93 (1978), 499–527.

³M. Eugene Sirmans, *Colonial South Carolina: A Political History, 1663–1763* (Chapel Hill, N.C., 1966); Jack P. Greene, *The Quest for Power: The Lower Houses of Assembly in the Southern Royal Colonies, 1689–1776* (Chapel Hill, N.C., 1963); Robert M. Weir, "'The Harmony We Were Famous For': An Interpretation of Pre-Revolutionary South Carolina Politics," *The William and Mary Quarterly,* 3rd Ser., XXVI (1969), 473–501 (hereafter *WMQ*).

⁴Walter B. Edgar and N. Louise Bailey, eds. *Biographical Directory of the South Carolina House of Representatives: The Commons House of Assembly, 1692–1775;* 2 vols. (Columbia, S.C., 1977).

⁵Many of Carolina's early settlers were from Barbados. See Richard Waterhouse, "England, the Caribbean, and the Settlement of Carolina," *Journal of American Studies,* 9 (1975), 259–281.

⁶David J. McCord and Thomas Cooper, eds., *The Statutes at Large of South Carolina,* 10 vols. (Columbia, S.C., 1836–1841), Vol. II, 683–691; *ibid.,* vol. III, 50–55, 135–40.

⁷*Ibid.,* III, 135–40.

⁸Sirmans, *Colonial South Carolina,* 239.

⁹David J. McCord and Thomas Cooper, eds., *The Statutes at Large of South Carolina,* Vol. III, 656–658, Vol. IV, 98–101.

¹⁰J. H. Easterby and Ruth S. Green, eds., *The Journal of the Commons House of Assembly,* November 10, 1736–June 7, 1739 (Columbia, S.C., 1951–1952), 168; McCord and Cooper, *Statutes,* III, 656–658; IV, 98–101; South Carolina Archives (hereafter, *S.C.A.*), Transcripts of Records in the British Public Record Office Relating to South Carolina (hereafter *B.P.R.O.*), Vol. XXII, 312; Vol. XXIII, 148–149.

¹¹McCord and Cooper, *Statutes,* Vol. III, 656–658, 692–693; Greene, *The Quest for Power,* 200.

¹²McCord and Cooper, Vol. IV, 266–268.

¹³*Ibid.,* Vol. IV, 298–302.

¹⁴*Ibid.,* Vol. II, 232–235; Vol. III, 50–55, 135–140.

¹⁵On the colony's system of local government, see Richard Waterhouse, "The Responsible Gentry of Colonial South Carolina: A Study in Local Government, 1670–1770," in Bruce C. Daniels, ed., *Town and County: Essays on the Structure of Local Government in the American Colonies* (Middletown, Conn., 1978), 160–185.

¹⁶Richard Waterhouse, "The Development of Elite Culture in the Colonial American South: A Study of Charles Town, 1670–1770," *The Australian Journal of Politics and History,* Vol. 28, Number 3 (1982), 391–404.

¹⁷J. G. A. Pocock, "Machiavelli, Harrington and English Political Ideologies in the Eighteenth Century," *WMQ,* 3rd Ser., XXII (1965), 549–583; Robert Weir, "'The Harmony We Were Famous For': An Interpretation of Pre-Revolutionary South Carolina Politics," *WMQ,* 3rd Ser., XXVI (1969), 473; Jack P. Greene, "Society, Ideology and Politics: An Analysis of the Political Culture of Mid-Eighteenth Century Virginia," in Richard M. Jellison, ed., *Society, Freedom and Conscience: The American*

Revolution in Virginia, Massachusetts and New York (New York, 1976), 26–52.

[18] Weir, "'The Harmony We Were Famous For,'" 474; *The South Carolina Gazette* (hereafter, *S.C.G.*), March 14, 1763.

[19] *S.C.G.*, April 21, 28; May 12, 19; June 2, 16, 23, 30; July 7, 14, 1733; December 10, 1764; Sirmans, *Colonial South Carolina*, 181–182.

[20] *S.C.G.*, December 12, 1774.

[21] Weir, 476; *S.C.G.*, October 5, 1765; October 4, 1768; April 4, 1774.

[22] McCord and Cooper, Vol. III, 2–4, 656–658; *S.C.A.*, *B.P.R.O.*, Vol. XXII, 312, Vol. XXIII, 148–149.

[23] George C. Rogers, ed., *The Papers of Henry Laurens*, Vol. IV (Columbia, S.C., 1974), 672; *The South Carolina Gazette and Country Journal*, October 4, 1768.

[24] *S.C.A.*, *B.P.R.O.*, Vol. II, 33–34.

[25] *Ibid.*, Vol. XXIII, 244–245, Vol. XXV, 14; Sirmans, *Colonial South Carolina*, 246.

[26] *S.C.A.*, *Commons House Journals*, Number I, Part I, 44; Number 33, Parts I and II, 9; J. H. Easterby and Ruth S. Green, eds., *The Journal of the Commons House of Assembly*, September 14, 1742–January 27, 1744 (Columbia, S.C., 1951–1952), 30.

[27] *S.C.G.*, January 6, 1748. In Virginia the voter turnout was much higher. See Lucille Griffith, *Virginia House of Burgesses, 1750–1774* (Northport, Alabama, 1963), 58–71.

[28] *S.C.A.*, *B.P.R.O.*, Vol. X, 87–91, 111–112, 195–196, Richard M. Jellison, "Paper Currency in Colonial South Carolina: A Reappraisal," *The South Carolina Historical Magazine* (hereafter *S.C.H.M.*), LXII (1961), 139–143; Richard M. Jellison, "Antecedents of the South Carolina Currency Acts of 1736 and 1746," *WMQ*, 3rd Ser. XVI (1959), 557; Sirmans, *Colonial South Carolina*, 148–157.

[29] *S.C.G.*, January 29, 1732; April 6, 1734; April 2, 1737; October 17, November 14, 1754; June 13, 1761; June 8, 1765; February 1, 1768.

[30] James Edward Smith, ed., *A Selection of the Correspondence of Linnaeus*, 2 vols. (London, 1821), Vol. I, 483.

[31] Sirmans, *Colonial South Carolina*, 245.

[32] Waterhouse, "The Responsible Gentry," 173.

[33] *S.C.A.*, *C.H.J.*, Number 5, pp. 2, 4, 5, 6, 9; *C.H.J.*, Number 37, Part I, 121–122; *S.C.A.*, *Public Records of South Carolina*, Old Vol. I, Part I, 30–31; Public Record Office (Great Britain), Co5/430/3; Easterby and Green, eds., *Journals*, November 9, 1736–August 3, 1739, 168; Easterby and Green, eds., *Journals*, September 14, 1742–January 27, 1744, 23.

[34] Sirmans, *Colonial South Carolina*, 241–242.

[35] *S.C.A.*, *B.P.R.O.*, Vol. XXXII, 404–405.

[36] *Ibid.*, Vol. XXXII, 37; *S.C.A.*, *C.H.J.*, Number 37, Part 2, 8–9; *S.C.G.*, October 10, 1768. This back-country dissatisfaction eventually culminated in the Regulator Movement. Not until 1775, however, with the calling of the Provincial Congress, did this area secure effective representation. See W. A. Hemphill and W. A. Wates, eds., *Extracts from the Journals of the Provincial Congresses of South Carolina, 1775–1776* (Columbia, S.C., 1960), 3–8.

[37] *The South Carolina Gazette and Country Journal*, October 4, 1768.

[38] Rogers, ed., *The Papers of Henry Laurens*, Vol. 6, 119; *S.C.A.*, *C.H.J.*, Number 38, Part I, 15, 69–70, Number 39, 16–17.

[39] British Museum, Add. MSS 33028 (Newcastle Papers), f.187; *S.C.A.*, *B.P.R.O.*, Vol. XXIII, 355; Carl Ubbeholde, *The Vice-Admiralty Courts and the American Revolution* (Chapel Hill, N.C., 1960), 6–7, 100.

[40] McCord and Cooper, Vol. III, 414–423; Greene, *The Quest for Power*, 156–157.

[41] Jack P. Greene, "The South Carolina Quartering Controversy, 1757–58", *S.C.H.M.*, L (1959), 193–204; Greene, *Quest for Power*, Chap. 8.

[42] The information on members of the assembly used in this section has been gleaned from a variety of sources including the Will Books, Inventories, Ship Registers, and Judgment Rolls in the S.C.A. The colonial newspapers were also useful. I am heavily indebted to Walter B. Edgar and N. Louise Bailey, eds., *Biographical Directory of the South Carolina House of Representatives*, Vol. II, *The Commons House of Assembly*, 1692–1775 (hereafter Edgar and Bailey, eds., *South Carolina Biographical Dictionary*).

[43] Philip M. Hamer and George C. Rogers, eds., *The Papers of Henry Laurens*, Vol. I (Columbia, S.C., 1968), 69–70, 259; S.C.A., B.P.R.O., Vol. XXXII, 378.

[44] Joseph Ioor Waring, *A History of Medicine in South Carolina, 1670–1825* (Columbia, S.C., 1964), appendix I.

[45] Edgar and Bailey, eds., *South Carolina Biographical Directory*, Vol. II, *The Commons House of Assembly*, 1692–1775, *passim*. In compiling this information, I have also used the genealogical data scattered through the volumes of the *S.C.H.M.*, and a multitude of family histories deposited in the South Caroliniana Library, Columbia.

[46] For lists of Carolinians educated at Oxford, Cambridge, the Inns of Court, and the Edinburgh Faculty of Medicine, see J. G. De Roulhac, "Southern Members of the Inns of Court," *The North Carolina Historical Review*, 10 (1933), 273–286; Willard Connely, "Colonial Americans in Oxford and Cambridge," *The American Oxonian*, 29 (1942), 75–76; Waring, *Medicine in South Carolina*, appendix I.

[47] *S.C.G.*, September 28, 1965; *The South Carolina Gazette and Country Journal*, October 4, 1708; June 27, 1769.

[48] *S.C.G.*, April, 1774.

[49] One other early-settled and wealthy parish in which one might have expected the wealthy and long-settled planter families to be predominant was St. Paul's. However, this was not so, perhaps because many of the old and wealthy families belonged to the nonconformist sects. Their representatives may have been unwilling to take the qualifying oath.

[50] *S.C.A.*, B.P.R.O., Vol. IX, 22–23; Waterhouse, "The Responsible Gentry," 166–168.

[51] *S.C.A.*, B.P.R.O., Vol. XXV, 13.

[52] See Greene, *Quest for Power*, 475–478. Greene has identified the leaders of the first and second rank in the Southern Royal Assemblies through his analysis of the membership of the important committees of these assemblies. For an analysis of Virginia's political leaders, see Jack P. Greene, "Foundations of Political Power in the Virginia House of Burgesses, 1720–1776", *WMQ*, 3rd Ser., XVI (1959), 485–506.

[53] Sixty-five percent of first-rank leaders were Charlestown residents.

[54] Sirmans, *Colonial South Carolina*, 247–248.

[55] *S.C.G.*, February 1, 1735; June 12, 1755; S.C.A., B.P.R.O., Vol. XXXII, 404–405.

[56] South Caroliniana Library (Columbia, S.C.), Manigault Papers, Folder 4.

[57] *S.C.A.*, *Upper House Journals*, Number 12, 62–65; Walter B. Edgar, ed., *The Letterbook of Robert Pringle*, 2 vols. (Columbia, S.C., 1972), Vol. II, 699–700; S.C.A., C.H.J., February 22; March 2, 1770.

[58] *S.C.G.*, November 7, 1741.

[59] Greene, *Quest for Power*, 475–488; Charleston Library Society, MS Journal of the Proceedings of the Charleston Library Society, 1759–1790; Waterhouse, "The Development of Elite Culture," 395.

[60] Greene, "The South Carolina Quartering Controversy," 193–204; Greene, "Bridge to Revolution: The Wilkes Fund Controversy in South Carolina, 1769–1775," *The Journal of Southern History*, XXIX (1963), 19–52.

[61] Diane Sydenham, "'Going Home': South Carolinians in England, 1745–1775," unpublished seminar paper, The Johns Hopkins University Library, 26–30; Robert M. Weir, "Who Shall Rule at Home: The American Revolution as a Crisis of Legitimacy for the Colonial Elite," *Journal of Interdisciplinary History*, VI (1976), 679–700.

[62] Robert M. Weir, "Harmony," 485; Rogers, ed., *The Papers of Henry Laurens*, Vol. 7, 225–226.

[63] William W. Freehling, *Prelude to Civil War: The Nullification Controversy in South Carolina, 1816–1836* (New York, 1968), 13.

At the Pinnacle of Elective Success: The Speaker of the House in Colonial America

[1] I have chosen the period of the Glorious Revolution as the starting point because, as Michael Kammen makes clear, "Beginning with the 1690's, the representative assembly can be said to have become a fixed feature of the English colonial administration." See Kammen, *Deputyes and Libertyes: The Origins of Representative Government in Colonial America* (New York, 1969), 57. Or, as Jack P. Greene states, "After the Restoration and especially during the years following the Glorious Revolution, the lower houses engaged in a successful quest for power . . . that made them paramount in the affairs of their respective colonies." See Greene, *The Quest for Power: The Lower Houses of Assembly in the Southern Royal Colonies, 1689–1776* (Chapel Hill, N.C., 1963), 33. The period of the Glorious Revolution can also be seen as an appropriate starting point in that Massachusetts received her royal charter then, Connecticut's legislature became bicameral in 1698, Rhode Island's in 1696, and New Hampshire's in 1692. William Penn granted the Charter of Privileges in 1701, and shortly thereafter the Lower Counties (Delaware) formed their own assembly. Bicameralism came to New York in 1691; the Jerseys, sharing New York's governor, came together in a single assembly in 1703. South Carolina's Commons House of Assembly first met in 1692. The older southern colonies experienced less significant changes in the period, though Maryland temporarily became a royal colony.

[2] In the corporate colonies and Massachusetts, the speakership was frequently a steppingstone to the court of assistants, the governorship, or both.

[3] Norman Cantor, *The English: A History of Politics and Society to 1760* (New York, 1967), 478.

[4] Robert Zemsky's remark concerning the leaders of the Massachusetts assembly in *Merchants, Farmers, and River Gods: An Essay on Eighteenth-Century American Politics* (Boston, 1971) applies with equal force to the other colonies: "The dozen or so men who controlled the Assembly's committees," Zemsky writes, "played much the same roles that cabinet ministers and coalition managers played in the eighteenth-century House of Commons or that the committee chairman and party leaders play in modern legislatures." In his article "Power, Influence, and Status: Leadership Patterns in the Massachusetts Assembly, 1740–1755," *William and Mary Quarterly* (hereafter *WMQ*), 3rd Ser., 26 (1969), 504, Zemsky points out that every Speaker "qualified in terms of committee assignments as a major house leader" before obtaining the office. Among the many studies that make essentially the same point with reference to the other colonies are Jack P. Greene, "Foundations of Political Power in the Virginia House of Burgesses, 1720–1776," *WMQ*, 3rd Ser., 16 (1959), 485–492; Sister Joan

de Lourdes Leonard, "The Organization and Procedure of the Pennsylvania Assembly, 1682–1776," *Pennsylvania Magazine of History and Biography*, 72 (1948), 215–239, 376–412 (hereinafter cited as *PMHB*), and George Edward Frakes, *Laboratory for Liberty, the South Carolina Legislative Committee System, 1719–1776* (Lexington, Kty., 1970), 4.

[5] One must go beyond the legislative journals to discover the ways in which a Speaker wielded influence. Jack P. Greene, ed., *The Diary of Colonel Landon Carter*, 2 vols. (Charlottesville, Va., 1965), gives rare insight into the machinations of Speaker John Robinson of Virginia's House of Burgesses. The Thomas Penn Papers, Historical Society of Pennsylvania, in letters from such proprietary agents as James Logan to his principal in England, are highly revelatory. Papers of the governors are another source, as are papers of prominent colonials. In addition, there are scattered references to the Speakers in Great Britain, Public Record Office, *Calendar of State Papers, Colonial Series, America and the West Indies* (London, 1860–).

[6] "Our Speaker," writes Lauros G. McConachie, referring to the national House of Representatives, "is premier and parliamentarian in one." See *Congressional Committees: A Study of the Origin and Development of Our National Life and Local Legislative Methods* (New York, 1898), 55.

[7] Onslow's "repeated election," according to Derek Jarrett [*Britain, 1688–1818* (New York, 1965), 183], "gave the office of Speaker a continuity which placed it above and beyond party politics." The ineffectual Sir John Cust served as Speaker of the House of Commons to 1770. He was followed by the highly partisan Sir Fletcher Norton. For Edward Mosely, see Joshua Sharpe Papers, Southern Historical Collection, University of North Carolina; for Philipse, see the Rutherford Papers, New York Historical Society; on Kinsey, the Thomas Penn Papers, Historical Society of Pennsylvania. Secondary works are likewise helpful. On Otis, for example, see John J. Waters, Jr., *The Otis Family in Provincial and Revolutionary Massachusetts* (Chapel Hill, N.C., 1968). See also Thomas Wendel, "The Speaker of the House, Pennsylvania, 1701–1776," *PMHB*, 98 (1973), 3–21.

[8] The author wishes to thank the following for their assistance in supplying data: Mr. Peter Perotti, Montclair, New Jersey; Dr. John Kukla, Virginia Historical Society, who kindly supplied information from his *Speakers and Clerks of the Virginia House of Burgesses* (Richmond, 1981); Ms. Dian Telian, Historical Society of Pennsylvania; Ms. Barbara Dege, New York Historical Society; Ms. Vicki Unimowicz, Newark, Delaware; Dr. Robert Sparks, Massachusetts Historical Society; Mr. Bruce Clouette, Connecticut State Library; Mr. Matthew Thomas, Colonial Poplin Research Center, Fremont, New Hampshire; Ms. Lisa Fink, Providence, Rhode Island; Professor William S. Powell, editor of the *Dictionary of North Carolina Biography*, who allowed me to see forthcoming Speaker biographies; Professor Edward C. Papenfuse, who allowed me to see materials gathered by his staff to be published in forthcoming volumes of *A Biographical Dictionary of the Maryland Legislature, 1635–1789*, of which he is chief editor. And special thanks to computer expert Alfred A. Aya, Jr.

[9] In one case, that of Elisha Cooke, Jr., of Massachusetts, Governor Shute refused to confirm an appointment. Although Cooke therefore cannot be said to have officially served as Speaker, he was elected, and the General Court attempted to do business under his speakership. I have thus considered him as having served during one year. The same is true for one year of New Hampshire's Richard Waldron, who was also denied confirmation.

[10] It was not unusual for an individual to have served as clerk previous to his attaining the Chair. Sir John Randolph, for example, served as Clerk of the House of Burgesses

sixteen years; Peter Beverly nine years; Benjamin Franklin in Pennsylvania, fifteen years.

[11] Edwin Bronner, "The Disgrace of John Kinsey, Quaker Politician, 1739–1750," *PMBH*, 65 (1951), 400–415.

[12] Sydney V. James, *Colonial Rhode Island* (New York, 1975), 121, 157, 171, 176.

[13] Walter B. Edgar and N. Louise Bailey, eds., *Biographical Directory of the South Carolina House of Representatives*, vol. 2: *The Commons House of Assembly, 1692–1775* (Columbia, S.C., 1977), 4.

[14] Alice Hanson Jones, *Wealth of a Nation to Be* (New York, 1980), 14; *South Carolina Biographical Dictionary*, 520–522, 554–556, 626.

[15] Greene, *Quest for Power*, 39–40.

[16] *Virginia Historical Register*, 1 (1848), 119–122.

[17] Purvis, "'High-Born, Long-Recorded Families': Social Origins of New Jersey Assemblymen, 1703–1776," *WMQ*, 3rd Ser., 37 (1980), 577–591; New Jersey Archives, 23, 175, 178, 472.

[18] Gary Nash, *Quakers & Politics: Pennsylvania, 1681–1726* (Princeton N.J., 1968), 55–56, 308.

[19] *Biographical and Genealogical History of the State of Delaware*, I (Chambersburg, Pa., 1899), 592; Harold Hancock, *Liberty and Independence: the Delaware State During the American Revolution* (Wilmington, Del., 1976), 29; George H. Gibson, ed., *The Collected Essays of Richard S. Rodney on Early Delaware* (Wilmington, Del., 1975), 187; *The National Cyclopedia of American Biography*, 16 (New York, 1918), 374; G. S. Rowe, "The Legal Career of Thomas McKean," *Delaware History*, 16 (1974), 41.

[20] Jones, *Wealth of a Nation*, 60.

[21] Edward M. Cook, Jr., *The Fathers of the Towns: Leadership and Community Structure in Eighteenth-Century New England* (Baltimore, 1976), 74.

[22] Typescript of Meshech Weare inventory, Rockingham County Courthouse, Sept. 20, 1786; Jones, *Wealth of a Nation*, 165.

[23] David Van Deventer, *The Emergence of Provincial New Hampshire, 1623–1741* (Baltimore, 1976), 22, 212, 281n.

[24] Among other useful studies are Bruce C. Daniels, "Family Dynasties in Connecticut's Largest Towns, 1700–1760," *Canadian Journal of History*, 8 (1973), 99–110; James, *Colonial Rhode Island*; and Zemsky, *Merchants, Farmers, and River Gods*.

[25] Jackson Turner Main, *The Social Structure of Revolutionary America* (Princeton, N.J., 1965), 282, 283.

[26] Daniels, "Family Dynasties," 105.

[27] Leonard Labaree's classic *Conservatism in Early American History* (Ithaca, N.Y., 1962; originally published 1948), 3, refers to the "veritable jungles of interwoven branches" that made up the "genealogical trees" of the ruling classes, particularly of New York and Virginia.

[28] Carl J. Vipperman, *The Rise of Rawlins Lowndes, 1721–1800* (Columbia, S.C., 1978), 53–54.

[29] Carl Van Doren, *Benjamin Franklin* (New York, 1938), 125.

[30] Edgar et al., eds., *Biographical Directory*, vol. 2: *The Commons House of Assembly*, 335.

[31] *Ibid.*, 37, 561.

[32] Eric E. Lampard, "American Historians and the Study of Urbanization," *American Historical Review*, 67 (1961–1962), 54.

[33] "Urbanization and the Development of Eighteenth-Century Southeastern Penn-

sylvania and Adjacent Delaware," *WMQ*, 3rd Ser., 24 (1967), 501.

³⁴ *Cal. St. Paps., Col. Ser.*, A. & W.I., 1731, 38 (1938), 256.

³⁵ Jackson Turner Main, *Political Parties Before the Constitution* (New York, 1973), 32.

³⁶ Greene, *Quest for Power*, though limited to the Southern colonies, details the many issues disputed by assemblies and governors. See also his "The Role of the Lower Houses of Assembly in Eighteenth-Century Politics," *Journal of Southern History*, 27 (1961), 451–474.

³⁷ Frank Eshleman, "The Public Career of John Wright," *Lancaster County Historical Society Publications*, 14 (1910), 251–282.

"Patronage Most Ardently Sought": The New York Council, 1665–1775

¹ *New-York Weekly Mercury*, April 5, 1756.

² For an appreciation of Alexander's range, see his correspondence with Cadwallader Colden in New-York Historical Society (hereafter cited NYHS), *Collections* L (1917)–LVI (1923), *passim*. Other obituaries, such as Joseph Reade's, use religious phrases. Reade was "an honest man and a good Christian" (*The New-York Gazette and Weekly Mercury*, March 4, 1771). This judgment on the *Brief Narrative* is from Michael Kammen's *Colonial New York: A History* (New York, 1975), 207.

³ William Smith, Jr., wrote that councillors were called "The Honourable." See William Smith, Jr., *The History of the Province of New York*, ed. by Michael Kammen, 2 vols. (Cambridge, Mass., 1972), I, 255 (hereafter cited as Smith, *History*).

⁴ Werner, *Civil List and Constitutional History of the Colony and State of New York* (Albany, 1889), 361–362; Carl Becker, *The History of Political Parties in the Province of New York, 1760–1776* (Madison, Wis., 1909, 1960), *passim*.

⁵ Douglas Greenberg, "The Middle Colonies in Recent Historiography," *The William and Mary Quarterly*, 3rd. Ser., XXXVI (1979), 426 (hereafter cited *WMQ*); Nicholas Varga, "New York Government and Politics During the Mid-Eighteenth Century," (Ph.D. diss., Fordham, 1960), 21, 248.

⁶ *Documents Relative to the Colonial History of the State of New York*, ed., by Edmund B. O'Callaghan and Berthold Fernow, 15 vols. (Albany, New York, 1856–1887), III, 188 (hereafter cited as DRHNY). Werner, *Civil List*, 361. I am not including the assembly of 1683, which was more like a false start, or the assembly called by Jacob Leisler.

⁷ Varga, "New York Government," 11. The quote is in Beverly McAnear, "Politics in Provincial New York, 1689–1761" (Ph.D diss., Stanford, 1935), 242; DRHNY, VI, 40–41.

⁸ *DRHNY*, IV, 965, V, 210, VI, 312.

⁹ NYHS, *Coll.*, LXVIII (1935), 253; William Smith, Jr., *Historical Memoirs from 16 March 1763 to 25 July 1778*, ed. William H. W. Sabine, 2 vols. (New York, 1956, 1958), I, 181 (hereafter cited as Smith, *Memoirs*).

¹⁰ *DRHNY*, III, 818–824, 827–833.

¹¹ Werner, *Civil List*, 362. Cases could be appealed to England if their value exceeded £500 sterling (Smith, *History*, I, 269). I would like to thank Herbert Johnson for suggesting this reason for the lack of attention to the council's judicial authority.

¹² *DRHNY*, VII, 810–811.

¹³ See Robert C. Ritchie, *The Duke's Province: A Study of New York Politics and Society, 1664–1691* (Chapel Hill, N.C., 1977); and Lawrence H. Leder, *Robert Livingston 1654–1728 and the Politics of Colonial New York* (Chapel Hill, N.C.,

1961) for information on financing. Sung Bok Kim, *Landlord and Tenant in Colonial New York: Manorial Society 1664–1775* (Chapel Hill, N.C., 1978), 61; *The Colonial Laws of New York from the Year 1664 to the Revolution*, 5 vols. (Albany, 1894–1896), I, 957; *DRHNY*, III, 846, VI, 597, 740; Dixon Ryan Fox, *Caleb Heathcote: Gentleman Colonist* (New York, 1926), 19; George Joseph Ruppel, "The Council and its Activities in Business, Politics, and Law in New York, 1664–1760," (Ph.D. diss., University of Pittsburgh, 1955), 138–139. For the confusion between public and private finance, see Michael Kammen, "A Different 'Fable of the Bees': The Problem of Public and Private Sectors in Colonial America," in John Parker and Carol Urness, eds., *The American Revolution: A Heritage of Change* (Minneapolis, 1975), 53–65.

[14] Smith, Jr., *History*, I, 255. The Sir Peter Warren quote is in Varga, "New York Government," 21.

[15] Smith, Jr., *History*, I, 254.

[16] *DRHNY*, IV, 307, 308, 387, 390, 396. The quote is in *DRHNY*, IV, 303.

[17] Lawrence H. Leder, "Military Victualling in Colonial New York," in Joseph R. Frese and Jacob Judd, eds., *Business Enterprises in Early New York* (Tarrytown, N.Y., 1979), 17, 26, 41. For more on the four independent companies, see Stanley Pargellis, "The Four Independent Companies of New York," in *Essays in Colonial History Presented to Charles McLean Andrews* (New Haven, Conn., 1931), 96–123.

[18] Ruppel, "The Council," appendix 7. The Colden quote is in NYHS, *Coll.*, LII (1919), 239; *DRHNY*, VII, 675; NYHS, *Coll.*, LIII (1920), 244–245, 45, 94; Smith, *Memoirs*, I, 54. The Clinton to Clinton letter is quoted in Stanley N. Katz, *Newcastle's New York: Anglo-American Politics, 1732–1753* (Cambridge, Mass., 1968), 179.

[19] The quote is in NYHS, *Coll.*, LV (1922), 117. Eric Wolf talks about the kinds of societies in which patron-client relationships flourish in "Kinship, Friendship, and Patron-Client Relations in Complex Societies," in Michael Banton, ed., *The Social Anthropology of Complex Societies* (ASA Monograph, New York, 1966), 1–22. On patronage, see also Katz, *Newcastle's New York*; and James A. Henretta, "*Salutary Neglect*": *Colonial Administration Under the Duke of Newcastle* (Princeton, N.J., 1972).

[20] Leder, *Robert Livingston*, 35; William Chazanoff, "Land Speculation in Eighteenth-Century New York," in Frese and Judd, *Business Enterprise*, 58, 62.

[21] NYHS, *Coll.*, LXVIII (1935), 125; LV (1922), 103; LVI (1923), 125, 163–164; Virginia Harrington, *The New York Merchant on the Eve of the Revolution* (New York, 1935; reprint Gloucester, Mass., 1964), 139–143; Smith, *Memoirs*, I, 102; for the remarks about Colden, see NYHS, *Coll.*, LXI (1928), 219, which is the letterbook of John Watts. *State Papers of Vermont: New York Land Patents 1688–1786 Covering Land Now Included in the State of Vermont* (n.p., 1947) VII, 163–164, 177–179.

[22] Letter to Darmouth is in *DRHNY*, VIII, 374. Letter to Schuyler is in Smith, *Memoirs*, I, 189.

[23] Moore to Conway in *DRHNY*, VII, 789.

[24] *DRHNY*, VI, 767, VII, 910, VIII, 59; Smith, *Memoirs*, I, 35, 44. The Colden quote is in *DRHNY*, VIII, 494.

[25] *Ibid.*, VI, 277. NYHS, *Coll.*, LIV (1921), 346–347; Smith, *Memoirs*, I, 35.

[26] *DRHNY*, III, 369.

[27] The Fletcher quote is in *DRHNY*, IV, 119. The Cornbury quote is in *ibid.*, V, 56. Hunter's quote is from *ibid.*, V, 478–479. Montgomerie's quote is in *ibid.*, 856–857.

[28] *Ibid.*, IV, 520, V, 886. On the Indian connection, see *ibid.*, V, 423, 713. William Johnson's Indian connections are well known. The Clinton quote is in *ibid.*, VI, 578.

[29] The council list was taken from Patricia U. Bonomi, A *Factious People: Politics and Society in Colonial New York* (New York, 1971), appendix D, but then pruned. Personal information on councillors came from a wide variety of primary and secondary sources. Most important were the *Dictionary of American Biography* (New York, 1957), hereafter cited as *DAB*; footnotes in the *DRHNY*, and Paul M. Hamlin and Charles E. Baker, *Supreme Court of Judicature of the Province of New York 1691–1704: Biographical Directory*, III (New York, 1959). Information on Cornelius Steenwyck is taken from *DAB*, XVII, 558–559 and Ritchie, *Duke's Province*, 44, 57, 129. For Thomas Topping, see NYHS, *Coll.*, XXV (1892), 111. For Lucas Santen, see Werner, *Civil List*, 180; and Ritchie, *Duke's Province*, 181, NYHS *Coll.*, XXV (1892), 201. This is a volume of will abstracts.

[30] NYHS, *Coll.*, LV (1922), 81–22; XXX (1897), 212–213.

[31] See Leder, *Robert Livingston*.

[32] *DAB*, I, 167–168. See also Henry Noble MacCracken, *Prologue to Independence: The Trials of James Alexander, American 1715–1756* (New York, 1964), 3, 4, 17, 20, 89. This filiopietistic biography has serious errors concerning Alexander's willingness to avail himself of patronage (*DRHNY*, V, 983n.).

[33] NYHS, *Coll.*, XXIX (1896), 386–388; *DRHNY*, V, 983n.

[34] The seventeenth-century figure of 41.7 is based on 18 of the total of 39 men who sat between 1665 and 1698. The range was between 26 and 60. For Maryland, see David W. Jordan, "Political Stability and the Emergence of a Native Elite in Maryland," in Thad W. Tate and David Ammerman, *The Chesapeake in the Seventeenth-Century: Essays on Anglo-American Society* (Chapel Hill, N.C., 1979), 241–273; and Lorena S. Walsh and Russel R. Menard, "Death in the Chesapeake: Two Life Tables for Men in Early Colonial Maryland," *Maryland Historical Magazine* 69 (1974), 211–227. For Virginia, see Darrett B. and Anita H. Rutman, "'Now Wives and Sons-in-law': Parental Death in a Seventeenth-Century Virginia County," in Tate and Ammerman, *The Chesapeake*, 153–182. For eighteenth-century New England, see Edward M. Cook, Jr., *The Fathers of the Towns: Leadership and Community Structure in Eighteenth-Century New England* (Baltimore, 1976), 103. Cook found the average age for selectmen was 42.7 years. The range for eighteenth-century New York councillors was between 23 and 70.

[35] Fox, *Caleb Heathcote*, 6, 8.

[36] I have calculated governors' tenures from Bonomi, A *Factious People*, appendix B. Native-born lieutenant governors and councillors who served as interim governors were excluded from the sample. James Kirby Martin, *Men in Rebellion: Higher Governmental Leaders and the Coming of the American Revolution* (New Brunswick, N.J., 1973), 15.

[37] Robert C. Maxwell and Philip Silverman, "The Nature of Deference," *Current Anthropology*, 19 (1978), 151.

[38] Ritchie, *Duke's Province*, 157–158.

[39] For John Lawrence, see James Riker, *The Annals of Newtown* (New York, 1852), 282; and *DRHNY* IV, 400. For the others, see *DRHNY* IV, 1181. Edsall appears in Riker, *Annals*, 284.

[40] Clinton quote is in *DRHNY*, VI, 413; NYHS *Coll.*, LIII (1920), 390.

[41] NYHS, *Coll.*, LXVIII (1935), 298, 123.

[42] There are probably more merchants, but I have no positive identification of them.

[43] On the professionalization of the bar, see Milton M. Klein, *The Politics of Diversity: Essays in the History of Colonial New York* (Port Washington, N.Y., 1974), 127–153; and "From Community to Status: The Development of the Legal Profession

in Colonial New York," *New York History* LX (1979), 133–156. See also Kammen, *Colonial New York,* 131. Information on Philip Livingston comes from E. B. O'Callaghan, *Calendar of New York Colonial Commissions* (New York, 1929), 18; Smith, *Memoirs,* I, 45.

[44] See Klein's work cited in note 43, *passim.* Smith, *History,* I, 268–272.

[45] Jackson Turner Main says that all councillors sitting between 1763 and 1776 lived in New York City, but he is not quite right. Cadwallader Colden, for example, resided in Ulster County. See Main, *The Upper House in Revolutionary America, 1763–1788* (Madison, Wis., 1967), 55.

[46] Ritchie, *Duke's Province,* 43, 114; Kammen, *Colonial New York,* 106; Harrington, *New York Merchants,* 38, 39; Bonomi, *Factious People,* 83 n. 36; Smith, *History,* II, 71; Smith, *Memoirs,* I, 217.

[47] *DRHNY,* IV, 119, III, 716n. 2; *DAB,* VIII, 491.

[48] *DRHNY,* V, 56, 458; VI, 209; VII, 916; V, 885, 974; VI, 153, LII 53; Smith, *Memoirs,* I, 145. Quote is from NYHS, *Coll.,* III (1919), 136–137. Kammen (*Colonial New York,* 311) says that Johnson never attended after 1753, but the "chronology and itinerary for Sir William Johnson, 1715–1774" in *The Papers of Sir William Johnson,* ed. James Sullivan (Albany, 1912), I, xix–xxxiii, suggests otherwise.

[49] *DRHNY,* VII, 328.

[50] McAnear, "Politics in Provincial New York," 404, 500; Katz, *Newcastle's New York,* 42. Main realizes that few placemen anywhere sat between 1763 and 1776. He finds only four colonies, all southern, where placemen gained importance on the eve of the Revolution. See Main, *Upper House,* 5.

[51] *DRHNY,* VI, 271. Main (*Upper House,* 56) called Horsmanden a placeman but I have not. While he was dependent, it was on the DeLanceys and not the governors, as his suspension demonstrates (*DAB,* X, 332).

[52] Ruppel, "The Council," appendices 2–9; *DRHNY,* VII, 464; VI, 119; V, 429.

[53] Smith, *Memoirs,* I, 145; Smith, *History,* II, 33.

[54] *DRHNY,* VII, 906.

[55] The mean age of death was 65 years, the median 64.6 years.

[56] *DRHNY,* V, 983n.

[57] Varga, "New York Government," 19.

[58] Jack P. Greene, "The Growth of Political Stability: An Interpretation of Political Development in the Anglo-American Colonies, 1660–1760," in Parker and Urness, eds., *The American Revolution,* 39–40; Robert M. Zemsky, "Power, Influence, and Status: Leadership Patterns in the Massachusetts Assembly, 1740–1755," *WMQ,* 3rd. Ser., XXVI (1969), 502–520.

[59] Bernard Bailyn, "Politics and Social Structure in Virginia," reprinted in Stanley N. Katz, *Colonial America: Essays in Politics and Social Development,* 2nd ed., (Boston, 1976), 139–140.

[60] Ritchie, *Duke's Province,* 100; MacCracken, *Prologue to Independence,* 17–22.

[61] Katz, *Newcastle's New York,* 42.

A Beleaguered Elite: The New Jersey Council, 1702–1776

[1] *The Votes and Proceedings of the General Assembly of the Province of New Jersey* (Philadelphia, 1751), Feb. 9, 1750/1 (hereafter cited as *Votes and Proceedings*).

[2] Bill of Indictment, Oct. 21, 1751, in William A. Whitehead et al., eds., *Archives of the State of New Jersey . . .* (Newark, 1880–1928), 1st Ser., VII, 612–613 (hereafter cited as *N.J. Archs.*).

[3] Dollens Hegeman, "The Petition of the Subscribers being a Committee chosen

and appointed by many Purchasers and Possessors of Lands in the Countys of Middlesex and Somerset" (1750), Robert Hunter Morris Papers, Box II, New Jersey Historical Society, Newark.

⁴"Journals of Andrew Johnston, 1743–1763," *Somerset Co. Historical Quarterly*, II (1913), 280; III (1914), 19.

⁵*Votes and Proceedings*, Oct. 23, 1751 and Feb. 10, 1752.

⁶This perspective runs throughout Edgar J. Fisher's *New Jersey as a Royal Province, 1738–1776*, Studies in History, Economics, and Public Law, XLI (New York, 1911); Donald L. Kemmerer's *Path to Freedom: The Struggle for Self-Government in Colonial New Jersey, 1703–1776* (Princeton, N.J., 1940) and James K. Martin, *Men in Rebellion: Higher Governmental Leaders and the Coming of the American Revolution* (New Brunswick, N.J., 1973), 23–25.

⁷A listing of all councillors and dates of service is in Kemmerer, *Path to Freedom*, 357–360. Six appointees who were never sworn in were excluded from this study. They are Peter Fretwell, John Harrison, Edward Hunloke, Samuel Leonard, William Morris, and Thomas Lechmere. Lechmere was a placeman and surveyor-general of customs. The other five all ranked among the wealthiest two percent of the population and, except for Fretwell, a Quaker, were all Anglicans.

⁸Royal Instructions to Lewis Morris, Apr. 14, 1738. *N.J. Archs.*, VI, 17–18. Nominations to the Council after 1736 are in Colonial Office 324/48, sections 1–4, Public Record Office, London. In only four instances were individuals other than the governor listed as recommendors.

⁹This statement is based on an analysis of 1,100 inventories probated between 1700 and 1730, edited in *N.J. Archs.*, XXIII. No adjustments for underrepresentation have been made, so these figures can be considered conservative in assessing the councillors' wealth relative to the entire population. Bequests were used to determine a councillor's wealth when no inventory was available. All monetary values are given in proclamation money, unless otherwise stated.

¹⁰This statement is based on an analysis of 1,400 inventories probated between 1761 and 1770, edited in *N.J. Archs.*, XXXIII, without adjusting for underrepresentation of poorer segments of the population. The mean value of the councillors' inventories, £3,069 Proclamation money, closely approximated the median.

¹¹Jackson Turner Main, *The Social Structure of Revolutionary America* (Princeton, N.J., 1965), 107. Donald J. Mrozek, "Problems of Social History and Patterns of Inheritance in Pre-Revolutionary New Jersey, 1751–1770," *Journal of the Rutgers University Library*, XXVI (1972), 12, 13.

¹²Alice Hanson Jones, "Wealth Estimates for the American Middle Colonies, 1774," *Economic Development and Cultural Change*, XVIII (1970), No. 4, pt. 2, 54.

¹³Thomas L. Purvis, "'High-Born, Long-Recorded Families': The Social Standing of New Jersey Assemblymen, 1703–1776," *William and Mary Quarterly*, 3d. Ser., XXXVII (1980), 594 (hereafter cited as *WMQ*).

¹⁴William Cosby to the Duke of Newcastle, Oct. 26, 1732, *N.J. Archs.*, V, 321.

¹⁵Smyth has been classified as a placeman (though other chief justices were not) because he was not a native of New Jersey, and obtained the position through his patronage connections in England. The other placemen included two surveyors-general of customs, two provincial secretaries, and one lieutenant governor of New York and New Jersey.

¹⁶Carl R. Woodward, *Ploughs and Politicks: Charles Read of New Jersey and his Notes on Agriculture, 1715–1774* (New Brunswick, N.J., 1941), 70–85.

¹⁷Aubrey C. Land, "Economic Base and Social Structure: The Northern Chesapeake

in the Eighteenth Century," *Journal of Economic History*, XXV (1965), 639–654.

[18] Included as proprietors are Lewis Morris (1702–1738) and David Ogden (1751–1776). They were not members of the group, but served as agents or provided legal counsel. They are included because of their close association with the eastern proprietors.

[19] Main, *Social Structure of Revolutionary America*, 107.

[20] Woodward, *Ploughs and Politicks*, 37, 97–98, 215.

[21] William Alexander to Samuel Allinson, Mar. 9, 1772, Allinson Family Papers, Folder 968, Haverford College Library, Haverford, Pa.

[22] Jackson Turner Main, *The Upper House in Revolutionary America, 1763–1788* (Madison, Wis., 1967), 70.

[23] *Ibid.*, 45. M. Eugene Sirmans, "The South Carolina Royal Council, 1720–1763," *WMQ*, 3d. Ser., XVIII (1961), 374.

[24] Sirmans, "South Carolina Royal Council," 237. Main, *Upper House in Revolutionary America*, 55.

[25] William S. Price, "Men of Good Estates: Wealth Among North Carolina's Royal Councillors," *North Carolina Historical Review*, XLIX (1972), 79.

[26] Lewis Morris to Lords of Trade, Jan. 28, 1744/5. William A. Whitehead, ed., *The Papers of Lewis Morris, Governor of New Jersey, 1738–1746* (New York, 1852), 219.

[27] Alan C. Valentine, *Lord Stirling* (New York, 1969), 278.

[28] For Coxe, see E. Alfred Jones, *The Loyalists of New Jersey in the Revolution* (Newark, N.J., 1927), 53–54. For Johnston, see "Sales of Land in Several Tracts & Parcels," West Jersey Society Papers, New Jersey Historical Society, Newark. For Stevens, see Lebanon Township. Tax List, *Genealogical Magazine of New Jersey*, XXXVIII (1973), 131. (Thirteen years after his council service ended, Stevens estimated his real estate to be worth £62,500 [Day Book of John Stevens, entries for 1789, Stevens Family Papers, N.J. Historical Society].)

[29] Purvis, "High-Born, Long-Recorded Families," 597, 606.

[30] On Morris's prejudices against Quakers, see Lewis Morris to the Duke of Newcastle, Oct. 18, 1740, *Lewis Morris Papers*, 122. On Belcher's Quaker connections, see Paul A. Stellhorn and Michael J. Birkner, eds., *The Governors of New Jersey, 1664–1974: Biographical Essays* (Trenton, N.J., 1982), 59. Belcher was unable to place many of his own preferences on the council because the Board of Trade overruled him, substituting persons nominated by Robert Hunter Morris.

[31] The remainder included 1.4 percent from Ireland and 3.0 percent whose immediate place of residence prior to settling in New Jersey is unknown.

[32] Purvis, "High-Born, Long-Recorded Families," 598.

[33] Leonard Family File, Genealogical Society of New Jersey Collection, Special Collections Department, Rutgers University Library. Paul Boyer and Stephen Nissenbaum, *Salem Possessed: The Social Origins of Witchcraft* (Cambridge, Mass., 1974), 124–125, discuss the Leonards's moral problems in detail.

[34] Probate records, genealogies, and biographical material in local histories were the major sources used. Fifteen councillors were the sons of former councillors, six were sons-in-law, two were grandsons, one was a brother, two were brothers-in-law, and two were nephews.

[35] A description of assembly leaders and the criteria used in identifying them is in Purvis, "High-Born, Long-Recorded Families," 604–607.

[36] Only 10 percent of New Jersey assemblymen sitting from 1703 to 1776 had fathers-in-law residing in other colonies, and only 2 percent were the sons-in-law of prominent politicians outside New Jersey (this latter figure excludes those who later became

councillors). Kinship connections outside of the colony became rare after 1730.

[37] Journal of the New Jersey Assembly, May 16, 1733. New Jersey State Library, Trenton.

[38] *Votes and Proceedings*, Nov. 22, 1744.

[39] *Ibid.*, Oct. 23, 1751 and Feb. 10, 1752.

[40] Livingston served continuously as governor from 1776 to 1790. Witherspoon signed the Declaration of Independence, as did Hopkinson. Kinsey became chief justice after the Revolution.

[41] Thomas L. Purvis, "Origins and Patterns of Agrarian Unrest in New Jersey, 1735–1754," *WMQ*, 3d Ser., XXXIX (1982), 600–609.

[42] *An Answer to the Council of Proprietor's Two Publications; Sett Forth at Perth-Amboy the 25th of March 1746, and the 25th of March 1747 . . .* (New York, 1747), 7.

[43] "The Humble Address and Representation of Several Members of His Majesty's Council . . . of New Jersey," Dec. 22, 1748; and "The Petition of the Council of Proprietors of the Eastern Division of New Jersey . . . ," Dec. 23, 1748, *New Jersey Archives*, VII, 190, 196. "Memorial of the Members of His Majesty's Council & of the General Council of Proprietors in His Majesty's Province of New Jersey, in America," July 30, 1751, Robert Hunter Morris Papers, Box II, N.J. Historical Society.

[44] Richard Smith to Richard Partridge, Oct. 20, 1749, *N.J. Archs.*, VII, 366–367.

[45] Address to the Governor, *Votes and Proceedings*, Mar. 7, 1748/9.

[46] *New-York Gazette; and the Weekly Mercury*, Jan. 22, 1770. *New-York Gazette: or, the Weekly Post-Boy*, Feb. 20, Mar. 5, 1770.

[47] *Votes and Proceedings*, Mar. 19, 1770.

[48] See the account of the incident given in the *New-York Gazette; or, the Weekly Post-Boy*, by Tobias Freeman, Feb. 26 and Mar 5, 1770.

[49] West Jersey's underrepresentation excluded many prominent Quakers, particularly the Smith family of Burlington. The Smiths were probably the driving force behind the petitions of 1751 and 1752 cited in n. 39; after members of this family began gaining appointment to the council, complaints about western underrepresentation ceased. Two Smiths sat on the council after 1757, as did a kinsman, Charles Reade. Quakers composed at least one-quarter of the upper house for two-thirds of the years from 1763 to 1775.

[50] Assembly Journal, June 30, 1730. *Votes and Proceedings*, Feb. 9, 1738/9. See sources cited in notes 1–3.

[51] Charles S. Sydnor, *American Revolutionaries in the Making* (New York, 1965), chap. 5.

[52] *N.J. Archs.*, XI, 558, n. He was recommended for a vacancy in 1735 but did not qualify, by paying the necessary fees, until 1738.

[53] Lewis Morris to Lords of Trade. Jan. 28, 1744/5. *Lewis Morris Papers*, 218. Wills was old and infirm, and Provoost was sixty-one, but Van Horne was only forty-seven. All were New Jersey residents when they resigned.

[54] David Ogden to James Alexander. Sep. 2, 1751. Quoted in James Alexander to Cf. [Chief Justice Robert] Morris. Sep. 6, 1751. Stevens Family Papers. New Jersey Historical Society. (Microfilm print # 486, reel 2).

[55] Lewis Morris to Lords of Trade. Jan. 28, 1744/5. *Lewis Morris Papers*, 219.

[56] The outbreak of hostility against Skinner did not become serious until 1772, four years after the loss occurred. Skinner's unpopularity did not become associated with other members of the conciliar elite, and the assembly chose another East Jersey proprietor, John Smyth, to succeed him (Larry R. Gerlach, "Politics and Prerogatives: The Aftermath of the Robbery of the East Jersey Treasury in 1768," *New Jersey History*, XC (1972), 133–168).

[57] Paulson's *American Daily Advertiser.* [Philadelphia] Feb. 13, 1815. Quoted in New Jersey Historical Society, *Proceedings,* L (1932), 272–273.

[58] Quoted in Gerlach, *Prologue to Independence,* 286.

[59] Richard P. McCormick, "The First Election of Governor William Livingston," N.J. Historical Society, *Proceedings,* LXV (1947), 92–100.

[60] C. Leonard Lundin, *Cockpit of the Revolution* (Princeton, N.J., 1940), 95.

[61] Main, *Upper House in Revolutionary America,* 143.

[62] *Ibid.,* 114–131.

Founders of an Oligarchy: The Virginia Council, 1692–1722

[1] Bernard Bailyn argues that successful men in early Virginia prior to midcentury failed to produce sons, that they had risen to status by "brute labor and shrewd manipulation" in a frontier or wilderness society, and that, by the time of Bacon's Rebellion (1676) new leadership, though broadly based on leading social and political families at the provincial level, was "too new, too lacking in the sanctions of time and custom, its leaders too close to humbler origins and as yet too undistinguished in style of life, to be accepted without a struggle." Bacon's Rebellion, he argues, was "the climactic episode" in a necessary period of adjustment. See Bailyn, "Politics and Social Structure in Virginia," in James Morton Smith, ed., *Seventeenth-Century America: Essays In Colonial History* (Chapel Hill, N.C., 1959), 90–115. See also Edmund S. Morgan, *American Slavery—American Freedom: The Ordeal of Colonial Virginia* (New York, 1975), *passim,* and Richard L. Morton, *Colonial Virginia* (Chapel Hill, N.C., 1960), Vol. 1.

[2] Bailyn, "Politics and Social Structure," 98–101.

[3] Leonard Woods Labaree, *Royal Instructions to British Colonial Governors, 1670–1776* (New Haven, Conn., 1930), Vol. I, 55.

[4] Resignation from the council was infrequent, occurring, with one exception, only as a result of ill health. The exceptional case was that of the elder Ludwell, who returned to England, where he died in about 1714. Removal from the council necessitated royal approval.

[5] Robert Beverley, *The History and Present State of Virginia* (Chapel Hill, N.C., 1947), 240–241. For a detailed account of the period, see G. L. Chickering, "The Governors' Councils of Virginia," (Ph.D. diss., University of Delaware, 1978); David Williams, "Political Alignments in Colonial Virginia Politics, 1698–1750" (Ph.D. diss., Northwestern University, 1959); and T. J. Wertenbaker, *Give Me Liberty: The Struggle for Self-Government in Virginia* (Philadelphia, 1958).

[6] Morton, *Colonial Virginia,* II, 412.

[7] Prior to 1682, appeals from the General Court (the governor in council) were heard by the assembly (the council and burgesses), but after 1692, for cases not involving life or limb, or not in excess of £300, there was no access beyond the General Court. Cases involving more than £300 could be appealed to courts in England.

[8] William Byrd to Charles, Earl of Orrery, July 5, 1726 in *Virginia Magazine of History and Biography,* XXXII, 27 (1924) (hereafter referred to as VMHB).

[9] "Report of the Journey of Francis Louis Michel from Berne, Switzerland to Virginia, October 2, 1701–December 1, 1702," trans. and ed. William J. Hinke, *VMHB,* XXIV (1916), 117–118.

[10] Richard Beale Davis, ed., *William Fitzhugh and his Chesapeake World, 1676–1701* (Chapel Hill, N.C., 1963), 175–176, 373–385; *VMHB,* VII (1900), 317.

[11] *VMHB,* XXI (1913), 395.

[12] *VMHB,* XXI (1913), 395–416.

[13] *William and Mary Quarterly,* 1st Ser., I (1892), 110 (hereafter cited as WMQ);

VMHB, I (1893), 174–178; V (1897), 44–45.

[14] *VMHB*, V (1898), 409; XXXII (1924), 18–22; *WMQ*, 1st Ser., VI (1897), 97–99.

[15] Will of Robert King Carter in *VHMB*, V (1898); 408–428, VI (1898), 1–22, 145–152, 260–268, 365–370; VII (1899); 64–68.

[16] Will of Mann Page, *VMHB*, XXXII (1924), 39–42.

[17] John Spencer Bassett, *The Writings of Colonel Byrd* (New York, 1901), xxviii–xxxv.

[18] Will of Nathaniel Bacon, York Records, deeds, Orders, Wills, No. 9, 1691–1692, Virginia State Library, Richmond.

[19] Will of Edmund Berkeley, *WMQ*, 1st Ser., VII (1898), 84–89.

[20] Hugh Jones, *The Present State of Virginia*, ed. Richard L. Morton (Chapel Hill, N.C., 1956), 74. Jones, an English clergyman, came to Virginia in the spring of 1717 to fill the chair of natural philosophy and mathematics at the College of William and Mary. In 1718 he became the chaplain of the House of Burgesses and in 1719 minister of the Jamestown church. He returned to England in 1721.

[21] York County Orders, Wills, etc., No. 17, 1729–1732, 33–34.

[22] *Ibid.*, No. 16, 1720–1729.

[23] Hinke, "Journey of Michel," 124.

[24] *VMHB*, VII (1900), 399.

[25] Robert Quary to the Board of Trade, June 16, 1703, Harleian Mss, CWF microfilm.

[26] Jones, *Present State of Virginia*, 70–71.

[27] *VMHB*, II (1895), 13; Davis, *William Fitzhugh*, 374.

[28] William G. and Mary Stanard, *The Colonial Virginia Register* (Albany, N.Y., 1902), 236–257; L. B. Wright and Marion Tinling, eds., *The Secret Diary of William Byrd of Westover*, 1709–1712 (Richmond, Va., 1941), 194.

[29] Chickering, "The Governors' Councils," Appendix 1; Stanard, *The Virginia Register, passim.*

[30] Chickering, "The Governors' Councils," Appendix 1.

[31] Chickering, "The Governors' Councils," 39–40.

[32] Beverley, *Present State of Virginia*, 247.

[33] Philip A. Bruce, *Institutional History of Virginia in the Seventeenth Century* (New York, 1910), II, 596.

[34] Beverley, *Present State of Virginia*, 246.

[35] Chickering, "The Governors' Councils," Appendix 1.

[36] Beverley, *Present State of Virginia*, 245.

[37] Chickering, "The Governors' Councils," Appendix 1.

[38] Beverley, *Present State of Virginia*, 245.

[39] Chickering, "The Governors' Councils," Appendix 1.

[40] While inspecting customs collection in Virginia in 1693, Edward Randolph wrote in exasperation to William Blathwayt, Secretary to the Lords of Trade and Plantations at Whitehall, "I tyre out my selfe in pursuing illegal traders but to no purpose." Randolph's complaint was that, even if he seized them, "No Court or Jury will find against them" (Admiralty courts were composed of members of the council). Later he complained, "I spend my money and my time most unprofitably here" and also wrote, "It's within my power to Rectify the great abuses [but] . . . the Collectors [regard] more their own fees than their Majesties Interest and care not how the Ship or M[aste]r be qualified provided they either give Security in the Country which they discharge by a false Certificate or produce a forged Certificate to them that may have given security in Engd." (Edward Randolph to Wm. Blathwayt, 14 July, 1693 and 30 July, 1693, *Blathwayt Papers*, II, folder 4 CWF).

[41] CO5/1316, f. 232, CWF microfilm.

[42] *Executive Journals of the Council*, Ed. H. R. McIlwaine (Richmond, Va., 1925–1945), II, 8th February 1704/5, 419–420.

[43] *VMHB*, XXIII (1915), 360–361.

[44] *Ibid.*, editor's note.

[45] Leonidas Dodson, *Alexander Spotswood* (Philadelphia, 1932), 158–159.

[46] Louis B. Wright and Marion Tinling (eds.), *The Secret Diary of William Byrd of Westover*, 1709–1712, (Richmond Va., 1941), 159.

[47] Nathaniel Blakiston to Philip Ludwell II, London, 18 April, 1711 in *VMHB*, IV (1896), 16.

[48] *Ibid.*, V (1897), 43–45.

[49] See Nathaniel Blakiston to Philip Ludwell II, London, May 28, 1709 in *VMHB*, V (1897), 45–47.

[50] Bassett, *Colonel Byrd*, xxii–xxiii.

[51] *VMHB*, II (1894), 124–130.

[52] Chickering, "The Governors' Councils," chap. 3.

[53] See Stephen Saunders Webb, "Army and Empire: English Garrison Government in Britain and America, 1569–1763", *WMQ*, 3d Ser., XXXIV (1977), 1–31.

[54] Cotton Mather, *An Appeal to the Men of New England* (Boston, 1689), 4.

[55] Dorothy Noble, "The Life of Francis Nicholson" (Ph.D. diss., Columbia University, 1958), 65.

[56] Robert Quary to the Board of Trade, June 16, 1703, Harleian MSS, CWF microfilm.

[57] From 1690 to 1720 the new population in Virginia was almost 50 percent black. See Chickering, "The Governors' Councils," 9–13.

[58] For a detailed account of the Lambeth Conference, see Chickering, *ibid.*, chap. 4.

[59] See Chickering, *ibid.*, chap. 5; and Williams, "Political Alignments in Virginia," chap 2.

[60] Spotswood to the Earl of Orkney, July 1, 1718, *Calendar of State Papers*, 1717–1718, Colonial Ser., America and West Indies (Cecil Headlam, London, 1933), XXX, 289–290. See also Chickering, *ibid.*, chap. 6 and Williams, *ibid.*, chaps. 4 and 5.

Index

Notes on Contributors

GRACE L. CHICKERING is Lecturer in History at the University of Delaware.

BRUCE C. DANIELS is Professor of History at the University of Winnipeg and Co-Editor of the *Canadian Review of American Studies*. He is the author of *The Connecticut Town: Growth and Development, 1636–1790* (1979) and *Dissent and Conformity on Narragansett Bay: The Colonial Rhode Island Town* (1983).

A. ROGER EKIRCH is Associate Professor of History at Virginia Polytechnic Institute and State University. He is the author of *"Poor Carolina": Politics and Society in Colonial North Carolina, 1729–1776* (1981) and *Bound for America: The Transportation of British Convicts To The Colonies, 1718–1775* (1986).

JESSICA KROSS is Associate Professor of History at the University of South Carolina. She is the author of *The Evolution of an American Town: Newtown, New York, 1642–1775* (1983).

THOMAS L. PURVIS is Andrew Mellon Fellow in History at the University of Pittsburgh. He is the author of *Proprietors, Patronage, and Paper Money: Legislative Politics in New Jersey, 1703–1776* (1986).

RICHARD ALAN RYERSON is Editor in Chief of the Adams Papers at the Massachusetts Historical Society. He is the author of *The Revolution Is Now Begun: The Radical Committees of Philadelphia, 1765–1776* (1978).

RONALD K. SNELL is a former member of the history faculties of the University of Oklahoma and San Diego State University. Presently he is a member of the staff of the Oklahoma House of Representatives.

ALAN TULLY is Associate Professor of History at the University of British Columbia. He is the author of *William Penn's Legacy: Politics and Social Structure in Provincial Pennsylvania, 1726–1755* (1977).

LORENA S. WALSH is a Research Fellow at the Colonial Williamsburg Foundation, Williamsburg, Virginia. She has published extensively on the agriculture and economy of the colonial Chesapeake and on family and community history in that region.

RICHARD WATERHOUSE is Senior Lecturer in American History at the University of Sydney. He has published extensively on colonial South Carolina.

THOMAS WENDEL is Professor of History at San Jose State University. He is the author of *Benjamin Franklin and the Politics of Liberty* (1974) and *The Call to Independence: Tom Paine's 'Common Sense'* (1976).

About the Book

This book has been composed in Electra by G&S Typesetters, Inc. of Austin, Texas. It was printed on Sebago Antique and bound by Halliday Lithograph Corporation of West Hanover, Massachusetts. Dust Jackets were printed by New England Book Components of Hingham, Massachusetts. Design is by Joyce Kachergis Book Design and Production of Bynum, North Carolina.

Wesleyan University Press, 1986.

DATE DUE

DATE DUE			
2 8 MAR 2007			